950
MOS

Mostyn, Trevor

Major political
events in Iran,
Iraq, and the
Arabian Peninsula,

35718

$27.95

MAJOR POLITICAL EVENTS IN
IRAN, IRAQ AND THE ARABIAN PENINSULA
1945–1990

MAJOR POLITICAL EVENTS IN
IRAN, IRAQ AND THE ARABIAN PENINSULA
1945–1990

Trevor Mostyn

Facts On File
New York • Oxford

MAJOR POLITICAL EVENTS IN IRAN,
IRAQ AND THE ARABIAN PENINSULA
Series editor: Thomas S. Arms
Copyright © 1991 by Trevor Mostyn

Facts On File Limited
Collins Street
Oxford OX4 1XJ
UK
or
Facts On File, Inc.
460 Park Avenue South
New York NY10016
USA

A British CIP catalogue record for this book is available from
the British Library

Library of Congress Cataloging-in-Publication Data
Mostyn, Trevor.
  Major political events in Iran, Iraq and the Arabian Peninsula, 1945–1990 / Trevor Mostyn.
    p.   cm. — (Major Political events series)
  Includes bibliographical references and index.
  ISBN 0–8160–2189–9
  1. Persian Gulf Region—Politics and government. I. Title. II. Series.
  DS326.M64 1991
  950—dc20   90–22491
                                                                       CIP

ISBN 0-8160-2189-9

Facts On File books are available at special discounts
when purchased in bulk quantities for businesses, associations,
institutions or sales promotions. Please contact the
Special Sales Department of our Oxford office on
0865 728399 or our New York office on 212/683-2244
(dial 800/322-8755 except in NY, AK or HI).

Jacket design by Richard Garratt
Typeset by Selectmove Ltd, London
Printed and bound in Great Britain by
Biddles Ltd, Guildford and King's Lynn

10 9 8 7 6 5 4 3 2 1

This book is printed on acid-free paper.

CONTENTS

35718

Acknowledgements

I am extremely grateful to the following colleagues who advised me on various aspects of the text although the usual caveat applies that any errors remaining are my own responsibility. Albert Hourani and Peter Mansfield read the introduction and Fakhreddin Azimi, Baqer Moin and Vahe Petrossian commented on certain years relating to Iran. Peter and Marion Sluglett commented on certain years relating to Iraq. Vahe Petrossian's articles in the Middle East Economic Digest (MEED) were an important source material as were books such as Marion Farouk-Sluglett and Peter Sluglett's *Iraq since 1958* and Shaul Bakhash's *The Reign of the Ayatollahs*. These and the many other sources that I have used are listed in the Bibliography. At Facts On File, I am very grateful to Tom Arms for initiating the series and to Sheila Dallas for her patience and help.

INTRODUCTION

When Iraq declared Kuwait its nineteenth *liwa* (province) on 8 August 1990, it argued that the present-day frontiers of the Gulf states had been drawn by the colonial powers – in particular Britain – and that one of these frontiers was simply being correctly, if brutally, redrawn. In order to understand the course of events which this book follows, it is necessary to look back to the powerful impact on the Gulf region which the West made in the nineteenth century, to understand the West's relationship with both the Ottoman Empire and the Iranian monarchy and to recognize the extent to which Western support for the state of Israel has undermined self-esteem in the Arab world.

This book covers major events between the end of the Second World War and the present day in three large states: Iran, Iraq and Saudi Arabia and six smaller ones: Kuwait, Qatar, Bahrain, the United Arab Emirates (UAE), Oman and the Republic of Yemen (former North and South). The period spreads itself through four extremely eventful decades. The late 1940s saw the emergence of Israel and the 1950s and the 1960s saw the total independence from the West of most of the Gulf states. The 1970s saw a boom era financed by escalating oil prices while the 1980s were dominated by the influence of the Islamic revolution in Iran. The 1990s have been flung into chaos by Iraq's invasion of Kuwait and the international war that followed it in January 1991.

British domination: Iran's humiliation

Between 1800 and the Second World War, most of the Gulf region came under various forms of European control, although until 1916 a great part of the region outside of Iran remained technically part of the Ottoman Empire ruled from Istanbul (formerly Constantinople). Iran remained independent in name, although in the mid-nineteenth century there was widespread resentment against the readiness of its monarch, Nadir al-Din Shah, to sell economic concessions to foreigners. This resentment led to a protest movement organized by the *ulema* (clergy) against a tobacco monopoly granted to a British subject in 1890.

The success of this movement brought about the alignment of the *ulema*, the bazaaris (or merchants) and the intelligentsia to limit the power of the Qajar shahs (or kings) and create a government that answered to a Western-style, elected assembly. Unfortunately, the achievements of the so-called constitutional revolution which came to a head in 1907 were never to be enjoyed, and the Qajars continued to rule autocratically. Following the end of the First World War, the British encouraged a Persian Cossack officer, Reza Khan (the father of the late shah), to seize power in 1921 and found a new autocratic dynasty, the Pahlavis, whose very name stressed Iran's imperial, pre-Islamic past. On 12 December 1925 Reza Khan crowned himself shah. The Pahlavis' continued autocracy and their attempts to bypass Islam fuelled widespread resentment and were to be the crucial factors leading to the Islamic revolution of February 1979 inspired by Ayatollah Khomeini.

The Arabian awakening

Although the intellectual awakening of the Arab world had its roots in Egypt and the Fertile Crescent (Syria, Lebanon, Palestine and Iraq), it has been argued that the first Arab movement with nationalist implications had emerged in what is now Saudi Arabia.

INTRODUCTION

In 1744 Muhammad ibn Saud, the chieftain of Dir'iyyah, a town north of the present Saudi capital of Riyadh, became the patron of a religious revivalist preacher, Shaikh Muhammad ibn Abd al-Wahhab. Abd al-Wahhab sought to cleanse Muslim society of the corrupt and mystical practices which had become widespread since the time of the Prophet Muhammad in the seventh and eighth centuries AD. Muhammad ibn Saud and Abd al-Wahhab were to lead a puritan reformation and campaign of territorial expansion that swept Arabia.

However, Saudi power was checked first by Egypt's semi-independent ruler, Muhammad Ali, and then by the Rashid clan who were based in the northern Saudi town of Hail. The Al-Saud (the Family of Saud) were eventually forced into exile in Kuwait. However, in 1902, after a dare-devil raid on Riyadh's Musmak Fort, the future King Abd al-Aziz (popularly known as Ibn Saud) managed to drive Ottoman forces out of eastern Arabia and establish his authority over the central region of Najd. All of the Saudi kings since Ibn Saud (Saud, Faisal, Khaled and the present King Fahd) have been his sons.

Ibn Saud galvanized his *ikhwan* (literally brothers), puritan soldiery, to spearhead his conquests. He seized Hasa, now the Eastern Province, from the Ottomans, but under British pressure and persuasion desisted from taking the western, Hejaz region containing the holy cities of Mecca and Medina, until the end of the First World War. However, after the Turkish leader, Mustafa Kemal (Ataturk), had abolished the caliphate (the spiritual leadership of Islam) in 1924 the Sharif Husayn of Mecca had what Ibn Saud considered the gross impertinence of claiming it, thus giving Ibn Saud his *casus belli* for invading the Hejaz. In 1926 Ibn Saud's armies took the Hejazi port of Jeddah and then the holy cities of Mecca and Medina. Having annexed the southern province of Asir in 1934, he was ruler of present-day Saudi Arabia.

Britain protects the shaikhs

The Arabian peninsula's eastern seaboard has had strong links with Britain since the eighteenth century. In 1776, during the Persian occupation of Basra, Britain's East India Company moved the southern terminal of its overland mail route to Aleppo, from Basra to Kuwait. As long as Istanbul recognized Britain's trade routes through the Gulf to India, Britain recognized nominal Ottoman control of the peninsula. The shaikh of Kuwait himself at times recognized Ottoman sovereignty (by paying tribute to the sultan), and Shaikh Abdullah ibn Sabah al-Jaber (1866–92) accepted the Ottoman title of *qa'imaqam* (district governor) in 1871. In 1899 his successor Shaikh Mubarak the Great, fearing an Ottoman invasion of Kuwait, signed a treaty agreement with Britain according to which Britain would defend Kuwait from external aggression.

The 'Pirate Coast' to the south (essentially the region of the present-day UAE) was to challenge Britain from its headquarters in Ras al-Khaimah. To secure its trade route to India, Britain signed truces with the tribal shaikhs in 1820, 1835 and 1853 when a 'treaty of maritime peace in perpetuity' established a 'perpetual maritime truce' on what now became known as the Trucial Coast or Trucial Oman. In 1838 and 1847 the shaikhs also agreed to abandon their customary slave-trading. A truce in 1892 further consolidated British authority at a time when Russia and France were showing increasing interest in the region. When Britain eventually terminated all its agreements on 1 December 1971, six of the Trucial States became the UAE, the seventh, Ras al-Khaimah, joining a year later.

Just as Iraq had claimed Kuwait in the 1930s, in 1962 and in 1990 on the basis of Kuwait's historic ties with Ottoman Basra, so Iran had long claimed the largely Shi'i islands of Bahrain. In 1861, 1880 and 1892 Bahrain's amir (ruler) secured his independence from Iran by signing treaties with Britain similar to those that Kuwait and the Trucial States had signed. The amir bound himself not to enter into any relationship with a foreign government without British consent. In 1913 the British and Ottoman governments signed a convention recognizing Bahrain's independence, although the islands remained under British administration. In 1923 the ruler was deposed and Britain's powerful Sir Charles Belgrave was appointed adviser to the new ruler, becoming the power behind the throne. In 1916 during the First World War Britain signed a similar treaty with Qatar whose ruler, Abdullah ibn-Qasim, had decided to support Britain against the Ottoman Empire which was allied to Germany. According to the agreement, Abdullah undertook not to cede, sell, lease or mortgage any of its territory without British consent, to have no relations with any foreign power without British consent, to accept the stationing in the Qatari capital, Doha, of a British political agent and to desist from piracy, the slave trade and arms traffic.

Iraq becomes a nation-state

After the Mongols destroyed the great Abbasid Empire and sacked Baghdad in AD 1258, Iraq had become a mere frontier province of the Mongol Khans of Persia. Various regimes followed but when the Safavid Ismail made himself the Shah of Persia and imposed Sh'ism (see Glossary) on his majority Sunni (see Glosssary) subjects, the Sunni Ottoman sultan saw this as a challenge and in the course of a campaign with Persia (as Iran was called until 1935) conquered Baghdad in 1535. Iraq was to remain, at least nominally, part of the Ottoman Empire (apart from a short period of further Persian rule) until the First World War and was divided approximately into the three *liwas* of Basra, Baghdad and Mosul. By 1800 there was a British Resident (Britain's senior political post in the region) at Basra and in 1802 a British consulate at Baghdad but until the reforms initiated in 1869 by Midhat Pasha, Iraq was little exposed to the West. It was with the emergence in 1908 of the reformist Young Turks that Arab nationalist sentiment began to flourish in cities such as Basra.

Arab hopes are disappointed

The First World War represented a period of dramatic changes for the region. In August 1914, shortly before war broke out, the Young Turks, who had come to power in Istanbul in 1908, made a secret treaty with Germany. They declared war on Britain, France and Russia in November. This meant that the allies were now at war with Istanbul throughout Arabia and the Near East. British forces landed at Iraq's peninsular town of Fao in November, taking the vital Shatt al-Arab waterway dividing Iraq from Iran. In the famous Arab revolt of June 1916, the British officer, T.E. Lawrence ('Lawrence of Arabia'), gave his support to Faisal, the son of the Sharif Husayn of Mecca, to lead a Bedouin army against the Ottoman Turks at Aqaba and from there to march on Damascus which was taken in October 1918. On 11 March 1917 the British had occupied Baghdad.

In 1917 a secret agreement reached the previous year (the Sykes-Picot agreement) was revealed to the world by the victorious Bolsheviks in Moscow who wanted to embarrass the imperial nations. It was a result of correspondence between the French and the British, and provided for the division of the Ottoman Empire if the allies won the war. Palestine would be internationalized, control of Mesopotamia (Iraq) and the ports of Haifa and Acre would go to Britain, and Syria and Lebanon would go to France. Yet, at the same time the British were promising the Sharif Husayn an independent Arab state in return for his support of the revolt. Even more significantly, in terms of the West's 'Great deception' of the Arabs, was the Balfour Declaration of 2 November 1917 in which the British government favoured 'the establishment in Palestine of a National Home for the Jewish people'. This was to become the basis on which the state of Israel was created in Palestine in 1948 and it has been a source of profound bitterness to the Arabs ever since.

INTRODUCTION

Britain and France divide the spoils

The war ended, and the January 1919 peace conference in Paris rearranged the frontiers of Europe. In 1924 Ibn Saud was to defeat the Sharif, the British doing nothing to protect their erstwhile ally. In March 1920 the Syrian National Congress proclaimed the Sharif's son, Faisal, king of Syria (including Palestine) but at the San Remo conference in April, the League of Nations parcelled out Syria, Lebanon, Palestine, Iraq and the newly-created emirate of Transjordan (later to become Jordan) as 'mandates', virtual protectorates, in approximate accordance with the now-notorious Sykes-Picot agreement. Iraq went to Britain and this led to a major uprising in Iraq which was not put down by the British until 1921. In March 1921 Faisal, whom the French had forced out of Syria as they took over their mandatory responsibilities, became king of Iraq. He was crowned on 23 August. His brother, Abdullah, was made amir of Transjordan on 1 April 1921.

The Second World War saw dramatic changes in the region once again as well as constant European interference. In July 1937, incidentally, Iraq had signed an important treaty with Iran providing for agreement on their mutual borders. Meanwhile, Iraq's relations with Britain began to deteriorate because of Britain's role in allowing the increasing settlement in Palestine of Jews fleeing Nazi persecution in Europe. German influence increased in Iraq and was to have a particular impact on an Iraqi army group later to be known as the Golden Square. In April–June 1941 an Iraqi lawyer and politician called Rashid Ali al-Gailani came to power and demonstrated pro-German sympathies, provoking the British occupation of Baghdad and Basra. Meanwhile, the Allies took Syria and Lebanon from the Vichy French, and in August Anglo-Soviet troops moved into Iran. On 16 September 1941 Reza Shah was forced to abdicate because of his apparently pro-German sympathies and was replaced by his son, Muhammad Reza.

The exodus of the Palestinians

After the war, the politics of the region were dominated by the influx into Palestine of hundreds of thousands of Jews from Europe, the creation of the state of Israel in 1948 and the first Arab-Israeli war which immediately followed it. The flight of up to one million Palestinians to neighbouring countries contributed to the dangerous political climate of the period. The humiliating defeat of the Arabs was a factor in provoking the Egyptian revolution in 1952 of young army officers. They were led by the charismatic Colonel Gamal abd al-Nasser who replaced the monarchy of King Faruk. Nasser's philosophies of pan-Arabism, Arab socialism and uncompromising hostility to Israel were to make him a hero with the Arab masses. His nationalization of the Suez Canal in 1956 and the subsequent humiliation of Britain and France made him a kind of Arab 'superman'.

Nasser: the super-star of Arab nationalism

In 1958 Egypt's union with Syria as the United Arab Republic (UAR) on 1 February 1958 appeared to be the first step in his dream of pan Arab unity. In July General Abd al-Karim Qasim led a revolution against the Iraqi monarchy in which the young King Faisal II, the regent, Abdulilah, and the prime minister, Nuri al-Said, were slaughtered. Iraq was to experience a period of violent conflict between the Communists and the Arab nationalist Ba'th Party and several reigns of terror. Today both Syria and Iraq are ruled, at least in principle, by mutually hostile groups of Ba'thists.

Nationalism and the search for cultural roots after long periods of Western domination lie at the heart of this period of Arab history. Nasser's success in championing independence was mirrored briefly by Muhammad Musaddiq in Iran who attempted to nationalize the

British-owned oil company which was based in Iran. But the forces against Musaddiq were too strong and the combined efforts of the West and Central Intelligence Agency (CIA) money eventually toppled him and brought the young Shah Muhammad Reza back to his throne.

Republicanism, exemplified by Nasser, and monarchism, exemplified by the no-less idealistic King Faisal of Saudi Arabia, were to confront each other in the long civil war in Yemen. No sooner had that come to an end than the Arab-Israeli war of 1967 saw Egypt's Sinai, Palestine's West Bank and Gaza Strip and Syria's Golan Heights absorbed by a conquering Israel. In the humiliation of that war lies many of the problems of the Arab world today.

When Nasser died in 1970 he was replaced by Anwar Sadat who was to make the dramatic peace mission to Israel in 1977 which led to the Camp David peace agreements two years later. Although most Arab states broke ties with Egypt over what they considered its treachery to the Palestinian cause, their fear of the spread of Islamic militancy after the 1979 Islamic revolution in Iran and the eight-year Iran-Iraq war which started in 1980, soon saw Egypt courted by its neighbours again. Iraq, in particular, found itself dependent on Egypt throughout the war. By the time of Iraq's invasion of Kuwait in August 1990, Egypt had once again become the pivot of the Arab world, this time leading a coalition of Arab states against Iraq.

The Islamic revolution

No event in modern Middle East history has been more momentous than the Islamic revolution in Iran of February 1979. The replacement of a Western-supported monarchy by a populist revolution with its roots in Islam was to inspire Islamic militants throughout the world and alarm Arab regimes. With the taking of the shah's palace in Tehran on 9 February, control of Iran was finally in the hands of revolutionaries inspired by Ayatollah Khomeini. The revolution had been the culmination of a year in which sometimes as many as three million unarmed people had defied imperial troops, at first every forty days (the Shi'i period of mourning), then almost daily, to demand the replacement of the shah's regime by an Islamic republic.

The seeds of the revolution were sown during the economic boom of the 1970s. After the Arab-Israeli war of 1973 and the quadrupling of oil prices which followed it, the shah believed himself able to fulfil his dream of turning Iran into a military and economic giant. The result was massive spending, raging inflation and severe shortages of food and consumer goods. Accelerating rural drift crippled agriculture while Westerners who poured into the country took the best jobs and brought with them cultural values that disturbed the country's Islamic identity.

The subsequent reduction of oil revenues forced cutbacks in the economy while severe power cuts in Tehran in the summer of 1977 affected every family and belied the myth that the nation was on the point of becoming a second Japan. Many Iranians saw their Muslim traditions increasingly eroded; the mosque benefited from this cultural backlash with women adopting the *hijab* (head covering) and *chador* (body-wrap) and students seeking security in Islam.

The election to the US presidency of the liberal Jimmy Carter in 1976 had encouraged the dissidents from the Mosque, the universities and the bazaar to meet for the first time in large, illegal gatherings. The mysterious death of Khomeini's son later in the year triggered suspicion that the shah's secret police, SAVAK, was responsible. When theology students demonstrated on 9 January 1978 against an article critical of Khomeini, the police killed six of the demonstrators. The Mosque promptly declared a traditional Shi'i 40-day mourning period which automatically associated the martyrs in people's minds with those of the early days of Islam such as Husayn and Hasan (the sons of the Prophet Muhammad's cousin and son-in-law, Ali) and the shah and his regime with their persecutor, Yazid. The demonstrations became bigger, the reprisals more brutal and the mourning periods almost constant. The shah responded with liberal measures but remained unwilling to reduce his own powers. The result of this indecision was disastrous: the pressure valves of dissidence being lifted while the security forces felt emasculated and panicked. Two traumatic events in 1978, the Abadan cinema burning on 19 August and the Jaleh Square massacre of 8 September had left the regime without any real remaining options. The burning of the cinema with 477 people locked inside was widely blamed on SAVAK while the Jaleh Square massacre in which up to 1,000 demonstrators were shot made any concordat between the regime and conservative religious leaders impossible. A day of anarchy in Tehran on 5 November was the prelude to the shah's final departure on 16 January. On 1 February Khomeini returned from France to a tumultuous welcome and within 11 days he was effectively the ruler of the country.

The siege by Islamic militants of the Great Mosque of Mecca in November 1979 was to serve as a warning against corruption and decadence among the ruling elites of the Arab states. The Iran-Iraq war which followed was to help the Iranian clergy keep the Islamic struggle alive and their own power-base secure. However the West, by supporting Saddam Husayn's Iraq, effectively created a new regional power that had become a potential threat to its Arab neighbours once the war had ended without advantage to either Iraq or Iran.

Saddam Husayn threatens the Arab dream

Arab moderates were horrified by Iraq's invasion of Kuwait because it seemed to expose as hollow the whole concept of Arab unity. Nevertheless, Saddam Husayn did not hesitate in claiming to be the very exemplar of Arab unity and nationalism. Kuwait, he maintained, had merely returned to its mother, Iraq. By linking any withdrawal from Kuwait with an Israeli withdrawal from the West Bank and Gaza, he managed to endear himself to the despairing Palestinians and draw the world's attention to the very heart of the grievance of the Arab world. He was also playing on the envy and disgust that many poor Arabs felt for the rich oil shaikhs of the Gulf. However bad Saddam Husayn's human rights record in Iraq might have been, his invasion of Kuwait seemed to win genuine support from the Arab masses, not only from Iraqis but also from Palestinians, Jordanians and Syrians. At the time of writing, whatever the outcome of the war raging in Iraq, the Middle East will never be the same again.

Note on transliteration
I have chosen as practical a transliteration system as possible. For names, I have used the classical Qasim rather than the anglicized Kassem, Abd al-Aziz rather than Abdul Aziz and Husayn in Arabic and Hussein in Persian. I have avoided elisions, writing Al-Sabah rather than As-Sabah.

Note on chronology
Where two unrelated events have occurred on the same date, I have repeated the date to introduce the second entry. On rare occasions where the exact date is unknown, I have simply inserted the month.

Organizations – e.g. the Revolutionary Command Council – are written in full for the first time in each year. Thereafter, the acronym – RCC – is used. Common Arabic and Persian words as well as acronyms are listed in the Glossary.

1 9 4 5

January In Saudi Arabia the California Arabian Standard Oil Company, owned jointly by the Standard Oil Company of California and the Texas Company, is re-formed as the Arabian American Oil Company (ARAMCO). In the same month work began on ARAMCO's Trans-Arabian pipeline (Tapline), running between the oilfields in Saudi Arabia's Eastern Province and the port of Sidon on the Mediterranean. Then the world's largest privately financed construction project, the pipeline was delayed while US Congress was being persuaded to approve the oil companies' plans.

A stumbling block was, and was to continue to be, Saudi anxiety about the growing political tension in Palestine caused by mass Jewish immigration. Indeed, ARAMCO briefly withdrew its backing for the pipeline while the US secretary of defence declared that unless the US had access to Middle East oil 'American motorcar companies would have to design a four-cylinder motorcar sometime within the next five years'. The Arab League reached a tentative agreement that pipeline rights would be refused to US companies so long as the US gave the Zionists unquestioned support. Nevertheless, work on the pipeline eventually began in January under the supervision of the US company, Bechtel, although it was not to be completed until September 1950. It was delayed by the first Arab-Israeli war which followed the ending of the British mandate in Palestine and the declaration of the new Israeli state in Palestine on 14 May 1948.

14 February King Abd al-Aziz (popularly known to foreigners as Ibn Saud) of Saudi Arabia meets US President Roosevelt on board USS *Quincy* in the Suez Canal's Great Bitter Lake. The meeting was extremely friendly and characterized by mutual respect. Roosevelt wanted to enlist the king's help over the question of Palestine. However, there was no real meeting point, the king arguing that the Jews should be given a part of Germany as reparation for the Nazi atrocities committed against them in the concentration camps in Germany, Poland and elsewhere during the Second World War.

17 February Ibn Saud meets the British prime minister, Winston Churchill, in the Grand Hotel du Lac on the shores of Egypt's Fayyoum Oasis. In contrast with the Roosevelt meeting, the Churchill meeting was strained, to say the least. As an indication of the shifting balance of power, prior to the Churchill meeting Ibn Saud had even asked Roosevelt if there was any US objection to it. For his part, Churchill treated the king with contempt, making a point of drinking alcohol – forbidden to Muslims and loathsome to the fundamentalist Ibn Saud – and smoking huge cigars in his face.

Saudi Arabia had declared war on Germany just in time to be eligible for admission to the new UN, and the US had by now almost completely replaced Britain as a world power. However, Roosevelt's successor, Harry Truman, was to take a far more pragmatic and, in Arab eyes, far less flexible line on the question of Palestine, making the famous remark to State Department officials in November: 'I'm sorry, gentlemen, but I have to answer to hundreds of thousands who are anxious for the success of Zionism; I do not have hundreds of thousands of Arabs among my constituents.' When the British Labour prime minister, Clement Attlee, succeeded Winston Churchill earlier in the year, Truman urged the immediate admission of 100,000 Jews to Palestine. Clement Attlee, keen to cultivate friendly relations with oil-rich Saudi Arabia, was loathe to upset Ibn Saud by allowing further Jewish immigration.

22 March The League of Arab States (Arab League) is founded in Cairo following a meeting at the Saudi port of Yanbu between Ibn Saud and King Faruk of Egypt. The protocol agreeing to establish it had been signed on 8 October 1944. In his capacity as Britain's foreign secretary, Anthony Eden had formally expressed British sympathy for Arab unity even earlier in a declaration of May 1941. It was with British blessing that the Egyptian prime minister, Nahas Pasha, had taken the initiative in July 1943 to convoke a meeting of Arab states in Alexandria to discuss the formation of the League. The war had weakened Britain and encouraged Arab determination to seek genuine independence.

Aware of the dangers to its oil interests in the region, Britain aimed to counter Arab militancy by co-operation rather than suppression. Thus, at a time when it was struggling to maintain a foothold in Saudi Arabia against US pressure, Britain found itself playing the role of discreet midwife to the creation of the League.

The League's seven founder members were Egypt, Lebanon, Iraq, Syria, Transjordan (later Jordan), Yemen (later the Yemen Arab Republic – North Yemen) and Saudi Arabia. Since then a further 14 Arab states were to join, plus Palestine which is today considered an independent state and is represented by the Palestine Liberation Organization (PLO) at League meetings. The League's first secretary-general was the Egyptian Abd al-Rahman Azzam Pasha (1945–52).

4 November In the Iranian province of Azerbayjan, the Democratic Party leader, Ja'far Pishavari, seizes power in a coup d'etat. Two battalions sent by the Tehran central government to regain control in Azerbayjan were halted by Soviet troops on 8 November near Qasvin. On 13 December an 'autonomous' government was set up in Azerbayjan with Soviet support. The Democratic Party's programme included the introduction of local Azeri Turkish into the schools and its adoption as the official language, the nationalization of the banks and the distribution of land to the peasants. In a separate development, on 15 December 1945, a Kurdish revolt took place at Mahabad in Iranian Kurdistan.

The Soviet decision to engineer revolts in Azerbayjan and Kurdistan had stemmed from the events of 1944 when the Tudeh (Communist) Party had launched a diplomatic offensive aimed at giving the Soviets an oil concession in northern Iran. The party called for 'positive equilibrium', an apparent euphemism for granting the Soviets an oil concession similar to that held by the Anglo-Iranian Oil Company (AIOC) in the south. At the end of October 1944 Dr Muhammad Musaddiq, later to be a controversial prime minister, had advocated 'negative equilibrium', stressing that no oil concessions would be negotiated while foreign troops (in this case implying Soviet troops) remained on Iranian soil.

10 January King Abd al-Aziz of Saudi Arabia (Ibn Saud) arrives in Egypt for a state visit to King Faruk. Ibn Saud's discussions with Faruk, and with the Egyptian prime minister, Nuqrashy Pasha, and members of the government, concentrated on the question of Jewish immigration into Palestine and the creation of the Arab League in 1945. In a joint statement published on 16 January the two monarchs associated themselves with all Muslim Arabs in their belief that Palestine was an Arab (rather than a Jewish) country and that it was the right of all Muslim Arabs to preserve it as such. They also confirmed their allegiance to the Arab League and to their goal of Arab unity. They agreed that every country had the right to decide its own future and to enjoy independence and that no Arab country would be an aggressor against another country.

13 January Ibn Saud receives a delegation of Palestinians headed by Jamal Husayni (a cousin of Hajj Amin, the Grand Mufti of Jerusalem) to whom he had confirmed that the question of the Arabs and Palestine was a concern for Islam and all Arab countries. Regarding Rashid Ali al-Gailani, who had led a revolt in Iraq in 1941 and who had escaped to Saudi Arabia, the king said that although he had disapproved of the revolt he could not refuse Gailani refuge. 'If our sister country [Iraq] demands that I should hand him over,' he said, 'I shall reply that he is sheltering under our protection and I would rather give up some of my sons instead.'

19 January The Iranian government appeals to the new UN Security Council to consider the matter of Soviet interference in Azerbayjan. The appeal came when delegates of Iran, Iraq and Saudi Arabia attended the first meeting of the UN General Assembly at London's Central Hall, Westminster. The Security Council promptly referred the question to direct negotiations between Iran and the Soviet Union.

14 February Qavam al-Saltaneh becomes the new Iranian prime minister. Soon after taking office, he spent two months in Moscow negotiating with Soviet Premier Stalin, and his foreign minister, Molotov, principally over Iranian refusal to accept Tudeh (Communist) Party members in the government or to recognize the Autonomous Azerbayjan Republic, which Iranian nationalists considered merely a Soviet satellite. Although the Soviet Union had returned the North Iranian Railway to the Iranian government on 30 January, it made no move to withdraw from Azerbayjan, and on 1 March it refused further requests that its troops leave the northern Iranian province.

24 March In the wake of the expiry of the Tripartite Treaty in Iran and the ordered evacuation of British and US forces, the Soviet Union commits itself to withdrawing all Soviet troops from Azerbayjan within five to six weeks. In addition, in April an oral understanding, confirmed by an exchange of letters between Qavam al-Saltaneh and the Soviet ambassador, was reached whereby a joint Soviet-Iranian company would exploit oil found in Azerbayjan. However, the Soviets did not withdraw and the Iranian government presented several notes protesting about this to the UN Security Council.

13 June An agreement signed between the Azerbayjani Republic and Tehran strongly suggests that the Iranian premier, Qavam al-Saltaneh, has conceded all essential points to the Azerbayjani Democrats in their bid for autonomy. In May the Soviet Union had finally fulfilled its promise to evacuate its troops from the northern province. According to the 13 June agreement the Azerbayjani Majlis (lower house) was to remain, the Republic's minister of the interior was to be called governor-general and Azeri Turkish was to remain the official language, although Persian would be taught in the high schools.

30 June Kuwait's ruler, Shaikh Ahmad al-Jaber al-Sabah, ceremonially inaugurates Kuwait's oil terminal and sends its first crude-oil export on its way by opening a specially installed silver valve which allows the tanker *British Fusilier* to take on its cargo. Meanwhile, the Dhahar ridge, the terminal area, was renamed al-Ahmadi and the port became Mina (Port) al-Ahmadi.

By June eight productive wells had been connected to Kuwait's first gathering centre. Together they were capable of producing 30,000 barrels of oil a day. Earlier in the year the state's first sea-loading line, a 12-inch line, had been built and a pier had been started.

Work was also proceeding on what was to become a 4,000-tons-a-day refinery, a power station and a seawater distillation plant.

The oil town of al-Ahmadi was now beginning to take shape. Oil revenues were to reach $760,000 by the end of the year, $2 million in 1947 and $5.95 million in 1948. In 1936 after four years of complicated discussions, Shaikh Ahmad al-Jaber al-Sabah had granted a concession to the Kuwait Oil Company which had been formed by the merger of two British and US companies – the Anglo-Persian Oil Company (later British Petroleum) and the Gulf Exploration Company (later Gulf Oil). Oil had been discovered in 1938 in Burgan, which was to prove one of Kuwait's richest oilfields. However, Kuwait's oil was not to be commercially exploited until after the end of the Second World War.

17 July Ayatollah Abul Qasim Kashani is imprisoned on the orders of the Iranian prime minister, Qavam al-Saltaneh, following his attack on the latter's suppression of press freedom in Iran. (Kashani was later to hold a charismatic influence over the Iranian crowds whose passions he would quickly inflame with his oratory). He had been incarcerated by the British in 1943 for his anti-British and pro-Nazi activities. He emerged from prison in 1945 as a hero among the radical clergy for his anti-British stand.

July Riots take place in Iraq when the British-directed Iraq Petroleum Company (IPC), based in Kirkuk, refuses its workers permission to form a union. After nine days of strikes for higher wages, the workers were gathered around a strike committee reading its report when armed police charged the meeting and killed 10 people. The violence came at the end of a period of reasonable liberalism under the ministries of Hamid al-Pachachi and Tewfiq al-Suwaidi between 1944 and 1946. During this period, 16 labour unions, 12 of which were controlled by the Iraqi Communists, were licensed. The biggest unions were formed at Basra Port and in the Iraqi railways which were under British management. Major strikes for higher wages took place on the railways in 1945, at the port in 1947 and again in the late 1940s. The July killings were to be seen as a foretaste of the great national uprising in the following year called *al-Wathba* (the leap).

1 August The Iranian premier, Qavam al-Saltaneh, includes three Tudeh (Communist) Party members in his cabinet. Tudeh Party members in Iran had now become free to act as never before and by 16 July, under their influence, 50,000 workers of the Anglo-Iranian Oil Company (AIOC) in Khuzestan had gone on strike. However, a perceptive few suspected that the ultimate goal of Qavam's apparently conciliatory strategy was really the destruction of the Tudeh Party and the re-incorporation of Azerbayjan into the Iranian state.

20 September The great Qashqai tribes of Fars province rise up and carry other tribes with them. It was later to become reasonably clear that the Iranian premier, Qavam al-Saltaneh, was party to the Qashqai unrest. The Qashqais' demands were all in conflict with Tudeh Party interests.

On 8 September the government had declared martial law in the Isfahan region after the alleged discovery of an anti-government plot hatched by the Bakhtiari tribes who had threatened to march on Tehran.

18 October Qavam al-Saltaneh forms a new Iranian cabinet without Tudeh Party members. In October the new Soviet-Iranian oil agreement had been presented to the National Assembly but was not ratified by the delegates. In November he went even further by suddenly arresting a number of their leaders in Tehran.

12 December The Azerbayjani Autonomous Provincial Assembly abandons resistance to Tehran as central government troops penetrate the province, taking its capital, Tabriz, on 13 December. The takeover was the culmination of the extraordinarily skilful year-long strategy of the Iranian prime minister, Qavam al-Saltaneh. By the time that the shah, who still did not enjoy substantial political power, signed his agreement to nationwide elections on 6 October, the once-powerful Tudeh Party had become neutralized. Qavam insisted that central government troops would have to oversee elections which he had put off to 7 December, arguing that the delay was necessitated by the country's disturbed state.

Throughout the year, Soviet pressure on Tehran had continued through the Tudeh Party, the Azerbayjani democratic movement and the Kurdish autonomy movement. Qavam al-Saltaneh had, by appointing Tudeh Party members to the Majlis and by demonstrating apparent sympathy with Communist ideals and empathy with the goals of the Azerbayjani republicans, managed to deceive the Soviets.

By November Qavam had cunningly ordered the army to march into Azerbayjan to supervise the elections. After token resistance the rebel regime collapsed. Ja'far Pishavari, the Azerbayjani rebel leader, escaped to the Soviet Union and was later reported to have been killed in a road accident near the Soviet Azerbayjani capital, Baku.

A little later the Iranian army overthrew the rebel regime, the so-called 'Mahabad Republic', in Kurdistan and the Kurdish leader, Qazi Muhammad, and his brother were hanged in the main square of Mahabad.

A Soviet-Kurdish cultural relations society had been founded in Mahabad in 1944, and in September 1945 the society had arranged for Mahabad's Kurdish notables to be sent to the Soviet city of Baku for indoctrination. The Kurdish People's Republic of Mahabad had been proclaimed on 15 December 1945.

1 9 4 7

7 March The Anglo-Iranian Oil Company (AIOC), the Standard Oil Company of New Jersey (Exxon) and the Socony Vacuum Oil Company (Mobil) form Middle East Pipelines to build and operate the 1,000-mile (1,609-kilometre) pipeline from the oilfields of Iran and Kuwait to the Mediterranean. The pipeline was distinct from the one which the Arabian American Oil Company (ARAMCO) planned to build from Saudi Arabia to the Mediterranean. Meanwhile, on 13 March ARAMCO completed its plans to re-develop Saudi Arabia's petroleum output. This involved the construction of a railway and deep-water port at Dammam and a 1,050-mile (1,689-kilometre) line from the oilfields to the Mediterranean. The end of the Second World War in 1945 had marked the beginning of uninterrupted expansion of the Saudi oil industry. Casoc, the partnership of Socal and Texaco founded in 1937 to handle the two companies' work in the Middle and Far East, had been named ARAMCO in 1944. In 1945 ARAMCO had set up the Trans-Arabian Pipeline Company (Tapline) to build the pipeline from the Saudi oilfields in the Eastern Province to the Mediterranean.

16 April Britain announces that all British forces will be withdrawn from Iraq before the end of the year.

4 May Iraq signs a 10-year treaty of friendship with Jordan.

1 June The Iranian government complains that the State Bank of the Soviet Union has not returned Iranian gold deposits and is therefore in breach of the Soviet-Iranian agreement of 24 May 1947. Soviet-Iranian relations were to deteriorate as the year progressed.

10 November The Soviet government protests at the Iranian government's nullification of the Soviet-Iranian oil agreement of April 1946. Iran was by then turning to the US for support. In October an agreement was signed with the US which provided for a military mission to be sent to Iran which would co-operate with the Iranian Ministry of War in order to enhance the efficiency of the Iranian army.

29 November The partition of Palestine into Arab and Jewish states is adopted by the UN General Assembly by a vote of 33 to 13, with 10 abstentions.

On 30 November six Arab delegations, including those of Iraq, Saudi Arabia and Yemen, walked out of the UN General Assembly in New York following the vote for the partition of Palestine. On 22 October several hundred Iraqi clerics had called for *jihad* (holy struggle), if necessary, in defence of Palestine. Reaction to the partition plan in Arab states was sometimes violent. From 2 to 5 December, rioting in Aden over the plan led to 111 deaths.

The Palestine problem had arisen out of the Balfour Declaration of 1917 in which Britain had looked 'with favour upon the establishment of a home for the Jews in Palestine'. However, at that time the Jews represented only 8 per cent of the population and it was not until 1933, with increasing Nazi persecution, that immigration accelerated. Arab opinion grew hostile as it became apparent that a Jewish state would be created at the expense of the Palestinian Arabs who then inhabited Palestine.

In April 1946 the British foreign secretary, Ernest Bevin, had decided to set up an Anglo-US commission of enquiry into the whole question. The commission had called for the continuation of the British mandate and the immediate admission of 100,000 Jews, but it criticized the existence of the Jewish underground which included terrorist groups such as the Stern Gang and the Irgun and was estimated to number 65,000 men in total. Britain had to deal with illegal immigration on a massive scale as well as a campaign of Zionist terrorism.

December Iran revives its claims to Bahrain. These were based on Iran's former hegemony over the island which had been superseded since 1820 by British influence. Iran's claims had been made at different intervals since the Al Khalifa clan had overrun the Iranian garrison on the island in 1783. The presence in Bahrain of a large Shi'i population helped to strengthen Iran's claims which were included in various appeals to the League of Nations Council between 1927 and 1936.

Britain defended Bahrain from these claims after 1869 when Shaikh Isa ibn Ali became ruler and Bahrain fell increasingly under British influence. A political agent was stationed in Bahrain when a series of treaties was made with the shaikhs in 1906, and in 1915 Shaikh Isa gave up his jurisdiction over foreigners in favour of political compromise. The Treaty of Jeddah between Britain and Saudi Arabia on 27 May 1927 appeared to have precipitated the first round of new claims over Bahrain since, according to the treaty, King Abd al-Aziz of Saudi Arabia had apparently recognized Britain's protectorate of the island. There were further Iranian protests when the Bahraini ruler granted oil concessions to US and British companies in 1930 and 1934.

In 1946 Britain's political residency, the centre of its regional power and influence, moved from Iran's port of Bushehr to Bahrain.

1 9 4 8

15 January The Iraqi prime minister, Saleh Jabr, initials the controversial Anglo-Iraqi agreement at Portsmouth which promptly provokes a spiral of bloody rioting in Iraq. Among Arab nationalists, bitter resentment had been fuelled by the partition of Palestine in 1947. The Portsmouth Treaty replaced the Anglo-Iraqi Treaty of 1930.

The main discussions surrounding the new agreement took place between May and December 1947 in Baghdad, and the Iraqi delegation left for Britain at the beginning of January. Before the delegation had arrived in England, Baghdad witnessed large-scale student demonstrations, apparently fomented by the Istiqlal (Independence) Party. However, when the terms of the agreement were announced on 16 January the riots became a virtual mass uprising. On 20 January a march of railway workers and slum dwellers was fired on by the police. Several people were killed.

On 21 January, in an astonishing volte-face the regent, Abdulilah, summoned a meeting at which the new agreement was rejected. On 27 January, a day after Jabr and his colleagues had returned from London, huge demonstrations in Baghdad developed into fighting between police and demonstrators and up to 400 people lost their lives. In the evening Jabr resigned and was replaced by another Shi'i, Muhammad al-Sadr, who held the post until June. Al-Sadr had been active in the 1920 revolution. On 19 February the Iraqi parliament was dissolved and new elections were called by the regent.

31 January The Soviet Union attacks Iran's 6 October 1947 agreement with the US. In a note to the Iranian government, the Soviet embassy interpreted the agreement as implying that all training of the Iranian army was now to be entrusted to the US military mission, that the US would acquire a monopoly of sensitive military positions and that the Iranian army would cease to be that of a sovereign independent nation since it was now subject to US influence. The note also claimed that US operations in Iran were aimed at transforming Iranian territory into a US military base. It added that the positioning of military establishments under US supervision near the Soviet border was incompatible with the Iranian-Soviet treaty which had been made in 1921.

4 February Iran rejects the Soviet allegations of 31 January in a note. The note explained that the 6 October 1947 agreement had been concluded for the purpose of employing a number of US advisers, that members of the US mission were forbidden to assume command or responsibility for staff in the Iranian army, and that they did not have a monopoly of Iran's sensitive military positions.

17 February Imam Yahya of Yemen (later to become the Yemen Arab Republic – North Yemen) is ambushed and machine-gunned to death together with his adviser Qadi Abdullah al-Amri while out on a drive outside the Yemeni capital, San'a. He was replaced as ruler by Abdullah ibn-Ahmad al-Wazir who had fallen out of favour with the imam because he was suspected of being ambitious for the imamate (the highest spiritual and temporal authority).

After being informed in Taiz of his father's murder, the imam's eldest son, Crown Prince Seif Ahmad, left Taiz with 180 faithful soldiers and a bag of gold. In San'a, meanwhile, two of the royal princes who tried to restore their family's power were killed by the Iraqi security chief, Colonel Jamal Jamil, who supported al-Wazir. Ministerial posts were given to Muhammad al-Zubeiri (a prominent member of the 'Free Yemenis' since

7

1944) and Ahmad Nu'man, who had escaped to Aden in 1944 along with al-Zubeiri. The rebel Prince Ibrahim was made president of the Consultative Assembly. In order to win support, Abdullah al-Wazir released all hostages, increased the army's salary and announced a programme of hospital and school building.

Neglecting to explain that Imam Yahya had been murdered, telegrams were sent to all Arab states requesting recognition of al-Wazir. A doubtful Arab League decided to send a delegation to study the situation. However, King Abd al-Aziz of Saudi Arabia, repelled by the killing of Imam Yahya, persuaded the delegation to remain in Riyadh. He kept them in his capital until Crown Prince Seif Ahmad's forces had reached and taken San'a on 14 March. In order to encourage the tribes to follow him and lacking ready money, Seif Ahmad had given them permission to loot San'a.

Seif Ahmad was officially recognized as imam by the *ulema* (clergy) and then by the foreign powers. Abdullah al-Wazir, Colonel Jamal Jamil and several others were publicly beheaded in San'a and their heads displayed to the public for more than a week. The coup, the first to take place in the Arab world since the Second World War, failed because of the revulsion caused by Imam Yahya's killing and general sympathy with Seif Ahmad. On 15 March the Arab League confirmed that Seif Ahmad was in control of San'a and had been proclaimed the imam. In May, resentful of the support San'a had given the rebels and anxious about the effects of the pillage, Seif Ahmad moved his capital to the safer region of Taiz to the south.

14 May At 4pm the Jewish National Council (Va'ad Leumi) proclaims the state of Israel in the Tel Aviv Modern Art Museum in the Rothschild Boulevard. The proclamation was broadcast by David Ben-Gurion, Israel's first prime minister, over Tel Aviv's newly opened Voice of Israel radio station.

Ben-Gurion said that the new state would be open to all Jewish immigrants, would be based upon the precepts of liberty, justice and peace taught by the Hebrew prophets, would uphold full social and political equality for all citizens without distinction of race, creed, or sex and would guarantee full freedom of education and culture. The declaration promised that the shrines and holy places of all religions would be safeguarded; pledged Israel to dedicate itself to the principles of the UN Charter; stated that Israel would seek admittance to the UN; promised the Arab inhabitants of Israel equality of citizenship and representation in all institutions of the Jewish state; and offered peace to all Arab countries.

15 May At midnight on 14/15 May the Arab sector of Palestine is simultaneously invaded by the armies of the surrounding Arab states from three sides. On the south it was invaded by Egyptian infantry and armoured formations which crossed the frontier and advanced into the Negev, in the east by the Transjordanian Arab Legion led by General Glubb (later Glubb Pasha) and in the north by Syro-Lebanese forces.

However, according to Glubb in *Peace in the Holy Land*, total Arab forces amounted to only 17,500 men against an Israeli strength of about 62,500. He estimated that Egypt fielded 10,000 men, the Arab Legion 4,500 and Iraq 3,000 whereas the Palmach (Israeli regulars) fielded 3,500, Hagana 55,000 and Irgun, one of the two main Jewish commando groups, 4,000.

Palestine had been partitioned into a Jewish and an Arab state; of the invading Arabs, only the Egyptians ever crossed the frontier of the Jewish state. The Jordanians entered only the Arab state. Lebanon took no part in the conflicts. Syria fought one border action at Samakh and then withdrew without entering Israel. The Iraqi token force of 3,000 engaged the Israelis across the River Jordan at Jisr al-Mejama. It then withdrew via Amman and joined the Arab Legion in defending the Arab state in the Nablus-Jenin-Tulkarm triangle. The Iraqis remained on the defensive throughout and never attacked the Jewish state.

May In Tehran, Ayatollah Sayyid Abul-Qasim Kashani encourages volunteers to fight 'Zionist Terrorism' and is supported by the Fedayeen-e Islam. In early January the Iranian *ulema* (clergy) had shown its muscle by issuing a *fatwa* (edict) that women must wear the *chador* (head-veil) while shopping. The prime minister, Ibrahim Hakimi, restricted his response by appealing to Ayatollah Muhammad Mousavi Behbehani, Tehran's clerical leader, to help stop zealot men from attacking unveiled women.

29 July Iran receives from the US a $26-million loan to equip the army and the police. On 22 March the Iranian government had protested against Soviet propaganda which sought to undermine its power and defended its improving relations with the US. However, the government showed leniency towards those who had tried to break away from Tehran's control with Soviet backing.

17 August Iran's Majlis (lower house) passes a bill providing for an amnesty for all involved in the 1945 Azerbayjan uprising, with the exception of those who held ministerial office in the Pishavari government or those found guilty of murder or robbery. In a further show of self-confidence, the government revived territorial claims. On 23 August the Iranian foreign minister announced that the government considered all arrangements among other powers relating to Bahrain null and void as long as Iranian sovereignty over the islands was ignored. Iran had started to revive its historic claims to Bahrain in December 1947.

12 October Iraq recognizes the Gaza government set up by the Palestine Higher Committee. Three days later, on 15 October, Saudi Arabia recognized the Gaza government. On 15 July the Iraqi Chamber of Deputies had passed a resolution that Zionism was punishable by imprisonment or death. In a letter to the British prime minister, Clement Attlee, and published in Farouk-Sluglett and Sluglett's book, *Iraq since 1958*, the British political agent in Iraq had written on 25 January: 'Iraqi opinion, in common with other Arab opinion, has grown steadily more and more concerned with what seems to them the manifest injustice of the National Home policy in Palestine . . . The man in the street and in the coffee house has been excited by the successive outrages in Palestine since the partition decision, and Palestine has formed one of the subjects of slogans shouted in all the recent demonstrations in Baghdad.'

1 9 4 9

4 February A press photographer named Fakhr Arai shoots and slightly wounds the 29-year-old Shah of Iran during his visit to Tehran University to commemorate the anniversary of its founding. As the shah started up the steps of the Faculty of Law building the assassin took a Belgian six-shooter out of a false camera and fired at him four times from behind. Three of the shots went through the shah's military cap and the fourth entered his right cheek. Generals, officers and policemen ran for cover, with nobody daring to help the shah until the assassin's gun jammed. The gunman was then attacked violently by the crowd and died of his wounds the following day.

The assassin's identity papers showed that he was almost certainly working for the *Parcham-e Islam* (Flag of Islam), a religious publication, and belonged to the journalists' union, then affiliated to a pro-Communist labour federation.

The shah sent his bloodstained uniform to be put on display in a glass case in Tehran's Officers' Club. Martial law was declared and the Tudeh (Communist) Party was banned. The shah then called on the Constituent Assembly to revise article 48 and allow him, at the government's request, to dissolve the Majlis (lower house). His decision was intended to reflect the bad economic state of the country and the fact that the Majlis had passed no budget for five years.

14/15 February Communist politicians are executed in Baghdad. The response of the Iraqi prime minister, Nuri al-Said, to opposition was given cruel expression when the secretary-general of the Iraqi Communist Party, Fahd, and two members of the Politburo, Husayn Muhammad al-Shabibi and Zaki Basim, were hanged in public in Baghdad, ostensibly for having continued to organize the Communist Party while in prison. They had all been in prison since their arrests in 1947.

15 February The Iranian Majlis reveals Iran's first economic plan, a seven-year development programme. The Majlis enacted into law the results of its study of a wide variety of economic development projects ranging from those aimed at increasing production, expanding exports and developing agriculture, to ones intended to improve public health and education. These goals were to be achieved within seven years.

4 March The Iranian government denies a Soviet allegation that the state is dominated by the military. Repeating accusations of the previous year, the note delivered by the Iranian Foreign Office to Sadchikov, the Soviet ambassador in Tehran, complained against persistent Soviet propaganda which alleged that Iran was under US military domination and had become a US base. The note pointed out that US officers in Iran were merely paid advisers. It rejected Soviet criticism of the Iranian government's suppression of the Tudeh Party, calling this criticism interference in Iranian affairs.

However, on 19 March, Moscow radio charged that aerodromes, ports and communication systems were being constructed in Iran to help US military and political expansion, and accused Iranian 'reactionaries' of waging a campaign of terror against those who raised their voices against Anglo-US domination of Iran. On 23 March the US secretary of state, Dean Acheson, said that the Soviet charges that Iran was being turned into a US base were 'false and demonstrably untrue'.

On 17 April it was reported from Tehran that Sadchikov, the Soviet ambassador, had left for Moscow 'on leave', the Soviet consulate-general at Tabriz and the other Soviet consular offices in Azerbayjan having been closed down on the same day. However, on 18 April it was announced that Nadir Arasteh, who had spent many years in the Soviet Union, had been appointed Iranian ambassador in Moscow.

7 April Elections for Iran's Constituent Assembly are completed, and on 11 May the shah takes an oath of loyalty to the new Iranian constitution. As the internal situation improved, however, feelings towards the Soviets continued to harden. In a statement to Reuters on 26 May the shah again denied that Iran was under a military dictatorship, adding that its form of government was based on the democratic pattern of the Western monarchies. He said that the recent constitutional amendments would guarantee the 'proper functioning of a truer democracy'.

23 June Iraq and Iran sign a mutual assistance treaty in Tehran.

12 October Foreign cultural missions outside Tehran are ordered to close. The move was clearly aimed at Soviet influence in Iran. Meanwhile, on 26 October Tehran announced that all diplomatic missions must henceforth refer to the country as Persia in English, and Perse in French, rather than Iran, which sounded too much like Iraq. The name had been changed from Persia to Iran on 21 March 1935.

14 October Saudi Arabia officially notifies the British government of its claim to nearly 50,000 square miles (129,500 square kilometres) of the deserts stretching eastwards from al-Hasa in regions regarded by the rulers of Qatar, Abu Dhabi and Muscat as their own. The most important of the towns covered by the claim was Buraimi, today Al-Ain in Abu Dhabi although the neighbouring Omani town is still called Buraimi. The incident came at a time of poor Anglo-Saudi relations to which British support for the new state of Israel had contributed.

Between 1947 and 1949 an Arabian American Oil Company (ARAMCO) survey party had entered the coastal region east of Qatar, exploring areas which the British government regarded as belonging to Abu Dhabi which Britain was committed by treaty to protect. Shaikh Shakbut, the ruler of Abu Dhabi, promptly complained about the trespass to the British political officer in Sharjah. However, King Abd al-Aziz (Ibn Saud) of Saudi Arabia had never accepted the demarcation line which had been formulated by Britain in 1935 and 1937.

Saudi Arabia's new claim of October involved four-fifths of Abu Dhabi's territory and included a corridor to the coast which contained the Liwa Oasis, the ancestral home of the Al bu Falah clan to which Abu Dhabi's ruling family belonged. It appears that ARAMCO itself played an important part in the Saudi claim, and although Ibn Saud was old and unlikely to have initiated the claim himself, it would have been a matter of honour for him to uphold it once it had been made.

On 30 November the British rejected the claim as totally unrealistic, taking as their premise the Anglo-Ottoman agreement of 1913/14.

4 November The Iranian court minister, Abd al-Hussein Hazhir, is shot at a mosque ceremony and dies the following day. Martial law, which had been lifted in August, was again imposed in Tehran and other towns. Hazhir was almost certainly the victim of the Fedayeen-e Islam, a militant Islamic underground organization founded in 1945 by a theological student called Sayyid Mujtaba Navab Safavi. The Fedayeen called for the implementation of of the Shari'a (Islamic law) and the banning of alcohol, cinema and other such amusements, opium and gambling and, it seems, even Western forms of dress.

Despite the instability created by the assassination and the martial law which followed, the shah left Tehran on 16 November for the US to meet President Truman and spend a six-week visit. On 30 December, President Truman's Point Four programme was announced promising economic and military assistance. Iran was to be a beneficiary.

7 November The Iraqi prime minister, Nuri al-Said, resigns. On 10 December a new Iraqi cabinet was formed by Ali Jawdat al-Ayyubi.

15 November Britain allows Iraq to draw hard currency to the value of $1 million a month on condition that it puts its hard currency at the disposal of the sterling-area pool.

1 9 5 0

15 January In a letter to US Republican Jacob Javits, the US secretary of state, Dean Acheson, defends British arms sales to Arab states. Acheson argued that the West must maintain friendship with the Arab world and satisfy its legitimate security requirements.

16 January The new Egyptian prime minister, Nahas Pasha, promises in his opening speech to parliament that his government will build up a stronger Egyptian army; try to make Britain withdraw its troops from the Suez Canal zone and the Anglo-Egyptian Sudan; end martial law; industrialize Egypt; and wipe out illiteracy.

23 January The Israeli Knesset (parliament) passes a proclamation designating Jerusalem as Israel's capital. The decision was widely condemned in the Islamic world since Muslims regard Jerusalem as the third holiest city after Mecca and Medina.

29 January Shaikh Abdullah al-Salem al-Sabah becomes ruler of Kuwait on the death of his cousin Ahmad al-Jaber al-Sabah at the Dasman Palace. Born in 1895, Shaikh Abdullah was married to Mariam, the daughter of Shaikh Jaber II, the ruler of Kuwait from 1915 to 1917. For more than two centuries Kuwait had been ruled by members of the al-Sabah family. In the twentieth century the succession has been shared by the families of two sons of Mubarak the Great, Jaber and Salem.

Shaikh Ahmad al-Jaber had ruled Kuwait from 1921 until 1950. Under his auspices the 1922 Uqair conference was held to define the boundaries between Iraq, Kuwait and Saudi Arabia. In 1936 Shaikh Ahmad granted a concession to the Kuwait Oil Company, formed from the merger of two rival British and US companies – the Anglo-Persian Oil Company (later British Petroleum – BP) and the Gulf Exploration Company (later Gulf Oil). Oil was first struck at Burgan which was to prove to be one of the world's richest oilfields.

The new ruler, Shaikh Abdullah, was noted for his moderation, belief in democratic traditions and his respect for education at a time when Kuwait was making its transition from being an obscure shaikhdom to becoming an influential modern state with an evolved welfare system.

1 February The Iraqi premier, Ali Jawdat Ayub, resigns. On 5 February a new cabinet was formed by General Tewfiq al-Suwaidi.

9 February Iran's first Senate (upper house) is convened. On the same day a new government was formed by General Ali Razmara.

27 February The state minister, Ali Asghar Hekmat, announces the dismissal of 60 high officials in the Azerbayjani province for corruption and cruelty following the flight of 120,000 Azerbayjani peasants from mistreatment in their villages.

2 March The Iraqi government announces that Jews who wish, may leave the country but will automatically forfeit their Iraqi nationality if they do so. On 10 March a new law froze the property and funds of 64,000 Jews who had earlier been deprived of Iraqi nationality because they had registered for migration to Israel.

15 March In sharp contrast with its neighbour Iraq, on 15 March Iran recognizes the new Jewish state of Israel, the second Muslim state to do so. Turkey had recognized Israel on

9 March, the same day on which Sweden had charged that Israel had made no real effort to find and punish the assassins of the UN mediator, Count Folke Bernadotte. Bernadotte had been killed by Jewish terrorists in 1948.

13 May Iraq announces that 50,000 Jews will soon begin a mass air migration to Israel. On 13 May a US company was reported to have been given permission to fly them there. On 14 May Israel admitted 1,027 Jewish immigrants from Rumania. On 20 May Operation Ali Baba began with the object of airlifting 60,000 Iraqi Jews to Israel. On 21 May it was announced in Tel Aviv that during the year 81,000 Iraqi Jews had come to Israel and 21,000 were still waiting in Iraq to leave.

14 May The Soviet ambassador to Iran protests to the Iranian government about alleged oil prospecting by foreign, and especially US, engineers in northern Iran. The Iranians agreed to halt the prospecting.

25 May Dr Muhammad Musaddiq, the newly re-elected First Deputy for Tehran (and later to lead Iran's National Front Party), gives a speech in the Majlis (lower house) in which he strongly attacks the shah's unconstitutional behaviour. He accused the shah of acting dictatorially and condemned the interference in government affairs of the shah's domineering twin sister Princess Ashraf as well as of the army chief-of-staff.

Musaddiq's speech was approved by most of the deputies and even sympathetically heard by Ali Mansur, the pragmatic and wily premier who was reputed to take bribes but was acceptable to the British because he seemed willing to sign the Supplementary Oil Agreement, which was supported by the Anglo-Iranian Oil Company (AIOC) but detested by the nationalists, in particular Musaddiq's National Front, as strongly favouring the AIOC at Iran's expense.

Although Mansur's premiership reflected the shah's reluctance to have a truly independent premier, the shah was angered by Mansur's attempts to placate the National Front. Following the nullification of the Tehran elections in mid-November 1949 the National Front had secured places at the top of Tehran's polls. Most of its support came from the urban middle class. It was admired as uncorrupt with no allegiance to a foreign power. Its immediate policy was to oppose the Supplementary Oil Agreement but its long-term policy was to root out ubiquitous British influence.

Mansur, meanwhile, seemed keen not to alienate the National Front and was reported to have offered Musaddiq the portfolio of finance which the latter refused. Mansur also invited the maverick and popular orator, Ayatollah Kashani, in exile in Lebanon since early 1949, to return to Iran.

10 June Recently elected as one of the Tehran deputies in the Majlis, Ayatollah Kashani makes a triumphant homecoming to Tehran from his exile in Lebanon as soon as he receives Premier Mansur's invitation to return.

17 June Arab League delegates, meeting in Cairo, sign a collective security pact obliging each member state to help defend any of the others against aggression.

26 June General Ali Razmara is appointed Iranian prime minister, but without the approval of parliament, in the place of Mansur. Mansur had lost the support of the US and Britain who had decided that he was 'spineless' and too ready to concede to Dr Musaddiq's National Front. The shah was frightened of a resurgence of Communism and had believed that Mansur's government would be unable to cope with the demonstrations which Ayatollah Kashani's return on 10 June was likely to inspire. Mansur had sought inaction as a solution to his dilemma while the British expected co-operation and the shah submission. A favourite of the shah, Razmara was responsible for ensuring the return of Azerbayjan to central government in Tehran and was favoured by the US as a strong man who could push forward social and economic reforms. The US State Department had informed the British that 'Razmara would be a distinct improvement on Mansur, and that he should be able to form a more stable and effective government.'

On becoming prime minister, Razmara issued a statement to the press which concentrated on the promises of reform which the shah had made at the opening of parliament in February. However, the measures that Razmara announced were considered Utopian by the cynics. They included the establishment of provincial, district and village councils; the elimination of unemployment; the guaranteeing of the independence of the judiciary; and the balancing of the budget. Nevertheless, Razmara's new government received a vote of confidence of 95 to 8.

27 July Iran bars Western and all other foreign correspondents from Azerbayjan province to 'avoid provocation to the Russians'. On 4 August Tehran sources reported a Soviet offer to negotiate a Soviet-Iranian trade and barter agreement.

7 August Saudi Arabia, Lebanon, Syria and Jordan protest to the UN with regard to the shooting incident on 24 July involving an Israeli fighter and a Lebanese airliner. The fighter killed two passengers and wounded seven.

11 August Major oil companies sign an agreement with Iraq providing for a royalty increase of four to six shillings per ton for the country's oil, giving Iraq $47 million in additional revenue on foreign concessions for the duration of the agreement.

13 August Iran and Pakistan agree to set up a joint boundary commission to fix the undemarcated sectors of their border.

14 August Israel secures an agreement with the AIOC whereby the company's Haifa refineries will supply their entire output of 800,000 tons for Israeli domestic use, thus saving Israel $3.5 million in foreign exchange for imported oil.

29 August Britain and Yemen initiate negotiations in London over the Yemen and Aden Protectorate border delineation.

August and September A $15-million loan to Saudi Arabia is announced by the US Export Import Bank. The loan was to purchase US equipment for transport, health and agricultural and other such projects.

3 September Iran reports the outbreak of a Kurdish revolt near the Iraqi border. Tehran blamed the uprising on Soviet propagated support for a separate Kurdish state. On the following day Kurdish tribesmen near the Iraqi border fought with Iranians after turning down an ultimatum to surrender arms and ammunition under the government's policy of disarming all the tribes. On 10 September Kurdish nationalists in Paris charged that the recent unrest in Iran arose from Tehran's attempts to appropriate much of the Kurdish harvest, to collect high taxes and to enforce an old royal decree giving the shah title to lands of the Javanrudi Kurds.

6 September Fifty US Jewish businessmen and community leaders meeting Israeli officials in Jerusalem promise that US Jews will provide $1,000 million worth of private financing for a three-year development and immigration programme in Israel.

12 September Egypt charges that Israeli troops have driven more than 6,000 Palestinians from their homes in southern Israel during the past 10 days, forcing them to go to Egypt. On 15 September Egypt complained to the UN Security Council that 'Jewish terrorism' had driven 4,000 Arabs out of Israel recently. On 16 September Israel asked the UN Security Council to consider complaints that Egypt and Jordan were 'officially and publicly threatening aggressive action' against the Jewish state. On 19 September an airlift of Yemen's 50,000 Jews to Israel was completed.

16 September Nuri al-Said forms a new Iraqi cabinet following the resignation of Tewfiq al-Suwaidi on 14 September.

3 October The Soviet Union agrees to return 11 tons of Iranian gold blocked since the Second World War in Soviet banks. In addition a Soviet-Iranian commission was set up to settle eight boundary disputes.

6 October It is reported from Lebanon that the 1,069-mile (1,720-kilometre) Trans-Arabian pipeline (Tapline) linking Saudi Arabia's Gulf coast with the Lebanese port of Sidon on the Mediterranean has been completed with the linking of its eastern and western segments in Jordan.

4 November The 1940 Iranian-Soviet trade agreement is renewed for one year. Sensitivity to the feelings of its giant northern neighbour influenced the Iranian government on 15 November to ban the state radio station from re-broadcasting foreign programmes, including those of the British Broadcasting Corporation (BBC) and Voice of America. Iran's head of press and propaganda was sacked after a programme was broadcast attacking the Soviet ambassador who had signed the new Iranian-Soviet trade treaty.

25 November The British-inspired Supplementary Oil Agreement is rejected by the Oil Committee of the Iranian Majlis. Iranians resented the agreement which they felt strongly favoured the British-controlled AIOC. Muhammad Musaddiq had led the Majlis committee since 26 June. General Razmara's government had failed to make its position on the agreement clear to Musaddiq and his followers who put most of Iran's troubles at the door of the AIOC and called for its nationalization. On 18 October Razmara had declared his support for the Supplementary Oil Agreement in the Senate.

November The Egyptian prime minister, Mustafa al-Nahas Pasha, demands the immediate British withdrawal from the Suez Canal zone and from the Anglo-Egyptian Sudan. Britain replied that the 1936 Anglo-Egyptian treaty providing for the stationing of troops in Egypt could be abrogated only by mutual consent.

13 December Ayatollah Kashani's proclamation calling for the nationalization of Iran's oil industry is published. Responding to British pressure, the finance minister, Ghulam Hussein Furuhar, defended the Supplementary Oil Agreement and attacked nationalization, although later, under heavy Majlis pressure, he withdrew his support.

21 December The 38-year-old Queen(-Mother) Aliya of Iraq dies in Baghdad of intestinal cancer.

29 December Aden's eastern state of Mukalla is placed under martial law after nationalist rioters attack the sultan's palace guard.

---

1 9 5 1

---

2 January The Arabian American Oil Company (ARAMCO) announces a new agreement with Saudi Arabia. The agreement increased the kingdom's oil revenues by one-third, to one-half of ARAMCO's net earnings.

20 January Britain and Yemen agree to establish diplomatic relations before the end of 1951, and a joint commission is to be set up to establish Yemen and Aden Protectorate borders.

28 January The Shah of Iran proclaims the sale of crown lands to the peasants, principally to gain popularity at a time when the country is becoming highly emotional on the question of the nationalization of the oil industry.

January In Iran, Ayatollah Muhammad Taqi Khansari and other clerics issue *fatwas* (edicts) in favour of the nationalization of Iran's oil industry.

1 February A UN General Assembly committee reports that it has obtained pledges totalling $882,000 from 12 countries excluding the US and Britain, towards a $55-million fund sought for the relief of Palestinian Arab refugees.

12 February The Shah of Iran marries the beautiful Soraya Esfandiary-Bakhtiari, the daughter of an Iranian nobleman and a German mother, making this turbulent period in Iran's history a turning-point in the shah's personal life. In 1939 the shah had married Princess Fawzia, daughter of King Faruk of Egypt, but the relationship had been unsuccessful and the marriage was eventually dissolved in 1948.

23 February The Israeli government reports that Israel's population is now 1.4 million, including 1.23 million Jews and 120,000 Muslims and Christians.

The Iran Oil Crisis: March

7 March The reformist prime minister, General Ali Razmara, is assassinated at the Masjid-e Soltani (Soltani Mosque) in Tehran when he attends the funeral of an ayatollah. His killer was Khalil Tahmasibi, a member of the fanatical Fedayeen-e Islam which had demanded the nationalization of the oil industry and bitterly attacked Razmara for not implementing it. The assassination was greeted by the crowds with jubilation and although Razmara had had several friends among the clergy, no cleric was willing to brave their wrath and read a sermon at his funeral.

8 March An oil commission appointed by Iran's Majlis (lower house), which had rejected the 1950 Supplementary Oil Agreement, submits a new report to it in which it suggests the nationalization of the oil industry.

12 March Iran's Majlis confirms the appointment of the former foreign minister, Hussein Ala, as the new premier following the assassination of General Razmara.

15 March Iran's Majlis passes a motion calling for the acceptance of the principle of oil nationalization and the elimination of foreign interests from the Anglo-Iranian Oil Company (AIOC).

20 March The Iranian Senate (upper house) unanimously approves the oil nationalization bill although only 27 out of its 60 members are present for the vote. On the same day the shah declared martial law in Tehran for two months and appointed General Hejazi military governor of the city. On 21 March oil workers went on strike at Bandar Mashur, the oil port built by the AIOC, and by 25 March the strike had spread to Abadan.

26 March The Arab League announces plans to establish a bureau in Cairo to tighten the Arab states' economic blockade of Israel.

The Iran Oil Crisis: April

20 March–4 April Iranian Premier Hussein Ala's new cabinet is announced in two stages. On 4 April Iran ordered the censorship of the foreign news dispatches that 'appear dangerous' to the nation's security or violated rules of decency.

3 April Iraq announces that the Iraq Petroleum Company (IPC), owned by an Anglo- US consortium, has agreed to pay higher royalties to protect its drilling concessions.

8 April Ala replies to a British note of 14 March, confirming that the Iranian oil industry is to be nationalized. On 12 April anti-British riots in Abadan ended in 11 deaths when the army fired into a crowd of demonstrators. On 17 April parliament passed a vote of confidence in Ala's handling of the crisis as well as his programme to nationalize the AIOC. On 20 April Communists and nationalists held anti-British demonstrations in Tehran, calling for the speeding-up of the government's oil nationalization programme.

Although anti-British strikes appeared to end on 24 April when 17,000 workers returned to their jobs, on 27 April Ala resigned on the grounds that he lacked support for his efforts to promote a compromise between Iranians backing oil nationalization and British demands for the protection of British interests.

Ala was replaced as premier on 28 April by Dr Muhammad Musaddiq, the National Front leader. The Majlis had recommended his selection by 79 votes to 12. Earlier in the day it had spelled out the steps for the Iranian takeover of the AIOC. After a 10-hour debate on the same day the Majlis agreed to a government takeover of all oil installations in the country. The British foreign secretary, Herbert Stanley Morrison, responded by assuring the British prime minister, Anthony Eden, that Britain would not hesitate to take appropriate action against Iran in the event of British oil interests being threatened.

14/15 April Mass demonstrations take place throughout Iran in favour of oil industry nationalization. On 19 April the Anglo-US discussions on the oil crisis were concluded. On 30 April Britain offered to accept nationalization of the $560-million AIOC, then 53 per cent British-owned, on condition that Iran agreed to provide Britain with oil.

28 April Shaikh Abdullah, the Kuwaiti ruler, asks the US and the British-owned Kuwait Oil Company to raise Kuwait's royalties to $200,000 a day.

The Iran Oil Crisis: May

1 May The shah gives his assent to the oil nationalization bill and formalizes the appointment of Musaddiq as premier. The AIOC responded to the nationalization decree by witholding £2 million in advance royalties from the Iranian government. On the same day the Tudeh Party staged a pro-Soviet demonstration in Tehran with 30,000 participants.

13 May Musaddiq claims that his life is being threatened by groups hostile to his nationalization campaign and seeks sanctuary in the Majlis building. After making a statement to the Majlis he collapsed. On 15 May his office sent a circular to all government offices announcing that the AIOC had been dissolved.

16 May Abul Qasim Rafi'i, the deputy head of the Fedayeen-e Islam, is arrested in Tehran. The police claimed that he said he would kill Musaddiq within the next three days. On 17 May the AIOC denied that it had employed agitators against Musaddiq.

18 June An agreement is signed in Jeddah between Saudi Arabia and the US permitting the US to use the Dhahran air base 'for maintenance, repair and other technical services to the US government aircraft' for a further five years.

The Iran Oil Crisis: June

22 June AIOC delegates leave Iran for the conference in London where letters are exchanged over the newly-formed National Iranian Oil Company's (NIOC) stringent demands of the previous day.

23 June The International Court at The Hague publishes its summing up of Britain's request that the AIOC remain in Iran. On 24 June AIOC tankers were forced to wait at port because tanker masters were refusing to sign Iranian receipts. On 25 June the British consul, Francis Shepherd, complained about Musaddiq's motion in the Majlis which had accused the general manager of the AIOC of sabotage and which had called for legislation to outlaw further such activity.

On 26 June the HMS *Mauritius* was ordered to the vicinity of Abadan as the US secretary of state, Dean Acheson, announced that events in Iran were moving towards disaster. On 27 June British AIOC staff were refused employment with the new NIOC. Acheson announced that the US sympathized with Iranian aspirations but that Iran should not proceed in this illegitimate way. On 28 June Tehran agreed to remove the anti-sabotage legislation if British technicians agreed to stay at their posts.

Meanwhile, the HMS *Mauritius* arrived on the Iraqi side of the Shatt al-Arab waterway to Iranian complaints that Britain had no right in time of peace to use Iraq as a base from which to to intimidate Iran. The NIOC took over Drake's (the AIOC head's) office in Abadan and the British staff promptly walked out. The Iranians appointed the Iranian Bazargan to replace Drake.

However, by stealth the AIOC tankers managed to discharge and leave, in one of the largest diversive moves of shipping ever made in peacetime.

The Iran Oil Crisis: July

1 July The house of Dr Seddon, the AIOC's chief representative in Tehran, is raided by the Iranian police in a search for documents proving 'efforts to bribe the Persian press'. On 2 July Drake met the British prime minister, Clement Attlee, as the Iranian embassy in London issued a statement assuring the British press that there was 'no anti-British feeling in Iran'. On 5 July the International Court at The Hague essentially supported the British case while Hussein Navab, the Iranian minister at The Hague, called the court's decision 'null and void'. On 6 July Britain accepted the Court's findings but the Iranians responded by saying that the Court was not impartial.

10 July Tehran sends a note to the UN secretary-general, Trygve Lie, challenging the competence of the Court while on 11 July Musaddiq welcomed a possible visit by US statesman Averell Harriman. At the same time the Iranian authorities at Abadan seized control of all AIOC links with the outside world. Even the AIOC's private telephone link with Basra was cut.

12 July Musaddiq threatens to publish secret AIOC documents and to take the dispute to the UN. Musaddiq initiated attempts at obtaining other sources of money. At the time Iran had £16 million deposited in British banks, $25 million in a US EximBank loan and a £22-million public loan in Iran. On 13 July Musaddiq sought emergency economic powers from the Majlis.

15 July Harriman arrives in Tehran as 15 people are killed by the police in demonstrations in Tehran, involving 15,000 Tudeh Party supporters against supporters of the Iranian Labour Party. On 16 July martial law was imposed in Tehran and on 31 July oil production at the Abadan refinery ceased entirely.

1 August In the UN Security Council, Britain demands that Egypt end its 'unjustified' and 'increasingly abusive' blockade of shipments to Israel through the Suez Canal. On 6 August the Egyptian foreign minister, Muhammad Salah al-Din, told parliament that Egypt would abrogate the 1936 Suez defence pact with Britain following the failure of the recent negotiations to amend it. On 1 September the Security Council asked Egypt to lift its blockade of shipping to Israel through the Suez Canal but Egypt refused to comply.

The Iran Oil crisis: August

3 August Britain accepts Harriman's formula for a solution to the Iranian oil crisis. On 4 August Britain's Lord Privy Seal Richard Stokes went to Tehran where he met Musaddiq and the shah, and on 6 August he had talks with the Iranian government. On 7 August he visited Abadan and on 13 August he presented the Iranian government with new British proposals, which it rejected on 15 August, insisting that AIOC assets be handed to it. On 22 August negotiations broke down. Stokes left Tehran on 23 August and Harriman on 24 August. On 28 August Harriman gave a press conference in London in which he called Iran's 'nationalist spirit and growing pride understandable'.

13 August An agreement is signed whereby the Iraqi government is to receive 50 per cent of oil-company profits. The other 50 per cent would go to the consortium of the Iraq Petroleum Company (IPC), the Mosul Petroleum Company and the Basrah Petroleum Company.

19

23 August The AIOC announces that all British, Indian and Pakistani staff will leave Iran, with only a skeleton staff remaining.

The Iran Oil Crisis: September

5 September Iran's Majlis decides to issue counter-proposals to the British offer, adding that if negotiations on the basis of these are refused, it will revoke all British residence permits. On 6, 9 and 16 September, speaking to a half-empty house, Iranian Premier Musaddiq asked the Majlis for a vote of confidence, but a quorum was prevented by the absence of many deputies due to 'ill-health'. Musaddiq told the Majlis that British agents were ubiquitous in Iran.

10 September The British treasury announces the withdrawal of certain trade and financial facilities accorded to Iran, causing the country severe economic problems. On 15 September Harriman added to the pressure on Musaddiq by refusing to pass new Iranian counter-proposals to the British. On 25 September the crisis developed with all British residents ordered to quit Iran within one week of 27 September.

By 27 September the Abadan refinery was entirely under Iranian control. However, in a pleasant and characteristic gesture, Musaddiq told the NIOC officials to take leave of the foreign technicians 'with the friendliest feelings'. On the same day Musaddiq again failed to win a vote of confidence in the Majlis for want of sufficient deputies to form a quorum.

Despairing of the Majlis, he stood on a chair outside the parliament building where he harangued the crowd, was garlanded with flowers and wept bitterly. He told the crowd that he would not leave office until the oil crisis was resolved and would, if necessary, resolve it without the support of parliament. At the end of the speech he was taken, fainting, back into the Majlis building.

28 September Britain decides to bring the crisis before the UN and on 1 October, by nine votes to two, the UN Security Council agrees to place on the agenda a resolution calling on Iran to respect the findings of the International Court regarding the oil crisis. A British official, Gladwyn Jebb, refuted the Iranian government's description of the AIOC organization as a 'gang of unscrupulous blood-suckers'.

The Iran Oil Crisis: October

3 October 280 members of the AIOC go on board HMS *Mauritius*. Six British destroyers had lain for some weeks at anchor in the Shatt al-Arab waterway waiting to take AIOC employees on board.

On 15 October Premier Musaddiq presented Iran's case to the UN Security Council and maintained that oil should help Iran but was in fact no benefit at all. He pointed out that of 1948 revenues of £61 million, Iran obtained only £9 million.

On 16 October he said that Britain wanted public opinion to believe that the 'lamb' (Iran) had menaced the 'wolf' (Britain), adding that Iranians in the oil-rich provinces lived in misery. Jebb replied that Musaddiq could not expect to have it both ways: enjoy foreign expertise, which Musaddiq admitted that Iran needed, and yet insist on unacceptable terms or else break contracts. Musaddiq then announced that the AIOC would never again operate in Iran, adding 'We are not prepared to finance other people's dreams of empire from our resources.'

10 October Rioters in Cairo sack British and other foreign businesses until they are stopped by police. On 8 October Egyptian Premier Nahas Pasha had asked parliament to endorse two decrees, one abrogating the 1936 Anglo-Egyptian treaty under which British troops defended the Suez Canal, and the other annexing Anglo-Egyptian Sudan to Egypt.

On 9 October Britain responded by warning that it would not recognize a unilateral renunciation of the 1936 treaty and would keep its troops in the Suez Canal zone by force if necessary. Britain's attitude was largely responsible for the riots on 10 October. On 16 October British troops battled with rioting Egyptians in the canal zone, with 12 deaths reported. On the following day Britain rushed 3,500 paratroops from Cyprus to Suez, bringing its garrison there up to 60,000. On 21 October Egypt protested in a note to Britain that British troops in Suez behaved as though they were patrolling a 'conquered country'. On 22 October Britain occupied Suez town. On 27 October Egypt formally notified Britain that it had abrogated the 1936 treaty. On 30 October the British prime minister, Winston Churchill, ordered 15,000 troops to the Middle East in a move to stem the violence.

6 November Britain accuses Egypt of violating the UN Charter by denouncing the 1936 Anglo-Egyptian treaty. On 15 November King Faruk formally assumed the title of King of Egypt and Sudan. On 18 November British troops clashed with Egyptian police in the Suez Canal town of Ismailiyya.

The Iran Oil Crisis: November

13 November The International Monetary Fund gives Iran a much-needed emergency credit of $7.75 million. On 16 November President Truman's press secretary confirmed that Musaddiq had requested a US loan, of perhaps $120 million.

On 25 November the Majlis gave Musaddiq a vote of confidence (90 to 0) but with 15 abstentions and 31 deputies absent. On 26 November the Senate also gave him a vote of confidence but again there were many absentees. He told the Majlis that Britain was trying to bring Iran 'to its knees' and that the US loan was 'under special consideration'. Jamal Imami, the opposition leader, made a violent attack on Musaddiq in the Majlis, accusing him of leading the country to bankruptcy and chaos.

16 November The British pro-vice-consul, Cyril Ousman, is shot dead at his own party in Jeddah by the 19-year-old eighteenth surviving son of Saudi King Abd al-Aziz (Ibn Saud), Prince Mishari ibn Abd al-Aziz. Alcohol had been served and a row had developed. According to custom and the king's command, Ousman's widow was offered the choice of Mishari's execution or 'blood money', but although tempted to choose the former, she was persuaded by friends to take blood money. The following year the king was to ban all alcohol from the kingdom.

21 November The Soviet foreign minister, Andrei Gromyko, sends a note to the Iraqi diplomatic representative requesting it not to join the Middle East Command sponsored by Britain, the US, France and Turkey. On 22 November Gromyko sent a similar note to the Saudi and Yemeni diplomatic representatives.

2 December Fighting breaks out in the Suez Canal zone between British troops and Egyptian dock workers following the end of a six-week dock strike. The clashes continued on 4 December, causing 65 deaths. The Egyptian government declared a state of emergency.

3 December The Kuwait Oil Company announces the conclusion of an agreement providing for an even division of profits with the ruler of Kuwait.

The Iran Oil Crisis: December

6 December Serious rioting breaks out in Tehran. As a result of mob violence, 15 newspaper editors and 15 opposition deputies took sanctuary in the Majlis building and refused to return home until they were safe from Mussadiq's National Front supporters. Meanwhile, Tehran's *New York Times* correspondent was expelled. On 9 December both supporters and critics of the government attacked its handling of the 6 December riots.

On 10/11 December Musaddiq condemned the violence and those who attacked the opposition offices in the riots. Opposition deputies, however, accused him of being a 'traitor, dictator and murderer'. The pro-British, anti-Communist leader of the opposition against Musaddiq, Jamal Imami, accused him of bringing the country to 'misery and the verge of revolution'. The meetings became so stormy that government and opposition deputies actually came to blows in the gallery of the Majlis and troops were called in to restore peace.

2–12 December Musaddiq reorganizes the cabinet. On 13 December the Reuters correspondent was expelled from Iran and on 30 December foreign travel was banned for Iranian nationals.

8 December Egypt recalls its ambassador to Britain as a protest against British actions in the Suez Canal zone.

22 December Iran concludes an oil supply agreement with Czechoslovakia. The agreement followed Britain's rejection of the 10-day limit for ordering Iranian oil.

24 December Libya officially gains independence under King Idris I, former ruler of Cyrenaica.

31 December Egyptian extremists announce that they will pay any 'partisan patriot' $2,800 for killing the British Suez Canal zone commander, General George Erskine, and $200 for killing any other British army officer.

1 9 5 2

The Iran Oil Crisis: January

1–13 January International Bank representatives visit Tehran and propose a temporary restoration of oil operations. However, on 3 January Musaddiq announced that the Bank's proposals were 'unacceptable'. On 4 January Amir Teymour Kalali, a close friend of Musaddiq, resigned as minister of the interior because the opposition had called for his impeachment and trial for organizing incidents in the 6 December riots.

9 January The Iranian government sends an insulting note by messenger-boy to the British embassy accusing it of interfering in national affairs. The embassy refused to accept the note. On 12 January the government called for the closure of all British consulates by 21 January, and on 20 January it sent the British embassy a second note saying that the Anglo-Persian treaty of 1857 was 'outmoded'.

15 January The Egyptian Chamber of Deputies passes a bill providing for life imprisonment for collaboration with foreign forces in Egypt.

21 January All British consulates in Iran are closed according to the request of the Iranian government which promptly declares a national holiday and 'liberation day'. On 23 January Sir Francis Shepherd left Tehran as British ambassador but Iran refused to accept Robert Hankey as his replacement, arguing that no British diplomat sent to Iran should have served in the British colonies. On 30 January the British Bank of the Middle East announced that its provincial offices were to close down on 30 April and its Tehran office on 30 July.

22–24 January Polling takes place for Iran's Majlis (lower house) elections. The results, announced on 11 February, gave Mussadiq's National Front a gain of 11 out of 12 seats for Tehran.

23 January The US State Department announces that military aid to Iran has ceased because Iran has failed to give the anti-Communist security pledge required by the 1952 Mutual Security Act. On 20 January, however, the US Point Four technical-aid programme for Iran had gone into effect. This provided Iran with $23 million without the signing of an implementation agreement placing the Iranian government under obligation to the US.

25 January British troops and Egyptian auxiliary police clash in Ismailiyya, leaving 42 Egyptians dead and 58 wounded. On 26 January the Egyptian government called out the army to quell the anti-British rioting while the king signed a decree placing the country under martial law.

31 January The Iranian government, desperately short of ready cash and goods, announces a barter deal to sell oil to Hungary.

1 February Egypt and Syria formally merge to form the United Arab Republic (UAR).

The Iran Oil Crisis: February

19 February Journalists, walled up in the Majlis building, leave unharmed, but opposition members remain within the protection of its walls. On 11 February an International Bank for Reconstruction and Development team arrived in Tehran. On 21 February the delegates flew to London.

22 February Iraq adopts a five-year, $470-million economic development programme proposed by a World Bank study mission.

The Iran Oil Crisis: March

20 March The US announces that it cannot justify financial aid to Iran, and on 27 March Musaddiq responds by saying that Iran is no longer pursuing a US loan. However, on 1 April, under the US Point Four programme, agreements for agricultural, health and educational projects in Iran worth $11 million were signed. On 28 March serious rioting broke out in Tehran and on 30 March martial law was imposed for one month. It was lifted on 12 April although on the following day the correspondent for the London *Times* was ordered to leave Iran.

The Iran Oil Crisis: April, May

20 April Iran lays claim to Bahrain, Kuwait and other areas of the Gulf. On 29 April Britain sharply refuted the legitimacy of these claims, stressing that it was bound to protect these states because of the treaties signed in 1820 and after. Iran's claims on Bahrain had always been ominous because of the many Iranians living on the islands and Bahrain's majority Shi'i population.

Bahrain was crucial to British interests, and even before oil had been struck there it had been considered as the most likely alternative to succeed Bushehr in Iran as the British headquarters in the Gulf. After 1927 the Iranians refused to give visas to British passport-holders with Bahraini or Kuwaiti stamps. The British responded to this after 1934 by allowing British passport-holders to bear two passports, one of which was valid only for journeys to Bahrain and Kuwait.

23 April The Iraq Petroleum Company (IPC) completes the pipeline from Kirkuk in northern Iraq to Syria's Mediterranean port of Banias.

25 April The US State Department announces the resumption of military aid to Iran. On 14 May Iran accepted the 1949 UN declaration on the settlement of international disputes but said that this did not apply to the British-Iranian oil dispute which was a domestic matter. On 21 May the Soviet Union warned Iran not to accept US military aid, but on 1 July Iran rejected the Soviet protest.

20 May The Iranian prime minister, Muhammad Musaddiq, suspends the Majlis elections.

17 June West Germany offers to pay $714 million for Israeli and other Jewish claims resulting from property damage inflicted by the Nazis.

2 July Israel announces that Jerusalem 'was, is and always will be' its capital. Israel was responding to Arab and other protests calling for the internationalization of the city.

The Iran Oil Crisis: July

5 July Musaddiq resigns as Iranian prime minister, as he is constitutionally bound to do, before being re-elected on the following day. On 16 July, however, he resigned once again when the Majlis would not vote him the plenary powers he requested. With the powers he had intended to impose a six-month economic austerity programme.

17 July Ahmad Qavam al-Saltaneh succeeds Musaddiq as prime minister and promises a quick resolution to the oil dispute. However, his appointment was followed by widespread rioting provoked by Mussadiq's supporters and on 21 July Qavam resigned.

Serious rioting followed in what parliament termed a 'national uprising', and Musaddiq thanked the crowds for 'saving the nation'. After his address Musaddiq fainted an occurrence which his supporters attributed to a medical condition, but which the Western press preferred to link with emotional instability.

22 July Crowds bearing false coffins demand vengeance against Qavam. National Front leaders called for his execution. On the same day Musaddiq was reappointed prime minister, and on 23 July Qavam was arrested in Qom but managed to escape from his guards. On 27 July Musaddiq formed a new cabinet in which the shah allowed him to combine the premiership with the ministry of war. In his inaugural speech, Musaddiq announced major reforms, particularly in landowner–peasant relations. However, the mob violence of 21 July and after made many Iranians believe that a coup d'etat was imminent.

23 July A coup forces the resignation of the Egyptian government. In what was to become a crucial revolution, an Egyptian military coup, headed in theory by the popular and avuncular army commander-in-chief, General Muhammad Neguib, forced the resignation of Premier Neguib al-Hillali and the appointment of the former premier, Ali Maher. Neguib said that the coup was aimed at ending government corruption. However, it later transpired that the mastermind behind the coup was a young army colonel, Gamal abd al-Nasser. On 26 July King Faruk was forced to abdicate and on 5 August the government seized his property, valued at $287 million.

The Iran Oil Crisis: August

7 August The Iranian Majlis elects as speaker Ayatollah Sayyid Abul-Qasim Kashani (see Biographies). The Fedayeen-e Islam supported both Kashani and Prime Minister Musaddiq but were also responsible for various assassinations. Since the previous year Musaddiq had regarded himself as a target because he was unable to satisfy their demands. These were the compulsory wearing of the *hijab* (veil for women), the dismissal of women employees, a ban on alcohol, and compulsory public prayers for government employees. The Fedayeen also demanded freedom of action for themselves and the release of their leaders.

11 August The Iranian Senate (upper house) grants Musaddiq emergency (and essentially autocratic) powers for six months. On 14 August the government issued a decree requiring police permission to hold public meetings and demonstrations. On 20 August the government re-imposed martial law in Tehran in order to end a week of fighting between the Tudeh (Communist) Party and radical nationalists.

21 August The Iranian government orders wealthy families to pay back taxes, traditionally ignored, or risk imprisonment and confiscation of property.

7 September The Egyptian army commander-in-chief, General Muhammad Neguib, forces the resignation of Premier Ali Maher and takes direct control of the Egyptian government.

The Iran Oil Crisis: September

17 September The Iranian parliament gives Prime Minister Musaddiq a vote of confidence following his report to it on the Anglo-Iranian oil dispute. On 24

September Iran demanded a payment of $137.2 million from the Anglo-Iranian Oil Company (AIOC) for the settlement of pre-nationalization debts. On 4 October Britain rejected the demand. On 8 October Iran modified the demand, asking Britain to pay $56 million in company debts before the start of negotiations on the dispute's settlement. On 15 September Britain rejected this latest proposal as 'unreasonable and unacceptable'. On 16 September Musaddiq threatened to sever relations with Britain although these were not formally broken off until 22 October.

28 October Following the Iraqi royal decree on 27 October dissolving parliament and ordering elections within 60 days, four out of the five leading parties (the Nationalists, the United Popular Front, the National Democratic Party and the Umma Socialists) put several demands in a letter of 28 October to the regent, Abdulilah. These demands included the direct election of parliamentary deputies instead of the existing method of indirect elections; a constitutional amendment allowing parliament instead of the king to dismiss cabinets; agrarian reforms similar to those introduced by Nasser's revolutionary regime in Egypt; the compulsory disclosure by private politicians of their source of wealth; the abrogation of the Anglo-Iraqi friendship treaty of 1928 (under which, for example, the British air force was allowed to maintain two bases in Iraq); and abstention from the proposed Middle East Command envisaged by the Western powers.

18 November Iraq's King Faisal II inaugurates the IPC's new oil pipeline from Kirkuk in Iraq to Banias in Syria.

22 November The Iraqi Communist Party leader, Baha' al-Din Nuri, organizes huge demonstrations in Baghdad known as the Intifada (the tremor). Martial law was promptly declared and on 23 November General Nur al-Din Mahmoud was appointed premier. The Intifada followed the resignation on the same day of the non-party cabinet headed by Mustafa al-Umari.

The rioters, who numbered about 20,000, staged anti-British and anti-US demonstrations, called for the dismantling of the Anglo-Iraqi treaty, wrecked the offices of the US Information Service and burned books and files. They smashed the offices of the Baghdad English-language *Iraq Times*, stoned the headquarters of the Constitutional Unionist Party and badly damaged the offices of the government-owned Iraqi Airways.

25 December The Arab League Political Commission issues a 'condemnation of the mere idea of an invitation to the Arabs to negotiate with the Israelis'. On 28 December Israel agreed not to conscript US citizens for military service, thus enabling them to retain their US citizenship under the McCarran Act.

---

1 9 5 3

The Iran Oil Crisis: January

6 January The Iranian Majlis (lower house) gives Premier Musaddiq a vote of confidence and extends his emergency powers. However, both were opposed by

Ayatollah Sayyid Abul-Qasim Kashani, and the break between the premier and Kashani now appeared to be complete. Meanwhile, later in the month there were clashes in Iran's holy city of Qom between the followers of Ayatollah Borujirdi and those of the more leftist and more junior cleric, Sayyid Ali Akbar Borqa'i. Borujirdi had been the focus of moderate clerical activity.

When, shortly after the attempt on the shah's life in February 1949, the Majlis, at the shah's behest, passed a law restricting political activity, the moderate ulema (clergy) rallied round the shah. On 20/21 February in that year Borujirdi had called a conference, attended by 2,000 clerics, which decided against political activism by the clergy and threatened to defrock any cleric who defied the directive. Musaddiq, increasingly provoked by Kashani who attacked the US at a time when the government was trying to give the impression of good relations, and who sent missions to Europe which appeared to question Iran's neutrality, exploited his own good relations with Borujirdi. He had made any insult to Borujirdi, Iran's senior ayatollah, a punishable offence while Kashani enjoyed no such protection, a source of deep humiliation to him.

19 January The Iranian parliament extends Musaddiq's power to govern by decree for a full year beginning on 9 February.

29 January Iraq's new coalition cabinet, headed by Premier Jamil al-Madfai, takes office, replacing that of General Nur al-Din Mahmoud.

29 January Iran terminates the Caspian fishing rights leased to the Soviet Union. On 31 January the Soviet monopoly on the sale of Iranian caviar ended when Iran refused to renew a 25-year pact for the joint operation of the Caspian Sea fisheries.

8 February The Iranian Majlis unanimously approves a bill forbidding the importation, manufacture, sale or use of alcoholic beverages throughout Iran. An amendment also banned the use of opium. The bill aimed to satisfy the dictates of Islam.

10 February The Iranian foreign minister, Hussein Fatemi, protests at Iraqi border-raids on Iranian tribes.

15 February Most of the 1,400 inhabitants of Turud in north-eastern Iran are reported killed in an earthquake.

Iran Oil Crisis: February

28 February The shah decides to leave the country 'for health reasons'. On the previous day Ayatollah Kashani had gathered together members of the Majlis to implore him to stay and had himself begged the shah's wife, Queen Soraya, to use her influence on her husband to persuade him. However, when on 28 February Musaddiq arrived at the palace to say farewell to the shah, both men were surprised by the shouting outside. Assuming that the shah was under threat, Musaddiq urged him to leave quickly. However, it soon became clear that the crowds were chanting 'Long live the Shah' and 'Down with Musaddiq'. The prime minister fainted and when he came round was led by Queen Soraya to the back door of the palace from where he could make a safe getaway.

Meanwhile Musaddiq's house was attacked, and, fearing his own murder, he was forced to escape from the mob dressed only in his pyjamas. As was the custom for those seeking safety, he took refuge in the Majlis building. After further pro-shah demonstrations, the shah decided to stay in Iran.

Some critics, according to Azimi in *Iran: the Crisis of Democracy*, maintain that the shah intentionally tricked Musaddiq by asking the premier to keep his journey secret but then deliberately leaking the details of it to the public. Kashani issued two letters publicly requesting the shah to abandon his trip and appealed to the people to prevent his departure. According to Azimi, the Association of Retired Officers (a group including military officers dismissed under Musaddiq) played a crucial role in the 28 February demonstrations by bringing in air-force lorries filled with peasants who supported the shah, from regions near Tehran where he had distributed crown lands, and by telling the crowds that Musaddiq had urged the shah to leave the country with the private intention of removing him from the throne as soon as he had departed.

1 March Musaddiq returned to Tehran as his followers clashed in the streets with pro-shah demonstrators. After four days of rioting by nationalist, royalist, Tudeh (Communist) and religious groups, Musaddiq managed to re-impose control.

3/4 March Saudi Arabia appeals to Britain over the Buraimi dispute. Saudi Arabia claimed that the area of the Buraimi Oasis within the Trucial States belonged to it. Britain had promised to maintain the region as a part of Abu Dhabi, the largest of the Trucial States.

22 March The Egyptian premier, Muhammad Neguib, calls upon all Egyptians to sacrifice themselves in the pursuit of Egypt's demand for the immediate unconditional withdrawal of British troops from the Suez Canal zone.

30 March The Kuwaiti ruler, Shaikh Abdullah al-Salem al-Sabah, opens the world's largest saltwater distillation plant in Kuwait city.

The Iran Oil Crisis: April

6 April Musaddiq accuses the Iranian royal court, in particular the dowager queen and the shah's twin sister, Princess Ashraf, of plotting against him and says that the shah must 'reign but not rule'. On 8 April the court minister, Hussein Ala, announced that the shah supported Musaddiq. However, Ala resigned on 23 April due to 'ill-health' and was replaced on 25 April by Dr Amini.

20 April Iran's energetic chief-of-police, Brigadier Mahmud Afshartus, disappears. He had formerly been an instructor at the Military Academy where, according to his enemies, he had earned a reputation for brutality. Some days later, on 26 April, he was found strangled in a roadside grave near Tehran. It was clear that he had been tortured to death in revenge for his alleged cruelties. It was also clear that the murder was intended as a message to Musaddiq.

2 May Faisal II, aged 18, formally assumes the royal prerogative as King of Iraq. The king took the oath before both the upper and lower houses of the Iraqi parliament assembled in joint session and in the presence of foreign representatives such as the Duke of Gloucester representing Queen Elizabeth of Britain, the Crown Prince of Saudi Arabia, the Amir

Saud, and the Crown Prince of Ethiopia, the Duke of Harar. On the same day his cousin in Jordan, Husayn, also reached the crucial age of 18 and acceded to the Jordanian throne. The accession of Faisal theoretically ended the regency of the Amir Abdulilah, the king's maternal uncle who had been regent because of Faisal's minority since 4 April 1939 when Faisal's father, King Ghazi, was killed in a car accident.

The Iran Oil Crisis: May

11 May The shah transfers some crown lands to the government, pre-empting the government's seizure of these. On 24 May the first reading of the bill aimed at limiting the shah's powers took place in the Majlis. When the bill reached the voting stage on 7 June there was an uproar and hand-to-hand fighting broke out within the Majlis chamber.

11 May The British prime minister, Winston Churchill, threatens to respond with force to any Egyptian move against the Suez Canal. On the following day the British admiralty reported the transfer of four destroyers and Royal Marine commando units from Malta to reinforce the Suez Canal zone garrison.

18 May The US secretary of state, Foster Dulles, says in Baghdad that he feels that the US has failed to pay enough attention to countries east of Turkey. He added that US policy would evolve as a result of his tour.

24 May Iran and Syria sign a treaty of friendship in Damascus.

The Iran Oil Crisis: June, July, August

30 June Ayatollah Kashani bitterly attacks Musaddiq in what is seen as the final step in the split between them. On 1 July the ayatollah was sacked as speaker of the Majlis and replaced by Dr Mu'azzami, a university professor who was more loyal to Musaddiq. When, on 27 July, Musaddiq called for a referendum on whether to retain the present Majlis, Kashani responded on 29 July by violently denouncing the referendum. On the same day, in a move that served to undermine Musaddiq's government, a letter was sent by the new US president, Dwight Eisenhower, rejecting Musaddiq's appeal for loans until the oil dispute had been settled. On 5 August Eisenhower was to feel constrained to criticize Musaddiq's collaboration with the Tudeh (Communist) Party.

19 July Kermit Roosevelt, the US Central Intelligence Agency's (CIA's) area chief in the Middle East, arrives in Iran by road from Iraq. By April the CIA had become the prime mover in a project, code-named Operation Ajax, to unseat Musaddiq in favour of the shah. From 1/2 to 8/9 August Roosevelt had a series of secret meetings with the shah in Tehran. They worked together on a plan that involved an alliance with the *ulema* (the Islamic clergy), the manipulation of crowds, the organization of publications, the monitoring of the opposition through hired agents, the consolidation of the support of royalist officers and overall co-ordination with Senator-General Fazlollah Zahedi and his friends.

Earlier in the year royalist military and gendarmerie officers had been busy planning Musaddiq's overthrow. They had been organized by Zahedi under the aegis of the secret Committee to Save the Fatherland. Most of the first recruits came from the

200 officers dismissed or retired by Musaddiq in the previous year. These men joined the so-called Retired Officers Club while Zahedi made contact with Britain's Military Intelligence 6 (MI6).

When Musaddiq cut diplomatic ties with Britain, MI6 left in Tehran a working group under a businessman called Asadollah Rashidian who had good contacts in Tehran's bazaar. MI6 also contacted the CIA since the US had the advantage of continuing to enjoy diplomatic relations with Iran. From that moment the movement to remove Musaddiq became a CIA campaign.

25 July The shah's twin sister, Princess Ashraf, arrives in Tehran. She had come, according to Queen Soraya's autobiography, to 'encourage us to act'. In Switzerland, where Ashraf had been on holiday, she had kept in close touch with Allen Dulles, the brother of Foster Dulles and the director of the CIA. The day after Princess Ashraf arrived in Tehran, Allen Dulles told journalists of the danger of Communism taking root on Iran.

3–10 August On 3 August in Tehran, and on 10 August in the rest of Iran a referendum is held by Premier Musaddiq to win approval for the dissolution of the present Majlis. Prior to this, 56 National Front supporters of Musaddiq had resigned from the Majlis on the grounds that opposition attacks on Musaddiq's policies had created a 'vicious atmosphere' which made parliamentary government impossible. Official government statements claimed that 166,607 votes had been cast in Tehran in favour of dissolving the Majlis to only 116 against, and that the figure in the rest of the country was 1,441,156 in favour of dissolution and a mere 694 against. This gave the government 99.93 per cent of the votes.

However, the voting procedure involved the provision of two separate voting booths, one for electors voting for the dissolution and one for those voting against. Each voter was obliged to write his name and identity-card number on his ballot paper.

August Nuri al-Said is re-appointed Iraqi premier by the regent and rules by decree, initiating a period of intense repression in Iraq.

10 August A mixed Soviet-Iranian commission is set up to resolve differences between the two countries.

16 August The shah and Queen Soraya fly to Rome from the Caspian Sea. They had flown from Tehran to the Caspian resort of Ramsar for a 'holiday' on 12 August, following the publication of the results of the referendum called by Premier Musaddiq. On 13 August and on CIA advice, the shah had sent orders dismissing Musaddiq and appointing senator General Fazlollah Zahedi, who had now gone into hiding, as prime minister.

The shah sent Colonel Nemotollah Nassiri, commander of the Imperial Guard, to Zahedi's hiding place to give him the message. The shah and Queen Soraya spent two nights in Baghdad, arriving in Rome on 18 August. Earlier on the day of 16 August the government announced that it had crushed an attempt by the shah's Imperial Guard to lead a military coup against it.

Following the shah's departure, Zahedi, now in hiding in hills north of Tehran, announced that the shah had appointed him prime minister before leaving Iran, having dismissed Musaddiq on 13 August. Zahedi called for the support of the army and emphasized that the shah's absence was only temporary. The government ordered police and troops to undertake an intensive search for Zahedi. When Colonel Nassiri had brought Zahedi the news of his appointment from the shah, he had ordered Nassiri to deliver Musaddiq his *firman* (decree) of dismissal. In Rome, meanwhile, the shah assured his Italian hosts that he was not asking for asylum and that he had not abdicated but that he was watching events 'very closely'.

According to the official Iranian government communiqué, at 11.40 pm on 15 August officers and men of the Imperial Guard had arrested two ministers, one of whom was the foreign minister, Dr Hussein Fatemi, and the other the deputy chief-of-staff, General Kiany. In addition, Colonel Nassiri, accompanied by tanks and four lorry loads of troops, had gone to Musaddiq's house to arrest him. However, Kiany had escaped and warned the security services who subsequently released the two ministers and arrested the ringleaders of the plot against the government. Although the comuniqué alluded to the complicity of the court, it made no reference to the shah himself.

Mussadiq posted government troops at all key points in Tehran and announced that the Majlis had been dissolved and that new elections for a lower house would take place after the drafting of an electoral law. On 16/17 August large pro-Musaddiq demonstrations against the shah took place in Tehran. Dr Fatemi wrote in his own newspaper *Bakhtar-e Imruz* that the shah was a 'serpent with beautiful spots' and that 'the people of this country want to see this traitor hanged'. The period was one of great confusion. While within Tehran street signs were being changed from Reza Shah Street to Republic Street and Pahlavi Street to People Street, pro-shah demonstrations were also taking place and police and government troops were putting down Tudeh demonstrations out of fear that the Tudeh would benefit from the confusion.

19 August Musaddiq is overthrown by the royalist forces commanded by General Zahedi and other army officers. On 18 August Tudeh Party gangs had set out to destroy statues of Reza Shah, the shah's father, in Tehran and desecrate his mausoleum at Hazrat Abd al-Azim, about eight miles (13 kilometres) from Tehran. However, on the following day Tudeh Party members obeyed orders to stay indoors.

Instead, large mobs from Tehran's bazaar (traditional market, one of the pivots of wealth) poured into the streets in support of the shah. They were led by Sha'ban bi-mukh (Sha'ban the Brainless) who ran a *zurkhanah* (a 'house of strength', or gymnasium) in Tehran. He frightened, persuaded or paid bazaaris to march in support of the shah. Gangs of youths were said to have distributed 10-riyal notes to anyone who shouted 'Long live the Shah'. In all they are said to have distributed $10 million in such bribes.

By mid-day the pro-shah rebels had seized control of Tehran and other leading cities. In a series of radio-broadcasts, army officers announced that Musaddiq's 'government of traitors and swindlers' had been overthrown, that all government buildings had been occupied and that all political prisoners had been freed.

Later in the day (19 August) Tehran radio announced that General Zahedi had ordered the arrest of all former ministers of the Musaddiq cabinet and that the shah would shortly be returning to Iran. Among those who broadcast on the station was Ayatollah Kashani's son who said that his father had welcomed the coup and the shah's return. Some 300 people were killed in Tehran during the coup. Most of the casualties, it appeared, had occurred when Musaddiq's supporters fought a last ditch battle from an underground bunker at his home which the shah's supporters had stormed and wrecked. Musaddiq had himself gone into hiding.

20 August Musaddiq is arrested, his house is gutted and destroyed and, still dressed in pyjamas, he is taken to the Officers' Club in Tehran. There he was told that the shah had ordered that his life be spared but that he be put on trial. According to an eye-witness, he was in bed when the attack took place and when he heard rifle-fire and the approaching tanks he pulled up the sheets and snuggled down giggling and saying '*Bebin che kar kardam*'

('Look what I've done !'). However, the story is probably apocryphal and an invention of his detractors.

22 August The shah returns, making a triumphant entry into Tehran. After his return to the city the shah broadcast a message of thanks to the people for 'rising to preserve the national traditions'. He continued that 'The same treacherous elements that attempted my life five years ago were seeking to divert our national struggle from its true course, so that we would share the fate of countries that exist with no spiritual life. I nurse no grudge in my heart, and extend clemency. But when it comes to violation of the Constitution which we are under oath to preserve – and this was forgotten by some – and to the dissolution of the Majlis, the disintegration of the Army and the dissipation of Treasury funds, the law must be carried out.'

23 August The shah tells the foreign press that Musaddiq has bequeathed a 'terrible situation' to the country, adding that the national treasury is empty and Iran's financial situation 'desperate'. Asked whether he would consider restoring relations with Britain, the shah said that it was still too early to say but that Iran wanted relations with all countries that respected 'our sovereignty and rights'.

In the internal sphere he said that emphasis would be given to land reform and that the distribution of crown lands to needy peasants would be resumed immediately. Asked about the situation of Musaddiq, the shah replied that he had been dismissed from office for trying to dissolve the Majlis illegally, that he was being kindly treated and that he would face two separate trials, one for crimes committed while he was prime minister and the second for resisting the legal government after he had been dismissed.

23 August General Fazlollah Zahedi forms a new government in Tehran. Meanwhile, it was announced in Tehran that the Iranian ambassadors in Paris and Baghdad, the minister in Brussels and the chargé d'affaires in Rome had been relieved of their posts.

25 August According to the new military governor of Tehran, stamps bearing the words 'Iranian Republic' are discovered at Tudeh Party offices. He added that the stamps indicated that Musaddiq had intended to proclaim a republic after the shah's flight to Rome. Meanwhile, Prime Minister Zahedi announced that, in defiance of foreign oil interests, he would discard Musaddiq's plan to sell Iranian oil abroad at half the prevailing world price. Musaddiq had made the offer to US and Japanese purchasers on 27 April on condition that payment was made in US dollars.

August Nuri al-Said is re-appointed Iraqi premier by the regent and rules by decree, initiating a period of intense repression in Iraq.

3 September With the shah firmly in power again, the US announces a $23.4-million grant for continued technical and military projects in Iran. It was the biggest Point Four expenditure ever made by the US for one country. On 5 September US President Eisenhower granted $45 million to Iran as emergency economic aid under the Mutual Security Act.

15 October The Saudi Arabian government imposes martial law to prevent attacks on US property by dissatisfied oil workers in the kingdom's Al-Hasa region, otherwise known as the Eastern Province. The strike, against the Arabian American Oil Company (ARAMCO) in Dhahran, ended on 26 October.

2 November In a message to Britain's foreign office, Iran proposes the restoration of diplomatic relations and further negotiations on the oil dispute.

3 November The Arab League secretary-general, Abd al-Khaliq Hassouna, threatens the US with the loss of its strategic bases and economic resources in the Middle East if it continues its policy of friendship with Israel.

8 November The trial of the former Iranian prime minister, Muhammad Musaddiq, begins in Tehran.

9 November King Abd al-Aziz of Saudi Arabia (known to Westerners as Ibn Saud) dies at the age of 73 (see Biographies). His 52-year-old son Saud became the new king. Abd al-Aziz ibn Abd al-Rahman al-Faisal was born in Riyadh in 1880, the son of the Amir Abd al-Rahman. Crown Prince Saud had been appointed prime minister on 11 October and had been the effective ruler during the last two months of his father's illness. The Amir Faisal (see Biographies), King Abd al-Aziz's second son, was proclaimed the new crown prince. Faisal had been viceroy of the Hejaz (western) region of Saudi Arabia and foreign minister and had often led Saudi delegations to the UN and to international conferences.

5 December Iran's diplomatic relations with Britain are resumed. On 19 December Iran's parliament was dissolved to prepare for new elections. Meanwhile, the shah embarked on the creation, with US backing, of a new secret police force called Sazman-e amniyat va ittilaat-e keshvar (Organization of National Security and Intelligence) but popularly known by its dreaded acronym SAVAK. The new organization was commanded by General Teymour Bakhtiar who had been involved in the re-conquest of Azerbayjan in 1941 and was a relative of Queen Soraya and an intimate of the shah to whom he showed an unquestioning loyalty.

21 December A five-man military court in Tehran convicts the former Iranian premier, Muhammad Musaddiq, of attempting to lead a revolt against the shah. He was sentenced to three years in solitary confinement.

1 9 5 4

13 January Egypt dissolves the extremist Muslim Brotherhood (Al-Ikhwan al-Muslimun) and arrests its supreme guide, Shaikh Hasan al-Hudeibi, and 77 other leaders for breaking a pledge to confine Brotherhood activities to religion and social work. On 30 January a revolutionary tribunal in Cairo sentenced the Wafd Party leader, Fuad Serag al-Din, to 15 years in prison for alleged corruption and abuse of power as a cabinet minister under former King Faruk.

16 January The US and Iran exchange ambassadors. The resumption of relations demonstrated that the nationalistic Musaddiq era was over and that Iran would now be increasingly aligned with the West.

1 February Ayatollah Sayyid Abul-Qasim Kashani attacks Iran's electoral process. Musaddiq's successor as Iranian premier, General Fazlollah Zahedi, responded to his criticism by calling him a 'hypocrite' and a 'demagogue'. Having supported Musaddiq during his early days in power, Kashani had later turned against him, welcoming his downfall and the return of the shah.

5 February The Israeli delegate, Abba Eban, asks the UN Security Council to impose sanctions against Egypt unless an Egyptian-imposed Suez Canal blockade of Israel-bound shipping is lifted. Probably in an attempt to lower the political temperature, on 8 February Egypt informed shipping firms that it would not blacklist merchants' vessels for stopping at Israeli ports if they did not visit Arab ports on the same voyage.

21 February Iran announces that it will not negotiate with Britain for settlement of the dispute over the nationalization of the Anglo-Iranian Oil Company (AIOC) holdings but will deal with representatives of a proposed international consortium which will market Iranian oil.

25 February Egypt's cabinet and Revolutionary Command Council (RCC) in Cairo announces the resignation of General Muhammad Neguib as president. The move was to be the start of a confusing power struggle in Cairo. The 37-year-old Colonel Gamal abd al-Nasser, who had discreetly master-minded the 1952 revolution against King Faruk, became head of government as president and prime minister. He promptly declared a state of emergency to guard against disorders in the form of pro-Neguib rallies. Neguib was confined to his home to prevent him from trying to start a movement aimed at regaining power.

On 27 February Neguib was restored to the presidency because some RCC members threatened that they would revolt against his ousting if Nasser retained both the prime ministership and the presidency. However, on 8 March Neguib was also reinstated as prime minister and Nasser again became his deputy.

25 February Syrian broadcasts announce the resignation of General Adib Shishekly, Syria's dictator-president since 1951. On 28 February Syrian officers restored Hachem al-Atassi to the presidency as the ousted Shishekly fled to Saudi Arabia.

11 March Elections to the Majlis (lower house) and the Senate (upper house) end in Iran. The elections had been marred by accusations of widespread electoral fraud. Gangs of hoodlums had toured polling districts, beating up hundreds of alleged Tudeh (Communist) Party members and anti-government voters. Dr Imami led the royalists.

13 March Dr Hussein Fatemi, foreign minister under the former premier, Dr Muhammad Musaddiq, is arrested and then stabbed by an angry crowd as he is carried away into custody in Tehran.

4 April The Arab League states adopt a resolution appealing to the rulers of the Western Aden Protectorate to refuse to commit themselves to any plan 'contradicting the national spirit'.

18 April Colonel Gamal abd al-Nasser replaces General Neguib as Egypt's prime minister, ending the power struggle that had been developing over several months. Neguib continued to hold the figurehead post of president.

25 April Iraq reports the conclusion of a military aid agreement with the US.

11 June In Cairo, Egypt and Saudi Arabia announce an agreement to pool their resources for the production of arms and military training.

15 June A £1.6-million Iranian order for agricultural equipment is placed with Britain. On 24 June a £5-million Iranian order for railway equipment had been placed with Britain.

8 July The Soviets complain in a note about US efforts to draw Iran into 'the aggressive military bloc' that was being created in the Middle East on the basis of the Turkish-Pakistani military agreement. The Soviets called Iran's attention to its 'obligations' under the Soviet-Iranian treaty of 1 October 1927 and asked for an Iranian explanation.

On 18 July Iran replied to the Soviets that possible Iranian membership in the Turkish-Pakistani accord did not constitute participation in an 'aggressive military bloc' as Moscow had claimed.

28 July Saudi Arabia and Britain agree to arbitration over the Buraimi Oasis dispute.

5 August The Iranian oil dispute appears to be settled as the government and the AIOC consortium initiate an agreement in principle. The oil companies had agreed tentatively on 19 December 1953 on the question of how to market Iranian oil once a settlement had been reached. It was understood that Britain was asking for 44 per cent in the consortium while the US had suggested 40 per cent for itself because it expected Iranian objections given that the AIOC had for so long been a symbol of foreign domination to Iranian nationalists.

After much haggling, the AIOC accepted a minority 40 per cent share although it was the biggest single share in the consortium. The 40 per cent which belonged to the US, on the other hand, was divided among Gulf Oil, Socony-Vacuum Oil (Mobil), Standard Oil of New Jersey and Texaco. The other 20 per cent was divided between Royal Dutch with 14 per cent and Compagnie Francaise des Petroles (CFP) with 6 per cent.

However, in spite of Iran's desire that it retain ultimate control of the fields, the agreement allotted only two seats out of seven on the board of directors, to Iranians. These two were nominated by the National Iranian Oil Company (NIOC). Moreover, although the board would act 'on behalf of Iran and the NIOC', the operating companies would determine and have 'full and effective management and control of all their operations'. Nationalist critics considered the agreement an act of 'denationalization', according to Rouhollah Ramazani in his book, *Iran's Foreign Policy; 1941–1973.*

11 August The Iranian premier, Fazlollah Zahedi, announces a five-year, $500-million programme to increase agricultural and mineral production. Both would be financed by oil revenues and US and World Bank loans.

17 August 2,000 British troops sail from Port Said in the first substantial withdrawal of British forces from Egypt's Suez Canal zone. On 30 August Britain lifted its three-year embargo on the sale of arms to Egypt.

10 October Dr Hussein Fatemi, who had been foreign minister under the former Iranian prime minister, Muhammad Musaddiq, is sentenced to death for treason against the shah. On 11 November he was executed. Many were shocked by the speed of his conviction and subsequent execution. However, he was the most radical of Musaddiq's followers and was said to have held both the shah and the shah's powerful twin, Princess Ashraf, in extreme contempt.

13 October The UN Relief and Works Agency for Palestine Refugees (UNRWA) reports that the number of Arab refugees on UN relief rolls has increased by 15,310 during 1954 to date. It said that the total number of Palestinian refugees was 887,058.

17 October The US ends its foreign aid mission to Saudi Arabia at the request of the Saudi government.

19 October Britain and Egypt sign a seven-year pact in Cairo replacing their 1936 treaty. The new agreement provided for the withdrawal of British forces from the Suez Canal zone over the next 20 months.

28 October The Iranian parliament completes the ratification of Iran's agreement with eight foreign oil companies to operate the Abadan oilfields. On 30 October the first AIOC shipment left Abadan since June 1951. On the same day an eight-company consortium and the Iranian government agreed to pay the AIOC $670,720,000 for its oil rights and properties in Iran.

31 October The Iranian premier, General Fazlollah Zahedi, introduces a government bill banning the Tudeh Party.

2 November The 32-year-old Prince Ali Reza, the shah's only full brother and heir presumptive to the Iranian throne, is killed when his small plane crashes in the Elburz Mountains north-east of Tehran.

On the same day the US had announced a $42.3-million grant and an $85-million loan for Iran to sustain the country's economy until its revived oil industry began to bring in revenues again.

3 November Iran is admitted by Britain to the £ sterling transferable account area.

14 November Egypt's RCC removes General Muhammad Neguib from the Egyptian presidency. The RCC charged that Neguib plotted with the extremist Muslim Brotherhood against the life of Premier Gamal abd al-Nasser. Nasser escaped an assassination attempt in Alexandria on 26 October. Four members of the Muslim Brotherhood were arrested as the suspected assassins. On 17 November the RCC, headed by Nasser, assumed the functions of the presidency. On 7 December Egypt executed six Muslim Brotherhood leaders for plotting to assassinate Nasser and seize control of Egypt.

3 January Iraq suspends diplomatic relations with the Soviet Union. The latter protested at the enforced closure of its legation in Baghdad.

5 January At a conference held in Aden, the Arab sultans and shaikhs of nine territories in the Western Aden Protectorate agree in principle to form a federation of their states within the Aden Protectorate. However, the acceptance of the proposals led to a severe deterioration in relations between Britain and Yemen.

6–14 January The Turkish prime minister, Adnan Menderes, visits Baghdad where he agrees on a mutual defence treaty with the Iraqi prime minister, Nuri al-Said. The treaty became known as the Baghdad Pact. Egypt and Syria promptly denounced the treaty.

22 January The prime ministers of Egypt, Syria, Lebanon, Jordan, Saudi Arabia, Yemen and Libya meet in Cairo to discuss the developments surrounding the Iraqi-Turkish defence treaty (to become the Baghdad Pact). Iraq's prime minister, Nuri al-Said, did not attend, claiming illness. However, after repeated calls from members of the conference, Nuri agreed to dispatch Fadil al-Jamali, a former Iraqi prime minister, accompanied by the vice-premier, Ahmad Mokhtar Baban, and the deputy foreign minister, Burhan al-Din Bashaiyan, who all arrived in Cairo on 26 January.

At the meeting the Egyptian premier, Gamal abd al-Nasser, accused Iraq of the intention to 'tie herself completely to the Western powers'. However, the Cairo conference was, by and large, a failure, and most of the states participating showed their willingness to compromise on the issue of the Pact.

25 January Cairo radio announces, in reference to the newly-agreed Baghdad Pact, that any alliance with Turkey, 'the friend of Israel', means an indirect alliance with Israel itself, and the betrayal of the Arab cause.

31 January Egypt executes Cairo surgeon Moussa Marzouk and Alexandrian teacher Samuel Azar, both convicted of being Israeli spies, in the wake of bomb attacks on British and US official establishments in Egypt. According to Robert Stephens in *Nasser*, the attacks were understood to have been organized by the Israeli military intelligence with the approval of the Israeli defence minister, Pinhas Lavon, but were to be made to appear the work of Egyptians.

8 February In a show of solidarity with Egypt, the Saudi Arabian premier, Crown Prince Faisal, says that if Egypt secedes from the Arab League collective security pact when Iraq signs its proposed defence treaty with Turkey, Saudi Arabia will immediately follow Egypt's initiative.

24 February The Iraqi premier, Nuri al-Said, and the Turkish premier, Adnan Menderes, go ahead as planned and sign the treaty of alliance, effectively creating the Baghdad Pact. On 25 February the new treaty was published. Observers saw the Pact both as a military weapon against Soviet influence in the Arab world, and as a political instrument of British and Iraqi power in the region. It was to have an important influence on every level of Arab political activity.

6 March In Cairo, Damascus and Riyadh, the creation a new Arab military, economic and political treaty is announced. This treaty was designed to supplant the Arab League collective security pact and to exclude Iraq. On 30 March Britain announced its intention of acceding to the Iraqi-Turkish Baghdad Pact and on 4 April the Anglo-Iraqi agreement was signed in Baghdad, making Britain a member of the Pact.

6 March Syria agrees to join Egypt and Saudi Arabia in a defence pact forbidding alliances with non-Arab countries.

24 March Iraq and the Iraq Petroleum Company (IPC) sign a new oil agreement, giving Iraq increased royalties of, in British money, about seven shillings a ton.

30 March The British foreign secretary, Anthony Eden, tells Britain's parliament that agreements linking Britain with the Turkish-Iraqi mutual defence pact (the Baghdad Pact) can serve as the basis for a general Middle East defence arrangement. However, on 16 April the Soviet Foreign Ministry was to charge that US-sponsored alliances in the Middle East threatened the Soviet Union's security. He warned that Soviet delegates might bring up the matter in the UN.

5 April Britain formally accedes to the Baghdad Pact. A special agreement had been signed between Iraq and Britain on 4 April, replacing the previous agreement of 30 June 1930 between the two countries. However, initial Iraqi and British hopes that Iraq would inherit the leadership of the Arab world under the overlordship of Britain were aborted. Egypt's opposition to the Pact had been unremitting and Syria had moved away from its orbit. The centre of gravity of Arab politics was now Cairo.

5 April The Iranian premier, General Fazlollah Zahedi, resigns for health reasons. On 7 April the shah appointed Hussein Ala as the new premier. In a further change, on 11 April the Iranian government dismissed Tehran's mayor, Gholam Hussein Ebtehaj, accusing him of poor administration of the Iranian capital.

18–24 April The famous Afro-Asian conference is held at Bandung in Indonesia. A total of 29 Asian and African countries attended. On 15 April Nasser had conferred in Rangoon with the Chinese premier, Chou en-Lai, the Indian premier, Jawharlal Nehru, and the Burmese premier, U Nu. In his opening remarks on 18 April the Indonesian president, Sukarno, had attacked racialism and colonialism. On 21 April the conference passed a resolution supporting Palestinian claims against Israel.

27 May A US report states that in the seven years of the US Marshall Plan from 3 April 1948 to 31 March 1955, Iraq has received $7,011,000 and Iran has received $205,538,000.

15 June Imam Seif al-Islam Ahmad of Yemen rallies loyal tribesmen and suppresses an army revolt led by the Amir Seif al-Islam Abdullah.

1 July The Pakistani premier, Muhammad Ali, announces that Pakistan will accede to the new Turkish-Iraqi mutual defence pact (the Baghdad Pact).

23 July Ahmad Qavam al-Saltaneh dies in Tehran at the age of 73. Qavam had been prime minister of Iran four times.

9–17 August King Saud of Saudi Arabia visits Iran. Diplomatic relations between the two countries were raised to embassy status during the visit.

15 August A US-Iranian treaty of friendship, economic relations and consular rights is signed, reflecting the rapidly improving relations between Iran and the West since the demise of Premier Muhammad Musaddiq.

18 August The Syrian parliament elects Shukri al-Quwatly as president. Al-Quwatly had been exiled from Syria after a coup in 1949.

22 August The French authorities report more than 1,000 deaths following three days of violent demonstrations in Algeria, still a part of Metropolitan France, and French Morocco. The riots marked the second anniversary of the dismissal of Morocco's nationalist leader, Sultan Sidi Muhammad ibn Youssuf. On the following day the French government called up reservists to reinforce colonial forces in the two French territories.

4 September Egypt confirms that the Soviet Union has offered to supply Egypt with military equipment. However, the Soviets asserted that no further action had been taken on the proposal. On 27 September, however, Egypt's President Nasser announced the conclusion of a foreign trade barter agreement with Czechoslovakia which provided for the exchange of Czech arms and Egyptian cotton. On 3 October the Israeli ambassador to the US, Abba Eban, urged the great powers to avoid disturbing the Middle East's military balance through arms sales to Arab countries. On 4 September the US secretary of state, Foster Dulles, said that he had protested to the Soviet foreign minister, Vyacheslav Molotov, in their recent talks, against the sale of Soviet and Czech arms to Egypt. A Soviet-Egyptian arms deal was announced on 27 September.

15 September Iraqi Premier Nuri al-Said's visit to Cairo ends all hopes of an Iraqi-Egyptian accord. Salah Salim, a leading member of the Egyptian military junta, was to tell the British writer Patrick Seale that Nuri al-Said had made it perfectly clear to Nasser that he could not depend on neighbouring Arab armies to defend Iraq and that the only way to defend his country was to make an alliance with the West. Nasser had replied that no such agreement could be made with Britain until at least two years had elapsed after Britain's final evacuation of its troops from the Suez Canal zone. Pakistan joined the Baghdad Pact in September.

16 September The Buraimi Oasis dispute between Saudi Arabia and the United Arab Emirates (UAE) reaches a deadlock when the arbitration tribunal's enquiry is suspended following the resignation of the British member, Sir Reader Bullard. Bullard claimed that the Saudi representative, Deputy Foreign Minister Shaikh Yusuf Yasin, represented Saudi Arabia and was not impartial.

4 October Abu Dhabi forces, commanded by British officers and supported by the Trucial Oman Levies, occupy the Buraimi Oasis. The British Foreign Ministry accused the Saudis of bribing the people of Buraimi in their attempt to overthrow the ruler of Abu Dhabi.

11 October Iran agrees to accede to the Baghdad Pact, joining Turkey, Iraq, Pakistan and Britain. Iran formally acceded on 3 November. On 12 October the Soviet foreign minister, Vyacheslav Molotov, protested at Iran's accession.

13 October Egypt confirms reports that the Soviet Union has offered to help finance the construction of a new dam on the Nile near Aswan in return for cotton, rice and other commodities. On 17 October, however, Egypt's ambassador to the US, Ahmad Husayn, pointed out to the US secretary of state, Foster Dulles, that Egypt would prefer US and World Bank financing to Soviet aid, with which to finance the dam. Nevertheless, on 20 October the first shipment of Czech arms arrived at Alexandria on a Soviet freighter.

13 October Egypt and Syria sign a mutual defence pact in Damascus. On 22 October the Israeli premier, Moshe Sharett, appealed to the West to avert the 'danger which looms over Israel as a result of the Czechoslovak-Egyptian arms deal'. On 24 October Sharret left Jerusalem for talks in Geneva with the foreign ministers of the Big Four.

25 October The Iraqi government signs a co-operation agreement with the US on the peaceful use of atomic energy.

27 October Egypt and Saudi Arabia sign a military pact. Meanwhile, Saudi Arabia's

Crown Prince Faisal said in Cairo that for the British to adhere to the arbitration agreement over the Buraimi Oasis dispute, and then to take the Buraimi Oasis by force was 'to throw dust in our eyes'. Nasser deplored the British attitude and 'wholeheartedly' supported Faisal's stand.

27 October The Iraqi foreign minister, Dr Jafar, announces that Iraq and Britain have agreed firstly that Iraq will buy £5 million worth of gold from Britain for payment in sterling, and secondly that Britain will provide up to $2 million to cover Iraq's obligations to the International Monetary Fund. Dr Jafar also declared that Britain might import Iraqi dates free of duty.

3 November David Ben-Gurion becomes prime minister of Israel. On the previous day he had presented a five-party coalition government to the Knesset (parliament), which included Moshe Sharett, the outgoing premier, as foreign minister. Ben-Gurion offered to meet Arab leaders, including Nasser, to avert 'dangers inherent in the present unstable situation'.
On 7 November Washington sources reported a US decision to sell Israel 'significant' quantities of arms.

17 November The Iranian premier, Hussein Ala, survives an assassination attempt.

20 November The Jordanian premier, Haza Majali, announces that Jordan will remain outside the Baghdad Pact despite strong pressure to join from Iraq and Turkey. On 21 November the Pact's first meeting was held in Baghdad under the chairmanship of Iraq's Premier Nuri al-Said.

21 November Egypt's finance minister, Abd al-Moneim al-Qaissouni, opens talks in Washington with representatives of the World Bank to seek financing of the $1,300-million Aswan High Dam project on the Nile.

28 November Iraq's 24,000-barrels-a-day first government-owned oil refinery at Daura on the Tigris, three miles (5 kilometres) south of Baghdad, is opened by King Faisal.

29 November Egypt and Syria complete plans for an anti-Israeli joint military command to be established in Damascus.

5 December Iran rejects Soviet protests against its accession to the Baghdad Pact. Iran declared that its membership was 'essential to Iran's prosperity' and that the Soviet protest constituted 'interference in Iran's internal affairs'.

16 December Serious rioting breaks out in Amman against Jordan's accession to the Baghdad Pact. On 19 December King Husayn granted Premier Haza Majali's request to dissolve parliament in preparation for elections based on the issue of Jordan's participation in the Pact.

17 December The US and Britain inform Egypt that they will finance the start of the $1,300-million Aswan High Dam project which is expected to take at least 15 years to complete. On 18 December the Soviet ambassador to Egypt, Daniel Solod, said in Cairo that the Soviet Union intended to contribute to the project.

29 December The membership of the tribunal, formed to arbitrate in the Buraimi dispute between Britain and Saudi Arabia, is announced. On 4 October Abu Dhabi forces, commanded by British officers and supported by the Trucial Oman Levies, had occupied the Buraimi Oasis.

---

1 9 5 6

---

1 January General Teymour Bakhtiar, the military governor of Tehran, says over 100 Tudeh (Communist) Party members have been arrested by the intelligence services. Meanwhile, the shah commuted to life imprisonment the death sentence on Dr Mortiza Yazdi, a founding member of the Tudeh Party. Dr Yazdi had been sentenced in September 1955 for treason. In an attempt to placate the Tudeh Party and the Soviets, Premier Qavam al-Saltaneh had made Dr Yazdi minister of health in his cabinet on 1 August 1946.

7 January Demonstrators opposed to Jordanian participation in the Baghdad Pact attack the US consulate in the Arab sector of Jerusalem but are dispersed by US marines. A curfew, which was to last until 14 January, was declared as a result of the unrest. On 8 January the US secretary of state, Foster Dulles, delivered a personal protest to the Jordanian chargé d'affaires in Washington against the 'inadequate' protection given to US property in Jordan. On 9 January Samir al-Rifai formed a new Jordanian cabinet following the resignation of Premier Ibrahim Hashim in the wake of the rioting.

8 January Hussein Makki, head of nationalizing the oil industry under the former Iranian premier, Muhammad Musaddiq, is arrested in connection with the assassination of General Razmara in 1951. Musaddiq's finance minister, Mahmoud Nariman, was also arrested. On 18 January four members of the Iranian Islamic militant group, the Fedayeen-e Islam, were executed for the attempted assassination of the present Iranian premier, Hussein Ala, on 17 November 1955. Also on 18 January Ayatollah Sayyid Abul-Qasim Kashani was held for questioning in connection with the assassination of General Razmara.

10 January Britain announces the transfer of 1,600 paratroopers to British Middle East headquarters in Cyprus 'in view of the disturbed position in the Middle East'.

11 January Syria, Egypt and Saudi Arabia offer to replace British aid to Jordan.

16 January The Egyptian premier, Gamal abd al-Nasser, proclaims a new constitution, thereby ending rule by the Revolutionary Command Council (RCC) established in the wake of the revolution in 1952.

27 January The US reporter, Osgood Caruthers, charges that Saudi Arabia is using its oil riches 'to foment disunity along lines that have followed almost to the letter the Soviet bloc's policies in the Middle East'.

28 January Eleanor Roosevelt urges the US to provide arms to Israel for its defence. In a statement made in New York and endorsed by former President Truman and Labour leader Walter Reuther, Eleanor Roosevelt urged the US to 'provide the defensive arms needed by Israel to protect itself against any aggression made possible or incited by the introduction of Communist arms'.

17 February The US State Department orders the temporary suspension of all shipments of arms to the Middle East. The order followed press reports that 18 M-41 Walker Bulldog tanks were being loaded in New York's Brooklyn for delivery to Saudi Arabia. However, on the following day the embargo was lifted in the wake of protests from the Saudi Arabian ambassador to the US, Shaikh Abdullah al-Khayyal, and the 18 tanks left for Saudi Arabia on 20 February. The Israeli ambassador to the US, Abba Eban, denounced the shipment. On 24 February the US secretary of state, Foster Dulles, claimed that sending US tanks to Saudi Arabia would help 'maintain internal security' in that nation, 'where there have been large-scale riots and disturbances at various points'.

2 March King Husayn of Jordan suddenly sacks the British commander of the Arab Legion, John Bagot Glubb. The king complained that Glubb had refused to reorganize the Legion and had ignored his order to plan for a counterattack in the event of an Israeli assault. However, observers saw pressure on the king from Jordanian nationalists, encouraged by Egypt's President Nasser's pan-Arabism, who wanted a Jordanian rather than an Englishman to run the army. On 5 March the Jordanian premier, Samir al-Rifai, said that Glubb's dismissal was 'a purely internal affair which Jordan felt she had a perfect right to perform'. The British prime minister, Anthony Eden, blamed Nasser for the sacking but observers of the day saw it as due to the 21-year-old king's desire to favour the young nationalist generation.
    On 6 March Saudi Arabia's King Saud, Egypt's President Nasser and Syria's President Quwatly began discussions in Cairo on ways of including Jordan's Arab Legion in their mutual defence pact. By the end of their talks on 13 March they had drafted plans for unified Arab action against 'Zionist aggression' and for Arab neutrality in East–West disputes.

6–11 March The meeting in Cairo between President Nasser, President Quwatly and King Saud follows the escalation of the Arab-Israeli problem.

15 March A five-year contract for the development and industrialization of the Iranian province of Khuzestan is signed in Tehran.

1 April Egypt's President Nasser indicates that he is considering a Soviet offer of long-range credit for the $1,300-million Aswan High Dam project.

2 April Iraq's King Faisal dedicates the Wadi Tharthar dam on the Tigris river, part of a $34-million flood control and irrigation project. On the following day a five-year development plan was approved by the Iraqi government. On 5 April the ninth barrage across the Euphrates was opened at Ramadi.

3 April Yemen announces that it is consulting with other Arab countries on ways of thwarting a British-sponsored plan for the creation of an Aden federation of rulers. However, on 23 April Britain agreed to open talks with Yemen on the latter's claims to Aden.

10 April The UN secretary-general, Dag Hammarskjold, arrives in Cairo at the start of talks with Middle East leaders involved in the Palestine problem. On 12 April the White House in Washington announced that President Eisenhower had sent personal messages to both Israel's Premier Ben-Gurion and Egypt's President Nasser urging restraint and outlining the current US policy of aid for the victim of aggression whichever side it should be.

16–19 April The second annual meeting of the Baghdad Pact is held in Tehran under the chairmanship of the Iranian prime minister, Hussein Ala. Britain was represented by its minister of defence, Sir Walter Monckton, and the US by the chief administration officer of the State Department and a former ambassador to Tehran, Loy Henderson.

21 April Nasser organizes a meeting in Jeddah between King Saud, the Imam Ahmad of Yemen and himself at which he persuades King Saud to give the imam money (possibly as much as £5 million) to buy arms from Communist sources. The agreement also covered a unified military command structure whereby the Saudi, Egyptian and Yemeni armies would be linked under the command of the Egyptian defence minister, General Abd al-Hakim Amer. Crown Prince Muhammad al-Badr of Yemen had been persuaded by Nasser's charm to court the Iron Curtain countries.

29 April The Food and Agricultural Organization announces that Saudi Arabia has advised the British Desert Locust Control mission to close its Jeddah headquarters and leave the country by 1 May. On 30 April it added that the Saudis had asked for non-British teams to be sent with the mission in future.

2 May The first television station in the Middle East is inaugurated in Baghdad. The service provided educational and cultural programmes and covered the Baghdad area.

22 May The US secretary of state, Foster Dulles, threatens to terminate US aid to the Aswan High Dam project if Egypt concurrently accepts Soviet aid.

13 June The Algerian nationalist leader, Ferhat Abbas, rejects cease-fire negotiations with France without recognition of Algerian sovereignty and independence as a minimum condition.

14 June Britain's 74-year occupation of the Suez Canal zone formally ends in a Port Said ceremony.

22 June Egyptians overwhelmingly approve Gamal abd al-Nasser as Egypt's president and vote for the acceptance of a new constitution in a national plebiscite. On the following day Egypt's ruling RCC was dissolved in preparation for a return to civilian rule.

1 July The Soviet Communist Party First Secretary, Nikita Krushchev, warns that 'war between Israel and the Arab states would mean World War III'. The warning was in an interview published by the Egyptian newspaper *Al Ahram*.

The Suez Crisis: July

19 July The US secretary of state, Foster Dulles, announces that the US has withdrawn a projected $56-million grant for the construction of the Aswan High Dam in Egypt. On 20 July the British Foreign Office announced the cancellation of a $14-million Aswan High Dam grant. On 21 July the Soviet foreign minister, Dmitri Shepilov, said that his government would 'consider favourably any Egyptian requests' for Soviet aid in the project. On 23 July the World Bank announced that its $200-million loan offer for the project had been contingent on the US and British grants and 'automatically expired' when they were withdrawn.

26 July In a speech in Alexandria, President Nasser nationalizes the Suez Canal Company, promising that shareholders would be 'duly indemnified ... at the estimated value' of their holdings. On 27 July France and Britain formally protested against the nationalization decree after the British and French prime ministers, Anthony Eden and Guy Mollet respectively, summoned their cabinet members and military leaders for emergency sessions. On the same day the Suez Canal Company called on banks holding the firm's assets to refuse to honour the nationalization decree.

On 28 July the British treasury blocked all Suez Canal Company and Egyptian assets in British banks. On 29 July Egypt banned all exports to Britain and its colonies and halted shipments of all sterling trade goods through the Suez Canal. On the same day the French government froze $1,285 million worth of Egyptian assets in France. On 30 July Britain halted all arms shipments to Egypt. On the same day Egypt revoked its embargo on sterling-area exports. On 31 July the US secretary of state, Foster Dulles, left for London to discuss the Suez situation with British and French leaders.

24 July The shah proclaims a national emergency as flooding in central and southern Iran claims 300 lives and leaves thousands homeless.

The Suez Crisis: August

1 August The Suez Canal Company notifies shippers that in view of the 'acts of force' it cannot be responsible for the canal's safe operation. On 2 August the US, Britain and France invited representatives of 24 states, including Egypt and the Soviet Union, to London for talks aimed at reaching an agreement on the international operation of the canal. However, on the following day Egypt rejected the invitation. On 3 August Queen Elizabeth of Britain signed a proclamation of 'great emergency' and empowered the British government to recall reservists for active service in the Suez crisis. On 5 August the Egyptian government did likewise.

On 6 August the Suez Canal Company gave its workers until 15 August to choose between loyalty to their contracts and collaboration with the '*de facto* authority' of the Egyptian government. On the same day Secretary of State Foster Dulles warned President Eisenhower that the Western use of force against Egypt would entail a possible war with the entire Arab world. On 9 August the Soviet Union agreed to attend the London conference but with the proviso that it would not accept 'restrictions or obligations'. On 12 August Britain launched an airlift of 5,000 troops to the Middle East.

4 August The former Iranian premier, Muhammad Musaddiq, is released after serving his three-year sentence imposed in 1953, but is promptly put under virtual house arrest in his village of Ahmadabad, near Tehran. He had spent his prison sentence in solitary confinement.

14 August US President Eisenhower names the State Department director-general, Raymond Hare, as the new US ambassador to Egypt, succeeding Henry Byroade. Hare was a reported exponent of a pro-Arab foreign policy. On 13 August the Arab League Council meeting in Cairo declared 'solidarity with Egypt in its determination to preserve its sovereignty' and said that the League would regard 'aggression against any Arab state to be an act of hostility directed against all Arab states'. In an ominous move on 23 August, the Soviet Union threatened to provide military aid to Egypt in the event of an attack by Britain and France.

25 August The National Iranian Oil Company (NIOC) discovers an 80,000 barrels-a-day oil well at Qom, the biggest found so far in Iran. The Aghajari well, the second largest, produced 50,000 barrels a day.

The Suez Crisis: September

5 September President Nasser presents his alternatives to the US proposal for the internationalization of the Suez Canal, expressing his readiness to agree on the formation of an international Suez advisory board as proposed by India at the London conference in August. On 14 September non-Egyptian canal pilots abandoned their Suez posts, leaving the canal's operation in the hands of a reduced force of Egyptian, Greek and Soviet pilots. Nasser claimed that Egypt could 'run the canal smoothly and efficiently' without British and French canal pilots. On 17 September the Arab League Political Committee meeting in Cairo approved resolutions supporting Egypt's seizure of the canal and condemning the Anglo-French 'military buildup' in the Middle East. On 24 September Saudi Arabia's King Saud and Syria's President Quwatly issued a joint statement in Cairo supporting Egypt 'in every attitude she takes' on the Suez question. On 27 September the International Monetary Fund granted Egypt a $15-million loan to meet foreign payment problems and help it pay for 250,000 tons of Canadian wheat.

14/15 September King Husayn of Jordan visits Baghdad where he discusses the 'Zionist' (Israeli) threat with Iraq's King Faisal and Prime Minister Nuri al-Said. On 19 September the Arab League secretary-general, Ahmad Shukairy, announced the initiation of talks between Iraq and Jordan on the possible stationing of Iraqi troops in Jordan as reinforcement against Israel.

20 September King Faisal and King Saud meet in Dammam. On 21 September the Middle East News Agency announced that Saudi Arabia had decided to buy from Egypt £E5 million in currency against the payment of $15 million to help Egypt since the blocking of her sterling balances. On 22 September Nasser, Quwatly and Saud met in Dammam, Saudi Arabia.

2 October The Iraq Petroleum Company (IPC) announces that it has abandoned work on a Lebanese oil-line spur and instead will link its Kirkuk oilfield with the Mediterranean via a new line through Syria which could carry nine million tons a year.

The Suez Crisis: October

1 October The British foreign secretary, Selwyn Lloyd, formally inaugurates the Suez Canal Users' Association at the opening of the third London conference on the Suez dispute, attended by ambassadors of the organization's 15 member states. On 2 October, however, the US secretary of state, Foster Dulles, conceded that there 'has been some difference' with Britain and France 'in our approach' to the Suez problem. The conference ended on 5 October after naming the US, Britain, France, Iran and Norway as members of the Suez Canal Users' Association Council.

On the same day the UN Security Council opened a debate on a complaint by France and Britain against the nationalization of the canal by Egypt. On 7 October Nasser warned that the dispute was a 'decisive test case for the UN' and would determine the organization's future effectiveness.

12 October Baghdad official sources say that Iraqi troops are ready to move into Jordan at short notice if requested. The Israelis showed concern since Iraq had refused to sign a separate armistice with Israel in 1948 and warned that Iraqi troops in Jordan would be considered a direct threat to Israel.

14 October The Israeli government expresses its 'alarm' at a British statement pledging fulfilment of its obligations to defend Jordan in the event of an Israeli attack. On 17 October Prime Minister Ben-Gurion told the Knesset (parliament) that Israel faced its greatest danger from 'the Egyptian fascist dictator', who 'does not conceal his intention to liquidate the state of Israel'. On the same day Egypt, Britain and France expressed willingness to continue negotiations on the Suez dispute.

14 October An Iraqi military mission headed by the regent, Abdulilah, arrived in Amman. On the following day the Jordanian government announced that Iraqi troops would not, after all, enter Jordan but would wait at the Iraqi-Jordanian frontier.

25 October Soviet tanks and Hungarian security police fire on unarmed crowds in front of the Hungarian parliament building in Budapest, causing an estimated 170 deaths. On 23 October an estimated 100,000 Hungarians had gathered in downtown Budapest to demand firstly the ousting of Communist Party First Secretary Erno Gero, secondly the formation of a new government by former Premier Imre Nagy and thirdly the withdrawal of Soviet troops from Hungary. By 27 October the fighting had spread throughout Hungary.

25 October Egypt, Jordan and Syria sign an agreement placing their armies under a joint command headed by General Abd al-Hakim Amer, the Egyptian commander-in-chief and war minister.

29 October The Israeli army advances more than 75 miles (121 kilometres) along the Suez Canal. An Israeli Foreign Ministry statement described the invasion as merely 'security measures to eliminate the Egyptian Fedayeen bases in the Sinai Peninsula'. On the same day and in a seemingly unrelated move, British and French naval units left Malta to 'cruise' in the eastern Mediterranean. On 30 October the Israelis announced that their attack on Egypt had now widened along a 70-mile (113-kilometre) front.

30 October An Anglo-French ultimatum is issued to Egypt and Israel to withdraw to a point 10 miles (16 kilometres) behind the Suez Canal. The Iraqi foreign minister informed the British, French and US ambassadors of his government's deep concern at Israel's attack on Egypt.

31 October Anglo-French forces attack Egyptian and Suez Canal zone installations and military bases. On the same day Israeli troops reached the banks of the canal and pulled back to the 10-mile (16-kilometre) limit imposed by the British-French ultimatum to both Egypt and Israel. On the same day Eisenhower opposed the attack on Egypt as an action 'taken in error' without consulting or informing Washington. He announced in a nation-wide broadcast that there would be 'no United States involvement in these present hostilities'. On the same day martial law was declared in Baghdad.

The Suez Crisis: November

1 November Egypt breaks off diplomatic relations with Britain and France and orders the seizure of all French and British property, including all installations registered with the Finance Ministry. On the same day Iraqi and Syrian troops entered Jordan.

2 November The Hungarian premier, Imre Nagy, reports that 'large Soviet military units' are marching towards Budapest, the Hungarian capital. On 31 October the new Hungarian government had called for the withdrawal of Soviet troops from Hungary. On the same day Hungarian troops had freed Josef Cardinal Mindszenty form detention and restored him as Roman Catholic primate of Hungary.

3 November The Anglo-French forces report 'the virtual destruction of the Egyptian air force as a fighting unit'. On the same day Egypt's President Nasser announced that all Egyptian troops are 'being withdrawn' from the Sinai Peninsula to defend the Suez Canal against Britain and France. On 4 November the Israeli Foreign Ministry said that Israel had 'no intention at present' of leaving the Sinai Peninsula and that the 1948 Israeli-Egyptian agreement was 'finished and dead'.

4 November Eight Soviet divisions with heavy air support attack Budapest and other Hungarian cities in order to wipe out the anti-Communist rebellion. Moscow then installed Hungarian Communist Party First Secretary Janos Kadar as premier of a new all-Communist cabinet.

4 November Baghdad announces that Iraqi troops have entered Jordan at Jordan's request. On 3 November Arabian American Oil Company (ARAMCO) officials said they had received reports that the Saudi-Mediterranean pipeline had been blown up at several points.

5 November Israeli military operations in Sinai effectively end, while an Anglo-French force invades the canal zone. Anglo-French paratroopers landed at the northern end of the canal and fought Egyptian forces estimated at three divisions with tanks. On 6 November Anglo-French commandos landed by sea at the Port Said and Port Fuad areas as a now-entrenched Israel declared a unilateral cease-fire. On the same day Prime Ministers Eden and Mollet accepted a cease-fire to become effective on 7 November. Also on 6 November Saudi Arabia broke relations with Britain and France while the Saudi government closed its oil pipeline to Bahrain and banned British and French tankers from using Saudi ports. On 7 November General Sir Charles Knightley, commander of the joint Anglo-French force in Egypt, declared a cease-fire in the Suez Canal zone. Rioters in Bahrain, angered by British and French activities in the Suez crisis, burnt down buildings and tried to set fire to the Roman Catholic church. Meanwhile, demonstrations against Britain and France in Kuwait led to a ban on meetings.

9 November Israel reluctantly agrees to withdraw from the Sinai under the UN cease-fire policing plan as the Anglo-French occupation force ends its Suez Canal zone buildup.

9 November Iraq breaks relations with France. On 13 November Iraq handed a note to all diplomatic representatives in Baghdad saying that the only solution to the Middle East crisis was the liquidation of Israel as a state, the return of its inhabitants to their former homes and the return to Palestine of the Palestinian refugees.

13 November The British War Office reports that 32 vessels have been sunk in the Suez Canal during the Egyptian fighting, 20 going down in Port Said harbour at the northern entrance to the canal.

13–15 November Arab heads of state and ministers meet in Beirut and call for the immediate withdrawal of the Anglo-French forces from the Suez Canal. King Faisal II and King Saud attended the meeting.

15 November In notes to Britain, France and Israel, Soviet Premier Bulganin renews his demand for the withdrawal of foreign troops from Egypt. He urged compensation to Egypt for loss of life and property at the hands of the invading Anglo-French forces. On the same day UN emergency forces landed in Egypt.

15 November The Tunisian premier, Habib Bourguiba, appeals for the dispatch of UN troops to Algeria to end 'butchery not less horrible than the butchery of Budapest'. On 22 October the French, fighting an escalating war against Algerian nationalists, had captured the rebel leader, Ahmad Ben Bella. On 25 November the French cabinet voted 'unanimous confidence' in the policy of military suppression of the Algerian nationalist movement.

17 November The Egyptian government places an estimated 15,000 British and French civilians under house arrest.

18 November The US secretary of state, Foster Dulles, attacks the Soviet Union for its attempted intervention in the Middle East and the 'promiscuous slaughter' brought on by its interference in Hungary. On 14 November President Eisenhower had denied that the US had encouraged the uprising.

19 November Reports from London say that British Prime Minister Anthony Eden is suffering from 'severe overstrain' and has cancelled all public engagements to avoid a possible nervous breakdown.

22 November The Soviet foreign minister, Dmitri Shepilov, warns that Western policy in the Middle East and Hungary has endangered the 'spirit of Geneva'.

24 November The UN General Assembly approves a resolution calling for the 'forthwith' withdrawal of British, French and Israeli forces from Egypt.

27 November The Jordanian prime minister, Sulayman Nabulsi, says the government intends to abrogate the 1948 Anglo-Jordanian treaty and wants, in principle, to accept the offer of financial aid from Egypt, Syria and Saudi Arabia in place of the annual British subsidy.

1 December King Faisal places Iraq under martial law and suspends parliament for one month in an attempt to prevent the opening of a general foreign affairs debate.

3 December Responding to US and UN pressure, a now-demoralized and humiliated Britain and France agree to evacuate their forces from the Suez Canal zone. On the same day UN Secretary-General Dag Hammarskjold ordered UN troops to be ready to replace the Anglo-French units in Egypt 'by the middle of December'.

4 December President Nasser claims in a published article that Egypt 'won the battle' against Britain, France and Israel.

9 December It is announced in Baghdad that Iraq has decided to withdraw troops from Jordan at Jordan's request. The troops were operating under the Iraq-Jordan-Syria defence agreement.

15 December Princess Shahnaz of Iran, the daughter of Shah Muhammad Reza Pahlavi of Iran, marries Ardeshir Zahedi, the son of General Fazlollah Zahedi who helped to overthrow the government of Prime Minister Muhammad Musaddiq.

16 December UN troops assume control over most of the sector of the Suez Canal zone invaded by Anglo-French troops. Meanwhile, the latter continued their withdrawal under increasing Egyptian harassment.

17 December A two-hour general strike takes place in Jordan against the policy of the Iraqi prime minister, Nuri al-Said. Telegrams were sent to King Faisal II calling for Nuri's resignation.

20 December Defending his Middle East policy before Britain's House of Commons (lower house), British Prime Minister Anthony Eden denies Labour Party charges that Britain engaged in a 'dishonourable conspiracy' with France and Israel against Egypt.

22 December The Syrian government orders 47 opposition leaders, including the former president, Adib Shishekly, to undergo court-martials on charges of 'preparing a pro-Iraq armed rebellion'.

23 December The Egyptian army units are greeted by massive civilian demonstrations of joy as they re-enter Port Said at the northern end of the Suez Canal.

31 December The US secretary of state, Foster Dulles, says that the US 'has a major responsibility to help prevent the spread to the Middle East of Soviet imperialism'.

1 9 5 7

1 January The Soviet Union denounces the 'Eisenhower Doctrine' for US aid to the Middle East as a plot to turn the region 'into a permanent hotbed of military conflict'. On the following day US President Eisenhower rejected Soviet Premier Bulganin's request for a five-power conference on a revised Soviet plan for international disarmament.

1 January The Egyptian president, Gamal abd al-Nasser, decrees the abrogation of the 1954 Anglo-Egyptian treaty which governed the evacuation of the Suez Canal zone and the maintenance of Britain's Suez zone military bases. On 8 January the US granted $5 million to the UN to help meet Suez Canal clearance costs, with Egypt promising its 'fullest cooperation and assistance' to the clearance operation. On 15 January Nasser announced the nationalization of all British and French banks and insurance firms in Egypt. The early part of 1957 was to see the expulsion of about 2,700 British and French subjects from Egypt. Some 14,000 Egyptian and non-Egyptian Jews were also driven into exile.

6 January The US Democrat, Senator Mike Mansfield, charges that the US administration's new Middle East programme is merely 'a continuation of the old Democratic policy of containment'. On 7 January President Eisenhower named former Republican James Richards to head a special mission to the Middle East to 'explain the cooperation we are prepared to give' under the new Eisenhower Doctrine. On 10 January the former US secretary of state, Dean Acheson, opposed the Eisenhower Doctrine as 'perilously like another approach to the brink' of a third world war. On 14 January the US secretary of state, Foster Dulles, warned that possible Communist aggression in the Middle East was 'the most serious threat we have faced over the last 10 years'.

9 January The British prime minister, Anthony Eden, resigns for health reasons. The 59-year-old prime minister's withdrawal from politics was ascribed to stress caused by the disaster of the Suez campaign which he had masterminded.

17 January The US State Department urges Britain and Yemen to employ 'the greatest restraint' in any attempt to end fighting underway in the Yemen-Aden Protectorate region. Earlier in the month the Yemeni representative at the UN had claimed that the whole of the Aden Protectorate was an 'integral part of the Yemen'.

18 January The Eisenhower Doctrine becomes the centre of controversy when the Soviet premier, Nikolai Bulganin, and the Chinese premier, Chou en-Lai, issue policy statements in Moscow warning that their countries will 'continue rendering support' for Middle Eastern countries opposed to the Doctrine. On 19 January Saudi Arabia, Egypt, Syria and Jordan issued a joint statement rejecting the Eisenhower Doctrine's 'vacuum theory' of Middle East politics. They maintained that Arab nationalism was 'the sole basis on which Arab policy could be formulated'.

23 January President Eisenhower says the US regards 'smaller [nuclear] weapons as an almost routine part of our equipment nowadays' and would almost definitely have to use them in the event of Middle East hostilities.

28 January Britain formally demands that Yemen 'cease forthwith' its 'aggression' against the Aden area.

1 February Saudi Arabia's King Saud ends two days of talks with US President Eisenhower and the secretary of state, Foster Dulles, on the Eisenhower Doctrine and Middle East politics. As the king sailed into New York Harbour he was greeted by a 24-gun salute. The visit, greatly welcomed by President Eisenhower if not by others, was to bring agreements on US military assistance to Saudi Arabia and on the continued US use of the Dhahran air base. However, on 27 January Robert Wagner, mayor of New York, said that King Saud was 'not wanted' in New York and on the following day he added that 'King

Saud is a fellow who says slavery is legal, that in the Air Force you can't have any Jewish boys, and that a Catholic priest cannot say mass'.

The Saudi minister of state, Yusuf Yasin, and the former finance minister, Muhammad Sorour Sabhan, carried out the negotiations with the US secretary of state, Foster Dulles. In line with the Point Four aid agreement reached in June 1951, the US agreed to strengthen the Saudi armed forces. At the same time King Saud endorsed the Eisenhower Doctrine.

2 February The Iraqi regent, Abdulilah, arrives in Washington where he starts talks with President Eisenhower. On 6 February King Saud met the Iraqi regent in Washington. On the same day President Eisenhower said that his recent talks with King Saud had cleared away 'much of the underbrush of misunderstanding' and made progress towards ' a peaceful . . . Middle East'.

5 February The US secretary of state, Foster Dulles, says that the US will give 'very serious consideration' to the application of sanctions against Israel if the UN calls for them. On 2 February the UN General Assembly had approved resolutions renewing demands for the Israeli withdrawal from Egyptian territory taken during the 1956 Suez war.

10–25 February Following his visit to the US, Saudi Arabia's King Saud visits Spain, Morocco, Tunisia, Libya and Egypt, arriving in Cairo on 25 February to attend the Conference of Arab Heads of State. There the king conferred with Egypt's President Nasser and Syria's President Quwatly in an attempt to reassure them that his friendship with the US was good for the Arab cause.

11 February The Soviet Union's Supreme Soviet proposes that the US, Britain and France join it in a declaration governing big power relations and policies in the Middle East. On 13 February the US Senate Foreign Relations and Armed Services Committees rejected President Eisenhower's request for authority to use US military force to repel Communist aggression in the Middle East.

17 February President Eisenhower warns that continued Israeli refusal to withdraw from Egyptian territory would be 'contrary to the overwhelming judgement of the world community'.

20 February Representatives of France, Italy, West Germany and the Benelux nations, meeting in Paris, approve provisions for the creation of a common market and the European Atomic Energy Community (Euratom). The two treaties were signed in Rome on 25 March, to become effective on 1 January 1958. No formal relations between the new European Economic Community (EEC), as the common market was named, and the Arab world were to develop until 1977.

22 February Britain accuses Yemeni forces of attacking Nejd Maizer in the Beihan area of the Aden Protectorate. By this time Imam Ahmad was extremely anti-British and he encouraged dissidence as far as possible within the Aden Protectorate and along the border. According to Edgar O'Ballance in *The War in the Yemen*, there were over 70 'incidents' in the Protectorate's Dhala State during February.

25–27 February The Cairo Conference, attended by President Nasser, King Husayn of Jordan, King Saud of Saudi Arabia and Syria's President Quwatly, agree on the following: Israel must withdraw behind the armistice lines; Palestinian rights must be upheld; aggressor states must compensate Egypt for their aggression; Egypt's ownership of the Suez Canal must be defended; solidarity must be maintained with Yemen against the British; Algeria's right to independence must be defended.

28 February The UN General Assembly adopts a resolution to continue UN assistance to 922,279 Palestinian refugees forced to leave Palestine since the creation of Israel in May 1948 and the first Arab-Israeli war that followed it.

2 March The US Senate rejects a resolution offered by Senator Richard Russell stating US intent to use armed force against Communist aggression in the Middle East.

5 March The US Senate passes a revised congressional joint resolution, embodying military and economic aid provisions of the Eisenhower Doctrine for the Middle East. On 9 March President Eisenhower signed a congressional joint resolution of Middle East assistance, authorizing him to extend economic aid and military aid to nations 'desiring such assistance'.

7 March The Egyptian Suez Canal Authority reopens the canal for daylight use of vessels of up to 500 tons. It announced that all ships that paid tolls to Egypt would be allowed transit through the canal.

9 March The flow of Saudi oil resumes to the Bahrain refinery for the first time since November when it was closed following the British-French Suez adventure. The price of Saudi oil had risen dramatically since the fighting, the new price of $2.12 a barrel representing the highest posting for Saudi crude since 1948.

11 March The US, Britain and France reject a Soviet proposal that the Big Four powers formulate a common policy on maintaining peace in the Middle East. Since the Suez campaign, the Soviets had greatly extended their influence in the region as the principal suppliers of arms and economic aid to Egypt, Syria and Iraq. They had first become a genuine rival to the US in the region when, from 1954 and culminating in the Suez crisis of 1956, they had supported the increasing neutralism of Nasser's Egypt.

13 March New Iranian legislation gives the franchise to women for the first time. Gradually women were to win the franchise in most Middle East states with obvious exceptions such as Saudi Arabia and Kuwait. In neighbouring Iraq, the League for the Defence of Women's Rights had come into being in 1952. The League's president, Dr Naziha Dulaimi, was to become the first woman cabinet minister in the Arab world when she became minister of municipalities in 1959.

13 March Jordan and Britain formally terminate their 1948 defence and mutual aid treaty. Observers believed that King Husayn of Jordan aimed to appeal to the pro-Nasser nationalist camp by ending the treaty.

19 March The Iraq Petroleum Company (IPC) agrees to lend Iraq an interest-free advance on royalties of £25 million.

19 March Egypt announces its intention of running the Suez Canal and collecting all canal dues. To the surprise of many, it was to succeed in both, although as a result of the 1956 imbroglio receipts did fall from £E29,396,000 in January–October 1956 to £E24,480,000 in April–December 1957.

22 March The US offers 'to participate actively in the work of the Military Command of the Baghdad Pact' under the congressional Eisenhower Doctrine resolution. The Pact had been shaken by the tensions arising from the Suez conflict. On 5 December 1956 the four Muslim members of the Pact had sought reassurance from the US that it would help them in times of need. On 21 December the Iraqi ambassador to Washington had sought a more concrete pledge of US support.

22 March The Algerian National Liberation Front announces plans to establish a provisional Algerian government to negotiate with France, on condition that France recognizes Algeria's right to independence. On the previous day the French authorities had claimed that the Algerian nationalist movement was on the point of defeat.

24 March Iranian bandits kill US aid officials Brewster Wilson and Kevin Carroll, Carroll's wife and two Iranian drivers, after ambushing their jeep in the Tangeorkheh Desert near the Pakistani border. On 6 April Pakistani militiamen captured a group of Iranian bandits whom they alleged to be the killers.

24 March Iraq announces the end of its boycott against Britain which it imposed following the Suez debacle.

25 March The Suez Canal is opened up for vessels of up to 20,000 tons. On 31 March the first regular convoy of ships to pass through the canal since November 1956 entered the waterway at Port Said.

27 March Following the Tehran talks between James Richards, specialist assistant to President Eisenhower on Middle East matters, and the Iranian Premier Hussein Ala, it was announced that the US government would increase military support to Iran and assist in joint projects which had been, or might be, approved by the economic commission of the Baghdad Pact.

28 March The Soviet Union warns Israel and France that a new attack on Egypt would threaten a broad military conflict 'with heavy consequences for the cause of peace'.

31 March An atomic energy training centre, built in Baghdad under the aegis of the Baghdad Pact powers, is opened by King Faisal. Most of the equipment had been supplied by Britain. Sir John Cockcroft, the director of Britain's Atomic Research Establishment at Harwell in England, became the chairman of the first scientific council of the Baghdad Pact Organization.

31 March The Saudi Arabian government declares that the use of the Gulf of Aqaba by ships visiting Israel's port of Eilat would be an 'encroachment on the sovereignty of Saudi Arabia and a threat to its territorial security'. The Jordanian port of Aqaba and the Israeli port of Eilat stand side by side at the head of the Gulf of Aqaba. Eilat is Israel's sole southern outlet to the sea. The western side of the Gulf of Aqaba is Egypt's Sinai Peninsula, and the eastern side is Saudi Arabia. Between 11 and 12 April the Saudis announced that they would prevent the Israelis from using the Gulf of Aqaba.

3 April Iran's Premier Hussein Ala resigns and is succeeded by Dr Manouchehr Eghbal, the minister of the court. Ala's resignation was said to be linked with the murder of three US citizens by a gang of bandits in south-east Iran on 24 March. The killings had led to the suspension of foreign aid activities in the region.

8 April A joint US-Iraqi communiqué on mutual support is issued following discussions in Baghdad between James P. Richards, the special assistant to President Eisenhower on the Middle East, and the Iraqis. On the following day Richards arrived in Riyadh.

14 April King Husayn of Jordan emerges victorious in the nation's power struggle after ordering the ousting and deportation of General Ali Abu Nuwar, the pro-Nasser army chief-of-staff, following clashes near Zarqa and Ajloun between pro-Nuwar and pro-King Husayn troops. On 13 April Abd al-Halim al-Nimr had formed a new Jordanian cabinet after the resignation on 10 April of Sulayman Nabulsi at the king's request. The king alleged that the army was being increasingly infiltrated by pro-Soviet elements. On 15 April Husayn Fakhri al-Khalidi, a former Jordanian foreign minister reportedly opposed to Soviet involvement in the Middle East, replaced at Nimr.

16 April The Iranian government orders the National Iranian Oil Company (NIOC) to 'avoid all transactions with Israel' and calls on it to prevent oil from being sent through the Gulf of Aqaba to the Israeli port of Eilat.

17 April The British foreign secretary, Selwyn Lloyd, announces that Britain will supply Iraq with five Hunter Mark VI jet aircraft.

21 April Egyptian press sources report that an Iraqi force has entered Jordan near Mafraq, a town 45 miles (72.5 kilometres) north-east of Amman. Observers saw the force as poised to support King Husayn against any pro-Nasser nationalist coup. On the previous day General Ali Hayari had resigned as the new Jordanian army chief-of-staff during a dispute with King Husayn. The king had designated General Majali as the new acting chief-of-staff. On 17 April the king had warned the Jordanian people in a broadcast that he would resist those 'who try to drive a wedge between me and you, between me and our army'. On 25 April King Husayn declared martial law throughout Jordan.

25 April The US orders the Sixth Fleet from French and Italian ports to the eastern Mediterranean. The US was acting to ensure the survival of Jordan's King Husayn against his leftist, pro-Nasser, nationalist opponents. On 26 April the US State Department said that the US had sent 'cautionary' advice to Jordan's Arab neighbours and Israel. On 29 April the Soviet Union charged that the dispatch of the Sixth Fleet was 'an open military demonstration against the countries of the Arab East'.

26 April The Syrian president, Shukri al-Quwatly, flies from Cairo to Riyadh to discuss the Jordanian situation with King Saud. Syria's alignment with the Soviet Union made her a threat to Jordan and in May Syrian troops serving under the joint Syro-Egyptian-Jordanian command were withdrawn from Jordanian territory.

3 May Lebanese press reports disclose that an Egyptian-backed plot to assassinate Saudi King Saud has been uncovered and crushed in the Saudi capital, Riyadh.

11–17 May King Saud visits Iraq in what appears to be a new era of friendship. King Husayn was also invited but was unable to come because of the dangerous developments in Jordan. On 15 May King Husayn asked Iraq and Saudi Arabia to grant Jordan $21 million in emergency loans or gifts to replace funds promised, but never delivered, by Egypt and Syria. On 16 May King Saud of Saudi Arabia, meeting in Baghdad with

General Majali, King Husayn's adviser and acting chief-of-staff, offered to visit Amman, the Jordanian capital, for talks on Saudi-Jordanian co-operation.

16 May The creation of a new opposition party called the People's Party is announced in Tehran, following the proclamation by the premier, Manouchehr Eghbal, of the introduction of a two-party system. The new party was headed by Asadulla Alam, the former minister of interior and labour, who had strong links with the shah. The new party was not taken seriously by those seeking a pluralist democracy.

18 May The Iraqi premier, Nuri al-Said, says that the Arab states will have to abandon neutralism and ally themselves with the West. Otherwise, they would be dominated by Moscow. He warned that Iraq would remain under martial law until Communist activities had been stamped out in neighbouring Syria and Jordan. Syria appeared to have fallen under the virtual army dictatorship of Colonel Abd al-Hamid al-Sarraj.

20 May In a note to Egypt, Saudi Arabia re-affirms its intention of barring Israeli shipping from the Gulf of Aqaba. The Saudis charged Israeli naval units with conducting manoeuvres in the Gulf. On 27 May Saudi Arabia complained to the UN Security Council that an Israeli plane and destroyer had violated Saudi Arabian territorial waters in the Gulf of Aqaba.

28 May The Iraqi premier, Nuri al-Said, ends the martial law imposed on November 1956.

3–6 June The Council of Ministers of the Baghdad Pact holds its third session in Karachi, under the chairmanship of the Pakistani prime minister, Suhrawardy. Among its decisions was one to implement extensive research work by the Joint Nuclear Training Centre at Baghdad. Nuri al-Said said that Israel was still the most serious source of danger in the Middle East because of her 'ambitious and sinister plans of expansion and aggression'. At the meeting on 3 June the US joined the Baghdad Treaty Military Committee. On 6 June the Council of Ministers announced their agreement on the creation of a joint military planning staff.

4 June Jordanian, Syrian, Yemeni and Saudi Arabian representatives, meeting in Cairo, sign an agreement providing for an Arab financial organization capitalized at $56 million for economic development of the entire region of Arab League states.

8 June The resignation of the Iraqi premier, Nuri al-Said, was followed on 17 June by the formation of a new government by Ali Jawdat al-Ayyubi which was sworn in on 19 June.

11 June Dad Shah, the Iranian bandit alleged to have killed three US citizens and two Iranian drivers in March, is killed in Iran's Baluchistan desert after a five-hour gun battle with the security forces.

22–24 June King Husayn of Jordan pays his third visit to Baghdad for discussions with King Faisal of Iraq. At the end of their discussions they pledged to defend each other and condemned intervention by other Arab states in their internal affairs.

23 June In a note distributed to US shipping companies, the US State Department affirms the 'right of free and innocent' navigation in the Gulf of Aqaba.

25 June Saudi Arabia recalls its ambassador to Syria in protest against criticism of King Saud and King Husayn by the Syrian defence minister, Khaled al-Azm.

1 July Egypt begins a shipment of jet aircraft to Saudi Arabia.

2 July Some 200 deaths are caused by earthquakes along Iran's Caspian Sea coast.

12 July King Husayn of Jordan and King Saud of Saudi Arabia order Muslims travelling to Mecca to perform the *hajj* to avoid the Gulf of Aqaba for safety reasons. They blamed 'aggressions by Israel in the Gulf waters' for having to close the usual Aqaba-Jeddah pilgrimage route.

22 July British troops move in to suppress an uprising against the sultan of Oman by the former imam of Oman, Ghalib ibn Ali. The sultan had requested British military assistance, which had successfully broken the back of the revolt by 22 July. By 19 July Ghalib controlled the Nizwa area but by 12 August the sultan's authority had been fully restored. The sultan's relations with the interior were governed by the 1920 Treaty of Sib. A new treaty of friendship with Britain, signed on 20 December 1951, recognized the full independence of the sultanate, officially called Muscat and Oman. Relations between Imam Muhammad ibn Abdullah al-Khalili and the sultan had remained friendly but on the imam's death in 1954 a rebellion broke out under his successor, Ghalib ibn Ali. Ghalib had sought foreign help to establish a new principality. In December 1955 the sultan's forces had managed to enter the main inhabited areas of Oman without any resistance. The sultan allowed the former imam to retire to his village but his brother, Talib, escaped to Saudi Arabia and then to Cairo where he set up the self-styled 'Omani Imamate'. By the summer of 1957 Talib had returned and established himself in the mountain areas around Nizwa.

25 July King Idris of Libya appoints the Iraqi officer, General Abd al-Ahmad Raghib, chief-of-staff of the Libyan army.

11 August Iran and the Soviet Union agree to co-operate on the joint use of the river Atrak that runs through Iran's north-eastern border with the Soviet Turkmen Republic.

17 August A leftist group of army officers, led by Colonel Afif Bizri, takes control of the Syrian government, replacing moderate army leaders. On the following day President Quwatly had talks in Cairo with Nasser after decreeing the dismissal of 10 moderate army officers. On 19 August Syria's foreign minister, Salah al-Bitar, claimed that Syria had been 'the target of destructive activities aimed at making her accept the Eisenhower Doctrine'. However, on 22 August Syria's defence minister, Khaled al-Azm, denied Western charges that Syria's military command had moved into the Soviet orbit. Nevertheless, on 28 August the Defence Ministry said that the Soviet leaders, Krushchev and Bulganin, would visit Syria before the end of the year. On 30 August the US embassy in Damascus announced that its consular and diplomatic staffs would be reduced.

26 August Saudi Arabia becomes a member of the International Bank for Reconstruction and Development and the International Monetary Fund.

8–12 September Italy's President Gronchi visits Iran as guest of the shah.

12 September Diplomatic sources in Washington report that Saudi Arabia's King Saud has sent US President Eisenhower a personal message urging moderation of the US administration's increasingly anti-Syrian position. The message sought assurances that the US would refrain from intervention in internal Arab affairs. On 14 September Ahmad Shukairy, the Saudi Arabian state minister and UN delegation chairman, said his government would side with Syria against an attack 'from whatever quarter'. On 15 September the Syrian army chief-of-staff, Afif Bizri, renewed charges of a US plot to attack Syria with Turkish help. He claimed that Turkey had massed two armoured divisions and one infantry division on the Syrian border. On 11 September Soviet Premier Bulganin accused Turkish Premier Adnan Menderes of deploying the Turkish army in preparation for a US-sponsored attack on Syria. On 14 September the Turkish defence minister denied the charges.

20 September French diplomats report that the Soviet Union has agreed to triple Syria's jet force of 40 MiG-17s and to provide 50 11-28 jet bombers. Soviet aid for Syria had escalated, representing a serious challenge to moderate Arab states supported by the West.

20 September The Soviet foreign minister, Andrei Gromyko, tells the UN General Assembly that the Soviet Union will not remain an 'impassive observer' while the West turns the Middle East into 'a permanent hotbed of conflict'. On 24 September, however, the US, Britain and France rejected Soviet proposals for a Big Four conference on the Middle East and on 27 September the US and five Baghdad Pact members agreed to expand the Pact's programme to counter Soviet penetration of the Middle East.

25 September King Saud pays a three-day visit to Syria. At the end of the visit, on 27 September, he declared that he deplored 'every aggression on Syria and on any other Arab country from whatever source it comes'.

19–26 October Syria accuses Turkey of trying to overthrow the Syrian regime with US help. On 13 October Egyptian troops were reported to have landed in Syria to support the regime against a threatened coup. President Eisenhower was later to confirm in his memoirs that the US and its Middle East allies had plotted to overthrow the regime in Damascus. Meanwhile, King Saud offered to mediate in the crisis; the Turks accepted his offer, but the Syrians rejected it.

28 October At the end of a 12-day visit to Iran by King Faisal of Iraq a joint statement is published pledging full support for the Baghdad Pact.

10 November Replying to Iraqi offers to mediate between Egypt and Jordan, Jordan's King Husayn accuses Egypt's rulers of having 'sold themselves to Communism' and having exploited 'Arab nationalism to divert Egyptian public opinion from the deteriorating situation at home'. On 8 November Egypt's press and radio had renewed pleas for Jordan's Palestinian refugees to overthrow the regime of King Husayn and destroy the Hashemite dynasty in Jordan. On 12 November Syria's Foreign Ministry warned that the revolt against King Husayn was imminent. On 14 November Iraq's King Faisal and Saudi Arabia's King Saud urged Egypt and Syria to halt the propaganda attacks against Jordan. On 19 November King Saud offered to mediate between Jordan and Egypt.

12 November It is announced in Tehran that the shah has instructed the government to put before parliament a bill declaring Bahrain to be the fourteenth Iranian province. On 14 November a British Foreign Office spokesman confirmed that Britain would safeguard Bahrain's independence. Bahrain, like Iran, was largely Shi'i and had been under occasional Iranian (Persian) rule from 1602 to 1782. In 1783 the Iranians were expelled by the Utub Tribe whose paramount family, the Al-Khalifas, became the independent shaikhs of Bahrain and have ruled Bahrain ever since, apart form a short break before 1810.

13 December An earthquake in western Iran completely destroys the village of Farsinaj, killing 1,266 people.

15 December A new Iraqi cabinet is formed by Abd al-Wahhab Mirjan, the speaker of Iraq's parliament, a close associate of Nuri al-Said and a strong supporter of the Baghdad Pact.

1 9 5 8

13 January Crown Prince Seif al-Islam Muhammad al-Badr of Yemen signs a $16.4-million loan agreement in Peking, providing for Chinese technicians to help in Yemeni road and factory projects. A Soviet mission arrived in Yemen in January 1957 and a Soviet legation opened at Taiz. Later in the year a Chinese mission arrived and a Chinese legation was opened at Taiz. Groups of Chinese workers were soon to follow. The Chinese were persuaded to build the San'a-Hodeida road, and by the end of 1958 there were 1,000 technicians and workers to Yemen. Athough the Chinese may have hoped for the development of lively political ties with Yemen, they were in fact to be deceived and few of their contracts were ever even paid for.

20 January Iraq, Iran, Pakistan and Turkey sign a convention in the Turkish capital, Ankara, providing for the co-ordination of Baghdad Pact members' customs services to combat smuggling and contraband trade in the area. On the following day the Pact's Economic Committee ended its five-day meeting with an appeal for more British and US aid. On 30 January the US secretary of state, Foster Dulles, told the Pact's council that US commitments under the Eisenhower Doctrine constituted a guarantee of US involvement which was equal to full US membership of the Pact.

25 January Iraq's parliament demands, and wins, an assurance from Premier Abd al-Wahhab Mirjan that Baghdad Pact membership will not compel Iraq to accept US missile bases. Mirjan had succeeded Ali Jawdat al-Ayyubi as premier in December 1957.

30 January British troops and aircraft clash with Yemeni forces on the Aden border after the Yemenis fire on a British frontier patrol. Yemeni subversion and direct attacks across the frontier had escalated since 1955. Since 1956 Cairo Radio had ceaselessly proclaimed that the British would be expelled from throughout the Arab world.

1 February The Egyptian president, Gamal abd al-Nasser, and the Syrian president, Shukri al-Quwatly, formally proclaim the union of Egypt and Syria as two *iqlims* (regions) of the United Arab Republic (UAR). On 5 February the Egyptian National Assembly and President Quwatly, as head of Syria's parliament, formally nominated Nasser to serve as the UAR's first president. On 21 February, in plebiscites in both countries, Egyptians and Syrians voted nearly unanimously to approve the establishment of the UAR with Nasser as president.

On 23 February Nasser announced in Cairo that the UAR would strive for 'complete liberation' of the Arab world, including the area occupied by Israel, 'from imperialism and its agents'. On 26 February he denounced the Iraqi-Jordanian union (the Arab Federation established on 14 February) as a 'false federation' aimed against the UAR.

The creation of the UAR was the fulfilment of Nasser's dream of pan-Arab unity. However, observers of the day saw it as being far from a union of hearts, and believed that it was due less to Nasser's ambition than a desire in both countries to control the spread of Soviet and Communist influence in the Arab world. When the union was proclaimed, President Quwatly was said to have told Nasser: 'You have acquired a nation of politicians; fifty per cent believe themselves to be national leaders, twenty-five per cent to be prophets, and at least ten per cent to be gods.' Nevertheless, the union had an electrifying impact on the other Arab states, inspiring admiration in some and fear in others. Jordan and Iraq were to form their own federation out of fear.

Although the Soviet Union welcomed the emergence of the UAR, it nursed private misgivings. The Syrian Communist Party was split by the union, although this did not prevent the Soviets from welcoming Nasser to Moscow on 28 April. On 29 January Egypt and the Soviet Union had signed an economic agreement.

14 February Confronted with the emergence of the UAR on 1 February, Jordan and Iraq proclaim the creation of a federal state uniting their two kingdoms called the Arab Federation. The decision was reached after four days of talks in Amman between Jordan's King Husayn and Iraq's King Faisal. Jordan's parliament ratified the new agreement on 18 February.

The articles of federation allowed Husayn and Faisal to retain sovereign power over their respective countries but provided for the unification of their armed forces, foreign policies, diplomatic corps, educational systems and customs administration. The currencies of both countries were to become one and economic co-operation was expected. Members chosen in equal numbers from both parliaments would unite to form a federal legislature. Baghdad and Amman would serve, each in turn for a period of six months, as the federal capital.

Soon Cairo and Damascus radios were to be raging against the 'imperialist stooges' of Baghdad and Amman. Saudi Arabia's King Saud quickly proclaimed that Saudi Arabia would join neither the UAR nor the Arab Federation. In an odd twist on 2 March, however, the medieval ruler of Yemen, Imam Ahmad, was to sign an opportunistic agreement with the UAR to form a federal union known as the United Arab States. The agreement had been announced on 2 February in Cairo by Nasser and Crown Prince Seif al-Islam Muhammad al-Badr of Yemen, although the imam's absolutist monarchy was to be retained.

17 February The Iranian prime minister, Dr Manouchehr Eghbal, announces the formation of a government majority party called the Nation Party. The purpose of the party was to give the impression in Iran of a pluralistic democracy.

28 February General Vali Gharani, former Iranian army intelligence chief, is arrested on the orders of the shah. General Gharani was seized with 33 other suspects on charges of plotting with 'a foreign power' against the Iranian government.

5 March Gamal abd al-Nasser, the president of the newly formed United Arab Republic of Egypt and Syria, accuses the Syrian-side finance minister, Colonel Abd al-Hamid Sarraj, of being paid £1.9 million to finance a military coup against the union. The plan was alleged to have involved the assassination of Nasser, with Sarraj becoming president of Syria.

6 March President Nasser appoints his first UAR cabinet. He named two Egyptians and two Syrians as vice-presidents but placed foreign affairs, defence and other key ministries in Egyptian hands. Meanwhile, King Saud denied any involvement in a plot against the UAR involving the Syrian Colonel Sarraj. On 12 March Nasser decreed the abolition of all Syrian political parties and associations.

10 March The Iranian foreign minister, Ali Gholi Ardalan, protests against a Saudi-Bahrain oil agreement giving Saudi Arabia rights to offshore oil exploration and development near Bahrain. On 12 November the shah had instructed the government to put before parliament a bill declaring Bahrain to be the 'fourteenth Persian [Iranian] province'.

13 March Saudi Arabian delegates to the UN conference on the Law of the Sea announce in Geneva that Saudi Arabia has formally extended its territorial waters to 12 miles (19 kilometres). The decision 'legally' closed the Gulf of Aqaba to Israeli shipping.

14 March The Iranian court announces the shah's divorce from Queen Soraya on the grounds that she cannot have children and that the shah must have a direct male heir.

18–19 March A draft constitution of the Arab Federation is approved by Iraq and Jordan. Iraq's King Faisal formally became the head and commander of its unified armed forces and Jordan's King Husayn the deputy head.

23 March Saudi Arabia's King Saud decrees that Crown Prince Faisal, who is already prime minister and foreign minister, should have increased powers in foreign and economic affairs. The decree meant that full executive authority was passed to Faisal from then on. This was welcomed by the Egyptian press which saw Faisal as more pro-Egyptian than Saud.

By the start of 1958 the government's debt was about 1,800 million Saudi riyals ($480 million), according to David Holden and Richards Johns in *The House of Saud*, of which 700 million riyals was owed to the Saudi Arabian Monetary Agency. Inflation was raging while capital was pouring out of the kingdom. Many doubted Saud's fitness to rule. His health was poor and, it was later to emerge, he was an alcoholic. At a time when monogomy was in fashion – the austere, disciplined Faisal had three wives throughout his life – the vast number of Saud's concubines and offspring was becoming a point of gossip.

18 April The Aden governor, Sir William Luce, orders the arrest of three leading citizens of the sultanate of Lahej for having contact with foreign powers and trying to make trouble in the Western Aden Protectorate. Muhammad Ali Jiffri was the main detainee. He had wanted to create a South Arabian League ruled by Sultan Sir Ali Abd al-Karim al-Abdali which would unite with the United Arab States, the new union of Yemen and the United Arab Republic of Egypt and Syria.

18 April Crown Prince Faisal of Saudi Arabia, recently installed as his country's executive ruler over his brother King Saud, announces that the Saudi government will pursue policies of 'positive neutrality' and will not join the United Arab Republic of Egypt and Syria nor the rival Arab Federation of Iraq and Jordan.

28 April President Nasser arrives in Moscow on the start of a three-week tour of the Soviet

Union in his capacity as president of the newly formed UAR. In a speech at a lunch given by the Soviet leader, Nikita Khrushchev, in the Kremlin on 30 April, Nasser paid tribute to Soviet aid which he said was without strings and involved no interference in the UAR's non-alignment. The two leaders signed a joint communiqué supporting the rights of the Palestinians and Algerians to self-determination and denounced British aggression against Yemen. Like Syria, Egypt was by now firmly aligned with Moscow against the West.

29 April Iran's Premier Manouchehr Eghbal submits to the Majlis (lower house) in Tehran a new US-Iranian oil agreement. The new agreement provided for a division of profits between the National Iranian Oil Company (NIOC: 75 per cent) and the Pan-American Petroleum Corporation, a subsidiary of Standard Oil Company of Indiana (25 per cent). On 1 June the shah gave his assent to the draft agreement. The terms of the agreement were particularly advantageous to Iran. They provided for expenditure of $82 million on exploitation activities within the first 12 years and the payment by the US company of a $25-million 'cash bonus' to the NIOC within one month of the agreement's ratification.

2 May A state of emergency is declared in Aden.

5 May The Iraqi general election results show an overwhelming victory for the government. The main issue was Iraq's federation with Jordan. The election of the 145-member parliament completed the constitutional revisions necessary for implementing the Arab Federation, the federal state of Jordan and Iraq.

11 May Saudi Arabia issues a royal edict aimed at regularizing cabinet practices as a first step towards a constitution. Soon after the fall of Mecca to King Abd al-Aziz's (Ibn Saud's) armies at the end of 1924, the late king had promised the creation of a Consultative Council (Majlis al-Shura) 'of the ulema [clerics], the dignitaries and the merchants'. The Council had been promulgated in 1926 in a decree which also promised a constitution. However, the latter had never materialized.

13 May The Arab Federation of Iraq and Jordan comes officially into being when the constitution is signed by the Iraqi and Jordanian kings in Baghdad. On the previous day it was ratified by the Iraqi parliament. The government of the new federation emerged with the installation of a federal cabinet headed by Iraqi Premier Nuri al-Said.

21 May The Lebanese president, Camille Chamoun, declares that the 'issue at stake' in Lebanon's current unrest is 'the existence of Lebanon as a free country in the Near East in which Muslims and Christians can live together in peace and concord'. On 24 May the Lebanese government formally appealed for the UN Security Council to halt 'the intervention of the UAR in the internal affairs of Lebanon'.

22 June Iranian Premier Manouchehr Eghbal informs the Majlis that an agreement has been concluded between the NIOC and Saphire Petroleum Limited of Canada for oil exploration in Baluchistan and for offshore rights in the Gulf of Oman.

2–11 July 2,500 people die in an earthquake in Iran south of the Caspian Sea.

5 July The former Ecuadorian president, UN Observation Group chairman Galo Plaza Lasso, says in Beirut that the present Lebanese conflict is 'a civil war with international overtones'. On 4 July the UN Observation Group had reported to the Security Council that its patrols had failed to prove UAR military support for Lebanese rebels and on 3 July the UN secretary-general, Dag Hammarskjold, had said that the UN had uncovered no evidence of 'mass infiltration' into Lebanon of arms or men from Syria.

10 July Britain deposes Sultan Sir Ali Abd al-Karim al-Abdali of Lahej, Western Aden Protectorate's dominant shaikhdom, for breaching his treaty with the British after he had shown himself willing to bring Lahej into the UAR. At the end of 1957 a confidential British government document recorded that the most dangerous anti-British dissident in the Aden Colony and Protectorate was Sultan Ali. He had rejected unification proposals for Aden and the western sultanates not, according to Robin Bidwell in *The Two Yemens*, because he was against a united South Arabia, but because he wanted to head it himself. He wanted Lahej to be pre-eminent and resented the way the British had made other rulers, such as the sharif of Bayhan and the Audhali sultan, his equals.

According to Bidwell, Sultan Ali's main weapon was the South Arabian League led by his close associate, Sayyid Muhammad Al-Jiffri, which called for the departure of the British and the creation of an independent state under Sultan Ali. Sultan Ali had met UAR President Nasser on the *hajj* to Mecca in 1955 and been impressed. Nasser had soon supplied Lahej with school teachers and other advisers until it became, in the words of an official report quoted by Bidwell, 'an outpost of Egyptian subversion'.

Many in Lahej believed that Sultan Ali would announce his adherence to the UAR but in April the British pre-empted him by entering Lahej and seizing the Jiffri brothers, while Sultan Ali, himself, went to London to protest. Almost immediately afterwards, the whole Lahej regular army deserted to Yemen with the sultanate's treasury. Sultan Ali ignored British 'advice' to return to Lahej and was, therefore, declared to be in breach of his treaty with the British and deposed.

14 July The Iraqi royal family is slaughtered in a bloody military coup and a republic is declared in Baghdad. The revolution was to be an important catalyst for events in the Middle East from henceforth.

On the night of 13 July Colonel Abd al-Salam Aref took control of the Iraqi army's Twentieth Brigade, of which he was one of three battalion commanders. The brigade surrounded strategic points in Baghdad, including Premier Nuri al-Said's house and the royal palace. Nuri escaped but King Faisal, Crown Prince Abdulilah and some female members of the royal family were lined up against the wall of the royal palace's courtyard and summarily shot.

On the morning of 14 July Brigadier (later General) Abd al-Karim Qasim, who headed the Nasser-style nationalist 'Free Officers' coup, and his deputy, Aref, proclaimed the end of the monarchy and the creation of a people's republic. A new cabinet was announced in which neither Communists nor Kurdish Democratic Party (KDP) members were invited to participate. Qasim became prime minister and effective president, Aref interior minister, and Naji Talib social affairs minister. The two parliamentary chambers were abolished and arrest warrants were issued for people associated with the *ancien régime*. The British embassy was sacked by the Baghdad mob and the British ambassador, Sir Michael Wright, was forced to move to a hotel.

Nevertheless, Aref tried to reassure foreign governments, while the new foreign minister, Dr Abd al-Jabbar Jomard, assured the West that the new regime's resumption of relations with the Soviet Union had no significance. Meanwhile, the UAR was the first power to support the new regime. President Chamoun of Lebanon called for support by the US marines and a grief-stricken King Husayn of Jordan (King Faisal's second cousin) passionately denounced the coup. Furthermore, on the day of the revolution two Jordanian ministers had been lynched by the Baghdad mob.

On 15 July the former Iraqi prime minister, Nuri al-Said, was captured, humiliatingly disguised as a woman, and was beaten to death by the Baghdad mob.

On the same day Iraq announced that it had withdrawn from its Arab Federation with Jordan.

On 19 July Iraq signed a defence pact with the Soviet Union.

15 July Two battalions of marines, numbering 1,500 in total, from the US Sixth Fleet land in Beirut in response to President Chamoun's appeal for help the previous day following the Iraqi revolution. Chamoun feared a pro-Nasser coup in Lebanon leading to civil war. The marines promptly assumed control of Beirut international airport. By 20 July there were 10,000 US troops in Lebanon.

On 16 July the British prime minister, Harold Macmillan, reported the transfer of British troops to Jordan to prevent a coup against King Husayn. On 17 July 2,000 men of the British Sixteenth Parachute Brigade and supporting units were flown from their bases in Cyprus to a camp near the Jordanian capital, Amman. They were escorted to Amman by 50 US navy fighters.

15 July UAR President Nasser is interrupted in his talks with Yugoslavia's President Tito by news of the US marine landings in Lebanon. On 16 July Nasser cut short his Yugoslav visit and went to Moscow. On 17 July he continued to Damascus where he met the new Iraqi leaders. On 18 July he gave a speech in Damascus in which he welcomed the Iraqi revolution.

16 July The Soviet Union denounces the British and US action in Lebanon and Jordan.

18 July Iranian and Turkish forces are placed on alert as Soviet armed forces begin manoeuvres in the Trans-Caucasian and Turkestan military districts.

19 July UAR President Nasser and the Iraqi deputy premier, Colonel Abd al-Salam Aref, sign a mutual defence treaty in Damascus.

19 July Responding to the anticipated effects of the Iraqi revolution, Britain reinforces its garrisons in Kuwait and Aden and lands 500 Royal Marine commandos in Libya. However, on 20 July the British foreign secretary, Selwyn Lloyd, and the US secretary of state, Foster Dulles, reportedly reached a decision in Washington ruling out military action in Iraq.

20 July Jordan breaks off relations with the UAR in response to the latter's recognition of the new Iraqi government.

21 July The Iranian and Soviet railway systems are linked with the opening of a junction at Julfa on the border between the two countries.

21 July The Israeli prime minister, David Ben-Gurion, tells the Knesset (parliament) that 'the menace of Israel's encirclement by Nasser has been greatly increased by recent events' in Iraq, Jordan and Lebanon.

26 July Iraq's President Qasim announces that elections in Iraq will be delayed until steps are taken towards land distribution, improved housing and an end to 'corruption'.

30 July Robert Murphy, deputy secretary of state and President Eisenhower's Middle East specialist, visit Amman before visiting Baghdad on 2 August where he is impressed by the integrity of President Qasim.

31 July The British foreign secretary, Selwyn-Lloyd, announces that Britain has agreed to help Oman strengthen its military forces and provide economic aid for development.

1 August King Husayn of Jordan announces the suspension of the Arab Federation of Iraq and Jordan following the Iraqi revolution.

2 August Britain and the US recognize the new regime in Baghdad. The agreement followed Iraqi assurances that the new regime would be bound by the UN Charter and 'its other international obligations'.

11 August The Israeli foreign minister, Golda Meir, warns that Israel will be forced to re-examine 'very seriously' its security position if UAR or Iraqi forces occupy Jordan.

17 August Crown Prince Faisal, the Saudi premier and executive head, and UAR President Nasser conclude three days of talks in Cairo. At the end of the talks, Faisal said that all 'misunderstandings are removed'. He even added 'Thank God our relations are so good now that if there were a cloud in the sky it has passed by.' The two leaders condemned 'the presence of any foreign forces on the territory of any Arab state'. Faisal had taken no public stand after the Iraqi revolution, even failing to condemn the execution of the Iraqi royal family, believing that Saudi Arabia's safest policy was one of non-alignment. The vogue of the period was Nasserist pan-Arabism and Faisal was astute enough to realize that monarchies were generally out of favour.

6 September The British Foreign Office announces that the sultan of Muscat and Oman has agreed to sell to Pakistan the small enclave of Gwadur on the Iranian border coast of Baluchistan.

7 September The new regime in Baghdad offers a political amnesty for those arrested under the previous regime and establishes relations with the Soviet Union, China and other eastern European countries.

12 September The new Iraqi deputy premier, Aref, is relieved of the post of deputy commander-in-chief of the Iraqi armed forces. The change reflected a power struggle in Baghdad, with President Qasim clearly in the ascendant. Aref had proved himself an outspoken supporter of union between Iraq and the UAR. On 30 September Aref was relieved of all his cabinet posts and was appointed ambassador to West Germany. At the same time two of Aref's supporters were dropped from the cabinet and there was a re-shuffle of ministerial appointments. On 12 October Qasim personally saw him off. However, Aref never went to Bonn but visited several other European cities before returning to Baghdad on 4 November.

21 September The Iraqi government announces the creation of a new military agency to censor all books and pamphlets published in the country.

7 October Nasser replaces the dual Egyptian-Syrian government system established for the UAR with a 21-member cabinet. On the previous day UAR Vice-President Sabri al-Assali resigned in protest against the increasing Egyptianization of the UAR civil service and the application in Syria of UAR restrictions. This was to be the beginning of a deterioration of relations between Egypt and Syria which was to end with the collapse of the new federation.

11 October Iraq signs a trade agreement with the Soviet Union.

23 October The Baghdad Pact offices are transferred from Baghdad to Ankara with retroactive effect from 17 October. Iraq's Qasim was not to bring Iraq formally out of the Pact until 24 March 1959.

31 October The Soviet Union denounces the new US-Iranian defence agreement. It claimed that the agreement had subjected the Soviet Union's 'southern borders' to 'immediate danger'.

31 October/1 November Serious rioting takes place in the Crater area of Aden. Five demonstrators were killed and 560 arrested, when mobs protesting against the imprisonment of two Arab journalists rioted and attacked British government and business offices.

4 November Iraq's former deputy leader, Aref, returns from Europe to Baghdad. There he visited President Qasim who offered him the ambassadorship to Britain. When Aref refused this offer he was arrested for 'conspiracy' against the state and condemned to death, although he was to be reprieved in February 1959 and Qasim was said to have visited him regularly in prison.

During November new harsh laws were imposed which were made restrospective to 1939 and sentences ranging from three years' imprisonment to death were handed down. On 10 November a Baghdad military tribunal condemned to death a former Iraqi premier, Fadil al-Jamali, and two former military leaders for alleged conspiracy to organize a West-backed coup in Iraq. On 13 November a Baghdad military court condemned to death a former Iraqi foreign minister, Burhan al-Din Bashaiyan, and on 20 November a former premier, Ahmad Mukhtar Baban, on charges of taking part in an anti-government conspiracy. Meanwhile, the five-year plan and the government's relationship with the Iraq Petroleum Company (IPC) were both revised.

22 November The Shah of Iran promises to retain Shaikh Sulman ibn Hamid al-Khalifa as Bahrain's governor-general if he accepts Iran's claims to sovereignty over the islands, still a British protectorate.

2 December Iraq expresses concern over US-Iranian talks on rebuilding the 'almost' dead Baghdad Pact defence alliance.

8 December Arrests are made in Iraq following a plot of which, one dubious report claimed, the British ambassador to Iraq, Sir Michael Wright, had warned President Qasim. The plot was to be led by Raghib Ali and his backers and was to to be carried out on 9 or 10 December. Money and arms to be used in the plot were allegedly seized.

On 15 December a Baghdad mob hurled mud, eggs and stones at the US assistant secretary of state, William Rountree, as he arrived for talks with President Qasim and other leaders of the Iraqi revolution.

On 16 December Baghdad Radio reported that the Iraq-Iran border had been closed and all communications between the two countries severed.

22 December The UAR and the Soviet Union sign an agreement in Cairo, providing for the Soviet construction of five airfields in Egypt and factories in the Suez Canal zone. On 24 December, in contrast, the UAR and the US concluded an agreement providing for the sale of $24.9 million worth of surplus US wheat and flour for UAR currency.

23 December UAR President Nasser's speech in Port Said attacking the Syrian Communists sets off a UAR media campaign against the new regime in Baghdad. President Qasim had become increasingly influenced by the Communists although they had no ministers in the government and were still banned as a party. The former deputy leader, Colonel Aref, had been the leading Nasserite in the new regime and with Aref gone, Qasim, although at first strongly influenced by Nasser, had edged away from him until a serious rivalry began to emerge between the two. Believing that Nasser was intriguing against him, Qasim leant more and more heavily on the Communists.

1 9 5 9

1 January The United Arab Republic (UAR) president, Gamal abd al-Nasser, orders the arrest of 200 Egyptian Communist leaders. This was to be the beginning of a fierce campaign against the Communists, whom he saw as threatening his dream of pan-Arab unity, and whom he derided for taking orders from Moscow.

14 January The Iraqi president, General Abd al-Karim Qasim, orders the leftist Iraq Students' Union and People's Resistance Force to halt their interference with the police authorities and to submit to the control of the Iraqi army. The government was becoming increasingly anxious about the street power that Communist front organizations were acquiring.

24 January During the trial in Baghdad of President Qasim's former deputy prime minister and minister of the interior, Colonel Abd al-Salam Aref, and of Rashid Ali, the military prosecutor refers to the discovery of 'another dirty plot by Aref'. On 2 February the trial was filmed on Baghdad television. Aref was accused of leading officers against the state between 4–5 November 1958, and of attempting to kill Qasim.

On 4 February the Iraqi military Supreme Court sentenced three leading officials of the overthrown regime of King Faisal to death for murder, torture and election fraud. On 7 February Baghdad Radio announced that Aref was to be executed for trying to kill President Qasim. They were referring to an incident in which he was alleged to have aimed a pistol at Qasim on the latter's return from Europe.

3 February The British Colonial Office announces that 6 out of 18 Western Aden Protectorate states have agreed on a constitution for a proposed Western Aden federation. The treaty was signed on 11 February by the governor of Aden, Sir William Luce, and the rulers of Bayhan, Fadhli, Aulaqi, Dhala, Lower Yafa and the Upper Aulaqi shaikhdom. The agreement specified that all previous agreements with Britain would remain in force and that British protection would cover the federation as a whole. The British would remain fully responsible for foreign affairs. London promised to provide financial and technical help and to maintain a federal army and national guard. However, the new federation was to be daunted by lack of natural resources and a heavy dependence on British aid.

6 February Six Iraq's cabinet ministers resign in protest against President Qasim's policies and against the death sentence passed on Colonel Aref. The ministers were said to hold anti-Communist views and to be favourably disposed to the UAR. They included Colonel Naji Talib, one of the leaders of the July revolution which overthrew the Iraqi monarchy.

8 February Iraq's President Qasim forms a new Iraqi government which excludes the right-wing nationalist Istiqlal (Independence) Party. The new cabinet consisted of six 'Free Officers' (referring to those who had carried out the coup in July 1958), five National Democrats and three Independents. The new ministers were said to be badly disposed towards the UAR and to favour a form of independent nationalism with a left-wing bias. Foreign observers considered the new cabinet as one favouring closer ties with the Soviet Union. One of the new ministers, Husayn Talbani, was a Kurd.

9 February The new Iraqi minister of national guidance (information), Husayn Jamil, suspends the Communist *Ittihad al-Sha'b* newspaper for two weeks for refusing to accept censorship, but Qasim cancels the order. Jamil promptly left Iraq for Delhi. Control of the ministry was then transferred to its permanent director-general. The rift represented increasing tensions within the government, particularly between those who sought unity with the UAR and those who were against it.

11 February Iraq's President Qasim indicates in a Baghdad address that Iraq will no longer honour its non-Arab military alliances, particularly the Baghdad Pact. Until now Iraq had, in principle, continued to belong to the Pact. It formally withdrew from it on 24 March.

5 March A US defence treaty is signed in Ankara with Iran, Pakistan and Turkey. On 8 March the Iranian Majlis (lower house) overwhelmingly approved a new US-Iranian bilateral defence agreement.

8 March An uprising in Mosul led by the commanding-officer of the Mosul Brigade, Colonel Abd al-Wahhab Shawwaf, is quelled by the Iraqi government. Shawwaf had forbidden a rally of Communist 'peace-partisans' in Mosul and many deaths were soon reported in subsequent street fighting between Communists and Arab nationalists. It was then announced that Colonel Shawwaf's troops had taken charge of Iraq's whole northern region and were preparing to march on Baghdad. A rebel government was said to have been set up in Mosul which called for the support of all Arab nationalists. It accused the Baghdad government of despotic conduct, particularly in its persecution of 'Free Officers' who had led the July coup against the monarchy, and of the expulsion of the July revolutionary council.

On 9 March, however, the Iraqi air force bombed Mosul and quickly ended the rebellion. Colonel Shawwaf, the brother of Major-General Muhammad Shawwaf, the minister of health, was reported to have been killed by officers loyal to President Qasim. Between 500 and 5,000 people (according to various estimates) were said to have been killed in the fighting.

The Baghdad regime accused both the Western powers and President Nasser of instigating the rebellion which led to a more anti-Western line on the part of the government. Qasim's supporters demanded Iraq's immediate withdrawal from the

Baghdad Pact and the breaking of relations with the UAR. The staff of the UAR embassy left Baghdad on 10 March.

16 March Iraq signs economic and technical co-operation agreements with the Soviet Union and Poland. Following the signature of the Soviet agreement, Soviet Premier Nikita Khrushchev said that Nasser was disappointed that Iraq had not joined the UAR.

1 April The German Democratic Republic (East Germany) signs a cultural and scientific co-operation agreement with Iraq in Baghdad, and on 2 April Poland signed an agreement of the same kind with Iraq in Warsaw. On 3 April the UAR deputy foreign minister, Farid Zayn al-Din, demanded that the Arab League take strong action condemning Qasim's regime for opening Iraq up to Soviet penetration.

8 April The Iraqi government announces that it has armed the Communist-dominated Popular Resistance Front and has extended its authority outside Baghdad to border regions.

23 April Oil ministers from nine Arab countries and emirates end the first Arab Petroleum Congress in Cairo. They called for increased Arab participation in oil transport, refining and marketing and a greater share in the industry's profits.

29 April The sultan of Lahej visits London to discuss a new federation. On 3 February the British Colonial Office had announced that 6 out of 18 Western Aden Protectorate states had agreed on a constitution for a proposed Western Aden federation. Lahej was not to join until October 1959 and Dathinah, Lower Aulaqi and Aqrabi until February 1960.

29 April The Communists demand participation in the new Iraqi government along with other 'loyal democratic parties and forces' but Qasim refuses to concede this.

2 May A state of emergency is declared throughout Aden Colony.

5 May Iraq and the Soviet Union sign a scientific and cultural co-operation agreement. On 16 April the Soviet news agency, Tass, had reported that Soviet economic aid to Iraq had begun with a $55-million loan.

5–7 May The shah makes a state visit to Britain, staying at Buckingham Palace as a guest of Queen Elizabeth. He confirmed Iran's adherence to the Baghdad Pact. However, he assured the London Foreign Press Association at the end of his visit that Iran 'will never grant military bases to any country'.

14 May Iraq's President Qasim says he is leading his country towards democracy and favours the eventual formation of political parties.

30 May The Iraqi Foreign Ministry terminates the 1954 military assistance pact with the US, the 1955 supplementary military aid agreement and the 1957 Iraqi-US economic assistance agreement. On the following day Britain completed its evacuation of the Habbaniya air base, and on 1 June the US embassy in Baghdad announced that Iraq had renounced US military aid. However, on 11 May Britain had announced its decision to supply Iraq with aircraft and arms.

15 June Dispatches from Aden report that rebellious troops have seized control of the Yemeni port of Hodeidah and of the inland town of Taiz, the Imam Ahmad's residence.

23 June Iraq withdraws from the £ sterling zone.

29 June The Iraqi Communists announce the formation of a United National Front with the National Democratic and Kurdish Democratic Parties. However, on 13 July Iraq's President Qasim reorganized his government without the Communists. This was to be an ominous signal for Iraq's Communists and the beginning of the end of Qasim's relationship with them.

14 July To celebrate the first anniversary of the Iraqi revolution representatives of all foreign governments except for France, Israel and Jordan are invited to Baghdad. The UAR turned down the invitation. On the same day fighting broke out between Turkomans and Kurds in the Kirkuk region of Iraq. Kurdish soldiers, led by the Communist-headed People's Resistance Force, were alleged to have massacred Turkomans. Order was not restored until 18 July. The Kurdish leader, Mulla Mustafa Barzani, had been allowed to return to Iraq with 400 followers in October 1958. During the spring of 1959 fighting had broken out between Barzani's tribe and other tribes.

23 July The Baghdad press announces that Rashid Ali had been sentenced to death on 17 December for planning a coup against President Qasim. It added that the UAR had agreed to supply the plotters with weapons.

26 July Describing Israel as a 'crime established by treachery and imperialism', UAR President Nasser tells an Alexandria rally that 'we will exterminate Israel if another conflict occurs'. On 28 July he reiterated his hopes for 'a decisive battle with Israel to avenge 1948' when he addressed a land-distribution ceremony near Alexandria.

29 July Iraq's President Qasim openly accuses the Communists of responsibility for the killings of 14 July and declares all-out war against them. He ordered the disbanding of the Communist-dominated Popular Resistance Organization. On 3 August Qasim claimed that 79 people had been killed in the clashes that took place between 14 and 18 July, of whom 40 were buried alive.

8 August UAR President Nasser tells a Cairo rally that he will not permit Israel to use the Suez Canal.

19 August In the Iraqi political trial which is presided over by Colonel Fadhil Mahdawi, five officers are condemned to be shot and one civilian to be hanged for their alleged part in the Mosul revolt. On 25 August the death sentences were carried out.

31 August–3 September President Nasser and Saudi Arabia's King Saud are reconciled when the latter visits Cairo and has his first meeting with Nasser since 1958. In that year the UAR had accused him of supporting an anti-Nasser plot designed to sabotage the Egypt-Syria union (the UAR). Following their meeting on 1 September a joint statement was published describing 'full cooperation' between the UAR and Saudi Arabia. They also agreed to maintain the Suez Canal blockade against Israel and to resume diplomatic relations with Britain which had been broken since the Suez crisis of 1956.

7 September The Arab League Council meeting in Casablanca calls for the continuation of the UAR's Suez blockade of Israel and the tightening of the Arab economic boycott of Israel.

16 September President de Gaulle offers Algeria the right to self-determination and proposes a referendum on the issue. In the referendum, Algerians would be able to choose between secession from the French community, integration with metropolitan France or internal autonomy.

20 September Thirteen alleged conspirators are hanged in Baghdad for their involvement in the Mosul revolt, after a televised trial in the People's Court. Four members of the *ancien régime* were also hanged. The conspirators included the 'Free Officers' Nadhim Tabaqchali and Rif'at al-Hajj Sirri. So far President Qasim had pardoned almost all of those previously sentenced to death but after the Mosul uprising he believed that he had to take firm action against his enemies. The executions broke Qasim's remaining links with the Ba'th Party.

28 September The foundation stone of Ittihad (Arabic, Unity) City, the capital of the new West Aden Federation, is laid by the sultan of Lahej, Fadl ibn Ali, in the presence of Aden's governor, Sir William Luce. On 1 October the state of emergency imposed in Aden in May 1958 was ended. On 5 October Lahej joined the new British-sponsored Aden Federation.

6 October The Saudi Arabian representative to the UN, Ahmad Shukairy, says the Arab states are willing to open negotiations with Israel on certain conditions. These conditions were Israel's compliance with UN resolutions on the rights of the Palestinian refugees, on the borders of Israel and on the internationalization of Jerusalem.

7 October Iraq's President Qasim is wounded and his chauffeur killed when five gunmen spray his car with machine-gun fire in downtown Baghdad. The assassins included the 23-year-old Saddam Husayn. The assassination attempt was considered the work of the Ba'th who were embittered by the executions which followed the Mosul uprising. Most of the plotters, including the Ba'thist secretary-general, Fu'ad al-Rikabi, escaped to Syria. On 15 October Baghdad's military governor, General Ahmad Salah al-Abdi, reported the suppression of a second plot to kill Qasim. Seventy-eight people were tried for the attempt which was made on 7 October and six were sentenced to death but the executions were never carried out.

9 October The Baghdad Pact Council of Ministers approves the formation of 'a permanent military deputies group' to begin operations in 1960.

21 October UAR President Nasser issues a decree giving the UAR vice-president, Field Marshal Abd al-Hakim Amer, full powers over the union's Syrian region.

2–6 November The Shah of Iran visits Jordan for talks with King Husayn. Although Iran had reluctantly recognized the new Iraqi regime on 30 July 1958, the revolution and with it the effective collapse of the Baghdad Pact worried Iran, making its relationship with pro-Western Jordan all the more important.

16 November Iraq's President Qasim endorses the proposed Fertile Crescent plan for the unification of Iraq, Syria and Jordan.

28 November The Shah of Iran warns that the border agreement made in 1937 with Iraq is intolerable and may be abrogated. The agreement gave Iraq sovereignty and toll rights over the Shatt al-Arab waterway which divides the two countries in the south.

4 December Iraq's President Qasim asks the Iraq Petroleum Company to relinquish most of its concession areas.

14 December An Anglo-Iraqi cultural agreement is signed in Baghdad, the first such agreement signed with a Western country by the new Iraqi regime.

16 December Iran and Iraq strengthen their border forces in the Gulf area, following conflicting claims concerning the Shatt al-Arab waterway.

21 December The 40-year-old Shah Muhammad Reza Pahlavi of Iran marries the 21-year-old Farah Dibah in a Muslim religious ceremony in Tehran. The new queen, the daughter of an Iranian army captain, had been a student of architecture in Paris. Their engagement had been announced on 23 November.

1 9 6 0

3 January Iraq's General Abd al-Karim Qasim presses for Iraq's rights in its territorial squabble with Iran. On 2 December he had demanded the return of the roadsteads outside the Iranian ports of Abadan, Khoramshahr and Khozabad on the Shatt al-Arab waterway. On 3 January the Iranians counter-claimed, demanding sovereignty over half the Shatt al-Arab which divides Iraq and Iran and leads into the Gulf waters. According to the 1914 and 1937 agreements, Iraq had full control of the waterway as far as the low-water mark on the Iranian side.

8 January The Iraqi president, General Abd al-Karim Qasim, publicly appeals to the Syrian people to free themselves from the 'despotic injustice' allegedly suffered under the Egyptian-dominated United Arab Republic (UAR).

9 January The UAR president, Gamal abd al-Nasser, formally inaugurates the construction of the Soviet-funded Aswan High Dam on the Nile.

24 January Armed Algiers 'pieds noirs' (meaning French colonist, literally 'Black Feet') rightists fight security forces, leaving 24 dead and 100 wounded. They were in revolt against French President de Gaulle's plan for Algerian self-determination which implied rule by the Muslim Arab majority. A state of siege was declared in Algiers. On 29 January de Gaulle made a dramatic speech calling upon Frenchmen everywhere 'to reunite with France' and end the uprising. By 1 February the European rebels had given up, having realized that de Gaulle had the support of the French army.

9 February Iraqi political parties are legalized for the first time since the 1958 revolution which swept away the monarchy and brought General Qasim to power. However, the parties had to operate under government licence. Qasim had announced on 2 January that political parties would be allowed in fulfilment of his promise made on 14 July 1959. Four new parties emerged: the National Democratic Party, the Kurdistan Democratic Party (KDP) led by Mulla Mustafa Barzani, the Communist Party (Titoist) and the Communist Party (Orthodox).

16 February UAR President Nasser urges Iraq's President Qasim to fulfil his pledges of co-operation against Israel by sending troops to the Syrian border. On a tour of the Syrian province of the UAR on 20 February, Nasser reiterated his pledge to lead a unified Arab effort to liberate Palestine. On 29 February the Arab League ended its Cairo conference. It had failed to resolve the UAR-Jordanian differences on the question of Palestine. On 12 March King Husayn of Jordan was to throw down the gauntlet to President Nasser by saying that Jordan would willingly join the UAR if the latter were genuinely 'prepared to open a final battle with the common enemy, Israel'.

13 March The Arab League Economic Council approves plans for an Arab-owned oil pipeline from the Gulf to the Mediterranean Sea.

18 March UAR President Nasser appoints seven new ministers to the UAR's Syrian regional cabinet, filling the vacancies created by the withdrawal of all the Ba'thist Party members from the government.

22 March Death sentences on anti-Qasim conspirators are commuted. On 26 December the trial of the conspirators in the 7 October coup against Iraq's President Qasim had begun. When the trial ended on 22 March, the death sentences on eight members of the old regime as well as the accused in the anti-Qasim plot were commuted.

27 March Iraq's President Qasim announces plans to train Palestinian Arabs for a war to restore their Israeli-occupied homeland, Palestine. On the same day the United Press Agency reported that at least five people had been killed in Baghdad in street fighting between Communists and Iraqi nationalists.

24 April Two large earthquakes in southern Iran kill an estimated 700 people.

4 May On 4 May a 41-year-old British businessman, Leslie March, is released from a Baghdad prison. He had been arrested on 9 October 1959 in connection with the attempted assassination of Iraq's President Qasim.

5 May The Shah of Iran appoints Dr Ali Amini as Iranian premier to replace Jafar Sharif-Emami. Sharif-Emami had resigned in the face of increasing student demonstrations against the government. On 9 May the shah dissolved parliament and empowered Amini to rule by decree pending new elections. On 11 May Amini announced a 15-point programme to counter official corruption and to save Iran from bankruptcy. The programme included land reforms, import restrictions, export incentives, the expansion of farm industries and a crackdown on corrupt office-holders. By 16 May hundreds of local officials, army officers and judges were reported to have been dismissed or arrested since the programme was announced.

7 May UAR President Nasser accuses US foreign policy of being under the sway of 'Zionist Jewish Israeli imperialism'.

23 May The Israeli prime minister, David Ben-Gurion, tells the Knesset (parliament) of the capture of SS General Adolf Eichmann, the alleged planner of the Nazi pogrom for exterminating the Jews in Europe. Eichmann was kidnapped by Israeli security forces in Argentine.

24 May UAR President Nasser decrees the nationalization of four leading Egyptian newspapers. He claimed that he was protecting them from foreign influence.

1 June Sir Charles Johnston, British ambassador to Jordan, replaces Sir William Luce as the new governor of Aden.

21 July The UAR's first national assembly, made up of 400 Egyptian and 200 Syrian delegates, convenes in Cairo.

24 July The Shah of Iran, Muhammad Reza Pahlavi, enrages his Arab neighbours with his *de facto* recognition of Israel. On 26 July the UAR broke off diplomatic relations with Iran and UAR President Nasser denounced the shah in a speech. On 28 July the Arab League declared a boycott of Iran. On 8 August the UAR congress of *ulema* (clergy) said that the shah had 'separated himself from the Islamic community' by siding with the 'enemies of God'.

12 August In New York, the UN announces its appointment of a neutral observer to the Buraimi Oasis. The oasis was being disputed by Saudi Arabia and Abu Dhabi, one of the seven Trucial States.

29 August The Iranian premier, Manouchehr Eghbal, resigns. His resignation came amid popular discontent over allegedly fraudulent elections which resulted in the retention of power by his National Party.

6 September King Husayn of Jordan claims that UAR President Nasser had advance personal knowledge of the conspiracy behind the assassination of his prime minister, General Hazza Majali. Majali was killed on 29 August by a bomb placed in his office. King Husayn appointed Bahjat al-Talhouni as Majali's successor.

10–14 September The oil producers meet in Baghdad and form the Organization of Petroleum Exporting Countries (OPEC). The meeting of oil representatives from Iraq, Kuwait, Iran, Saudi Arabia, Venezuela, as well as observers from Qatar and the Arab League, had initially met to formulate a unified policy towards the unilateral decision of the major oil companies to lower the price of oil. The UAR was not invited because of disagreements among members on the question of its control since 1956 of the Suez Canal. Jordan and Lebanon were not invited because of the pipelines passing through their territories. Between 17 and 22 October the Arab League sponsored the second Arab Petroleum Congress in Beirut. Shortly after this, on 2 November, the Iraqi spokesman Dr Muhammad Salman Hasan announced that he had been informed by the oil companies that they would not reduce prices again without the consent of the producers.

17 October The Egyptian authorities report that Suez Canal operations during 1959 yielded a profit of over $47 million. This was 16 and a half times the amount paid in royalties to Egypt in the last year, 1955, before the canal was nationalized.

31 October A male heir is born to the Shah of Iran, Muhammad Reza Pahlavi.

8 November John F. Kennedy defeats Nixon by a narrow margin to become the thirty-fifth president of the US. The 43-year-old Kennedy was the youngest man and the first Roman Catholic to win the nation's highest office.

21 December King Saud of Saudi Arabia announces his acceptance of the resignation of his brother Faisal as prime minister and assumes the premiership himself. King Saud had given Faisal the premiership and other powers in March 1958 and the astute Faisal had introduced reforms, created a cabinet system and given the press greater freedom. However, by 1960 the relationship between the two men had become severely strained and it was further exacerbated by the activities of the 'Free Princes' led by Prince Talal ibn Abd al-Aziz who was decrying corruption in the Saudi monarchy from his base in Nasser's Egypt (UAR). By promising reforms in the kingdom, King Saud managed to win the reformist princes' support for ousting Faisal. On 25 December Mecca radio announced that Saud had ordered the formation of a national council to draw up a constitution.

1 9 6 1

8 January French President de Gaulle's referendum on Algerian self-determination wins over 72 per cent approval. However, French rightists saw the referendum as the abandonment of Algeria to the rebels.

10 January Voting begins for new elections to the Iranian Majlis (lower house). The elections held the previous summer had been annulled by the shah because of allegations that they had been rigged. The new elections were contested by Iran's only two legal parties, the National Party (Mellyum) led by Manouchehr Eghbal and the People's Party (Mardom). However, supporters of the National Front were quick to claim that even the new elections were rigged. In response to these protests the security police closed their headquarters on 30 January.

16 January The governor of Aden, Sir Charles Johnston, announces at the opening of the new session of the colony's legislative council that the British colonial secretary, Ian McLeod, has approved the ministerial system for Aden.

21 February The Shah of Iran inaugurates the new Majlis, announcing that it must pass new electoral laws.

26 February King Muhammad V of Morocco dies of heart failure at the age of 51 while undergoing minor surgery. His son is proclaimed King Hasan II.

12 March Dr Jafar Sharif-Emami forms a new Iranian government.

16 March The Saudi Arabian government announces that it will not allow the US to continue using the Dhahran air base when the present lease expires on 1 April 1962. It had been a five-year agreement from 1957. Crown Prince Faisal had appeared to approve the renewal of the lease. A controversial angle of the situation had been the Saudi refusal to allow US Jews to work at the air base which had led to protests on the part of

US Jews. Meanwhile, Saudi Arabia was still benefiting from US assistance, with total aid received so far having reached $50 million.

27 March Imam Ahmad, the ruler of Yemen, is shot and seriously wounded by an unknown assassin while on an inspection tour of the Red Sea port of Hodeidah. On 8 April officials in Yemen announced that five Yemenis had been sentenced to death for participating in the assassination plot.

27 March Ayatollah Muhammad Hussein Borujirdi, who has been Iran's *Marja-e taqlid* (spiritual 'source of imitation') for 16 years, dies. According to Baqer Moin in his biography of Khomeini, Borujirdi's death represented a watershed in clergy–state relations as the country closed down in mourning to a background of enormous marches. The shah, who had often conferred with the ayatollah in the early days until his land reforms upset the relationship, committed the gaffe of sending a telegram of condolence to Grand Ayatollah Muhsin Hakim in Najaf, an Arab and an Iraqi, rather than to one of the leading ayatollahs in Qom.

With Borujirdi gone, clerical leadership of the conservatives went to the triumvirate of Ayatollahs Muhammad Reza Golpaygani, Shehab al-Din Marashi-Najafi and Muhammad Kazem Shariatmadari, the senior clerics in Qom. The centrists disagreed with Borujirdi's ruling to keep out of politics although they had rarely defied it. They concentrated on the educational and social aspects of Shi'i institutions. Their most important spokesmen were Ayatollahs Murtaza Motahhari and Muhammad Husseini Beheshti who were both in Tehran. They had contacts with Ayatollah Mahmoud Taleqani. The group stood for popular participation in the parliamentary process and the limiting of the shah's powers.

In Qom, meanwhile, the radical viewpoint was being expressed by Hojatolislam Ruhullah Mousavi Khomeini, who argued that the shah had violated the constitution by failing to call new elections within a month of the dissolution of the Majlis. He also claimed that the shah's agricultural reforms would damage the interests of the traditional bazaar since the agricultural co-operatives that were to handle both production and marketing were to be financed by the US.

2 May The Iranian police open fire on a crowd, killing several people when striking teachers protest in Tehran. The prime minister, Jafar Sharif-Emami, resigned in protest at the police apparently having fired without government orders. The shah appointed the 58-year-old Dr Ali Amini to form a new cabinet and on 8 May warned that Iran faced 'economic poverty' because its vast resources were being squandered. Amini had served under Dr Musaddiq and headed the delegation which negotiated the settlement of the Anglo-Iranian oil dispute in 1954.

On 9 May the government banned all public meetings and demonstrations in Tehran and on 11 May it announced a package of reforms. These included limits on land ownership, the prosecution of officials guilty of corruption and the prosecution of those guilty of rigging elections. On 9 May the shah dissolved parliament and gave Amini six months of rule by decree so that he could draft a new electoral law. The shah argued that elections at the present time were too risky. On 22 May the shah had even appealed to the public to suggest how electoral laws might be improved.

13 May Four Iranian generals, including General Kia, are arrested for interfering in the elections and misappropriating public funds. The generals were booed by the crowds as they were led away.

15 May In an extraordinary government volte-face, the leader of Iran's teachers' strike, Darakhshesh, is made minister of education and on 18 May the National Front was allowed to hold a meeting calling for immediate elections.

23 May Iran's new agriculture minister, Dr Hasan Arsanjani, announces that the government intended dividing all state-owned lands among the peasantry within one month and then splitting up the large estates. If there was any delay, he warned, there was the danger of a 'bloody, red revolution'.

19 June Britain's Lord Privy Seal Edward Heath announces that the 1899 Anglo-Kuwaiti agreement was being abrogated as from this day. On 27 June Kuwait applied for membership of the Arab League. The abrogation of the Anglo-Kuwaiti agreement promptly exposed Kuwait to external threats (from Iraq).

On 25 June the Iraqi president, General Abd al-Karim Qasim, announced that Kuwait had been part of the Ottoman province of Basra and was now, therefore, a part of Iraq. Iraq, he said, did not recognize the 'forged treaties' of 1899. He then announced that he had appointed the ruler of Kuwait as its *qa'imaqam* (effectively viceroy). Qasim argued that Ottoman Kuwait came under the administrative control of the governor of Basra.

Kuwait responded by saying that it would defend its territorial rights fully. On 28 June Britain guaranteed Kuwait its support and on 30 June, following reports of Iraqi troop movements in the south, the Kuwaiti ruler, Shaikh Abdullah al-Salem al-Sabah, formally requested British help under the newly signed protection agreement.

On 1 July the rapid buildup of British troops began with an advance force of 600 British commandos and a squadron of air-force jet fighters. On the same day the UN Security Council met to discuss the emerging crisis. On 2 July the Iraqi representative to the UN, Adnan Pachachi, denounced, with Soviet backing, the dispatch of British troops. With French support, Britain argued that its action was legitimate in view of its treaty obligation to Kuwait. On 4 July Iraqi infantry forces and tank units were said to be massing near the Kuwaiti border but no fighting was reported. On 6 July British military spokesmen reported that they doubted whether Iraqi troops would attack Kuwait in the face of the 4,000 British troops now stationed there.

On 4 July the Arab League considered Kuwait's application, and on 7 July, in an apparent volte-face, Qasim told newsmen in Baghdad that Iraq had never intended to use force to press its claim. On 10 July a Kuwaiti goodwill mission arrived in Cairo for talks with UAR President Nasser. On 14 July Qasim reiterated his claims at a military graduation speech and, as if to stress the point, on 26 July three British soldiers were captured by the Iraqi army in the border area with Kuwait.

On 12 August the Kuwaiti ruler signed an agreement with Muhammad Ali Hassouna, the secretary-general of the Arab League, according to which the Arab League bound itself to defend Kuwait's integrity. On 13 August the Kuwaiti ruler sent a letter to the British political agent, Sir William Luce, formally requesting the withdrawal of the British forces. On 22 September Kuwait and Britain exchanged ambassadors. British forces began leaving Kuwait on 19 October although their withdrawal was temporarily suspended on 21 August in the face of renewed Iraqi threats against Kuwait.

20 July French troops fight their way into the Tunisian town of Bizerte, following the French refusal to evacuate its military base there. The Tunisian president, Bourguiba, promptly severed relations with France. Reports on 23 July estimated that 670 Tunisians and 30 French troops had been killed in three and a half days of fighting. Declarations of support for Tunisia from many Arab states were reported during the ensuing days.

27 August Ferhat Abbas is replaced by the militant Ben Youssef Ben Khedda as premier of the rebel Algerian provisional government.

10 September Some 4,000 Arab League troops are airlifted to Kuwait to replace the withdrawing British forces.

11 September The Saudi Arabian cabinet is re-shuffled as the rift between the king and the crown prince develops. Prince Talal was replaced by Prince Muhammad ibn Saud as minister of defence and civil aviation. The change seemed to reflect a rapprochement between King Saud and Crown Prince and Prime Minister Faisal who wanted the reformist-minded Prince Talal out of the centres of power. Princes Talal, Abd al-Muhsen and Badr were given, respectively, the portfolios of finance and national economy, interior and communications. Abdullah Tariki became head of the new ministry of petroleum and mineral resources. Ibrahim Suwayl became foreign minister.

17 September The Iraqi government announces the suppression of a separatist revolt by Kurdish tribesmen in northern Iraq.

28 September A military coup in Syria leads to its secession from the United Arab Republic (UAR) which it had formed with Egypt in 1958. The Syrian leaders had had a meeting with Egyptian Field Marshal Abd al-Hakim Amer in which they had complained that Egyptian officials had been constantly preferred over Syrian officials within the federation. UAR President Nasser called off Egyptian resistance to the uprising several hours after it had begun. On 29 September Syria's new revolutionary command installed Mahmoud al-Kuzbari, a conservative law professor, as the head of the new all-civilian cabinet. Nasser told a Cairo crowd that he had suspended resistance against the Syrian revolt 'so that no Arab blood would be shed'. On 30 September the new Syrian government ordered the expulsion of all Egyptians, both civilian and military.

1 October UAR President Nasser breaks ties with Jordan and Turkey after both countries recognize the new Syrian regime. On 5 October Nasser announced that he had given up all claims to Syria as part of the UAR. On 13 October Syria resumed its independent UN seat.

5 October The Shah of Iran gives the Pahlavi Foundation, which he had created on 28 September, about £47.5 million in properties. These included most of the shah's villages and farms, hotels, his holdings in the Iranian fleet of six oil tankers, and all his stocks and shares. The Foundation's administrator, Asadollah Alam, said that it was 'the most momentous revolutionary and historic act of its kind taken by any monarch in any country'.

The personal assets the shah gave away are said to have amounted to $135 million. He was to tell the British newspaper the *Sunday Express* in 1965 'I have given my personal fortune away, or at least 90 per cent of it.' Under pressure from the then Iranian prime minister, the nationalist Dr Muhammad Musaddiq, in February 1953 the shah had handed property inherited from his father to the government in return for a payment of 60 million riyals to be paid to the Pahlavi Foundation annually. Although a charity, the Foundation never disclosed details of its income or expenditure. On 11 November, when neither the Majlis nor the Senate were in session, the shah announced that he had the right under the constitution to initiate legislation and prepared to push through his land reform bill in the face of recalcitrant landowners. On 9 October he created the Pahlavi Dynasty Trust.

13 October Imam Ahmad of Yemen abdicates in favour of his son, Premier Seif al-Islam al-Badr.

19 November UAR President Nasser, Indian Prime Minister Nehru and Yugoslav President Tito meet in Cairo for a one-day conference on the world problems facing neutralist nations.

25 November Iraq's former deputy premier, Colonel Abd al-Salam Aref, is pardoned by Iraq's President Qasim. Aref had been sentenced to death in February 1959 for plotting to assassinate Qasim.

29 November The Aden governor, Sir Charles Johnston, hands over the Aden Protectorate levies to the Federation of Arab Emirates in the south.

30 November The Soviet Union vetoes Kuwait's application for membership of the UN on the grounds that its identity is entirely linked to Britain. Iraq called the veto a slap in the face for British imperialism. On 30 December Kuwait held its first elections.

12 December Negotiations between the Iraqi government and the Iraq Petroleum Company (IPC) are aborted over modifications to the concession agreement. The IPC rejected the demands of Iraq's President Qasim. Iraq's Law 80 of 1961 reclaimed the unexploited areas of the IPC's concession.

Later in December heavy fighting recommenced between the Iraqi army and the Kurds. The Kurdish rebellion under the president of the Kurdish Democratic Party (KDP), Mulla Mustafa Barzani, had started in March. By September the rebellion had spread to affect one-third of Iraq. It was suppressed but flared up again in December.

15 December A Jerusalem court sentences Adolf Eichmann to death by hanging for his involvement in the slaughter of up to six million Jews by Nazi Germany during the Second World War.

24 December UAR President Nasser announces that the UAR (formally Egypt and Syria, now only Egypt) will nationalize all foreign-owned farm lands for the benefit of the peasants. On 26 December Yemen's ties with the UAR were formally dissolved, leaving Egypt as the sole remaining member. Egypt was to keep the name for a decade.

1 9 6 2

6 January The Kuwaiti minister of finance, Shaikh Jaber al-Ahmad al-Jaber al-Sabah, announces Kuwait's decision to form the Arab Economic Development Fund with an initial capital of £50 million.

15 January The Shah of Iran signs a land reform bill providing for the government to buy large estates and sell them back to the peasants.

22 January Soldiers and paratroopers occupy Tehran University following unprecedented student unrest. By the end of the day, one is dead, 218 are injured and 300 students are in prison. Earlier in January the announcement of cuts in government scholarships had been followed by serious student unrest. Students had poured through the streets crying 'Down with [Prime Minister] Amini, down with corrupt and vicious government.' The university chancellor, Dr Ahmad Farhad, condemned the tactics of the military on 22 January.

23 January The Iranian premier, Ali Amini, says that the recent student protestors in Iran were provoked by elements opposed to agrarian reform – the shah had signed the legislation in question on 15 January – and by the Tudeh (Communist) Party. However, former army security chief, General Teymour Bakhtiar, who left Iran at the shah's request on 26 January, foresaw great danger. In Rome on 28 January, he said that 'unless the Shah acts soon to restore constitutional rights and allows free elections, there will be a very serious revolution in Persia'. He added that Amini had neither the capacity nor the real intention of carrying out the land reform programme. In February and March Amini was to make a tour of western Europe, visiting Bonn, Paris and London.

28 January Iran's Premier Amini tells newsmen that his government holds the Soviet Union responsible for inciting the anti-government student riots in Tehran between 21 and 23 January.

15 March The creation of a unified Arab military force and a pan-Arab economic council is proposed by the Iraqi prime minister, General Abd al-Karim Qasim, and the new Syrian president, Nazem al-Qodsi, following two days of talks in Rutba, Iraq.

16 March Mecca radio announces that Saudi Arabia's Crown Prince Faisal, a brother of King Saud, has been promoted to deputy premier and foreign minister, although King Saud retains the premiership. The change reflected the debate taking place within the Saudi royal family over Saud's competence to rule.

18 March France and the Algerian provisional government jointly announce the signing of a truce ending the seven-year Algerian war of independence. Ahmad Ben Bella and four other prominent rebel leaders, imprisoned by the French since 1956, were released following the truce. On 19 March Algeria's European underground terrorist group, Organisation Armée Secrète, declared open warfare on the de Gaulle government for betraying them. On 23 March de Gaulle ordered the French army 'to crush without pity the armed insurrection'.

28 March The Syrian army seizes control of the government in a bloodless coup. Army spokesmen said that the new government would restore 'constructive and just socialism' and renew friendly relations with 'dear Egypt and sister Iraq'. On 31 March, however, pro-Nasser army officers in northern Syria launched a counter-revolt against the armed forces high command which had carried out the coup. On 3 April the revolt against the new rulers ended when the ruling junta agreed to their demands for clemency towards the deposed president, Nazem al-Qodsi, and for a popular referendum on whether Syria should rejoin the United Arab Republic (UAR).

8 April In a national referendum, French voters overwhelmingly record their approval of President de Gaulle's peace agreement with the Algerian rebels.

13 April The deposed Syrian president, Nazem al-Qodsi, is reinstated by the same military junta which overthrew him on 28 March.

2 June Iraq orders the recall of US ambassador, John Jernegan, in protest against US recognition of newly independent Kuwait to which Iraq had laid territorial claims.

6 June The new Syrian prime minister, Bashir al-Azmah, proposes a restoration of Syria's union with the UAR under a new federal constitution guaranteeing the Damascus government greater sovereignty and autonomy. However, on 23 June Azmah withdrew his proposal, arguing that it may not have had the full backing of Syrian public opinion.

3 July French President de Gaulle issues a proclamation recognizing the full independence of Algeria after 132 years of French rule. The proclamation followed the announcement of the results of the 1 July referendum on Algeria in which almost six million Algerians voted for independence against 16,534 who voted against. De Gaulle transferred sovereignty to the Algerian provisional executive headed by Ben Youssef Ben Khedda, and on 11 July Ahmad Ben Bella returned to Algeria.

17 July Iran's Prime Minister Amini resigns and is replaced on 20 July by Asadollah Alam. Alam was determined to push through the shah's largely unpopular land reform programme. Amini apparently resigned after failing to reduce Iran's $70-million budget deficit. The Soviet Union at once became less critical of Iran and on 15 September the two countries exchanged notes assuring mutual non-aggression. This followed shortly after an earthquake on 1 September that devastated Qasvin and Hamadan and cost 10,000 lives. Alam called it the greatest catastrophe in Iran's history. On 3 September Alam went to Qasvin to see for himself and the shah's eldest sister, Princess Shams, took over the relief operations. The army was to play a major role in the rescue operations.

23 July At a time of heightened tension between militantly socialist and pan-Arab Egypt and conservative Saudi Arabia, the Saudi Prince Talal ibn Abd al-Aziz, one of the reformist princes, cables President Nasser to congratulate him on the tenth anniversary of the Egyptian revolution. Some weeks later, at a press conference in Beirut, Talal announced that he and his half brothers Muhsen and Nawwaf had agreed to liberate their slaves and concubines of which, he told the press, he himself had 50 and 32 respectively. A furious King Saud withdrew Talal's passport on 16 August. In sympathy with him, his half brothers Fawwaz and Badr and his cousin Saud ibn Fahd handed their passports in as well. At his press conference in Beirut Talal had called for democracy in Saudi Arabia based on a system that was moderate rather than left wing. He maintained that there was nothing personal about his disagreements with King Saud.

On 19 August Talal, Fawwaz, Badr and Saud ibn Fahd settled in Cairo where they were later joined by Muhsen. There they became known as the 'Free Princes'. Talal claimed that Nasser, who was to exploit them for propaganda purposes, had made the formation of a league of Free Princes a condition for allowing them to stay in Cairo. Crown Prince Faisal, who was determined to have no opposition within Saudi Arabia, was probably glad to see them settle in Egypt.

Relations with Nasser's Egypt had reached an all-time low. In May the Saudis refused to accept the *Kiswa* (the hand-woven covering for the *Ka'ba* in Mecca which Egypt had traditionally supplied each year for the *hajj* – pilgrimage). The *Kiswa* was accompanied by 110,000 Egyptian pilgrims but the Saudis claimed that they had refused to accept it on the grounds that the fabric was of too poor quality to cover the *Ka'ba*, the cube around which the pilgrims make their seven-fold circumambulation.

Shortly before this incident, Cairo had alleged that a Saudi vessel had fired at Egyptian fishing boats in the Red Sea. The Saudis had responded to this by ordering that the return of Egyptian workers, a process that had started in 1961, be speeded up.

Increasingly vulnerable to Egyptian propaganda and the UAR lobby, on 29 August the Saudis announced that Jordan and Saudi Arabia have decided on close military, political and economic co-operation. According to the agreement, they were to create an immediate joint military command in a move which some saw as a challenge to the UAR.

23 July–16 August At the London conference Aden agrees to accede to the Federation of South Arabia on or before 1 March 1963.

3 August Huge crowds turn out to welcome Ahmad Ben Bella as he returns to Algiers for the first time since his capture by the French in 1956. On 7 August Ben Bella effectively became Algeria's premier.

29 August Saudi Arabia and Jordan jointly announce a plan to merge their armed forces and to co-ordinate their national economic policies.

15 September The Soviet daily *Izvestia* reports that Iran has promised the Soviet Union not to allow the establishment of foreign rocket bases on Iranian territory.

18 September Imam Ahmad, the ruler of Yemen, dies and is succeeded by his son, Crown Prince Seif al-Islam Muhammad al-Badr. However, on 26 September a Yemeni military faction overthrew the government of the new imam. Rebel sources erroneously claimed that Badr had been killed during the coup. The overthrow of the new imam was to be the spark which led to a five-year civil war in which Egypt would support the republicans and Saudi Arabia the monarchists.

28 September Algeria's newly elected premier, Ahmad Ben Bella, pledges to build a 'Socialist Algeria'. On 29 September the new Algerian government was recognized by the US.

2–8 October Saudi Arabian pilots defect to the UAR with their aircraft. On 17 October, as the situation deteriorated, Crown Prince Faisal was called in as prime minister. He promptly dismissed the cabinet. King Saud had been prompted to bring back his extremely able brother at a time of heightened tension with Egypt and in Yemen where a coup had taken place with the aim of establishing a democratic republic and when Prince Talal and his supporters were calling from Cairo for constitutional reforms in Saudi Arabia. On 31 October Faisal announced his new government and became commander-in-chief of the Saudi armed forces. On 6 November he made public his ten-point reform programme.

The point within the programme that made news was the abolition of slavery. At the time there were 30,000 slaves in the kingdom. According to David Holden and Richard Johns in *The House of Saud*, Faisal had himself manumitted his slaves long ago although his government had refused in 1956 to subscribe to the UN Supplementary Convention on slavery. Later Faisal complained that few of his slaves had wanted their freedom as slaves in the kingdom enjoyed a fairly privileged position and slavery was approved of in the Qur'an.

7 October Yemeni sources report that fighting has erupted between forces of the ruling military junta and royalists loyal to the overthrown Imam al-Badr. Royalist leaders denied earlier reports that the imam had been killed during the 26 September coup.

7 October Iranian women are given the franchise by the Asadollah Alam government. According to the new laws, every mentally healthy Iranian over the age of 20 could vote, with the exception of people such as policemen, judges and senior civil servants. Prior to the new law, voters and candidates had to be male, Muslim and swear an oath by the Qur'an. The new law abolished all these requirements, and the 'Qur'an' was replaced by the expression 'The Holy Book' to include Zoroastrians, Christians, Jews and other minorities such as Bahais. For the clergy this was clearly a challenge to Shi'ism which the shah was constitutionally obliged to defend.

According to Baqer Moin in his biography of Khomeini the franchise was an important turning-point in the shah's relations with the clergy. Ruhullah Mousavi Khomeini and other ayatollahs sent the shah a telegram of complaint on the following day. This represented Khomeini's entrance into active politics. On the same day he held an important meeting with Ayatollahs Shariatmadari and Golpaigani at the house of Mortaza Ha'eri, the elder son of Ayatollah Abd al-Karim Ha'eri. The shah sent a telegram after six days, referring to them humiliatingly as hojatolislams rather than as ayatollahs. He wished them well in their 'non-interference' in political activities and asked them to take account of the times they were living in.

4 November The first UAR aerial bombardments of Najran in southern Saudi Arabia are reported. Meanwhile, a military alliance was formed between Saudi Arabia and Jordan. On 10 November the first UAR naval and air attack was made on Jizan, a south-western Saudi port. Later in the month a joint defence pact was signed between the UAR and Yemen.

6 November Saudi Arabia breaks diplomatic ties with the UAR because of alleged attacks on Saudi territory by UAR naval units fighting alongside republican forces in Yemen. On 10 November Yemen's deposed Imam Muhammad al-Badr appeared before news reporters at an undisclosed site in north-eastern Yemen to quash rumours that he had been killed. On the same day the UAR signed a five-year mutual defence pact with the new republican regime in the Yemeni capital, San'a.

On 25 November US President Kennedy was reported to have offered a plan for a settlement of the Yemen conflict. His proposal apparently called for the withdrawal of UAR troops serving with Yemen's new republican regime and the suspension of Saudi and Jordanian aid to the Yemeni royalist forces. On 27 November rebel Yemeni royalists asked for a UN investigation into charges of UAR aggression in Yemen.

28 November The Saudi prime minister, Crown Prince Faisal, rejects the recent Yemen peace proposal of the US and asserts that the deposed Imam Muhammad al-Badr is about to recover his role as Yemen's legitimate ruler.

2 December Ayatollah Khomeini challenges the shah in a keynote speech at the Faiziya seminary in which he criticizes the shah's reforms and calls for an Islamic constitution in Iran.

9 December Iraq's President Qasim tells a Syrian press delegation that he could 'occupy it [Kuwait] militarily in half an hour. It was under my thumb.' He was referring to Iraq's longstanding territorial claims on Kuwait.

19 December The US recognizes the new republican regime in Yemen after the latter had pledged to honour the previous Yemeni regime's international obligations. On 20 December the UN seat reserved for Yemen was given to the Yemeni republican government.

1 9 6 3

4 January Sources in Cairo report that the United Arab Republic (UAR) has reversed its decision to withdraw its troops from Yemen in view of alleged preparations by Saudi Arabia to increase aid to Yemen's royalist forces. In December 1962 the US had recognized the new Yemeni Republic in the hope that it would become secure enough for UAR troops to be withdrawn. However, the UAR president, Gamal abd-al Nasser, was soon to become increasingly entangled in a bitter civil war. He was to be quoted as saying in despair that he could not cope with Yemenis 'who are republicans in the morning and royalists in the evening'. Meanwhile, King Husayn of Jordan joined Saudi Arabia in criticizing US recognition of Yemen's new republican regime. Fifty nations had followed the US decision to recognize the new regime. Nasser had unsuccessfully attempted to persuade Britain to recognize it in exchange for the new republic dropping its claims to the British-protected South Aden Protectorate. On 7 January Saudi Arabia called for the immediate withdrawal of all foreign troops and military aid from Yemen as a first step towards the holding of an internationally supervised plebiscite to resolve the Yemeni civil war.

6 January The Shah of Iran launches his *Inghelab-e Safid* (white revolution), a six-point plan which includes land reform, the emancipation of women and a literacy programme. On 23 January a huge demonstration against the reforms and the referendum on the reforms started in the Tehran bazaar, an important centre of power. Ayatollahs Khonsari and Behbehani announced that the bazaar would remain closed for three days in protest. Violence began in Bouzarjomehri Street with baton charges. Crowds shouted slogans such as 'The clergy is victorious. Death to the enemies of Islam.' The 75-year-old Khonsari was isolated from the crowd and abused and humiliated by the police. As a result he was not to enter active politics again. Behbehani was threatened by the police chief and did not emerge from the mosque.

16 January Britain and Saudi Arabia announce an agreement to resume diplomatic relations which were severed by Riyadh after Britain's Suez invasion in 1956. The Saudi decision was clearly prompted by its need for British support for its pro-monarchist stand in the Yemeni civil war.

16 January An agreement merging the British colony of Aden with the adjoining British-protected 11-state Federation of South Arabia is signed in the city of the federation's capital, Al-Ittihad. Hasan Ali Bayoomi was appointed chief minister. The Aden Protectorate was renamed the Protectorate of Southern Arabia.

24 January The Shah of Iran visits the holy Shi'i city of Qom, south of Tehran, in the wake of clerically-led rioting following the announcement of his reform programme. He was not greeted by clerics at Qom, and the bazaars and theological schools remained closed. In his speech he called the clergy 'Always a stupid and reactionary bunch whose brains have not moved.' He accused them of being led by UAR President Nasser and said that they were 'one hundred times more treacherous than the Tudeh (Communist) Party'.

26 January The results of the shah's *Inghelab-e Safid* (white revolution) referendum are returned. Although the turnout was low, the government claimed that 5,598,711 voted in favour of the reforms and only 4,115 against. Ayatollah Ruhullah Khomeini gave a speech attacking the reforms as anti-Islamic.

8 February The Iraqi president, Abd al-Karim Qasim, is overthrown in a coup and executed the following day. His deputy, Abd al-Salam Aref, was nominated as president. Aref refused Qasim's plea for clemency despite the fact that Qasim had pardoned him in 1961 after he had been sentenced to death for trying to kill Qasim. Aref formed a new cabinet under the premiership of Brigadier Ahmad Hasan al-Bakr. When the conspirators broadcast over the radio on 8 February there were demonstrations all over Baghdad in favour of Qasim and there was bitter resistance in the poorer parts of the city, in particular Karkh, Karrada and 'Aqd al-Kird. It took a further 24 hours for the rebels to take the Ministry of Defence where Qasim, who had refused to supply weapons to his own followers who mobbed the square in front of the ministry, made his last stand. As many as 1,000 people were said to have been killed in the fighting.

The coup had been carried out by Nasserites and the Ba'th Party. Founded in Damascus in 1944 by three French-educated Syrian intellectuals, Michel Aflaq, a Greek Orthodox Christian, Salah al-Din Bitar, a Sunni Muslim, and Zaki al-Arsuzi, an Alawi, the Ba'th at first developed as a liberation movement during the French mandate over Syria. However, after the Second World War it developed into a pan-Arab movement, distinctive in its belief that the individual Arab states were all part of a single Arab nation. Its key slogan was 'One Arab nation with an Eternal Mission.'

The period of Ba'th power in Iraq which followed the 8 February coup was to see some of the most terrible violence witnessed in post-War Middle East. On 13 May Ba'th cabinets were established in both Iraq and Syria which excluded Nasserites who were removed and their leaders arrested for alleged conspiracy. Mass trials saw the purging by execution of Communists and former supporters of Qasim. From 5 to 7 June a Syrian delegation visited Baghdad for talks on an international Ba'thist conference.

10 February Yemen demands the closing of the British legation in the South Yemeni town of Taiz in apparent retaliation for Britain's refusal to recognize the new republican regime of Abdullah Sallal.

26 February UN officials announce that the UN under-secretary, Ralph Bunche, has been sent to Yemen in an effort to resolve the continuing civil war between republicans and royalists. On 28 February Yemen's president, Abdullah al-Salal, asked the UN Security Council to halt alleged British 'aggression' on behalf of the royalists.

4 March For the second day running, UAR (Egyptian) warships are reported to have shelled the southern Saudi port of Jizan near the Yemeni border. On 7 March the US formally warned the UAR that its attacks on Saudi Arabian territory threatened the relationship between them. However, Muhammad Habib, the UAR press attaché in Washington, said the attacks were legitimately aimed at destroying Yemeni royalist supply lines in Saudi territory.

7 March A pro-Nasserite army coup in Syria topples the government of Khaled al-Azam. Salah al-Din Bitar was named the new prime minister and the new regime was promptly recognized by the UAR and Iraq. On 9 March the UAR and the new regime exchanged messages stressing the restoration of friendly relations.

8 March The Shah of Iran appoints Hasan Ali Mansur as the new prime minister. He was the leader of the Hezb-e Iran-e Novin (the New Iran Party), one of the two official parties.

He spoke of a reconciliation with the clergy and he was soon inundated with demands for the release of Ayatollah Khomeini and others and the repeal of anti-Islamic laws. Soon after he came to power, Khomeini was released.

10 March The ruling Iraqi Revolutionary Command Council (RCC) proposes the establishment of a joint military command consisting of Iraq, Syria, the UAR, Algeria and Yemen.

14 March Over 1,500 people demonstrate in front of the Iraqi embassy in Moscow to protest the new Iraqi government's current anti-Communist campaign.

16 March Representatives of Iraq, Syria and the UAR end two days of meetings in Cairo on a proposed military, political and economic merger of the three countries.

1 April Syria's ruling RCC decrees a state of emergency to curb extreme pro-Nasser demonstrators in support of an immediate union with the UAR.

11 April The leaders of the UAR, Iraq and Syria, announce agreement on the merger of the three nations as a federal United Arab Republic. The announcement followed four days of constitutional talks in Cairo.

On 23 April Jordanian police in Jordan's capital, Amman, clashed with pro-Nasser, anti-monarchist demonstrators demanding Jordan's entry into the new federation. On 27 April student demonstrators even occupied the Jordanian embassy in Baghdad.

On 29 April Jordan declared a state of emergency along its borders in an attempt to prevent anti-monarchist infiltrators from entering the kingdom.

30 April The UN secretary-general, U Thant, announces that the UAR and Saudi Arabia have tentatively accepted a UN plan for the withdrawal of their forces from Yemen. Yemen also endorsed the proposal.

3 May Pro-Nasser ministers resign from Syria's Ba'thist-dominated government amid a growing dispute over which faction will represent Syria in the proposed federation with Iraq and Egypt. A similar crisis between Nasserite and Ba'thist factions was reported in Iraq. However, on 4 May Cairo sources reported an indefinite postponement of military unity talks among the three countries. The talks were to have begun on 12 May.

6 May In a *Pravda* editorial the Soviet Communist Party expresses support for the efforts of Kurdish tribesmen to establish an autonomous state in Iraq. According to observers, the policy reflected Soviet displeasure over the anti-Soviet actions of the new Iraqi regime.

8 May At least 50 people are killed in the northern Syrian city of Aleppo as police try to break up pro-Nasser mobs demanding the ousting of the ruling Ba'th Party. On 14 April the Syrian premier, Salah al-Din Bitar, completely reorganized his cabinet in an attempt to cope with the growing conflict between Ba'thists and Nasserites for control of the government. On 22 May the government reported that it had thwarted an attempted coup by pro-Nasser army officers.

11 May Five pro-Nasser ministers resign from the Iraqi cabinet of Prime Minister Ahmad Hasan al-Bakr. On 25 May Baghdad radio reported that a pro-Nasser coup aimed at overthrowing the government had been crushed. On the following day the government announced that 11 out of the 26 people arrested in the alleged coup had been executed.

14 May Kuwait is admitted as the 111th member of the UN.

16 May The Shah of Iran tells a Lions Club meeting in Tehran that his revolution is going to be stained with the blood of innocent people: 'unfortunately', he said 'many people will have to be punished: Society must make this sacrifice'.

28 May Yemeni royalist forces launch an offensive against Yemeni republican troops. The offensive broke a tacit cease-fire which had been in effect since the ratification of a UN agreement on 30 April providing for the apparent withdrawal of Saudi Arabia and the UAR from the civil war. Meanwhile, on the same day US officials urged the UN secretary-general, U Thant, to renew his peace efforts in Yemen. On 11 June the UN Security Council approved U Thant's plan to send a 200-man UN observation team to Yemen to supervise the withdrawal of UAR troops and Saudi Arabian aid.

4 June From 4 to 7 June at least 100 people are killed in demonstrations in Tehran following the arrest on 4 June of Ayatollah Khomeini. From 26 May to 3 June, during the month of Muhurram, Khomeini had visited different mosques from which he attacked the shah's regime. In June, on the eve of the martyrdom of Hussein (the son of Ali, the Prophet Muhammad's cousin and son-in-law; Ali was married to the Prophet's daughter, Fatima) at Kerbela, Shi'ism's most emotive feast, he made an attack on the shah in which he drew a parallel between the shah and the tyrannical eighth-century Caliph Yazid whose army had killed Hussein. Anti-government riots led by Khomeini and other religious leaders followed.

In August political pressures forced the shah to release Khomeini who was then kept under house arrest.

9 June Saudi Arabian officials claim that on the previous day UAR planes from Yemen bombed the Saudi Red Sea port of Jizan, killing 30 people.

10 June The Iraqi government announces that it has launched a major offensive against Kurdish tribesmen in Iraq's northern province. On 15 June Baghdad radio announced that the army had captured 14 Kurdish villages. On 16 June two Kurdish members of the Iraqi cabinet resigned in protest against the government's resumption of hostility against the Kurds. On 26 June Kurdish sources claimed that Syrian MiGs were helping the Iraqi air force in its renewed campaign to suppress Kurdish rebels.

16 June The US *New York Times* quotes diplomatic sources as estimating that the number of Soviet military technicians in Yemen now exceeds 1,000.

22 June A British army group from Aden is attacked by tribesmen after they accidently crossed into Yemeni territory. Four British soldiers were reported killed.

23 June Twenty-eight Communists are executed by the Iraqi government for their alleged role in atrocities during the abortive 1959 coup in Mosul.

3 July The Iraqi government announces that it has crushed an armed attempt by a group of Kurdish tribesmen and 'Moscow agents' to take over military installations near Baghdad. On 5 July Iraqi soldiers reported that they had driven dissident Kurdish tribesmen to within 20 miles (32 kilometres) of the Iranian border. On 9 July the Soviet Union formally protested against what it called Iraq's 'genocidal' campaign against Kurdish tribesmen.

18 July The Syrian army crushes an attempt by pro-Nasser elements to overthrow the ruling Ba'thist government. As many as 70 people were reported killed and several hundred others arrested. On 22 July UAR President Nasser renounced the 17 April agreement to merge Egypt, Syria and Iraq into a new United Arab Republic. He cited the continued rule in Syria of what he called the 'fascist' Ba'th Party as the reason for the renunciation.

21 August The Iraqi president, Abd al-Salam Aref, arrives in Cairo on an official visit to the UAR aimed at a reconciliation between the Syrian Ba'thist regime and the UAR (Egypt). On 26 August Aref and his delegation continued to Damascus and on 2 September an Iraqi-Syrian defence co-operation agreement was announced, reflecting the Ba'thist character of both regimes. At the same time Iraq's relations with the Soviet Union were on the mend. On 17 September a Ba'th Party newspaper accused Nasser of dictatorial powers and of violating the federation agreement. Ten days later, on 28 September, the Syrian Ba'th Party declared its avowed aim of Syria and Iraq forming a 'popular socialist democratic state'. On the following day the Iraqi defence minister, General Ammash, had talks in Damascus with Syria's General Hafez on the proposed federation's plans. On 31 October the semi-official Egyptian daily *Al-Ahram* said that Egypt refused to have any dealings with the Syrian regime.

15 September Kuwait and Syria establish diplomatic relations and pledge the maximum political and economic co-operation. Kuwait assured Syria of its support in the fight against Israel. On 24 September the Kuwait national assembly approved a loan of 30 million dinars to Iraq.

17 September The Iranian general elections see overwhelming success for the National Union, a coalition of parties pledging support for the shah's six-point reform programme which had been approved at the January national referendum. The National Front and the Tudeh (Communist) Party both called for a boycott. Khomeini and other clerics who had been arrested at the time of the 5/6 June riots had been released on 2 August on condition that they did not interfere in politics although they remained under a form of house arrest. Between 16 and 20 October President de Gaulle paid a state visit to Iran, and on 13 December an agreement was signed in Paris providing for French credits worth 300 million francs towards Iran's third five-year development plan.

4 October Iraq at last recognizes Kuwait's complete independence. In Baghdad, Premier Hasan al-Bakr and the Kuwaiti premier, Dr Sabah al-Salam al-Sabah, signed an agreement and announced that ambassadors would soon be exchanged.

18 November A second coup in Iraq gives President Aref complete power. On 21 November General Yahya formed a new government. Aref eased out the right wing of the Ba'th from the government and increased links with Nasser, although he dropped his earlier demands for immediate union with Egypt. From 5 to 23 October an international Ba'thist conference had been held in Damascus which had called for the federal union of Iraq and Syria.

By 13 November, after a rocket had exploded in Aref's bedroom, Iraq was in a state of virtual civil war. On 18 November troops led by the president's brother, Brigadier Abd al-Rahman Aref, entered Baghdad and were joined by troops from the Rashid barracks. The president then formed a new revolutionary council comprising himself, the deputy commander-in-chief of the army, Brigadier Hardan Takriti, and four other army chiefs. To some extent the coup, engineered by the president and his brother, reflected anti-Ba'thist reaction within the professional officer class.

President Aref quickly announced that he sought friendly relations with Syria and the UAR and wanted to settle the Kurdish question. On 11 November the Syrian premier, Salah al-Din Bitar, had resigned at a time when Syria was divided between the proponents and opponents of the union with Egypt in the UAR.

6 December In an ominous development it is announced in Baghdad that every Iraqi Jew must register with the department of travel and nationalities. They would be supplied with an identity card which would show that they wanted to retain their Iraqi nationality.

10 December A state of emergency is declared in the South Arabian Federation following a bomb attack at Aden airport targeted at the British high commissioner for the administration of the South Arabian Protectorate, Sir Kennedy Trevaskis. Trevaskis was about to leave for London when the attack occurred.

---

1 9 6 4

7 January The UN secretary-general, U Thant, maintains that the Middle East is one of the world's major trouble spots. Speaking at New York's Columbia University, he called for continued UN efforts to control tensions growing out of the Yemeni civil war and the Arab-Israeli conflict. In September 1963 U Thant had conceded that his peace-making efforts in Yemen had failed. The Arab League mediators who succeeded him in October were to fare no better since they were unwilling to parley with the royalists and were rejected by the Saudis. At US instigation, in December U Thant sent another negotiator to Riyadh, San'a and Cairo but Crown Prince Faisal of Saudi Arabia was to reject this and all other attempts at mediation.

10 February A cease-fire between Iraqi troops and rebel Kurdish tribesmen is announced by the leaders of both sides. Pledges to resume negotiations in a final settlement were also exchanged. The new Iraqi premier, Tahir Yahya, who had been in contact with the Kurdish rebels, reopened negotiations. Although no agreement was reached, two communiqués were released simultaneously on 10 February by the Iraqi president, Colonel Abd al-Salam Aref, and the Kurdish Democratic Party leader, Mulla Mustafa Barzani. The Iraqi communiqué affirmed 'the national rights of the Kurds' within a unified Iraqi state: the release of political prisoners; the lifting of the economic blockade of the Kurdish region; the re-establishment of local administration to resume its duties and restore order and security; the reconstruction of demolished areas in the north; and fair compensation to individuals in certain areas.

23 February Prince Talal ibn Abd al-Aziz of Saudi Arabia, the leader of the Saudi 'Free Princes', returns to his own country where he is reconciled with King Saud. His three brothers and a cousin also returned to make similar apologies. Talal had made his peace indirectly with Crown Prince Faisal, his sternest critic, late in the summer of 1963 through the mediation of Talal's mother, Munaiyer. On 23 October, during his exile in Cairo, Talal had announced plans 'to establish a national democratic government and to leave the people free to choose the kind of government they prefer'. He saw the present Saudi regime as 'steeped in backwardness, under-development, reactionary individuals and tyranny'. Faisal, shortly to become king, was never to forgive Talal for his treachery although he did allow him to carry on his business affairs in Saudi Arabia in peace.

1–3 March A United Arab Republic (UAR) delegation headed by Egypt's Field Marshal Abd al-Hakim Amer visits Riyadh for talks with Crown Prince Faisal and other Saudi leaders. Their discussions produced agreements to exchange diplomatic relations and drop territorial claims on Yemen which should remain independent; and that Faisal would visit the UAR at the end of April for talks with the UAR (Egyptian) president, Gamal abd al-Nasser, aimed at a definite solution of the Yemeni problem. Relations had been broken in October 1962 during the early days of the Yemeni civil war. At that time Algeria and Iraq had mediated between the UAR and Saudi Arabia.

28 March The British air force bombs Harib Fort, close to the Yemeni border, in retaliation for a series of Yemeni machine-gun and bomb attacks on Beihan State, a member-state of the South Arabian Federation (SAF). After dropping warning leaflets in Arabic, eight Hunter jet aircraft destroyed the fort with rockets and cannon-fire in a 10-minute assault. The attack was the culmination of a series of incidents along the border. During the first three weeks of March Yemeni Soviet-made Yak and Ilyushin aircraft had made several bomb and machine-gun attacks on Beihan. On 20 March the British government had protested to the Yemenis, warning that serious consequences would follow any further assaults. On the same day it was stated in Aden that British air-fighter patrols would provide protection for the Beihan region, following requests from the SAF for air protection, guaranteed under the terms of the its defence treaty with Britain.

28 March The Saudi Arabian royal family council votes to reduce King Saud to a mere figurehead monarch. This move gave full effective control of the Saudi kingdom to Crown Prince and Prime Minister Faisal, the king's half brother and son of King Abd al-Aziz by his wife Tarfa bint Abdullah.

According to decrees issued on 30 March, Saud was deprived of all executive, legal and administrative powers and his private allowance was cut by half to 183 million riyals ($40 million).

7 May The British prime minister, Alec Douglas-Home, repeats Britain's determination to defend South Arabia and Aden from attacks by dissident tribesmen and Yemeni border forces. However, on 11 May the UN Special Committee on Colonialism adopted a resolution asking Britain to halt its military activity in the SAF. On 23 April UAR President Nasser, arriving in Yemen on a goodwill visit, had pledged unceasing efforts 'to expel Britain from all parts of the Arab world'. Meanwhile, in May a joint force of about 3,000 men, known as Radforce, and comprising British and federal troops, had been built up in the Radfan area by Brigadier Robert L. Hargroves, commander of the Aden garrison. By the spring the British in the Radfan area had secured the Aden-Dhala road and had established British and federal troops in strategic positions on high ground overlooking areas controlled by dissident tribesmen. From the end of the year onwards, there was an increase in terrorist attacks in Aden by the National Front for the Liberation of the Occupied South.

24 May A Soviet agreement to lend the UAR $277 million is announced by President Nasser at a farewell dinner marking the end of Soviet Premier Khrushchev's two-week visit to Egypt. However, in a speech at the Soviet-built Aswan Dam on 16 May, Khrushchev criticized Arab leaders for concentrating on 'Arab unity and nationalism' at the expense of fraternal unity with socialist movements throughout the world.

26 May Iraq's President Aref and UAR President Nasser sign an agreement for the creation of a joint presidency council and military command. In their communiqué, they denounced the 'terrorist regime in Syria'. Syria had abrogated its military treaty with Iraq on 28 April. On 16 October Aref and Nasser were to agree on the setting up of a joint political body which was to be ratified on 20 December. On 14 July Aref announced the formation and charter of the Iraqi Arab Socialist Union. In his speech he proclaimed the UAR as the 'nucleus of Arab unity.' Meanwhile, the Iraqi prime minister, Lieutenant-General Yahya, formed a new cabinet and announced that Iraq was 'a socialist and democratic republic deriving its democracy and socialism from the Arab and Islamic heritage'.

28 May The first congress of Palestinian refugees opens in the Jordanian sector of Jerusalem and agrees to form the Palestine Liberation Organization (PLO). The congress resolved that the Palestinian problem would be resolved only in Palestine and by force. Between 9 and 19 September 1963 the Arab League Council had appointed the new PLO leader, Ahmad Shukairy, as the Palestinian delegate to the council.

3 July The UN secretary-general, U Thant, announces a two-month extension of the UN observation mission in Yemen, where fighting between UAR-supported republicans and Saudi-supported royalists continues. On 4 July Britain promised to grant independence to the SAF 'not later than 1968'. On 13 July the UAR and Yemen signed a policy co-ordination agreement 'as a step towards complete unity'.

5 September The second Arab summit opens in Alexandria. With the exceptions of Lebanon, Morocco, Saudi Arabia and Tunisia, its 13 members were represented by heads of state. On 11 September the summit agreed on a head-waters dam construction plan, designed to prevent Israel from diverting the River Jordan's waters to the Negev Desert. On 13 September the Israeli government warned that it would not tolerate this. On 14 September UAR President Nasser and the Saudi prime minister, Crown Prince Faisal, announced an agreement to end their nations' intervention in the Yemeni civil war. On 16 September it was reported from Yemen that a cease-fire had been achieved. On 13 August Iraq, the UAR, Jordan, Kuwait and Syria had signed an agreement in Cairo providing for the creation of an Arab common market but it was never to materialize.

16 October UAR and Iraqi leaders issue a joint communiqué, announcing that steps will be taken towards 'political unification' of the two countries within two years. On 26 May they had formed a special council to explore means of unifying their two governments. Meanwhile, on 24 October Iraq indicated its new recognition of Kuwait's independence by signing a trade and economic agreement with Kuwait.

2 November Crown Prince Faisal becomes the king of Saudi Arabia following the deposition of his brother Saud. The ailing king had served as little more than a figurehead since March. Faisal did not express his apparent feelings of disgust for the former king but restricted himself to saying: 'Saud is our brother and we shall do our best to ensure his comfort'. In early 1965 Saud was to leave the kingdom for Beirut and Cairo, before going on to Athens where he settled in a seaside hotel for the remainder of his life.

2 November The Shell Group announces that it has found commercial quantities of oil in Oman and the decision is announced to develop Oman's oilfields. Shell also announced that it was going to build an 156-mile (251-kilometre) pipeline from the new field at Natih-Fahud to Saih al-Malih on the Gulf of Oman near Muscat. Oman hoped to export between six and seven million tons of oil a year by the second half of 1967. Oil exploration had started in 1954 when Petroleum Development Oman, the first company to produce oil in Oman, established a beachhead at Duqm on the south-eastern coast. Drilling started in 1957 at Fahud, but the first hole was dry. Three further holes were drilled in 1960 at Ghaba, Heima and Afar. In 1962 oil was found at Yibal, in 1963 at Natih and in 1964 at Fahud.

4 November Ayatollah Ruhullah Khomeini is arrested for 'instigating against the country's interests, security, independence and territorial integrity' and for his opposition to the shah's new reform programme. He was taken to Tehran's Mehrabad airport and put on a plane bound for Turkey where he was to spend more than a year with a Turkish family in Bursa near Istanbul. After that he was sent to the holy Shi'i city of Najaf in Iraq. His application to settle in Najaf was to be accepted by the shah because he believed that there Khomeini would be overshadowed by more senior ayatollahs.

Meanwhile, the Iranian government passed legislation which granted US military forces in Iran immunity from Iranian law, thus preventing the courts from hearing complaints against foreigners. Khomeini strongly denounced the act, saying: 'They have reduced the Iranian people to a level lower than that of an American dog.' Within weeks of his banishment to Turkey, tapes of his utterances were being smuggled to Iran.

6 November Iraq's rebellious Kurdish tribesmen are reported to have proclaimed the creation of a Kurdish state in northern Iraq, under the leadership of Mulla Mustafa Barzani. Political negotiations between the Baghdad government and Kurdish representatives had recently collapsed in Baghdad.

When Britain had given Iraq its independence in 1932, its guarantees to Iraq's Kurds were not recognized by the new government in Baghdad who feared that this would set a dangerous precedent to its large Shi'i communities in southern Iraq. It put down ensuing Kurdish revolts with the help of British airpower. In the mid-1930s Barzani emerged as the leader of the new Kurdish separatist movement. He was expelled from Iraq in 1945 but returned in 1958, following the revolution which overthrew the monarchy and brought General Abd al-Karim Qasim to power. Barzani helped Qasim in return for winning Qasim's help against fellow Kurdish leaders. Barzani also managed to restore his leadership of the Kurdish Democratic Party (KDP). He then broke with Qasim and fought successive Iraqi governments until 1970 when the Ba'th agreed to discuss an autonomy agreement. However, negotiations continually failed, largely over the question of oil-rich Kirkuk which the Kurds maintained should be in their autonomous region.

8 November The Yemeni president, Abdullah Sallal, announces a formal cease-fire in the two-year-old civil war between republican forces and royalist forces of the deposed Imam al-Badr. However, throughout November and December sporadic fighting was reported between the two sides. On 27 December Yemen's entire 25-member cabinet was reported to have resigned in protest against Salal's allegedly corrupt rule and against the continued presence of 40,000 UAR troops in Yemen.

1 9 6 5

21 January The Iranian prime minister, Hasan Ali Mansur, is mortally wounded when a young man fires four shots at him at point-blank range outside the Majlis (lower house) building in Tehran. He was hit by two bullets, one in the throat and one in the stomach, and died in hospital on 26 January. The alleged murderer, Muhammad Bokhara'i, was arrested on the spot and his alleged accomplices, Morteza Niknezhad and Reza Saffar-Harandi, were arrested later in the day. According to reports from Tehran, Bokhara'i was a follower of Ayatollah Ruhullah Khomeini, the Shi'i cleric who had been a key figure in the riots of 1963. The reason for the killing appeared to have been partly Khomeini's expulsion from Iran to Turkey in November 1964. But Mansur was the focus of more general unpopularity, as he was considered too pro-US and his monetarist policies had angered many.

Among those arrested in the wake of the killing, was Hojatolislam Hashemi Rafsanjani, who was to become Iran's post-revolutionary speaker and later, president. When Ayatollah Husseini Beheshti also fell under the suspicion of the Organization of National Security and Intelligence (SAVAK), fellow followers of Khomeini arranged for him to go to Hamburg in West Germany where he was to spend the next five years. However, the possibility that the assassination was the result of a conspiracy was eventually ruled out, and no other country appeared to be involved.

The finance minister, Amir Abbas Hoveida, was appointed acting premier on 27 January, while retaining the finance portfolio. On 9 May, after a 12-day trial in camera, a military tribunal in Tehran sentenced four men to death by firing squad for the murder of Mansur. Six others were sentenced to life imprisonment with hard labour, and three more to prison terms ranging from five to ten years with hard labour. All the accused were reported to be members of the extremist right-wing Fedayeen-e Islam. On 16 June Muhammad Bokhara'i and his alleged accomplices were executed.

30 March It is announced that the Finns have won Iraq's Tigris Dam project. Imatran Voima, the Finnish state-owned power company, won the 700-million-fmks project to build the dam 35 miles (56 kilometres) north of Mosul. It was expected to take seven years to complete and would be the fifth biggest dam in the world.

3 April The Iraqi army launches an offensive against the Kurdish nationalists led by Mulla Mustafa Barzani, the third such attack since 1961. Tanks and armoured cars occupied the town of Sulaimaniyya. Kurdish sources claimed that in random firing 60 people had been killed and several hundred wounded. Two days later, between 40,000 and 50,000 Iraqi troops, supported by aircraft, opened a general offensive along a 250-mile (402-kilometre) front from Khanaqin in the east to Zakhno in the west.

10 April A soldier of the Imperial Guard, Reza Shamsabadi, fires shots in the direction of the Shah of Iran as he is stepping out of his car outside Tehran's Marble Palace where he has his office. The shah was unhurt and Shamsabadi was killed in an exchange of shots with the other guards. He and five others arrested were said to have subscribed to the 'extremist Communist ideology'. Of 14 men accused of complicity in the attempt two were to be sentenced to death by firing squad on 1 November. Of the other 12 one was to be sentenced to life imprisonment, 9 were to receive sentences ranging from three to eight years and 2 were to be acquitted. On 27 December the two sentenced to death were to have their sentences commuted to life imprisonment while the student sentenced to life imprisonment was to have his sentence reduced to 10 years' solitary confinement. Despite this apparent clemency, it was generally believed that most of the suspects were tortured by SAVAK.

June The ruler of Sharjah, Shaikh Saqr ibn Sultan al-Qasimi, is deposed by his family and succeeded by his cousin Shaikh Khaled Muhammad al-Qasimi. A statement from his family said that 'by his scandalous behaviour and the neglect of the welfare of his people', Shaikh Saqr was no longer worthy to be ruler. However, many believed that he had been deposed because of his sympathies with Nasserism and applauded his work in developing the Sharjah education system.

After being deposed, he visited Baghdad and Cairo where he was received by the Iraqi and United Arab Republic (UAR) governments as well as the Arab League. He announced that he would seek Arab League support for his reinstatement. Previously, he had maintained that he had no differences with his family and had said that Britain was trying to isolate the Trucial Coast from the influence of the Arab League and had tried to persuade him to refuse Arab League aid. The British Foreign Office spokesman denied these allegations, saying that this was a 'straightforward case of the deposition of an unpopular Ruler by family consensus'. He went to live in exile in Cairo until his return in 1972 and his unsuccessful attempt to wrest the leadership from his nephew, Shaikh Khaled ibn Muhammad. Shaikh Saqr had been recognized as Sharjah's ruler by the British in 1951 after the death of Shaikh Sultan ibn Saqr and the failure of Shaikh Sultan's brother Muhammad to become ruler.

24 August At the end of a meeting in Jeddah which began on 22 August, UAR President Nasser and Saudi Arabia's King Faisal sign an agreement on an immediate cease-fire in the Yemeni civil war. The agreement also called for a plebiscite to be held no later that 23 November 1966. UAR troops would leave Yemen within 10 months of 23 November 1965. On 22 August Mecca radio had called their talks 'friendly and brotherly'.

It was announced on 4 September that the Yemeni republican president, Sallal, would lead the Yemeni delegation to the Arab summit in Casablanca. On 20 July Nasser had had a meeting in Cairo with the Saudi under-secretary for foreign affairs, Omar Saqqaf. Nasser announced that he wanted to withdraw Egyptian troops from Yemen within six months but that if Britain and Saudi Arabia continued to provoke Egypt, Egypt would have to 'liquidate the points of aggression'.

In Yemen the year had seen a stream of royalist successes in the field. They took Jebel Razeh and Bait Ma'aran in late January, Harib on 10 March, Sirwah on 24 May, Qaflah (the Hashid Federation heartland) on 14 June, Jihanah on 24 July and Marib on 25 July.

15–16 September The Iraqi prime minister and commander of the air force, Brigadier Aref abd al-Razzak, attempts to seize power by force in Baghdad. After the failure of his coup he fled to Cairo. According to unofficial reports, troops from the Abu Ghuraib army camp advanced on Baghdad in the early hours of 16 September in order to take control of the radio station and other key points but were repelled by an armoured force hastily assembled by President Aref.

Since July most of the opposition to President Aref had come from a group described as Nasserites who were associated with the Arab Nationalist Movement, a pan-Arab organization which recognized President Nasser as leader of the Arab socialist revolution but often operated independently of Cairo to whom they were frequently an embarrassment. The Nasserites wished to accelerate the union with the UAR, they opposed the war against the Kurds, opposed a settlement that had almost been reached between the government and the oil companies and regarded Aref as too lukewarm in applying nationalization laws introduced in July 1964.

In a statement published in Cairo on 21 September, Nasser disassociated himself from the coup and recognized Aref as the legitimate ruler of Iraq.

25 September UAR President Nasser cancels a meeting with the British foreign minister, George Thomson, in protest at Britain's suspension of the constitution in Aden. The constitution was suspended and the British high commissioner took over personal rule after Aden ministers refused to condemn the Adeni freedom movement, the National Liberation Front, for its assassination of the speaker of the Adeni parliament. Egypt believed that the timing of the suspension, while Thomson was in Cairo, was designed as a personal snub to Nasser, the key supporter of anti-British activities in Aden.

23 November In accordance with the Jeddah agreement of 24 August, 25 Yemeni republicans and 25 royalists meet at Harad in Yemen, a few miles from the Saudi border. The so-called Harad conference began on 24 November. Their mandate was to discuss the nature of the plebiscite on the future form of a Yemeni government and the foundation of a provisional government. The republican side was led by Abd al-Rahman al-Iriani, a member of the republican council. The royalist delegation was led by Ahmad al-Shami, who had been foreign minister in the royalist government.

In view of republican objections the royalists agreed to exclude members of the Hamid al-Din family (descendants of Imam Hamid al-Din Yahya who died in 1890). This concession was said to have been made under Saudi pressure. Both the UAR and Saudi Arabia were represented by two observers each. However, the conference was, from the very start, deadlocked. The republicans insisted that the provisional government should operate within a republican framework and that the Hamid al-Din family should be excluded from it. The royalists countered with their understanding that the Jeddah agreement involved a provisional government that was neither republican nor imamic and should contain an equal number of royalists and republicans. The royalists also demanded the immediate withdrawal of UAR troops from Yemen to be followed by an immediate plebiscite. The republicans replied that they had no objection to a plebiscite but that time was needed to arrange the evacuation of UAR troops.

The conference broke up on 24 December as Ramadan (the fasting month) had begun, but it was agreed that it would resume on 20 February 1966. It was also agreed that both sides would respect the armistice while retaining their military positions and would refrain from hostile propaganda against each other.

24 November The ruler of Kuwait, Shaikh Abdullah al-Salem al-Sabah, dies aged 73. He was succeeded by his 51-year-old younger brother Shaikh Sabah al-Salem al-Sabah who had been prime minister since January 1963.

21 December A £100-million Saudi defence order with Britain is announced in London and Jeddah. The order, which went to the British Aircraft Corporation, Associated Electrical Industries and Airwork Services, was the largest order that Britain had ever received.

1 9 6 6

27 January During a visit to Jordan from 27 January to 2 February, King Faisal of Saudi Arabia denies that he planned a political alliance to challenge the role of the United Arab Republic (UAR) president, Gamal abd-al Nasser, in the Arab world. He claimed that the conference of Muslim countries which he had recently called for might be compared with the Vatican Council and that its aim was 'to integrate Islam in the context of the modern world'. He would convene it in his capacity as protector of Islam's holy places (Mecca and Medina). From 8 to 14 December 1965 Faisal had paid an official visit to Iran at the end of which it had been announced that the shah and the king would invite all Muslim countries to a conference to further their unity of views and to defend their common interests.

The UAR and other Arab republican regimes immediately read into the statement an attempt by Faisal to challenge Nasser's leadership of the Arab world by forming an alliance of conservative states against the Socialist regimes. King Husayn of Jordan had visited Tehran from 26 to 28 September and, according to the Jordanian prime minister, Wasfi al-Tall, his aim was to draw Iran and the Arab states closer together in line with the request of the heads of state taking part in the Casablanca summit. Faisal made a return visit to Jordan from 27 January to 2 February. Following his visit, Nasser attacked the plan for an Islamic conference in a series of statements in February and March, and suggested that the UAR might repudiate the Arab solidarity pact concluded at the summit.

22 February Britain's Labour government publishes its white paper announcing that Britain intends to leave Aden in 1968. Within hours of the announcement, the UAR President Nasser declared that 'we can stay in Yemen for one year or two, three, four or five years . . . There was an announcement today that the British had decided to grant independence in 1968. Well, we shall stay there until after 1968.'

By remaining on the borders of the South Arabian Federation (SAF), Nasser apparently hoped to influence the victory in the South for his Front for the Liberation of Occupied South Yemen (FLOSY) allies. Meanwhile, in the South, acts of terrorism continued. On 24 February a gunman murdered the president of the South Yemeni Trade Union Congress, Ali Husayn al-Qadhi. On 26 February British troops broke up a demonstration of about 1,000 rock-throwing rioters in Aden and on 20 March a gunman murdered William Hunn, a British official, in South Yemen. On 13 April an assassin killed Yemen's acting president, Abdullah al-Iriany.

23 February Syrian radicals led by Major-General Salah Jadid oust the prime minister, Salah al-Din Bitar, in a bloody coup. On 1 March Major-General Hafez Asad became Syria's defence minister. On 27 February the Syrian Ba'th Party congress elected its 16-member leadership group. Between 1963 and 1966 a power struggle took place between the more conservative Ba'th in Syria who had steered the party since its early days, and younger members who wanted the party to adopt more radical policies. These, often called the neo-Ba'th, emerged victorious in the 23 February coup. The coup saw a split between the Iraqi and Syrian Ba'th. In 1957 the Iraqi Ba'th had joined the National Front with the Communists and other parties, and welcomed General Qasim's 1958 revolution. However, the Iraqi Ba'th fell out with Qasim over his increasing distaste for union with Egypt, and after the party's attempt on his life in November 1959 they went underground.

22 March Addressing a rally at Suez, UAR President Nasser repeats his promise that the Egyptian army will remain in Yemen until the Yemeni revolution can defend itself. He again warned that Egypt would strike at 'the bases of aggression'. He strongly attacked the Saudi plan for an Islamic conference which he saw as an attempt by King Faisal firstly to form an alliance of conservative Muslim states, in opposition to the revolutionary Arab republics, secondly to pursue against the latter a policy of 'encirclement' directed by the 'Western colonialist countries', and thirdly to contest his own leadership of the Arab world.

In his speech on 22 March Nasser said: 'But how can I undertake a battle for Palestine side by side with these people? Each of them carries a knife and wishes to cut our throats because of our socialism. The reactionary forces in the Arab countries are more afraid of the Arab revolutionaries than of Israel . . . If these reactionaries continue to ally themselves with imperialism, we shall end the Casablanca solidarity pact and call on the revolutionaries to resume the struggle.'

Although Nasser was committed by the Jeddah agreement of 24 August 1965 to the withdrawal of Egyptian troops from Yemen by 23 November 1966, Britain's announcement in February that it would evacuate Aden by 1968 gave him an increasing incentive to remain there and increase Egypt's revolutionary influence in the region. On 21 February Saudi Arabia had appealed for US diplomatic and military aid if Egypt resumed fighting in Yemen. On the previous day a scheduled round of peace talks had failed to take place because the royalist delegation allied with Saudi Arabia had refused to attend. On 22 February Nasser had threatened to keep his estimated 70,000 troops in Yemen for another five years unless an acceptable Yemeni government was established.

In a further speech on 24 March Nasser said: 'Shall we surrender to Faisal or stay ten years in Yemen? I say we shall stay twenty years. I now say we shall strike against whoever intervenes in Yemen . . .' In his May Day speech, Nasser was to promise to help the Yemenis to regain the Saudi Arabian border towns of Jizan and Najran. On 5 May the North Yemeni government asserted that the towns had been taken by force in 1930 and that they would be retaken by force if necessary.

13 April President of Iraq since February 1963, Field-Marshal Abd al-Salam Aref is killed when the helicopter he is flying from Al Qurnah to Basra crashes in the desert near his destination during a sandstorm. All nine passengers and the crew of two were killed. The victims included the minister of the interior, Abd al-Latif al-Darraji, and the minister of industry and planning, Mustafa Abdullah. Aref had played a leading role in the 1958 coup which led to the overthrow of the monarchy and the murder of King Faisal as well as in the 1963 coup which led to his installation as president after the overthrow and execution of General Qasim.

On 17 April several hours after he was buried with full military honours, his younger brother, Major-General Abd al-Rahman Aref, was sworn in as his successor. Like his brother, the new president was a career army officer and had assisted in Qasim's overthrow in 1963. He had also helped to put down the Ba'th uprising in November 963 and towards the end of 1965 was credited with having prevented a pro-Nasser coup. He had been acting chief-of-staff since 1963.

On 18 April Dr Abd al-Rahman al-Bazzaz formed a new cabinet as prime minister. The new foreign minister was Dr Adnan Pachachi, a former Iraqi representative at the UN. The other major cabinet change was the appointment of Major-General Shaker Mahmoud Shukri, previously Iraqi ambassador in London, as the new defence minister in place of Major-General Abd al-Aziz al-Okeili.

Al-Okeili had called for all-out war against the Kurds in the north and the late president had himself been committed to a strong military line. Both the new president and Dr

Bazzaz, however, were thought to favour a more conciliatory line. It had become evident, in any case, that the army, over two-thirds of which was engaged in the campaign against the Kurds, had failed to destroy the rebel Kurdish forces. Following the death of President Abd al-Salam Aref, Kurdish rebel radio announced that the Kurdish leader, Mulla Mustafa Barzani, had ordered a month's truce to give the government time to reflect on the Kurds' demands for autonomy. Although Dr Bazzaz announced in a speech on 25 April that the Kurds had a right to retain their nationalism, he ruled out any possibility of separatism and on 27 April the new president rejected Barzani's offer of negotiations.

31 May The Kuwaiti National Assembly confirms Prime Minister Jaber as crown prince.

22 June At a US press conference, King Faisal of Saudi Arabia shocks his listeners when he says 'Unfortunately, Jews support Israel and we consider those who provide assistance to our enemies as our own enemies.' Many considered his remarks to be anti-Jewish rather than merely anti-Israeli, an important distinction. Responding to these reactions, on 25 June the king clarified his statement by adding 'We are not against the religion of the Jews but against the Zionists and the Jews who help the Zionists.'

Like Saud in 1957, Faisal was snubbed by New York's Mayor John Lindsay who cancelled a dinner engagement with Faisal in deference to his pro-Zionist electorate. Even the state governor, Nelson Rockefeller, announced that he would not make a courtesy call on Faisal.

29 June The new Iraqi president, Abd al-Rahman Aref, announces that the leader of Iraq's Kurds, Mulla Mustafa Barzani, has agreed to a 12-point peace proposal. On the following day the president crushed an attempted coup led by Brigadier-General Aref Abd al-Razzak.

9 July Egyptian President Nasser says that the Arab countries will never accept Israel as a neighbour.

30 July Two Yemeni-based Egyptian jets, strafe government buildings in Bahrain.

6 August Iraq's President Abd al-Rahman Aref names Naji Talib to form a new cabinet. On 9 August the president told his ministers that the Iraqi economy must make room for both the public and the private sectors.

6 August The ruler of Abu Dhabi, the 61-year-old Shaikh Shakbut ibn Sultan, is deposed by a family conclave and replaced by his younger brother, Shaikh Zayed ibn Sultan al-Nahayan. According to the acting British resident in the Gulf, H.G. Balfour-Paul, Shakbut, ruler since 1928, was deposed for governing inefficiently and for failing to use the state's wealth for the benefit of the people. After his deposition, Shakbut was given temporary asylum in Bahrain.

In June 1965 the ruler of Sharjah, Shaikh Saqr ibn Sultan al-Qasimi, had also been deposed by his family. He had been succeeded by his cousin, Shaikh Khaled Muhammad al-Qasimi.

Abu Dhabi was one of the seven Trucial States which had been under British protection since the nineteenth century. The others were Dubai, Ajman, Fujairah, Ras al-Khaimah, Sharjah and Umm al-Qaiwain. Britain was responsible for their external relations and defence. Otherwise they were self-governing. Abu Dhabi's offshore fields were operated by Abu Dhabi Marine Areas, owned two-thirds by British Petroleum (BP) and one-third by the Compagnie Française des Petroles (CFP). The onshore fields were owned by a subsidiary of the Iraq Petroleum Company (IPC) in which BP, Shell, CFP, Standard Oil of New Jersey, and the Gulbenkian interests held shares. Oil had been discovered in Abu Dhabi in 1960 and production had begun in 1962.

16 August An Iraqi air-force pilot defects to Israel by flying his Soviet-built MiG-21 to an undisclosed Israeli air base.

20 November The Arab countries vote to cut investment links with Ford and Coca-Cola because of their ties with Israel.

23 November It is announced in Amman that King Husayn of Jordan has accepted an offer by King Faisal of Saudi Arabia to place 20,000 Saudi troops at his disposal. These would be stationed permanently at Saudi Arabia's northern town of Tabuk from where they would be able to enter Jordan promptly if Husayn requested them. Jordan's Prime Minister Wasfi al-Tall, however, refused on 28 November to comment on reports that Saudi troops had already entered Jordan.

In a Cairo broadcast on 22 November, the Palestine Liberation Organization (PLO) chairman, Ahmad Shukairy, called on King Husayn to allow the PLO to defend Jordanian frontier villages, and gave an assurance that the PLO did not intend to seize power in Jordan. However, King Husayn rejected the offer, telling Paris's *Le Monde* on 24 November 'I do not see why I should offer my head to the executioner.' On the following day Shukairy denounced Husayn as a 'murderer', a 'tool of imperialism', an 'atheist' and an 'enemy of Islam and Arabism'.

1 9 6 7

11 January A former Yemeni republican official says he saw Egyptian planes stage gas attacks in Yemen on 11 December 1966. On 5 January nine Egyptian Ilyushin bombers were reported to have bombed the Yemeni mountain village of Kitaf, some 30 miles (48 kilometres) from the Saudi border, with phosgene poison gas three weeks earlier. The Yemeni royalists invited the international press to Kitaf to see for themselves.

7 February United Press International (UPI) reports that the Soviet Union is to supply Iran with Soviet arms. On 5 October 1965 a draft agreement had been initialled under which the Soviet Union would build a steel mill near Isfahan with an annual capacity of between half a million and 1.2 million tons. The agreement, first announced by the Iranian prime minister, Amir Abbas Hoveida, on 6 July 1965, had been discussed during the shah's visit to the Soviet Union between 21 June and 3 July of that year. A joint communiqué at the end of his visit had stressed the willingness of both countries to develop further good-neighbourly relations and to extend economic, technical and cultural co-operation.

On 26 June the Soviet president, Mikoyan, had stated that the Soviet Union 'appreciates the Persian [Iranian] government's statement that Persia will not allow foreign missile bases of any type to be set up on her territory and will never be a means of aggression against the Soviet Union'.

12 February The South Arabian Federation (SAF) information minister, Abd al-Rahman

Girgirah, accuses Egypt of fomenting trouble in Aden. Rioting had broken out in the Federation on 10 and 11 February and British troops had clashed with nationalist demonstrators in Aden. On 26 February an assassin killed the Adeni Legislative Council member, Sayyid Muhammad Hasan, in Aden. On the following day a bomb killed six people in the city and on 28 February competing Arab nationalist forces clashed in the streets. On 1 March British troops killed two Arab demonstrators. On 7 March an Arab mob set fire to the headquarters of a rival political group in the city.

On 2 April riots broke out as a three-man UN mission visited Aden. On 15 April fighting erupted between the Front for the Liberation of South Yemen (FLOSY) and the National Liberation Front (NLF), the two Arab groups competing for power in anticipation of Britain's scheduled departure from Aden in 1968. On 26 April 3,000 Yemenis attacked the US Agency for International Development in Aden.

17 March Seventeen Yemenis are beheaded in Riyadh's Deera Square, after confessing to having carried out acts of sabotage in Saudi Arabia. They had been captured in January and accused of planting bombs in the Saudi capital, Riyadh, at Prince Fahd's Nasariyah Palace, at the Zahra Hotel and under a bridge which King Faisal was scheduled to cross. Towards the end of 1966 various bomb explosions were reported in the kingdom. Three went off in Riyadh, including one outside the Dammam beach palace of Saud ibn Jiluwi, Hasa province's ruthless governor. During a three-day Arabian American Oil Company (ARAMCO) strike in spring 1956, Ibn Jiluwi was reported to have shown his mettle by having three of the strikers publicly beaten to death.

The perpetrators of the bomb attacks on 17 March were believed to have been influenced by the ideological war of words between the UAR (Egyptian) president, Gamal abd al-Nasser, and King Faisal, which was at its height. Faisal's call for an Islamic pact at the end of 1966 had particularly enraged Nasser. The Constituent Assembly of the Muslim World League which had convened in Jeddah to discuss the pact had called for Muslims everywhere 'to denounce this murderous war in which Muslim kills his Muslim brother' and deplored the persecution of the Muslim Brotherhood in Egypt. Nasser denounced the pact as an imperialist conspiracy and claimed that it was an attempt to revive the British-sponsored Baghdad Pact.

23 April Former King Saud flies to San'a, the Yemeni capital, to extend full recognition to Yemen's President Sallal who, in his turn, greets Saud as the 'legal King of Saudi Arabia'. Saud gave Sallal's regime $1 million. President Nasser had arranged for Sallal's return to San'a in August 1966, and from the moment of his arrival Sallal had unleashed a reign of terror against his rivals. On 13 December Nasser had given Saud permission to leave his Athens exile and to move to Cairo, from where the Egyptian leader could more easily exploit him for propaganda purposes.

Saud told Nasser, Abd al-Hakim Amer and Anwar Sadat that he had not abdicated the Saudi throne, but that the *ulema* had forced his deposition illegally'. The US Central Intelligence Agency (CIA), he claimed, had also been involved in the plot to depose him. To ingratiate himself further with Nasser he lent Egypt $10 million and donated money to the families of the Yemenis executed on 17 March.

For his part, Nasser wanted both to create unrest in Saudi Arabia and to weaken the kingdom's role in the Yemeni civil war. On 12 May Saudi Arabia claimed that Egyptian planes had, the previous day, again attacked the Saudi border town of Najran.

Between 10 and 13 February Egypt had sequestered the property held in Egypt of King Faisal and 210 other Saudi citizens. It did not confiscate the property of former King Saud or those who 'voluntarily chose' to live in Egypt. Egypt's action followed a Saudi government decision on 9 February to revoke the operating licences of two Egyptian banks in Saudi Arabia, the Bank of Cairo and Bank Misr. On

11 February Saud said that by closing the two Egyptian banks and by other recent actions, King Faisal was 'behaving like a frightened man who has lost his sense of proportion'.

18 May Egypt demands that UN troops leave their positions in the Sinai Peninsula. On 19 May the UN acceded to Egypt's demand to withdraw its troops from both the Gaza Strip and Sharm al-Shaikh at the southern tip of the Sinai Peninsula. On 20 May reports indicated that Egypt had deployed about 58,000 troops along its border with Israel and that Israeli tanks had also moved to the border zone. On 21 May Israel completed partial mobilization of its reserves while Egypt announced total mobilization. On 22 May Nasser threatened to halt all Israeli shipping through the Gulf of Aqaba. On 23 May the Israeli premier, Levi Eshkol, warned that an Egyptian blockade of the Gulf of Aqaba would constitute 'an act of aggression' against Israel. On the same day US President Johnson announced that the US considered the Gulf of Aqaba 'to be an international waterway'. On 25 and 26 May the Israeli foreign minister, Abba Eban, met President Johnson in Washington.

24 May A force of 20,000 Saudi Arabian troops crosses into Jordan, and on 25 May all Saudi forces are placed on the alert. On 26 May Iraq said that its troops were moving into Syria to reinforce Syrian troops poised on the Israeli border. On 28 May President Nasser ruled out a negotiated peace in the Middle East until the Palestinians were returned to their homes in Israel (termed by Nasser 'Occupied Palestine').

During the last days of May there were various explosions in Saudi Arabia aimed at the US presence in the kingdom. Despite the escalating ideological conflict between Nasser and Faisal, the latter now had no choice but to declare his support for Egypt and make gestures of solidarity as the Arab states prepared for war with Israel.

1 June Iraqi air-force jets take off from the Habbaniya air base to fly to front-line positions in an 'undisclosed' Arab country bordering Israel (clearly Jordan). On the previous day Iraqi troops and armoured units were reported to be moving into Jordan to take up positions alongside Jordanian troops on the Israeli border. On 30 May King Husayn had made a dramatic visit to Cairo where he had signed a defence treaty with Nasser during a six-hour visit. The treaty stipulated that each country would consider an attack on the other as an attack on itself, and that both Egyptian and Jordanian forces would be under the overall command of the Egyptian chief-of-staff.

Meanwhile, the Iraqi chargé d'affaires in London told the British Foreign Office that in the event of Western countries aiding Israel against the Arab states, Iraq would nationalize Western oil companies in her territory and break off diplomatic relations with Britain and the US. Saudi Arabia and Kuwait also threatened to suspend oil shipments to all Western countries who aided Israel. In Tehran, meanwhile, the Iranian government issued a statement expressing support for the Arab states and saying that it would support and respect the legitimate rights of the Palestinian people as provided for by the UN resolutions.

2 June The Palestine Liberation Organization (PLO) chairman, Ahmad Shukairy, calls for a *jihad* (holy struggle) 'for the liberation of Palestine and the cleansing of our land from infidels'. Addressing a large Muslim congregation in the Haram al-Sharif Mosque in Old Jerusalem, he said that the Arabs wanted 'fighters, not Beatles' and called upon Arab women to don battledress, adding that 'this is no time for lipstick and miniskirts'.

The Arab-Israeli War (The 'June' War)

5 June Israel attacks Egypt and Jordan, wiping out the Egyptian air force – destroying 374 planes – in several hours, and driving deep into Jordan and Egypt's Sinai Peninsula. Israel took the Sinai capital, El Arish, fought intense tank battles with Egypt along a 200-mile (322-kilometre) front and fought the Jordanian army (formerly the Arab Legion) in Jerusalem. King Faisal told the Saudis to prepare for the 'decisive battle'.

6 June Israel continues its rout of Egyptian forces in Sinai but meets fierce resistance in the Old City of Jerusalem, then annexed to Jordan. On the same day Nasser closed the Suez Canal to all shipping and severed relations with the US and Britain. King Faisal addressed a public rally on Riyadh racecourse in which he said, 'We consider any state or country supporting or aiding Zionist-Israeli aggression against the Arabs in any way as aggression against us.' He cried out passionately 'To jihad, citizens! To jihad, citizens! To jihad, nation of Muhammad and the Islamic peoples.'

Meanwhile, a Saudi brigade moved towards Jordan but by the time it reached Jerusalem King Husayn's army had been driven across the River Jordan by the Israelis who were only to accept a cease-fire when they had full control of the West Bank (of the River Jordan) and Syria's Golan Heights. Nasser accused the US and Britain of helping Israel and three Arab oil producers promptly cut oil supplies to both countries. The UN Security Council called for an immediate cease-fire.

Saudi Arabia reluctantly joined the other Arab oil producers in suspending oil supplies to the US and Britain. The decision had been taken after Cairo radio had alleged that US and British planes had taken part in the surprise attack which destroyed Egypt's air force. The accusations were clearly nonsense and both Nasser and Husayn soon dropped them while Faisal had never believed them in the first place. However, Faisal felt obliged to show solidarity by joining a collective Arab embargo against the US and Britain.

Anti-US riots erupted in Dhahran on 7 June, a day which ARAMCO employees were later to call 'Rock Wednesday'. Students from Dhahran's College of Petroleum and Minerals attacked the military section of Dhahran airport and the US Officers' Club which had been evacuated just in time. They also attacked the exterior of the US consulate and a number of houses of senior ARAMCO employees. Eventually the national guard intervened and the day ended without bloodshed.

7 June Israel assumes virtual control of Sinai, the Arab section of Jerusalem and most of the West Bank as Jordan accepts a cease-fire. Israeli troops marched across Sinai to the Suez Canal and took Sinai's southern fortress town of Sharm al-Shaikh. On 8 June Egypt, with the remains of its army now trapped behind Israeli lines, accepted the UN's cease-fire order.

Earlier in the day Israel had killed 10 US sailors in a torpedo attack on its communications ship *Liberty* after, it claimed, mistakenly identifying it as an Egyptian ship.

After Syria had accepted the UN cease-fire on 9 June, Israel bombed Damascus and advanced into the Golan Heights.

9 June A weeping President Nasser announces his resignation in a television broadcast to the Egyptian people. However, enormous demonstrations calling for him to stay on immediately filled the streets of Cairo and Beirut and by dawn on 10 June Nasser, following pressure on him by Egypt's National Assembly, had agreed to withdraw his resignation.

10 June All the combatants accept a cease-fire as Israel halts its 12-mile (19-kilometre) advance into Syria at the town of Qunaitra. However, the cease-fire was rejected by King Faisal who had little sympathy with Nasser and commented to an Arab diplomat: 'If someone throws stones at a neighbour's windows he should not be surprised or complain if the owner comes out and beats him with a stick.'

14 June Israel announces that it was holding 5,499 Arab prisoners. Reports indicated that the Arabs held 16 Israeli prisoners. Total war casualties on both sides were estimated at 100,000.

On 28 June Israel formally merged the Old City of Jerusalem (east Jerusalem), conquered in the war, with the city's Israeli sector (west Jerusalem).

16 June Agence France Presse reports that Egyptian troops have started to withdraw from Yemen. On 19 June Yemeni royalist sources reported that the Egyptian garrison at San'a had been withdrawn.

3 July British troops re-enter Aden's Crater district from which they had been expelled on 20 June when violence had increased in Aden. This followed the British announcement that the SAF would be granted its sovereignty on 9 January 1968 but that British military forces would remain in the area, at least temporarily. On 21 June British troops clashed with Arab gunmen in Aden.

On 5 July the SAF Supreme Council appointed the information minister, Husayn Ali Bayoomi, as the federation's first prime minister, but by 28 July pressures and threats by two radical political groups had forced him to abandon his attempts to form a caretaker government pending independence.

15 July The presidents of Egypt, Algeria, Syria, Iraq and Sudan meet in Cairo to discuss the consequences of the Arab defeat. On 16 July the five presidents vowed 'to eliminate the consequences of imperialist Israeli aggression in the Arab homeland'. On 17 June foreign ministers of 13 Arab states had met in Kuwait to plan a joint political strategy in the wake of the Arab defeat.

31 August Nasser and Saudi Arabia's King Faisal announce the formation of a three-nation committee to supervise the withdrawal from Yemen of Egyptian troops. They were speaking at the conference of 13 Arab leaders which began in the Sudanese capital, Khartoum, on 29 August. The two men met at the house of the Sudanese prime minister, Muhammad Mahgoub. Following Egypt's devastating defeat in the Arab-Israeli war of June, Nasser was in a weak position.

At the conclusion of the conference on 1 September the Arab leaders agreed to commit themselves to no peace with Israel, no negotiations with Israel and no recognition of Israel. To enable them to stick to their word it was agreed that Kuwait would grant £55 million, Saudi Arabia £50 million and Libya £30 million each year to provide Egypt with £90 million, Jordan with £40 million and Syria with £5 million. On 3 September, however, Kuwait decided to resume oil shipments to Britain and the US. These had been under boycott since the start of the war.

26 October The Shah of Iran is formally crowned in the Iranian capital, Tehran.

5 November A bloodless coup by Yemen's high command overthrows Yemen's President Sallal while he is in Iraq. At the time of the coup Sallal was en route to the Soviet Union where he was ostensibly to attend the government's fiftieth anniversary celebrations. Sallal visited Nasser on the way but was given a cool reception, and on his leaving Cairo, Nasser sent an open message to the commander-in-chief of Egypt's remaining forces in Yemen, ordering him not to block a coup against Sallal should there be one.

The coup which followed brought to power a group of moderate republicans with Qadi Iriani as chief-of-state and Mohsen al-Aini as prime minister. However, hopes that the coup would augur the end of the civil war were dashed when the royalists launched an all-out attack on San'a which was almost to succeed.

22 November The UN passes Resolution 242 on the Arab-Israeli problem.

28 November Britain grants independence to the SAF. On 1 November the SAF's two rival liberation groups, the NLF and FLOSY announced their agreement to negotiate jointly with Britain, but on 2 November renewed fighting broke out between them. On 11 November Britain agreed to negotiate with the NLF, recognizing it as the SAF's sole representative. On 24 August reports indicated that the NLF had seized control of one of the SAF provinces as it fought to establish supremacy over FLOSY.

On 26 November British troops began to leave the SAF and on 30 November the newly installed NLF president, Qahtan Muhammad al-Sha'bi, was proclaimed president of the SAF, whose name was changed to the People's Republic of South Yemen.

1 December The PDRY challenges the British cession of the Kureia Muria islands to Oman. On 3 December it declared its right to use 'all possible means' to recover the islands. On 6 December it expressed concern about royalist military successes in North Yemen but added that it would not intervene militarily. On 4 December the San'a (North Yemeni) government had conceded for the first time that fighting was raging around the city and on 5 December the royalists claimed to have shot down a Soviet plane. On 15 December Egypt completed its evacuation of Yemen.

15 December Egypt's Field-Marshal Abd al-Hakim Amer, who had long urged Nasser to abandon Yemen, commits suicide after an unsuccessful coup against his erstwhile close friend. Nasser had sacked Amer as commander-in-chief of the Egyptian armed forces after the Israeli victory in June.

18 December Of the 10 members of the PLO Executive Committee, 6 demand the resignation of Chairman Ahmad Shukairy. On 13 October Shukairy had declared that Arab guerrilla raids on the West Bank of the River Jordan were only 'the first phase of a popular Palestinian war'. In contrast, on 5 November King Husayn of Jordan asserted that the Arab states were willing to recognize Israel's right to exist but only after it had withdrawn from occupied Arab territory. On 24 December Shukairy resigned.

19 December Britain announces that it will renew diplomatic relations with Egypt.

24 December Iraq and the Soviet Union sign an agreement for the Soviet development of Iraqi oil deposits.

1 9 6 8

9 January The agreement setting up the Organization of Arab Petroleum Exporting Countries (OAPEC) is signed in Beirut. It was agreed that the headquarters would be in Kuwait and that the organization would concern itself with the economic and commercial interests of its members but not with political matters which would continue to be treated within the context of the Arab League. The decision to establish OAPEC was made at the end of 1967 to represent the special interests of the Arab oil-producing countries. It was to be additional to the wider-based Organization of Petroleum Exporting Countries (OPEC), and separate from the Arab petroleum congresses which were held approximately biennially. The formation of OAPEC had been announced in Jeddah on 21 December 1967 with Kuwait, Libya and Saudi Arabia as its initial members. Other early members were Algeria, Bahrain, Egypt, Iraq, Qatar, Syria, Tunisia and the United Arab Emirates (UAE).

16 January In a speech to Britain's House of Commons (lower house), the prime minister, Harold Wilson, announces further severe expenditure cuts and Britain's intention of withdrawing completely from the Gulf region by 1971.

Britain's new policy was largely a response to rank-and-file Labour Party criticism of annual increases in Britain's defence spending. Wilson responded to these criticisms with cuts and in a white paper published on 16 February 1967 further cuts were planned. Britain's intention to withdraw from the Gulf was strongly criticized by King Faisal of Saudi Arabia when he visited London in May 1967.

One of the problems that had to be tackled was the defence agreement with Kuwait of 19 June 1961 which provided for British assistance to Kuwait in the event of her being attacked. An exchange of letters in May was to remove this defence clause from the agreement with effect from 13 May 1971. It was also now widely realized in the region that the Shah of Iran would from then on regard himself as the obvious 'policeman' of the Gulf.

17 January Bahrain and Saudi Arabia announce that they will build a causeway linking the main island of Bahrain with Saudi Arabia.

27 February The rulers of the seven Trucial States (Abu Dhabi, Dubai, Sharjah, Ajman, Ras al-Khaimah, Fujairah and Umm al-Qaiwain), Bahrain and Qatar end a three-day meeting (25–27 February) at which they agree to form a federation of nine Arab Emirates with effect from 30 March. The meeting, in response to Britain's decision to withdraw British military forces from the 'Persian' Gulf by 1971, followed an earlier decision of 19 February by Dubai and Abu Dhabi to federate under a common flag and share joint foreign policy, defence and citizenship. The invitation was made by the rulers of Abu Dhabi and Dubai who, it seems, wanted to extend the federation beyond the seven Trucial States to include Bahrain and Qatar. It was probably the idea of Dubai's ruler, Shaikh Rashid, to include Qatar which was then ruled by his son-in-law, Shaikh Ahmad ibn Ali Al-Thani, who had helped Dubai generously with grants and loans. Abu Dhabi enjoyed similarly cordial relations with Bahrain whose currency it used from 1966 to 1972.

28 February King Faisal says that the Saudi government will help North Yemeni royalist forces in view of the alleged intervention of Syria, the Soviet Union and South Yemen in the North Yemeni civil war. In a note to the Arab League, North Yemen's republican government had alleged on 31 January that Saudi Arabian armoured and artillery units had occupied coastal areas of north-western Yemen. If the Arab League failed to prevent the intervention, it said it would refer the matter to the UN Security Council. On 3 January the Beirut correspondent of the London *Times* had commented that 'it was probably inevitable that Saudi Arabia would take advantage of the withdrawal of the Egyptian expeditionary force. Indeed, there is serious doubt about how completely King Faisal's government ever abstained from helping the Royalists.'

On 6 February a major battle had begun between royalist and republican forces around the Yemeni capital, San'a. On 8 February republican forces had lifted their siege on the royalists and on 19 February both North and South Yemen claimed that their forces were attacking the royalists in the North. On 13 January a three-nation Arab commission had appealed to Syria, Saudi Arabia, the Soviet Union and Iran not to interfere in North Yemen's internal affairs.

Under the agreement concluded in Khartoum on 31 August 1967 by the United Arab Republic (UAR) president, Gamal abd al-Nasser, and Saudi King Faisal it had been agreed that UAR (Egyptian) forces would be withdrawn by 9 December. On 5 November the republicans' first president, Sallal, had been overthrown in a military coup and replaced by a presidential council headed by Abd al-Rahman al-Iriani. Then, with implicit Saudi backing, the Yemeni royalists had launched two unsuccessful attacks on San'a in November and December. To challenge the threat, the republicans secured military aid from the Soviet Union and formed a defence cabinet headed by General Hasan al-Amri.

2 April The Soviet premier, Aleksei Kosygin, arrives in Iran for an official visit. On 5 April Iran and the Soviet Union announced their opposition to the proposed British-sponsored Gulf federation. In a joint communiqué on 7 April, they expressed similar views on the Middle East, South-East Asia and European security. On 18 February Abu Dhabi and Dubai had announced merger plans, and on 27 February nine of the Gulf states had agreed to form a union when Britain withdrew its forces from the area at the end of 1971.

29 May The Israeli foreign minister, Abba Eban, declares that Israel will not return the territories occupied in 1967 until the Arab states are ready to sign peace treaties with Israel. On 5 March King Faisal had accused Israel of dishonouring Muslim shrines in East (Old) Jerusalem. On the following day the Israeli mayor of Jerusalem, Teddy Kollek, criticized the Israeli government for extending to East Jerusalem its practice of blowing up the homes of suspected Palestinian guerrillas.

On 11 May, in its first broadcast, the Palestinian commando organization Fatah had announced that its ultimate aim was to free the whole of Palestine, and not merely to end the Israeli occupation of Arab regions (the West Bank, Gaza, Sinai and the Golan Heights) seized during the Arab-Israeli war of 1967.

17 July A military coup overthrows the government of the Iraqi president, Abd al-Rahman Aref. On 21 July the Iraqi foreign minister, Nasser al-Hani, said that Iraq would not resume relations with the US. On the following day he said that the agreements made with a French oil company remained in force despite the coup. On 6 April France had agreed to sell to Iraq 54 Mirage fighter bombers. However, on 9 July Iraq announced its rejection of foreign bids to develop its sulphur deposits and, on 10 July, its rejection of bids to develop its North Rumailah oilfields.

At dawn on 17 July, tanks, armoured cars and infantry units surrounded the presidential palace where they met resistance from Aref's presidential guard. Major-General Ahmad Hasan al-Bakr, a former prime minister and vice-president, per-suaded Aref to resign after two warning shots had been fired at the palace. A safe conduct was agreed to and Aref was escorted to the airport and placed on a plane bound for London where the British government gave him a three-month visa.

The Arab defeat in the Arab-Israeli war of 1967 had led to serious unrest in Iraq and to fundamental changes in government policy. The foreign press attributed Aref's downfall to his failure to win popular support on this and other issues, to his inability to settle the Kurdish question, to the widespread allegations of corruption levelled at Prime Minister Lieutenant-General Taher Yahya's government, formed on 10 July 1967, to general dislike of UAR influence on Iraq and to popular anger at the economy's stagnation. Many cases of alleged corruption concerned large sums of money received by Iraqis as 'commission' for deals between the Iraq National Oil Company (INOC) and the French state oil company ERAP which had been given a concession to exploit large oil-bearing regions of Iraq.

Following the government's overthrow, it was announced on 28 July that a Revolutionary Command Council (RCC) had taken control of the country. The council consisted of three Ba'thist generals, Major-General Ahmad Hasan al-Bakr, Lieutenant-General Hardan Takriti and Lieutenant-General Saleh Mahdi Ammash and four colonels – Colonel Abd al-Razzak al-Nayef, Lieutenant-Colonel Ibrahim Abd al-Rahman al-Daoud, Colonel Hamad Shehab and Colonel Sa'doun Ghaidan. Foreign observers believed the coup to be a result of a conspiracy between the right wing of the Ba'th Party and a group of young army officers who after the Arab-Israeli war of 1967 had formed a secret organization calling itself the Arab Revolutionary Movement.

27 July South Yemeni dissident forces cut the country's main road. On the following day the government announced that an armed revolt had broken out against it. On 16 May the government had announced that on 20 March it had crushed a revolt led by dissident army elements, and on 26 March it had announced the purging of 150 army officers in the wake of the March attempted coup.

20 August An estimated 200,000 troops of the Warsaw Pact nations invade Czechoslovakia under cover of darkness. On 27 August President Ludvig Svoboda and Communist Party First Secretary Alexander Dubcek returned to Prague where Svoboda was said to have threatened suicide.

31 August Severe earthquakes shake north-east Iran on 31 August and 1 September. The authorities estimated that between 18,000 and 22,000 people had died.

10 September The deposed Imam Muhammad al-Badr of Yemen returns to North Yemen, after two years of exile in Saudi Arabia, in order to resume his command of the royalist forces in preparation for a new offensive against the republicans. On his return, his cousin the Amir Muhammad ibn Husayn took command of the royalist forces around San'a. Reports from Beirut suggested that after the amir's military failure in January the royalist tribes had threatened to defect to the republicans if the imam in person did not return to lead them. At the beginning of September King Faisal of Saudi Arabia was reported to have agreed to subsidize the royalist forces for a further three months but with the stipulation that this was the last such payment he would make to them.

A conflict had developed at the start of 1968 between the republican government headed by General Hasan al-Amri and the left-wing republicans. The latter controlled the Popular Resistance Front (PRF), a para-military organization formed in December 1967 to defend San'a from the royalists. The PRF were believed to be receiving arms and money from South Yemen's ruling party, the National Liberation Front (NLF). The split among the republicans was largely based on a religious divide; the republican government drawing much support from the traditional Shi'i Zaidi Muslim tribes of the North while the left-wingers relied on the Sunni Shafi'is of the South.

2 December Iraqi troops stationed in Jordan shell an Israeli border settlement. On the same day Israeli planes attacked the Jordanian town of Irbid, some 40 miles (64 kilometres) north of Amman. On 3 December the Iraqi troops exchanged artillery fire with the Israelis. Israeli planes again struck targets in Jordan.

13 December Iraq's RCC sets up a Revolutionary Court in Baghdad to try 'spies, agents, enemies of the People, and counter-revolutionaries' shortly before two Iraqis – one a soldier, the other a lawyer – accused of spying for Israel, were subjected to a television trial. In televised 'confessions' the defendants said that the alleged espionage network had been directed from Basra by two Iraqi Jews, and that the US Central Intelligence Agency (CIA) and the Central Treaty Organization (CENTO, of which Baghdad was a member) were implicated. Meanwhile, President al-Baqr promised that 'no spy will live in Iraq' as the press and radio violently attacked the US, Israel, imperialism and Zionism.

On 11 November Dr Nasser al-Hani, a recent foreign minister, and a moderate, was found murdered in Baghdad. The Western press surmised that he had been arrested and murdered by the Ba'th Party's security apparatus. On 18 December it was reported that the former prime minister and foreign minister, Dr Abd al-Rahman al-Bazzaz, and a former defence minister, General Abd al-Aziz Okeili, had been arrested on charges of alleged participation in an 'Israeli-American spy network' and that their property and that of 66 others had been confiscated.

1 9 6 9

27 January Fourteen Iraqis, nine Jews, are publicly hanged in Baghdad after being convicted as 'Israeli spies' in a series of show trials. On 28 January the International Commission of Jurists said that it was 'very perturbed' over the hangings, while on 31 January the Egyptian newspaper *Al Ahram* restricted itself to saying that they should not have been carried out in public.

In December 1968 a special revolutionary court in which no defence lawyers appear to have been allowed, and whose judges were not legally qualified, had been established to try what the court referred to as the 'enemies of the people'. The court was to sit through 1968 and 1969 by the end of which 53 people had been executed, many in public. Some were to be forced to confess their 'crimes' on television.

The trials were seen to be aimed at discouraging opposition to the regime at a time when President al-Baqr and Saddam Husayn (Takriti), a rising star, were emerging to positions of supreme power. Saddam Husayn had, through shrewdness and ruthlessness, risen from virtual obscurity in 1966 to the second most important position in the state apparatus.

Most of Iraq's Jewish community had migrated to Israel in 1948/49, leaving only 3,000 in Iraq.

3 February The Fatah Palestinian commando leader, Yasser Arafat, is elected chairman of the newly formed executive committee of the 11-member Palestine Liberation Organization (PLO). On 6 February the authoritative Egyptian newspaper *Al-Ahram* said that he had announced plans to move a large part of his guerrilla forces from Egypt and Syria to Jordan. In a statement he made after his election at a PLO meeting in Cairo, Arafat pledged to intensify the 'armed revolution in all parts of our Palestinian territory to make of it a war of liberation', adding that 'We reject all political settlements.' A short, bald, highly active man who always wears a black-chequered *kaffiya* (Arab head-dress), Arafat had founded Fatah, the Palestinian commando unit, in 1963. In 1967 he just escaped capture by the Israelis while organizing resistance cells in Jerusalem.

At the time of his election, the PLO was thought to number three battalions made up of 3,800 men in Egypt, 3,000 in Syria and 1,200 attached to an Iraqi division in Jordan. On 13 February Fatah officials had reported in Cairo that the Israeli defence minister, Moshe Dayan, had sent a message to Arafat informing him that he was ready to meet the PLO leader. The officials said that the Israelis had released an Arab prisoner to carry the message to Arafat. On 16 February Arafat and the PLO's Executive Committee conferred in Amman with Jordan's King Husayn. It was believed to be the first meeting between Husayn and a PLO executive chairman.

23 February Former King Saud of Saudi Arabia dies in Greece. Despite a natural aversion to his brother who had virtually bankrupted Saudi Arabia during his time as ruler, King Faisal sent an aircraft to fetch his body and intoned verses from the Qur'an over it before it was interred in an unmarked grave near that of their father, King Abd al-Aziz (Ibn Saud), the founder of modern Saudi Arabia. According to Holden and Johns in *The House of Saud*, Faisal had wanted to disinherit Saud's sons but bowed to opposition from other members of the Al Saud, the Saudi ruling family.

3 March Golda Meir is nominated as Israel's interim prime minister in the wake of the death of Levi Eshkol on 26 February. On 17 March she was sworn in as Israel's fourth prime minister.

17 March Reports indicate that Syria has permitted the stationing of 6,000 Iraqi troops on its territory.

2 April Iran ends diplomatic ties with Lebanon because of its refusal to extradite an Iranian official wanted for alleged corruption.

10 April King Husayn of Jordan proposes a six-point peace plan for the Middle East involving the recognition by Arab countries of the state of Israel. Addressing the National Press Club in Washington, the king proposed that the Arab countries recognize Israel and lift all obstacles to Israeli navigation in the Suez Canal and the Gulf of Aqaba, provided that Israel withdraw from the territories occupied in the Arab-Israeli war of 1967 and accept the 22 November 1967 Resolution 242 of the UN Security Council.

19 April Iran declares void the 1937 agreement granting Iraq control of the Shatt al-Arab waterway on the grounds that Iraq had allegedly violated its provisions for many years. Iraq responded by maintaining that the entire waterway was Iraqi territory, the government describing Iran's action as a 'unilateral action contravening the principles of international law'. In abrogating the treaty, Iran's Foreign Ministry had alleged that Iraq had, for years, unilaterally collected river tolls on the waterway – which runs from the confluence of the Euphrates and Tigris to the head of the Gulf – without giving Iran a share as provided under the treaty. The ministry added that tolls would no longer be paid by Iranian ships to Iraq and that Iranian vessels would no longer comply with an Iraqi requirement that all vessels using the waterway fly the Iraqi flag. On 22 April Iran sent through the waterway several freighters which refused to pay tolls in defiance of Iraqi demands. On 25 April it sent through two more such freighters.

Apparently as a reprisal for Iran's action, Iraq had brutally expelled over 10,000 Iranians living in Iraq by mid-May. On 12 May the Iranian government presented a note to the UN Security Council protesting at the 'arrests, expulsions and tortures' inflicted by the Iraqis on those Iranians who were being expelled.

6 June On 5/6 June the Saudi security forces arrest officers of the army following what they allege to be an armed plot against the monarchy. The alleged plotters' immediate targets were air-force officers based in Jeddah, Riyadh and Dhahran, and the largest proportion arrested were from the squadron of Lockheed C-130 transport aircraft with its headquarters at Jeddah. Those arrested included figures such as Dawood Romahi, the commander of the Dhahran air base.

In June and July at least 60 members of the Saudi air force, army and police and some 60 civilians were to be arrested. Senior officers believed that the plot had been uncovered following a CIA tip-off but with hindsight it seemed unlikely that either the CIA or Britain's MI6 had any foreknowledge of it.

The plot took place against a background of disillusionment among young, educated Saudis. This social group had become disenchanted with the puritan diktat of 'Wahhabism' (more correctly 'Unitarianism', Saudi Arabia's strict Islamic code); the kingdom's slow rate of progress; government inefficiency; and ubiquitous corruption. The newly emergent middle class resented the concentration of wealth in the hands of the princes while many Hejazis resented discrimination in favour of Najdis whom they considered far less sophisticated. (The Hejaz is the kingdom's western region and includes the holy cities of Mecca and Medina as well as the cosmopolitan port of Jeddah. The Najd, whose chief city is the Saudi capital, Riyadh, is the birthplace of the Al-Saud (the 'Saud Family') and 'Wahhabism'.

The Shi'is of the kingdom's Eastern Province, Hasa, desperately poor in the heart of the kingdom's oil-rich region, felt even fiercer resentments. Moreover, petroleum revenues, which made up to 90 per cent of the kingdom's wealth, rose only marginally in 1969 while grants to the key 'frontline states' with Israel, Egypt and Jordan, represented over one-tenth of this revenue. At the same time defence consumed about one-third of the kingdom's budget. A threat was also posed by the kingdom's shadowy Arab Nationalist Movement made up of Marxists and the Ba'th Socialist Party.

22 June The South Yemeni president, Qahtan al-Sha'bi, is overthrown in a bloodless coup. President Sha'bi had been South Yemen's president since independence in November 1967. His functions were taken over by a five-man presidential council. Reports indicated that the situation in the South Yemeni capital, Aden, was normal and that although Sha'bi was confined to his house, he was under no further restrictions. His ousting was the culmination of a power struggle between moderate and left-wing factions within the ruling National Liberation Front (NLF), which had resulted in victory for the left-wingers.

Six days before his overthrow, President Sha'bi had dismissed his interior minister, Muhammad Ali Haithem, who enjoyed considerable army and security forces support. The dismissal led to four days of intense discussions within the 41-member Supreme General Command of the NLF, ending with the president's 'resignation' and a victory for Haithem's faction. Haithem became a member of the new five-member presidential council. Among other things the new presidential council announced that relations with the socialist block, and particularly with the Soviet Union, would be a 'guiding principle' of the new government.

1 September The Libyan military ousts the monarchy and proclaims a republic. A group of revolutionary army officers led by a 28-year-old sulbaltern named Mu'ammar al-Qadhafi, seized power in Tripoli while King Idris, the 70-year-old monarch, was in Istanbul. Although a spokesman for the royal family said that the coup was of 'no importance', Crown Prince Hasan Rida broadcast from Libya the renunciation of his title and his support for the new regime. The officers proclaimed a republic in the name of 'freedom, socialism and unity' dedicated to the struggle against colonialism. Qadhafi was to become Libya's formal prime minister on 16 January 1970.

22 September An Islamic summit conference, hosted by Saudi Arabia and Morocco, opens in Rabat to discuss the fire at Jerusalem's Al-Aksa Mosque on 21 August. The fire, started by a 28-year-old gentile Australian and Christian fundamentalist, Denis Michael Rohan, caused considerable damage, destroying, among other things, a twelfth-century cedarwood *minbar* (pulpit) given by Salah ad-Din (Saladdin). The mosque is Islam's third most holy shrine after the great mosques of Mecca and Medina.

Built on the site where the Caliph Omar was said to have prayed after the Arab conquest of Jerusalem in AD 636, the mosque forms part of the Old City of Jerusalem's *Haram al-sharif* (sacred precinct), known by Jews as the Temple Mount. The media in Amman, Baghdad, Damascus, Cairo and other capitals denounced Israel as responsible for the fire and called for a *jihad* (holy struggle) against Israel. As firemen doused the flames, Palestinians in Jerusalem chanted 'Death to Israel' and praised Fatah, the Palestinian commando organization. In consequence, the Israeli authorities imposed a day-long curfew in the vicinity of the shrine.

Following the fire, Arab leaders called an Islamic conference to discuss the protection of holy places under Israeli occupation. When the conference ended on 25 September, it adopted a resolution which was essentially a recapitulation of UN resolutions on the status of Jerusalem and on other Middle East issues. The resolution's preamble said 'The painful events of August 21, 1969, which, because of the fire, caused extensive damage to the sacred Al Aksa mosque, threw into the deepest anguish more than 600,000,000 Muslims all over the world.'

29 November Reports reveal that Saudi Arabian and South Yemeni forces have clashed in recent weeks. On 1 December their two air forces fought along the border between the two countries. On 9 November Saudi Arabia had reportedly authorized its forces to cross into South Yemeni territory to fight the forces of its southern neighbour.

18 December The United Arab Republic (UAR) president, Gamal abd al-Nasser, and Saudi Arabia's King Faisal meet in Cairo. However, on 23 December Nasser walked out of the Moroccan conference of Arab leaders because of Saudi Arabia's refusal to increase its financial support to Arab armies (of which the most important was the UAR's). On 24 December Arab leaders left the Moroccan capital, Rabat, as talks collapsed.

1 9 7 0

7 January Iraq, Egypt (United Arab Republic –UAR), Libya and Algeria sign an agreement to co-operate in oil policies, including dealing with foreign companies. On 22 May Algerian, Libyan and Iraqi cabinet ministers met in Algiers to sign an accord for co-operation in the oil industry.

21 January Baghdad radio announces that a plot to overthrow the regime had been crushed on the previous night and that the conspirators had been arrested. The plot was generally thought to have been the work of right-wing, pro-Western groups within the armed forces who were opposed to the government's increasingly pro-Communist policies, as well as to its plans for a peaceful settlement with Iraq's large and volatile Kurdish minority in the north.

According to the Iraqis, the Third Secretary at the Iranian embassy in Baghdad, Daoud Taher, first communicated with the conspirators on 15 April 1969. Then, on 28 September a representative of the Iranian government made further contact with them at the Iranian embassy in Kuwait. After this meeting, the Iraqi authorities claimed that 3,000 submachine guns, 650,000 rounds of ammunition and two mobile radio transmitters had been supplied to the rebels by the Iranian government. Moreover, they claimed secret correspondence between the alleged plot leader, Major-General Abd al-Ghani al-Rawi, and the conspirators had been transmitted through the Iranian embassy in Baghdad. According to Britain's *Guardian* newspaper, a loyal Iraqi officer had infiltrated the group and helped to bring into the plot officers who were faithful to the regime, as well as officers the government wished to test.

On the night of 20 January (the night of the proposed coup) the 300 officers involved in the plot were driven, unarmed, from the Rashid military camp to the Presidential Palace. Their arms, they were assured, had been sent on ahead. Once in the palace they were surrounded by troops and seized.

On the following day a special court was set up and between 21 and 24 January four batches of conspirators were tried before it. Those sentenced to death were executed immediately and altogether 44 men were executed. According to newspaper sources, this brought the total number of people executed in Iraq since January 1969 on conspiracy or espionage charges to 98.

On 22 January the Iranian ambassador to Iraq, Dr Izzatalla al-Amili, and four members of his staff were ordered to leave Baghdad within 24 hours. The staff of the Iranian consulates in Baghdad, Basra and Kerbela were expelled at the same time. An Iranian diplomatic note of 28 January alleged that the Second Secretary at the Iranian embassy in Baghdad, Abd al-Khaliq Bushehri Zadeh, had been kidnapped and tortured. On his release, Zadeh claimed that he had been seized at gunpoint on the street on 20 January, blindfolded and taken to the vice-president's office where he was questioned in the presence of the vice-president and General Teymour Bakhtiar.

Bakhtiar, Iran's former army security chief, had been exiled by the shah in 1962, and was reported in September 1969 to have set up his headquarters in Baghdad and to have begun recruiting volunteers to form an armed underground movement to overthrow the shah. He had been sentenced to death in absentia on 22 September.

11 March Iraq agrees to grant the Kurdish people autonomy in a manifesto which, observers believe, aims at giving the Ba'th Party enough confidence to resume its verbal and physical attacks on the Iraqi Communists. On 23 March the body of Muhammad Ahmad al-Khadri, a prominent Baghdad Communist, was found in the street.

Following the suppression of the January plot against the regime, on 24 January the Revolutionary Command Council (RCC) issued a decree reaffirming its support for the 1966 agreement and its desire to settle the Kurdish question peacefully.

14 May The Iranian Majlis (lower house) ratifies the UN endorsement of Bahrain's independence by 186 votes to 4, and on 18 May the Senate ratified it unanimously. Iran thereby renounced all its historic claims to the islands. Bahrain had refused to order a formal plebiscite on the issue but had agreed to Britain's proposal to take note of Bahraini public opinion under UN auspices. On 30 March, therefore, the UN secretary-general's personal representative and director-general of the UN office in Geneva, Vittorio Winspeare Guicciardi, arrived in Bahrain where he conferred on the issue until his departure on 18 April. On 2 May he had told the UN: 'My conclusions have convinced me that the overwhelming majority of the people of Bahrain wish to gain recognition of their identity in a fully independent and sovereign state free to decide for itself its relations with other states.'

23 May Royalists are admitted to North Yemen's presidential council and cabinet, following their peace agreement with the republicans which represented the end of the Yemeni civil war. Some 30 leading royalists returned to North Yemen on 23 May after eight years of exile in Saudi Arabia. On the same day it was announced that Ahmad Ben Muhammad al-Shami (the royalist government-in-exile's foreign minister) and Muhammad Nu'man had been appointed to the presidential council and that four royalists had entered the government. It was also announced that 12 former royalists had been nominated to the Consultative National Assembly which had been increased from 45 to 68 members.

It was thought that negotiations for an end to the civil war had been initiated by Saudi Arabia in its desire to balance its reasonable relations with North Yemen with its hostile relationship with Marxist South Yemen (the PRSY). The agreement seems to have involved the appointment of royalists to administrative and diplomatic posts in exchange for an agreement from them that Imam Muhammad al-Badr and members of his family would not be allowed to return.

23 July Sultan Said ibn Teymour, the 60-year-old ruler of Muscat and Oman, is overthrown by his son Sultan Qaboos ibn Said in a palace coup masterminded by the British Foreign Office. On 10 August the new Sultan Qaboos changed the name of the country from the Sultanate of Muscat and Oman to the Sultanate of Oman to stress the nation's unity.   With the apparent support of local tribesmen, the coup took place in the Dhofari capital of Salalah from where the cloistered Sultan Said ruled. The sultan was slightly wounded during the coup and on the following day was flown to Bahrain for immediate medical treatment and thence by a British air-force plane to London, where he was admitted to hospital on 26 July.

Sultan Qaboos, whom the British government formally recognized as ruler on 29 July, issued a proclamation on 26 July saying that he had 'watched with growing dismay and anger the inability of my father to use the new-found wealth of his country for the needs of his people' and for this reason he had taken control. He promised to set up a modern and forceful government as quickly as possible. He had taken over a nation which had only 12 hospital beds, seven miles (11 kilometres) of asphalt roads and three primary schools. Under his father's lugubrious rule, radios and spectacles had been banned, civilians were forbidden to drive cars and a curfew was imposed in Muscat every night.

Britain signed a treaty of protection with the then sultan in 1798 and Britain's subsequent domination of Oman was not challenged even by the US which had signed a treaty of commerce and friendship in 1834, although it was to close its legation in 1915. In 1932 Britain deposed Sultan Teymour in favour of his son, Said, whom it supported totally in 1951 in his dispute with Saudi Arabia over the Buraimi oasis, and in 1954 when Britain helped him quell an internal rebellion by the Imam Ghalib ibn Ali. After the sultan retired to his palace in Salalah, British civil servants virtually ran Oman's administration.

31 July A spokesman for the Iraqi RCC announces Iraq's 'categorical rejection of all plans aimed at liquidating the Palestine cause and the rights of the Palestinian people to return to their own land, particularly the latest American proposals'. Baghdad was referring to a recent US peace plan which the Egyptian president, Gamal abd al-Nasser, had accepted in a speech on 24 July. Responding to attacks on his acceptance by Baghdad radio on 2 August Nasser delivered a message to the Iraqi president by Cairo radio, saying he sometimes wondered 'why your forces on the [eastern] front never receive an order to clash with the enemy, why your planes never raid his positions, and why the enemy never opens fire against your forces or sends his warplanes against them'. Clearly addressing the Iraqi criticisms, the Cairo daily newspaper *Al Akhbar* commented on 28 July on 'those who talk but don't fight ... who raise their voices but never their weapons ... who talk about the front but keep away from it'.

August General Teymour Bakhtiar, the founder of Iran's secret police, the Organization of National Security and Intelligence (SAVAK), and a relative of Queen Soraya, is murdered on a hunting expedition in Iraq. On a flight out of Tehran, two men, bandying pistols, hijacked the plane on which they were passengers, forcing it to land in Baghdad. They claimed that they wanted to join Bakhtiar's ongoing fight against the shah. Bakhtiar welcomed them and some days later they all went off hunting in an area of Iraq some 20 miles (32 kilometres) from the Iranian border. There one of the hunters shot Bakhtiar through the back. The hunters then fled to Iran.

SAVAK was created in 1957 with US help, and Bakhtiar became its first chief. He built up massive dossiers of leading figures and when it became clear that Queen Soraya would not bear a son, he was even reputed to have nursed dreams of power. He was popular with the US and deeply feared by Iranians. Despite his charm and dapper dressing, he was said to enjoy watching the torture that was SAVAK's regular method of obtaining information.

28 September President Gamal abd al-Nasser of Egypt dies, aged 52. Nasser had been president of Egypt since 1954 and of the UAR since 1958. After the devastating defeat of the Arabs by the Israelis in the June 1967 war, his health had deteriorated and he had paid repeated visits to the Soviet Union for medical treatment. On 15 October, in a nationwide plebiscite, Anwar Sadat was elected president to succeed Nasser.

15 October The Iraqi vice-president and air corps chief air marshal, Hardan Takriti, is stripped of all power by Iraq's RCC. Meanwhile, on 21 October an estimated 12,000 Iraqi troops, stationed in Jordan since the Arab-Israeli war of June 1967, began to withdraw.

13 November Right-wing army officers led by the defence minister, Hafez al-Asad, seize control of the Syrian government. On 19 November Asad was named president. On 27 November Syria agreed to join the proposed federation with Egypt, and on 13 December Syria, Egypt, Libya and Sudan signed an accord placing their armies under joint command.

26–28 December The second conference of foreign ministers of Islamic countries meets in Karachi. The conference was represented by 22 countries including Iran, Kuwait, Lebanon, Libya, Morocco, Saudi Arabia, Somalia, Tunisia, Turkey, the UAR (Egypt) and North Yemen. The secretary-general of the Arab League and a representative of the Palestine Liberation Organization (PLO) were also present as observers. Iraq, Sudan, Syria and South Yemen boycotted the conference and Shaikh Zayed, the ruler of Abu Dhabi, who wished to attend as an observer, was refused on the grounds that Abu Dhabi was not yet independent of British control after the Iranian delegate had complained on these grounds.

Among other resolutions the conference agreed to condemn the Israeli occupation of Sinai, the West Bank and the Golan Heights, to restore 'the people of Palestine to their rightful homeland' and to denounce Zionism as 'a racial, aggressive and expansionist movement . . . constituting a permanent threat to world peace'. The conference also instructed the UAR to make a study for proposals to establish an Islamic bank, and agreed in principle to establish an Islamic international news agency.

1 9 7 1

29 January The Trans-Arabian Pipeline (Tapline) is reopened after a 270-day closure. The closure was thought to have entailed the loss to consumer countries of about 130 million barrels of oil and nearly $35 million in fees to the four countries – Saudi Arabia, Jordan, Syria and Lebanon – through which it passed. Beirut sources said that total additional charges incurred by Tapline in all four countries would raise the cost of pumping Saudi crude to the Mediterranean by about 10 cents a barrel.

The pipeline had been closed since 3 May 1970 when, according to the Syrians, it was breached by a bulldozer. However, political differences between Saudi Arabia and Syria – as well as Syria's need for higher fees – hampered efforts to repair the line. The more moderate policies of the Hafez al-Asad government which came to power in Syria in November 1970 were thought to have induced the Tapline company to renew its efforts to have the line reopened. The pipeline's maximum capacity was then 480,000 barrels a day.

10 February The Kurdish Revolutionary Party (KRP) announces that it has dissolved all its organizations and merged with the Kurdish Democratic Party (KDP) led by Mulla Mustafa Barzani in order to strengthen Kurdish unity. At a meeting in December 1970 the KRP had decided on a united Kurdish movement.

The KRP was formed in 1964 under the leadership of Jalal Talabani and Ibrahim Ahmad after a split had developed within the KDP in which Ahmad had been secretary-general and Talabani a politburo member. According to Barzani, members of Talabani's group made an attempt on his son's life in December 1970.

On 2 February the Iraqi news agency had reported that Mahmoud Uthman, a spokesman for the KDP, had said that regular meetings were being held between the KDP and Iraq's ruling Ba'th Party on the implementation of the 11 March 1970 declaration which had (in principle, if not in fact) ended the war with the Kurds.

14 February The Tehran producer-consumer conference boosts Gulf oil revenues. A five-year agreement between six Gulf oil-producing countries and 23 international oil companies was announced in Tehran on 14 February. The producing countries, all Organization of Petroleum Exporting Countries (OPEC) members, were Abu Dhabi, Iran, Iraq, Kuwait, Qatar and Saudi Arabia. The oil companies announced on the same day that the agreement established security of supply, and stability in financial arrangements, for the five-year period 1971–75, and would yield the Gulf states concerned an estimated additional revenue of over $1,200 million in 1971, rising to about $3,000 million in 1975.

The agreement also established at 55 per cent the tax rate for Gulf exports of crude oil whose posted prices were uniformly increased at Gulf terminals by 35 cents a barrel, including 2 cents a barrel in settlement of freight disparities. There was also to be a new system of gravity differentials. To deal with inflation, posted prices were to be raised by 2.5 per cent on 1 June 1971 and on the first day of each of the years from 1973 to 1975. In addition the companies would increase the crude posted price by 5 cents a barrel on 1 June 1971. Thereafter, an increase of 5 cents per barrel would be added on 1 January in each of the years from 1973 to 1975, to reflect increasing demand for crude oil during the agreement. The chief negotiator on the consumer side was British Petroleum's (BP's) Lord Strathalmond and on the producers' side the Iranian finance minister, Jamshid Amouzegar.

3 March Commenting on a statement made by the British foreign secretary, Sir Alec Douglas-Home, on British policy towards the Gulf, an Iraqi foreign ministry spokesman said that 'the Arabian Gulf and Arab emirates are Arab territory, and guaranteeing the sovereignty of that territory is an Arab responsibility'. He added that 'Iraq demands that British withdrawal from that area and the liquidation of the imperialist presence should be complete.'

On 1 March Douglas-Home had told the House of Commons (lower house) that Britain offered the Arab emirates of the Gulf a treaty of friendship to replace the existing defence treaties which would cease to operate by the end of 1971. The only immediate Gulf reaction came from Shaikh Rashid of Dubai who told the London *Times* on 3 March that he regarded the withdrawal of British forces by 1971 as a 'disappointment'. Nevertheless, he said that he believed that a Gulf federation could be formed if it embraced the Trucial States and Qatar but omitted Bahrain.

On 3 March the Kuwaiti deputy foreign minister welcomed Britain's announcement, but on the same day an Iraqi foreign ministry spokesman added an acid note, saying that the emirates should 'steer clear of foreign military alliances and protection'. Complete responsibility for the area should be 'handed over to its people' and Britain should withdraw 'not only from the north but also from the south of the Gulf'.

On 11 March the rulers of Abu Dhabi, Dubai and Qatar were reported to be holding 'informal but crucial' talks in Dubai on the projected union.

On the same day the Iranian foreign minister, Ardeshir Zahedi, said ominously that he hoped the British government would 'hand over' the islands of Abu Musa and the two Tunb islands. On 17 February the shah was reported to have threatened to take them over 'by force if necessary', Iran's policy being 'indisputable ownership of the islands'. Britain regarded Abu Musa as Sharjah's property and the Greater and Lesser Tunbs as Ras al-Khaimah's.

One of the factors which caused the breakdown of the meeting in October 1970 of deputy rulers of the nine states involved in the Gulf federation plan was Bahrain's insistence that members of the proposed federal assembly should be elected by universal suffrage, on the grounds that the increasing political development of Bahrainis made this essential.

4 March The Kuwaiti government agrees to resume its $45-million annual subsidy to Jordan. However, on 5 March and again on 9 March the *Kuwait Daily News* said that it had learnt from reliable sources that there was no question of the aid being renewed until an assurance had been received from Bahi Ladgham, chairman of the Arab Supreme Follow-up Committee, that fighting between the Jordanian government and Palestinian commandos had ceased. The subsidy had been withdrawn in September 1970 when Jordanian and Palestinian forces commando clashed, restored in December and suspended again in January 1971 when Jordanian forces came into conflict with the guerrillas once again.

12 March General Hafez al-Asad, who seized power on 13 November 1970, is approved by national plebiscite as president of Syria. On 16 March Syria and Egypt formed a joint military command. On 7 January the new president had stressed the importance of confidence between the Syrian people and the regime and described freedom of the citizen and respect for the dignity of the individual as 'essential human values'.

22 March Mainland ('Red') China and Kuwait establish diplomatic relations. On 13 March the US State Department had reported that China had established a military mission in South Yemen in what was clearly an increasing involvement in the Arab world. On 7 February London's *Sunday Times* had reported that 'Chinese ships carrying men and supplies are arriving regularly in Aden ... With loans totalling £23 million and welfare and economic aid programmes, Peking is vigorously challenging Soviet influence in the area. About 300 miles [483 kilometres] of roads and bridges and textile works are being built under Chinese direction. Peking also delivers medical supplies for use by Chinese doctors in Aden's new hospital.'

According to the Chinese news agency, Hsinhua, Chinese exports to the Arab world totalled about $200 million in 1970 and aid to the Arab world, estimated at about $212 million 'during the last decade', now accounted for about 26 per cent of total Chinese foreign aid.

30 March The former Iraqi vice-president, Air-Marshal Hardan Takriti, is assassinated in Kuwait. Takriti, who had been relieved of all his posts and exiled to Algeria in October 1970, was shot as he stepped from the car of the Iraqi ambassador to Kuwait, Midhat Ibrahim Jum'a, to enter a hospital. Jum'a was beside him but was not hurt. Takriti's body was flown to Iraq, and on the following day his funeral was held in Takrit, north of Baghdad. Reuter reported from Kuwait on 31 March that five men had been arrested as suspects. An Iraqi security team arrived on the night of 30 March to help in investigations.

In July 1968 Takriti had been able to exploit his popularity with the army and air force to win their support for a coup which brought the Ba'th Party back to power. He was then given the posts of army chief-of-staff, defence minister and deputy prime minister. In April 1970 he was appointed one of Iraq's two vice-presidents. His dismissal and exile in October 1970 was attributed to his opposition to using the 12,000 Iraqi troops stationed in Jordan to support the Palestinian commandos in Jordan's civil war in September. He was said to have clashed with his cousin Saddam Husayn (Takriti), the regime's strongman and the leader of the Ba'th Party's civilian faction, who may have wanted to weaken the military group by ousting his cousin.

17 April Egypt, Syria and Libya announce the formation of the Union of Arab Republics, a federation that would have to be approved by plebiscites in each country.

5 June Britain's special envoy to the Gulf region had told the rulers of Sharjah and Ras al-Khaimah that Iran will occupy 'by force if necessary' the island of Abu Musa and the Tunbs by the end of 1971. Quoting 'well-informed sources', the Kuwait daily newspaper *Al-Khalij* (The Gulf) said that Sir William Luce had advised the rulers to negotiate with Iran which was willing to offer compensation for the islands' inhabitants plus a percentage of oil revenues from offshore drilling. The two rulers told Luce that although they did not have the military power to defend the islands they considered them Arab territory and felt responsible for their defence.

On 11 March the Iranian foreign minister, Ardeshir Zahedi, had said ominously that he hoped the British government would 'hand over' the islands. On 17 February the shah was reported to have threatened to take them over 'by force if necessary', Iran's policy being 'indisputable ownership of the islands'. Britain regarded Abu Musa as Sharjah's property and the Greater and Lesser Tunbs as Ras al-Khaimah's but, it appears, was unwilling to defend them on behalf of its allies.

6 June The South Yemeni premier, Muhammad Ali Haithem, announces his support for Gulf revolutions. He said in an interview with the Aden news agency that South Yemen would always support the armed revolution led by the Popular Front for the Liberation of the Occupied Arabian Gulf (PFLOAG). Clearly referring to the proposed federation of the Trucial States, Bahrain and Qatar, he denounced conspiracies 'to break up the Gulf area into tribal entities, subject to Saudi and Iranian influences, through the establishment of false federations without the consent of the Arab people of the Gulf'.

By the second half of June there was increasing speculation that despite the efforts of Kuwait and Saudi Arabia to accelerate the establishment of the Federation of Arab Emirates and the UAR's (Egypt's) support for its formation, Bahrain and Qatar would remain outside it.

10 June Iran's ruling Iran Novin Party retains control of both houses in parliamentary elections.

26 June Saudi Arabia's King Faisal and UAR President Sadat end a week of talks aimed at strengthening Arab unity against Israel. The two leaders also met the PLO chairman, Yasser Arafat. In a joint communiqué on 26 June they recorded their agreement on 'the seriousness of the present stage' and gave warning of the 'ferocity' of the coming battle with Israel. Their communiqué ended: 'There will be no peace in the Middle East until Jerusalem and other occupied Arab territories are liberated and the Palestinian people recover their usurped rights.'

5 July The British ambassador in Baghdad, H.G. Balfour-Paul, is informed that two members of his staff must leave the country for spying. According to the Iraqi news agency, Wing-Commander Hugh Harrison, acting defence attaché, and George Rolleston, a First Secretary, had 'been connected . . . with a spy ring and had engaged in a plot to overthrow the regime'. On 6 July Roderick Clube, First Secretary for economic affairs, was given 24 hours to leave the country on the grounds that he was also involved. On 8 July Britain gave three members of the Iraqi embassy in London a week to leave Britain.

18 July It is announced that Iraq has decided to close its borders with Jordan to both road and air traffic and has asked Jordan to withdraw its ambassador from Baghdad because of the renewed fighting between government forces and Palestinian commandos. In a memorandum sent to the Arab League secretary-general on 20 July, Iraq called for Jordan's expulsion from the League. In a statement on 19 July the Jordanian prime minister, Wasfi al-Tall, had said that during the previous week's fighting about 2,300 out of an estimated 2,500 Palestinian guerrillas had been killed and that they had lost all their bases. He concluded that Jordan was now 'free of guerrillas'. On 13 July the Jordanian army had opened an all-out attack on Palestinian commandos based in northern Jordan.

On 2 June Jordan's King Husayn had at last ordered a final crackdown on Palestinian guerrillas whom he saw as a serious threat to his regime. On 13 January Lebanese press reports that Saudi troops stationed in Jordan had supported the Jordanian army in clashes with Palestinian guerrillas, were strongly denied by a Saudi embassy spokesman in Beirut.

He said that such 'baseless rumours' could 'only serve the Israeli enemy and its schemes directed against the Arab nation'.

On 30 March King Husayn had called upon 13 Arab heads of state to meet in Amman and witness the devastation caused by Palestinian commando attacks. On 6 April the Jordanian army and Palestinian commandos clashed for the second time in two weeks, in Amman and around Irbid. On 7 July the US defence secretary, Melvin Laird, announced plans to increase US military aid to Jordan.

On 9 July the Jordanians and Palestinians had reached an agreement to end the latest round of fighting. The peace was to be shortlived although on 13 August Saudi Arabia and Egypt did launch efforts to mediate.

18 July Abu Dhabi establishes a $160-million fund to provide economic aid to other Arab countries.

14 August Bahrain's ruler, Shaikh Isa ibn Salman al-Khalifa, announces Bahrain's independence. He said that since plans for a nine-emirate federation had come to nothing, Bahrain had decided to end all her treaties with Britain, declare Bahrain a sovereign independent state with the right to conduct its own foreign affairs, apply at once for membership of the UN and the Arab League and ask Arab, Islamic and other friendly nations to recognize Bahrain as a free and sovereign Arab state.

In London the Foreign Office welcomed Shaikh Isa's declaration and on 15 August Britain signed a treaty of friendship with the new state. Under a decree issued on the same day the ruler's title was changed to that of amir. The 'British political agency' became the 'British embassy' and it was announced that the British political agent, Alec Stirling, would soon be given ambassadorial rank. The British political resident, Sir Geoffrey Sarthur, would stay in Bahrain until British forces were finally withdrawn from the Gulf at the end of the year.

On 14 August the UAR formally recognized Bahrain as an independent state, and on the same day messages of congratulation were received from King Husayn of Jordan, President Bakr of Iraq and the Shah of Iran. On 15 August similar messages were received from King Faisal of Saudi Arabia and the amir of Kuwait. A bad note was struck, however, by South Yemen who said that the 'fake independence of Bahrain' was 'no more than the implementation of an imperialist and reactionary plan prepared in agreement with the British government, the United States and reactionary quarters in the area'.

1 September Qatar proclaims itself independent. A statement by the ruler, Shaikh Ahmad ibn Ali al-Thani, and broadcast by the prime minister, Shaikh Khalifa ibn Hamad al-Thani, said that Qatar had decided to end its contractual relationship with Britain and all agreements pertaining to it and to seek immediate membership of the Arab League and the UN.

Nevertheless, the statement added that a nine-emirate federation (with the Trucial States and Bahrain) still presented the best means of strengthening 'close brotherly ties' between the nine states and other countries in 'the greater Arab homeland' as well as the strongest guarantee of stability in the Gulf region.

On 3 September Qatar signed a treaty of friendship with Britain in Geneva. The British Political Resident in the Persian Gulf, Sir Geoffrey Arthur, exchanged notes ending Britain's former treaty relations with Qatar, which dated back to 1916, before signing the new agreement. The new treaty did not involve any military commitment by Britain but provided for consultation on defence where the need arose.

On 4 September Shaikh Ahmad changed his title from ruler to amir. In a separate decree he announced the establishment of a foreign ministry and the appointment of Prime

Minister Shaikh Khalifa as foreign minister. On 6 September the British ambassador, Edward Henderson, presented his credentials to the prime minister in the absence of the amir. On 7 September Qatar applied for membership of the UN.

Of the Arab states, South Yemen was the only state to voice opposition to Qatar's admittance by the Arab League, maintaining that both Qatar and Bahrain were still dominated by 'political and military colonialism'. The PFLOAG called the League's decision a means of consolidating 'the frail entities set up by Britain in the territory of the Gulf'.

2 September The UAR, which has been Egypt's official name since its abortive union with Syria in 1958, becomes the Arab Republic of Egypt (ARE) under a constitutional proclamation. The proclamation was made a day after a referendum in Egypt had approved the country's membership of the Federation of Arab Republics. On 20 August the leaders of Syria, the UAR and Libya had signed a constitution for the proposed Federation of Arab Republics.

On 1 September voters in all three countries 'agreed overwhelmingly' to approve the Federation. According to the Egyptian minister of the interior, Mamdouh Salem, 99.98 per cent of Egypt's population voted in favour. On 4 October Egypt's President Sadat was selected as the Federation's first president.

8 September Tapline, the pipeline from Saudi Arabia to Lebanon, is damaged in Jordan in an explosion caused by Palestinian guerrillas from Syria, according to Jordanian government sources. Tapline, which carried 475,000 barrels a day of crude oil from Saudi Arabia through Jordan and Syria to Lebanon's Zahrani refinery, had already been breached four times since the 1967 Arab-Israeli war.

12–16 October A week of parades, ceremonies and festivities in Iranian cities celebrates the 2,500th anniversary of the foundation of the Persian empire and monarchy by Cyrus the Great. Iran's ancient capital, Persepolis, 30 miles (48 kilometres) from Shiraz, was the focus of the festivities which attracted one of the largest gatherings of heads of state ever assembled.

The celebrations were inaugurated by the shah in the presence of Empress Farah, the 11-year-old Prince Reza, members of the government, many guests and some 2,000 troops. About 40 heads of state were present at the 15 October celebrations as guests of the empress. They included kings, queens, sultans, shaikhs and amirs. Among them were the Duke of Edinburgh and Princess Anne representing Queen Elizabeth of Britain. On the evening of 15 October a banquet was held in the 'tent city' of Persepolis at which the toast of the Persian empire was proposed by the shah, with the emperor of Ethiopia, Haile Selassie, replying on behalf of the guests.

4 November Iranian interior ministry officials say that more than 6,000 Iranians have been expelled from Iraq in the past five weeks. The officials were speaking to journalists at a 650-tent camp established at the Iranian town of Borujerd near the Iraqi border to provide temporary shelter for the refugees. Some of them complained that they had been tortured and had had their property confiscated by the Iraqi security authorities.

The officials told reporters that 33,000 Iranians had been ordered out of Iraq since 1969 when the dispute over navigation rights in the Shatt al-Arab waterway, separating the two countries, had arisen. However, on 26 October the Iraqi interior minister, Lieutenant-General Sa'doun Ghaidan, had denied that Iraq was 'undertaking a collective deportation of Iranians and Kurds of Iranian origin'.

119

26 November In Jeddah, Saudi Arabian, Jordanian and Palestinian commando delegates fail to come to an understanding in a meeting aimed at resolving their differences.

28 November In Cairo Jordan's Premier Wasfi al-Tall is shot dead by three Palestinian gunmen apparently belonging to a secret association called the Black September Organization. In an interview on 29 November one of the guerrillas, Munzer Sulaiman Khalifa (who was acknowledged to have drunk some of Tall's blood), said that the assassination was in retaliation for the killing of Palestinians in Jordan. 'Nobody,' he said, 'who has caused harm to the Palestine cause anywhere in the Arab world . . . will escape unpunished.'

30 November Iran occupies the Greater and Lesser Tunb islands without any agreement with the ruler of Ras al-Khaimah, Shaikh Saqr. Ras al-Khaimah police resisted the invasion and four of them as well as three Iranian soldiers were reportedly killed in the attack. Shaikh Saqr promptly complained to the Arab League and the British government about the invasion.

On the previous day the ruler of Sharjah, Shaikh Khaled, announced that he had reached agreement with Iran over the disputed island of Abu Musa. According to the agreement, Iranian forces would be stationed in certain parts of Abu Musa and have full jurisdiction over these areas but the rest of the island would remain under Sharjah's jurisdiction and flag. Both Sharjah and Iran recognized a 12-mile (19-kilometre) territorial waters limit and it was agreed that the US company Buttes Oil and Gas would continue to explore for oil onshore and offshore. Revenue from the operations would be divided equally between Sharjah and Iran, and Iran would give Sharjah £1.5 million a year until the emirate's annual receipts from oil totalled £3 million. In accordance with the agreement, Iranian troops landed on Abu Musa on 30 November.

On the same day Baghdad radio announced that Iraq had decided to break off diplomatic relations with Britain and Iran because of Iran's 'flagrant aggression, in collusion with Britain' against the Greater and Lesser Tunb islands. Baghdad radio reported on 5 December that the Iraqi Foreign Ministry had ordered the British ambassador, H.G. Balfour-Paul, and the chargé d'affaires at the Iranian embassy, to leave Baghdad by 12 December, and their respective staffs to leave by 16 December.

2 December The United Arab Emirates (UAE) (Abu Dhabi, Ajman, Dubai, Fujairah, Sharjah and Umm al-Qaiwain, all the Trucial States except Ras al-Khaimah) is proclaimed a free and sovereign state at a meeting of its six rulers in Dubai. Shaikh Saqr of Ras al-Khaimah was present at the ceremony. The ruler of Abu Dhabi, Shaikh Zayed, was elected president and the ruler of Dubai, Shaikh Rashid, vice-president, both for an initial five years. Shaikh Rashid's son and heir, Shaikh Maktoum, was appointed the UAE's first prime minister.

The first cabinet was formed on 9 December. The new UAE had an area of about 15,400 square miles (40,000 square kilometres) and a population of about 250,000. On 2 December a treaty of friendship between the UAE and Britain was signed by Shaikh Zayed and by the British political resident in the Gulf region, Sir Geoffrey Arthur.

The UAE was accepted as the eighteenth member of the Arab League at an emergency session which had been convened at the request of Iraq, Syria and Ras al-Khaimah on 6 December to discuss Iran's occupation of the the three Gulf islands. On 8 December the UAE's application for UN membership was approved unanimously by the UN Security Council and agreed by the UN General Assembly on the following day. The only hostile voice was that of South Yemen. On 10 December the UAE took its seat as the 132nd UN member. On 6 December Britain's first ambassador to the UAE, Charles Treadwell, had presented his credentials to Shaikh Zayed.

2 December The amir of Ras al-Khaimah, Shaikh Saqr, appeals to Arab states to force Iran off the Greater and Lesser Tunb islands which it had seized on 30 November. Shaikh Saqr appealed to Libya and Kuwait to repel the Iranian forces that had occupied the islands. Although Shaikh Saqr's messages to Libya and Kuwait were the only ones recorded, it was understood that he had written in similar terms to the leaders of all the Arab League states.

On 10 December his son and heir, Shaikh Khaled ibn Saqr, arrived in Benghazi where he told journalists that he had come to 'explain the situation regarding Iran's occupation of the Arab islands . . . and to ask fraternal Libya to back and support us'. On 8 December Libyan radio quoted the Libyan premier, Major Abd al-Salam Jaloud, as saying in a newspaper interview 'The Libyan Arab republic asked permission from the Iraqi authorities to land airborne forces at Basra Airport, preparatory to moving them to the islands. The Iraqi authorities approved Libya's application, but some in the Gulf refused.' He continued, 'Iran's ambition will not end with the occupation of the three islands. It plans to take control of the entire Gulf.'

On 7 December Libya had nationalized all holdings of BP for its alleged complicity in Iran's seizure of the islands.

9 December The former Egyptian vice-president, Aly Sabry, and three others are sentenced to death in Cairo for attempting to overthrow Egypt's President Sadat in May. The sentences were immediately commuted to life imprisonment by Sadat.

27 December Delegates from 18 members of the Arab League hold talks in Cairo in an effort to co-ordinate their military and economic attacks on Israel.

30 December 60,000 'Iranians' are deported from Iraq. It was reported that Iraq had expelled a further 60,000 Iranians from its territory over the past few days and that these included women and children. The reports added that convoys of buses had taken them in freezing conditions to the border and left them there. In a speech on 31 December the deputy chairman of the RCC, Saddam Husayn (Takriti), said that Iraq was deporting all aliens who had entered Iraq illegally.

---

1 9 7 2

---

1 January Sultan Qaboos of Oman announces that the prime minister, Tariq ibn Teymour, has resigned due to ill-health and that the sultan has taken over the premiership. Unconfirmed reports suggested differences between the two men over recent months. However, on 31 January the sultan was reported to have asked for ibn Teymour's return to Oman from abroad.

3 January Kuwait decrees that health care for all citizens and foreign residents in Kuwait will be free. Under a decree published on 23 December 1971, free health care was similarly available to all in Qatar.

6 January In a controversial move, Bahrain grants the US the use of its naval base. It was announced in Washington that Bahrain had agreed to lease part of its naval base, formerly used by Britain, to the US as a station for the latter's still small Middle East fleet of one flagship and two destroyers manned by 260 men. However, US State Department officials stressed that the agreement, originally signed on 23 December 1971 but not publicized at Bahrain's request, involved no political or military commitment.

At a press conference on 19 January the Kuwaiti foreign minister, Shaikh Sabah al-Ahmad al-Jaber, refused to comment on reports that the US had rented part of Bahrain's base, but added that Kuwait was opposed to the establishment of any foreign bases in the Gulf region and 'would not accept them at all'.

13 January Union Oil of California is reported to have made its first offshore oil discovery off the coast of Ras al-Khaimah. Ras al-Khaimah's ruler, Shaikh Saqr, visited the oil rig where he was told that studies were being carried out to determine whether oil was present in commercial quantities.

19 January It is reported that Iran has sent a memorandum to the UN Commission on Human Rights asking for effective measures to be taken to protect the remaining Iranian community in Iraq after the recent expulsions. On 3 January the Iranian authorities reported a daily influx of 1,000 refugees.

On 9 January the Iranian English-language newspaper *Kayhan International* said that the deportations had dropped after violent protests by Kurdish villagers in north-eastern Iraq. There had been clashes in which 13 Kurds and six Iraqi policemen had been killed and some 10,000 Iranians awaiting expulsion at the border had been returned to their homes in Kerbala, Najaf and Kazemain.

The Iraqi Interior Ministry claimed that on 14 January two Iranian army detachments had attempted to cross the border into Iraq but had been driven back by Iraqi police and frontier guards but the report was dismissed as 'ridiculous' by Iran's deputy information minister, Farhad Nikoukhah.

On the same day a spokesman for the Iranian security forces said that 120 Iranians faced trial by a military court on charges of sabotage, espionage and subversion. They had all been arrested over the past five months, had been 'trained in Iraq and East Germany', and had 'received arms and ammunition from the Iraqi Ba'thist regime for sabotage and disruption in Iran'. The spokesman added that they had tried to kidnap the shah's nephew, Prince Shahram, as well as the US ambassador, and had robbed a number of banks.

25 January The 45-year-old ruler of Sharjah, Shaikh Khaled ibn Muhammad al-Qasimi, is found shot dead in his palace after rebel forces holding him hostage surrender to security guards and members of the recently formed Union Defence Force (UDF). Some 18 rebels led by Shaikh Khaled's cousin, Shaikh Saqr ibn Sultan, who had been deposed as ruler in June 1965 and had since lived in exile in Cairo, attacked the palace on 24 January with hand grenades. However, the ruler's brother, Shaikh Saqr ibn Muhammad, surrounded the building with local forces, and fire was exchanged throughout the night. At dawn the rebels surrendered and were taken to Abu Dhabi where United Arab Emirates (UAE) President Shaikh Zayed said they would stand trial. Reports suggested that up to nine members of Shaikh Khaled's family were killed in the revolt. A British officer seconded to the UDF, Captain Cameron, was shot in the leg.

An attempt on Shaikh Khaled's life had been made in July 1970 when explosives were planted under his chair. In December 1971 shots were fired at Shaikh Saqr ibn

Muhammad, Sharjah's deputy ruler, but only grazed his shoulder. Shaikh Saqr had represented his brother, Shaikh Khaled, in receiving the Iranian landing party which had taken over part of Abu Musa island on 30 November, an action which had angered many nationalists.

On 7 February Iraq firmly denied a report that arms used in the attempted coup on 25 January had been shipped from Basra with Iraqi connivance.

On 25 January Sharjah's new ruler, Shaikh Sultan ibn Muhammad, said in a public audience that he intended to rule according to the liberal principles of his predecessor and to retain Sharjah's membership of the UAE. In an interview published on 2 February he said that he would keep to his brother's agreement with Iran on the partial occupation of Abu Musa, but would try to achieve a new understanding with the shah on the issue.

Shaikh Khaled, whose family had ruled Sharjah for two centuries, had been a paint merchant when he deposed his cousin, Shaikh Saqr, in 1965. He was obsessed by Sharjah's development and committed to turning it into a modern state. He introduced electricity and an efficient irrigation system, realizing the importance of agricultural development in a state without oil wealth.

29 January It is announced in Aden that the two rebel forces in Dhofar – the Popular Front for the Liberation of the Occupied Arabian Gulf and the National Democratic Front for the Liberation of Oman and the Arabian Gulf, had merged in a new organization to be known as the Popular Front for the Liberation of Oman and the Arabian Gulf (PFLOAG).

10 February Ras al-Khaimah is accepted as the UAE's seventh member. The UAE, then consisting of Abu Dhabi, Ajman, Dubai, Fujairah, Sharjah and Umm al-Qaiwain, was proclaimed a sovereign state on 2 December 1971. Ras al-Khaimah's ruler, Shaikh Saqr, had rejected membership when the federation's establishment was agreed by the other six Trucial States in July 1971. However, he had now dropped his early conditions for membership: that all members should break off relations with Iran over its seizure of the Tunb and Abu Musa islands and that Ras al-Khaimah should be given equal voting and veto rights in the Consultative Assembly with the larger and wealthier emirates of Abu Dhabi and Dubai.

17 February A Lebanese newspaper reports that 10 suitcases seized at Manama airport contain machine guns and other weapons. Classified as diplomatic mail, the suitcases were carried by an Iraqi diplomatic official, Abd al-Hamid Kharbit, and contained machine guns, hand grenades, bazookas, small arms and ammunition. Kharbit was quoted as telling the Bahraini authorities that the arms were gifts from the Iraqi government to the leaders of Bahrain in view of 'their well-known love of hunting'.

On 18 February Lamya al-Nayif, wife of a former prime minister of Iraq, General Abd al-Razzaq al-Nayif, was shot in the chest and shoulder when she threw herself between her husband and three men armed with Sten gun and pistols. They had knocked at the door of Nayif's London flat. They ran away when Mrs Nayif called for help from a window. On 19 February an Iraqi called Yahya Qasim was arrested and charged with attempted murder. Nayif had taken part in the Ba'thist coup which overthrew the government of President Aref, and was made prime minister on 20 July 1968. But on 30 July he was dismissed and exiled for 'crimes against the nation'.

On 27 February three Iraqis were arrested in Cairo after they had allegedly attempted to kill Brigadier Arfan Abd al-Qadir Wajdi, an Iraqi political refugee who had once commanded the Military Academy in Baghdad. Egyptian interrogation of the three men is said to have shown that they were Iraqi security officers who also intended to murder two other Iraqi exiles in Egypt. On 29 February it was reported that a further 17 Iraqis had been arrested by the Egyptian police, and had made known details of a large-scale plot to kill Iraqi refugees. The Egyptian newspaper *Al-Ahram* said that they had revealed that the operation was organized in Baghdad by Nazim Kazar, head of Iraq's security service.

22 February The ruler of Qatar, Shaikh Ahmad ibn Ali al-Thani, is deposed in a bloodless coup by his cousin Shaikh Khalifa ibn Hamad al-Thani. The coup took place while Shaikh Ahmad was in Iran on a hunting trip. According to Qatar radio it took place 'with the blessing and support of the ruling family, the armed forces and the people'. Among other things, the 55-year-old Shaikh Ahmad had provoked resentment by being absent from the capital, Doha, when Qatar was proclaimed independent. The 37-year-old Shaikh Khalifa, who held the oil and finance portfolios as well as being prime minister and deputy ruler, was already regarded as the state's effective ruler.

Of Qatar's population of about 150,000, some 500 were members of the al-Thani ruling family. Of these all the males drew incomes on reaching the age of 12. Oil royalties made up about 90 per cent of the state's revenue.

23 February After flying to South Yemen and releasing all the passengers and crew, five Palestinian hijackers of a Lufthansa jet surrender to the South Yemeni authorities. On 25 February the West German government admitted that it had paid a $5-million ransom to gain the release of the jet which was hijacked on 21 February en route from New Delhi to Athens with 172 passengers aboard (including Joseph Kennedy III, the son of the late US senator, Robert Kennedy).

13 March South Yemen claims that North Yemeni troops, instigated by Saudi Arabia and the US, have massed along its borders. On 11 March North Yemen had accused its Southern neighbour of massing along its borders, shelling its territory and violating its air space. On 3 April South Yemen proposed mutual troop withdrawals to ease border tensions.

Many tribal leaders and right-wing politicians fled from South to North Yemen and Saudi Arabia after the National Liberation Front (NLF) took power in Aden in 1967. With the support of the Saudi and North Yemeni governments, some then recruited tribesmen to raid South Yemen. Sources in Lebanon reported that 4,000–5,000 so-called 'mercenary' tribesmen were based in camps along the Saudi border with South Yemen.

17 March Fatah, the principal Palestinian commando group, calls for the removal of the Jordanian regime. The call came in response to King Husayn of Jordan's proposals for a federated state of Jordan and the West Bank (of the River Jordan). On 28 March King Husayn met US President Nixon in Washington where he outlined his plan for the federated state.

20 March The Saudi news agency reports that the South Yemeni government has invited 40 members of the Front for the Liberation of Occupied South Yemen (FLOSY) to reconciliation talks, only to have them murdered when they crossed the border from North Yemen. On 26 March the North Yemeni embassy in Lebanon had issued a statement accusing South Yemeni forces of machine-gunning guests at a wedding in North Yemen, killing 60 and wounding others. The statement added 'If the Aden authorities persist in this policy, civil war will follow.'

21 March The Iraqi president, Ahmad Hasan al-Bakr, is quoted as saying that a union of Iraq, Egypt and Syria would 'continue to be the most sublime aim of the Arab masses in all parts of the Arab homeland'. On the same day Saddam Husayn (Takriti), vice-chairman of the Revolutionary Command Council (RCC), arrived in the Syrian capital, Damascus, with a delegation to discuss the union. He was received by Syria's President Asad on the same evening. Discussions between the ministers – the first in six years between Iraqi and Syrian government representatives – continued daily until 26 March when Saddam Husayn and his party went on to Cairo. There he had talks with Egypt's President Sadat and other Egyptian ministers. The Egyptian press suggested that Iraq was contemplating joining the Federation of Arab Republics rather than uniting with Egypt and Syria in a separate federation that excluded Libya.

28 March A spokesman for PFLOAG is quoted by Aden radio as saying that Saudi Arabia had helped put down the recent strikes in Bahrain. It said that 'the reactionary Saudi Arabian authorities' had sent agents to Bahrain to help in suppressing the strikes, seeking to 'protect the tottering regime' in Bahrain.

On 13 March workers demonstrating in sympathy with the strikers at Manama airport damaged cars and buses and flung stones at commercial premises.

9 April In Baghdad, Iraq's President Bakr and Soviet Premier Aleksei Kosygin sign a 15-year treaty of friendship and co-operation. On 17 April a communiqué was released stating that an Iraqi delegation, led by Saddam Husayn (Takriti), vice-chairman of the RCC, and including the oil and minerals minister, Sa'doun Hamadi, had been in Moscow since 10 April and had concluded an agreement under which the Soviet Union would supply Iraq with more military and economic assistance.

14 April Baghdad radio reports that Iraqi forces have clashed with Iranian troops in eastern Iraq, citing a series of conflicts starting on 11 April. On 15 April some members of Kuwait's National Assembly called for an official denunciation of Iran's 'aggression against Iraqi territory' while others demanded that Kuwait should sever diplomatic relations or at least cut off economic ties with Iran. On 16 April Tehran responded to the Iraqi claims by saying that Iranian forces had merely repelled attempts by Iraqi troops to occupy frontier posts in Iranian territory.

23 April It is announced that Umm al-Qaiwain, one of the seven emirates forming the UAE, has decided to sue the Sharjah Petroleum Company (SPC) for allegedly infringing drilling rights in the Gulf's offshore waters off the island of Abu Musa. A government spokesman said that the SPC, acting on behalf of Sharjah and Iran, was preparing to drill in waters nine miles (15 kilometres) from the island. He also said that the decision to start legal proceedings had been taken only after mediation had failed.

Offshore drilling rights in the region of Abu Musa had been in dispute between Umm al-Qaiwain and Sharjah, and between Buttes and Occidental Petroleum, for the previous two years. When Sharjah and Iran divided the island between them in November 1971, they agreed that Buttes should explore within a 12-mile (19-kilometre) territorial waters limit and that any revenue from its operations should be shared equally between them.

3 May Reuter reports that the ruler of Dubai, Shaikh Rashid, has signed an agreement with a new New York organization, John McMullen, and a local firm, Abd al-Rahim Galadari Brothers, to establish a company to build the biggest dry dock between Europe and the Far East, in Dubai. The dock would cost about £27 million, take over three years to build and provide facilities for tankers of up to 400,000 tons.

5 May The Omani air force bombs gun sites in South Yemen which borders Oman's Dhofar province. The Ministry of Defence in Muscat said that the attack was made after South Yemeni forces had fired machine guns and mortars across the border for 36 hours at a fort in Habrut, an Omani border post about 60 miles (97 kilometres) inland from the Indian Ocean, killing six Omani soldiers and wounding four. It was the first Omani attack on South Yemen since the Dhofar rebels launched their South Yemen-supported rebellion against the Omani sultan. On 12 May the London *Times* reported that the Omani government had launched a further offensive in Dhofar in an effort to gain control of the province before the June monsoon.

On 9 May a statement issued by the South Yemeni embassy in Beirut said that British-piloted fighter planes had attacked positions in South Yemen near the Omani border, killing five soldiers and wounding others. It was announced in Aden on 12 May that the South Yemeni government had protested to the UN about what it termed 'repeated attacks by British forces on its territory'.

On 6 May Britain announced that technical assistance to North Yemen which was valued at about £22,000 in 1971 was likely to increase to about £90,000 in 1972.

30 May Three Japanese guerrillas, in the name of the Palestinian cause, open fire on civilians at Israel's Lod Airport, killing 26 and wounding 76.

1 June Iraq nationalizes the Iraq Petroleum Company (IPC) after failing to reach an agreement with it on terms for its nationalization. IPC produced about 10 per cent of Middle East oil. British Petroleum, Royal Dutch Shell, Standard New Jersey/Socony Mobil and the Compagnie Francaise des Petroles (CFP) each had a 23.75 per cent share in the IPC's ownership. Iraq's President Bakr announced on the same night that a new organization, the Iraqi Company for Oil Operations, was being formed to take over IPC's assets in Iraq, valued at £136 million, and its activities.

The nationalization edict did not apply to the IPC's associates, the Basrah and Mosul Petroleum Companies.

On 20 June the Organization of Arab Petroleum Exporting Countries (OAPEC) members agreed to lend Iraq and Syria $169 million to help meet exchange shortages arising from their nationalization of oil production.

On 21 May the Kuwaiti minister of state for cabinet affairs told reporters that Kuwait fully supported Iraq in its dispute with the IPC and on 3 June Kuwait's National Assembly called for united Arab support for Iraq in its dispute with the company.

11 June Twenty-two people are believed killed and 12 seriously wounded in fighting between tribesmen of the UAE emirates of Fujairah and Sharjah. The clash occurred in the UAE's eastern region, where Sharjah owns the three enclaves of Husn Dibba, Khor Fakkan and Kalba, which all stretch into Fujairah's territory. Units of the Union's Defence Force of the federation imposed a cease-fire and took up positions between the combatants.

On 17 July it was announced in Abu Dhabi that a final settlement had been reached over the dispute.

18 June In Paris, vice-president of Iraq's RCC, Saddam Husayn, says that France has agreed to buy 23.75 per cent of the oil produced from the now-nationalized Kirkuk field for a period of 10 years and on the terms prevailing before Iraq's nationalization of the IPC on 1 June. An Iraqi spokesman also said that the two countries had discussed French purchases at 'world commercial prices' of crude oil in excess of the 23.75 per cent already agreed. On his return to Baghdad on 19 June Saddam Husayn said that Iraq would not allow any of the partners in the IPC to take action against France. 'We will not tolerate any sanctions' he said. '. . . in such an event we would put all our oil resources at the disposal of France, including those exploited by the IPC in southern Iraq by the Basrah Petroleum Company.' Iraq was offering France favourable terms in recognition of France's support for the Arabs in the Arab-Israeli conflict.

On 21 June the Kuwait National Assembly unanimously approved a £15,175,000 loan to Iraq and Syria to 'stabilize their economies' after their recent oil company nationalizations.

2 July The US and the Yemen Arab Republic (North Yemen) formally announce the resumption of diplomatic relations severed since the 1967 Arab-Israeli war.

11 July The Popular Front for the Liberation of Palestine (PFLP) claims responsibility for a grenade explosion that wounds nine people in Tel Aviv's central bus station. On 31 May the PFLP had claimed responsibility for the attack on Israel's Lod airport in which, on 30 May, three Japanese gunmen killed 26 people and wounded 76.

16 July It is announced in the Syrian capital, Damascus, that the government has agreed that oil from Iraq's Kirkuk fields should be pumped across Syria through the IPC pipeline terminating at the Syrian port of Banyas. Iraq had nationalized the IPC on 2 June. The pipeline was taken over by the Syrian Company for Oil Transport. On 18 July it was announced in Beirut that Lebanon was prepared to buy the Lebanese section of the line 'if Iraq insisted on national control'. The pipeline carrying crude oil from northern Iraq to the Mediterranean had two terminals, one at Banias in Syria and the other at Tripoli in Lebanon.

18 July Egypt's President Sadat announces that he has expelled Soviet military advisers and experts. He expressed his frustration at not obtaining the arms he needed to defeat Israel. By 5 August, most Soviets, amounting to about 15,000 Soviet military advisers and 25,000 dependants, had left Egypt.

2 August The Libyan head-of-state, Mu'ammar Qadhafi, and Egypt's President Sadat agree to establish a unified political leadership by 1 September.

5 September King Husayn bitterly criticizes the Palestinian commando attack on Israeli athletes at the Munich Olympics. When West German forces opened fire on the commandos, 11 members of the Israeli Olympic team were killed.

13 September US officials report that the Soviet Union and Syria have agreed to establish Soviet naval facilities in Syria and to airlift Soviet men and arms to the base.

30 September A broadcast from South Yemen states that rebels have captured some villages with the assistance of forces from North Yemen. On the same day North and South Yemen called on the Arab League to mediate in their border dispute. On 1 October South Yemen reported that its troops had captured the border village of Qataba in North Yemen. However, in one of those extraordinary volte-faces that was to become characteristic of the two Yemens, on 28 October they agreed to merge as one nation and signed a pact in Cairo to that end.

18 November Twelve Arab League delegates and a representative of the Palestinians conclude a four-day meeting in Kuwait in which they agree to give MiG aircraft to Syria to help in its conflict with Israel.

1 9 7 3

20 January The Trans-Arabian Pipeline (Tapline) is breached in Saudi Arabia by an explosion between the Rif'a and Shuba pumping stations. The flow of oil through the pipeline was stopped until 24 January when repairs to it were finished. Although Tapline had been damaged by explosions several times in Jordan, Syria and Lebanon and had been closed for 100 days after the 1967 Arab-Israeli war, this was the first time it had been damaged by an explosion in Saudi Arabia. At the time the 760-mile (1,223-kilometre) pipeline carried about 480,000 barrels of Saudi crude oil a day to the Zahrani refinery in Lebanon.

7 February Abu Dhabi reaches an eight-year agreement to permit the tanker operator, Japan Line, to transport Gulf crude oil directly to Japan. On 9 January Abu Dhabi's oil and industry minister, Mani ibn Said al-Otaiba, referred to the 26 December 1972 agreement between the British Petroleum Company (BP) and the Japanese Overseas Petroleum Corporation (JOPC) under which the latter gained a 30 per cent interest in offshore oil produced by Abu Dhabi Marine Areas. He pointed out that no agreement could be properly concluded without the approval of the Abu Dhabi government which reserved its right to compensation from BP.

1 March Eight members of the Palestinian Black September group take over the Saudi Arabian embassy in Khartoum, holding six hostages to demand the release of Arab prisoners in various countries. On 2 March the group killed the US ambassador, Cleo Neel, Jr, the departing chargé d'affaires, George Moore, and the Egyptian-born chargé at the Belgium embassy, Guy Eid. On 4 March, however, the guerrillas ended their siege and surrendered to Sudanese officials. On 6 March the Sudanese president, Muhammad Ga'afar al-Nimeiry, accused the Palestinian commando group Fatah of being the principal force behind the takeover and the killing of the diplomats. On 12 March it was announced that Sudan would indict the guerrillas for premeditated murder.

On 24 March Jordan reported that the jailed Fatah leader, Abu Daoud, had confessed that Black September was in fact merely a camouflage for commando operations carried out by Fatah, the mainstream group headed by Yasser Arafat. On 21 April Arafat was to take over the leadership of the Palestine Liberation Organization's (PLO) political and government relations.

Black September had started operating with the 1971 assassination of the Jordanian prime minister, Wasfi al-Tall. From then on, most terrorist attacks on behalf of the Palestinian cause were carried out by the group or else by George Habash's Popular Front for the Liberation of Palestine (PFLP).

4 March The Iranian prime minister, Amir Abbas Hoveida, unveils a record $10,100-million budget based on an expansionist economic policy providing for 'more guns and more butter'. The budget foresaw a 47 per cent increase in defence expenditure. He promised to build up the defence forces to 'one of the most formidable in the world'. On 25 February it had been reported that Iran was paying the US in cash for eight squadrons of F-4 Phantom fighter-bombers for delivery over the next three or four years in addition to about 141 new F-5 fighter-bombers, some 489 helicopters and other equipment. It was also reported that Iran required several hundred more US personnel. Since the British withdrawal from the Gulf, Iran had become important to the US because of its potential stability, and what Washington described as its 'generally progressive attitudes'. Moreover, the Soviet Union had increased its activity in the Middle East and was providing Syria and Iraq with weapons.

29 March Saudi Arabia sends nearly 20,000 troops into Kuwait to help defend its borders against Iraq. On 20 March Iraqi and Kuwaiti troops had clashed along their disputed frontier. Iraqi-Kuwait relations had never fully recovered from General Qasim's attempt to annex Kuwait in 1961 when Saudi troops had been in the forefront of Arab League forces which had replaced British forces.

10 May In a $625-million deal, Britain agrees to modernize the Saudi Arabian air force.

15 May Iraq, Kuwait, Libya and Algeria temporarily halt the flow of oil to the West in a symbolic protest against the existence of Israel. On 16 April the Saudi Arabian petroleum minister, Shaikh Ahmad Zaki Yamani, had reportedly warned US secretary of state, William Rogers, that oil shipments to the US would not increase unless the US helped find a solution to the Middle East crisis which was satisfactory to the Arabs.

On 18 April the Libyan head-of-state, Mu'ammar Qadhafi, had predicted that the Arabs would use oil as a weapon in their struggle with Israel. He was to repeat this prediction on 13 May at a Tripoli news conference. On 9 April in Tripoli, representatives of Western oil companies and the Organization of Petroleum Exporting Countries (OPEC) had failed to reach an agreement on crude-oil price increases.

24 May In Tehran a consortium of Western oil companies surrenders full control of its operations within Iran to the Iranian government. On 20 March Iran's Shah Muhammad Reza Pahlavi announced the nationalization of the foreign-operated oil industry.

26 May Egypt reports that at least 30 people have been killed in four days of border clashes between North and South Yemen.

2 June In Geneva a group of Western oil companies agrees to increase the posted prices of crude oil by 11.9 per cent to 8 of the 11 OPEC members.

1 July The Iraqi regime crushes a coup led by the dreaded Iraqi security chief, Nazim Kazar. It was thought that the attempted coup was an attempt by a civilian faction within the Ba'th Party to oust the president, Hasan al-Bakr, and the military faction of the party. As a result of the coup, more power was given to the president, and a National Front was formed between the Ba'th Party and the Iraqi Communist Party.

Capitalizing on the absence of most of the Ba'th Party leadership to greet the returning President Bakr, the notorious Kazar invited the defence minister, Hammad Shihab, and the interior minister, Sa'doun Ghaidan, to 'a banquet'. On arrival they were pushed into a cellar. Kazar and his followers went to the airport to kill the president but, failing to do so, took the ministers hostage and eventually made for the Iranian border. Sighted by Iraqi forces, Kazar killed Shihab and severely wounded Ghaidan before being captured.

On 7 July the regime announced that Kazar and 21 others had been tried and executed. On 10 July Shibli Aisami, assistant secretary-general of the Iraqi Ba'th Party, noted (without irony) that the experience would encourage the party to 'cling even more tenaciously to democracy, legality and morality' (see Farouk-Sluglett and Sluglett, *Iraq since 1958*).

On 17 July Iraq announced plans to re-establish a 100-member legislature, its first representative government in 15 years.

20 July Palestinian guerrillas hijack a Japan Airlines jet, with 137 passengers aboard, shortly after take-off from Amsterdam and order it to Dubai. However, on 24 July, after three days on Dubai's airstrip, the guerrillas took the hijacked plane to Libya, released the passengers and crew, then blew up the plane.

23–27 July The shah visits the US where concern with the oil problem is the 'No. 1 topic to be discussed between him and the President', according to the US *Washington Post*. The security of the Gulf was stressed during the visit by US President Nixon who described the shah as 'a world statesman of the first rank'. The US seemed prepared to supply Iran with sophisticated weaponry in exchange for a larger US quota of Iranian oil.

31 July A contract is signed in Tehran under which the National Iranian Oil Company (NIOC) formally takes over ownership and control in the Consortium area of south-west Iran. The Consortium (British Petroleum (BP), Royal Dutch Shell, Gulf Oil, Socony, Mobil, Exxon, Standard Oil of California, Texaco, Compagnie Francaise des Petroles (CFP), and a group of independents) was to set up a new operating company, Oil Service Company of Iran. In January the shah had declared that the 1954 agreement between the NIOC and the Consortium would be terminated because Iran was no longer happy with the arrangement. On 26 February it was announced in London that a 'general understanding' had been reached between the shah and the Consortium in St Moritz. This 'general understanding' was worked into an agreement that was signed on 24 May.

10 August Israeli jets force an Iraqi Airways passenger jet to land near the Israeli port of Haifa but release it after a two-hour security check. On the following day the Israeli defence minister, Moshe Dayan, justified the forced landing on the grounds that suspected Palestinian guerrillas were aboard. On 15 August the UN Security Council voted a resolution condemning the incident.

12 August The Iranian premier, Amir Abbas Hoveida, and Soviet officials end a week-long conference in Moscow, at the end of which they issued a joint statement confirming that questions involving the Gulf region should be resolved by Gulf countries without outside interference.

25 August An armed Yemeni hijacks a Yemeni Airways airliner and forces it to fly to Kuwait where he surrenders after the Kuwait government assures him that he will not face prosecution.

7 September Palestinian commandos threaten the lives of four Saudi hostages seized in Paris on 5 September. They said they would kill them unless Saudi officials helped secure the release of Abu Daoud, a Fatah leader serving a life-term in Jordan for terrorism.

7 September The Saudi Arabian petroleum minister, Shaikh Ahmad Zaki Yamani, calls for a revision of the 1971 Tehran agreement to permit higher prices for oil-producing nations. The call came at a time when the world was preparing for the Arab oil producers' possible use of its oil weapon. On 16 September OPEC had ended a two-day conference by announcing that it would demand higher prices from Western oil companies in forthcoming negotiations and on 11 September Organization for Economic Co-operation and Development (OECD) representatives had held a secret meeting in Paris on pooling their resources in case of an Arab cut-back of oil exports. On 18 September Shaikh Yamani warned the US of a possible oil cut-off if it failed to resolve the Arab-Israeli dispute, reiterating King Faisal's warning on 30 August that he might halt Saudi oil supplies to the US because it supported Zionism.

2 October The Iranian government announces the crushing of a plot to kidnap and assassinate the shah and his family.

6 October At the start of the 'October' War (known to Israelis as the Yom Kippur War and to the Arabs as the Ramadan War) Egyptian troops cross the Suez Canal by pontoon bridges into Sinai, taking Israel by surprise.

7 October Iraq announces the nationalization of Exxon and Mobil in retaliation for US support of Israel. On 9 October Egypt urged Saudi Arabia to stop oil production at US-run wells if the US made moves to re-supply Israel.

10 October Joining Syria and Egypt, Iraq and several other Arab states announce the sending of combat units to the Golan Heights and the Suez Canal to confront Israel. Britain announced an arms embargo on both sides.

11 October After a week of bloody battles, the Israelis claim to have pushed the Syrians off the Golan Heights. However, the Egyptians claimed sweeping victories after crossing the Suez Canal on pontoons and driving the Israelis nine miles (15 kilometres) back into the Sinai desert. Meanwhile, Israeli troops reached Sassa, some 20 miles (32 kilometres) from Damascus.

13 October In their first battle with Iraqi troops, the Israelis destroy nearly a complete Iraqi tank division in a battle 12 miles (19 kilometres) into Syria. On the same day Jordan declared war on Israel and King Husayn of Jordan announced that his force of 68,000 men would be sent into battle. On 14 October an Israeli communiqué reported the halting of the Egyptian drive across the Sinai desert. Saudi Arabia joined the war against Israel with the disclosure that an undetermined number of Saudi troops was in Syria. On 15 October the US announced a massive airlift of arms to Israel to counter Soviet aid to the Arabs. On 16 October Egypt's President Sadat announced that Egypt's goal was not the elimination of Israel but the regaining of territory lost in the 1967 Arab-Israeli war. On 17 October at the White House, President Nixon discussed Middle East peace prospects with the foreign ministers of Saudi Arabia, Kuwait, Morocco and Algeria. On the same day a massive tank battle between Arab and Israeli tanks erupted on both sides of the Suez Canal. On 18 October Sadat ended two days of private talks in Cairo with Soviet Premier Kosygin on a possible cease-fire.

17 October Eleven OPEC members agree on a co-ordinated programme of oil production and export cuts to force the US to alter its Middle East policy. On the same day six of the largest Gulf oil-producing countries agreed to raise the price of their crude oil by 17 per cent and taxes paid by oil companies by 70 per cent. On 19 October Libya halted shipments of crude oil and petroleum products to the US because of its support for Israel and raised oil prices from $4.90 to $8.25 per barrel to other nations. On 20 October Saudi Arabia halted oil shipments to the US for the same reason. On

21 October Iraq responded to the Netherlands' support for Israel by nationalizing the former's portion of the Basrah Petroleum Company. On the same day Kuwait, Bahrain, Qatar and Dubai announced their cut-off of oil supplies to the US, making the Arab oil boycott virtually complete.

On 26 October the US *New York Times* reported that major oil companies estimated that Arab oil shipments had been cut by 20 per cent from pre-war levels. On 30 October Libya became the seventh Arab state to cut oil supplies to the Netherlands.

On 1 November Saudi Arabia reduced its oil production by 5 per cent. On 5 November, following a two-day meeting in Kuwait, OAPEC announced a 75 per cent reduction of its September oil output for November.

On 6 October European Economic Community (EEC) foreign ministers called on Israel to return to the 22 October cease-fire lines in an effort to avoid the boycott.

22 October The UN Security Council passes resolution 338, calling for a cease-fire based on talks held in Moscow between the US secretary of state, Henry Kissinger, and the Soviet leader, Leonid Brezhnev. The cease-fire was immediately accepted by Egypt, but only on condition that Israel also adhered to it. On 25 October the Security Council approved a resolution to establish a peace-keeping force to ensure the implementation of the cease-fire.

On 23 October Israeli troops, who had crossed the Suez Canal on 15 October, had encircled Egypt's 111 Corps approximately 20 miles (32 kilometres) inside Egypt. On the same day Israel's Prime Minister Golda Meir had accepted the UN cease-fire. On 24 October fighting in the northern sector of the war virtually stopped as Syria accepted the cease-fire.

8 November Five US oil companies agree to build a petroleum refinery for the NIOC on the Gulf.

The Arab Oil Embargo: November and December

9 November The US secretary of state, Henry Kissinger, ends a two-day stay in Saudi Arabia where King Faisal tells him that the oil embargo against the US will not be lifted until Israel withdraws from Arab territories occupied since 1967.

On 17 November the Saudi petroleum minister, Ahmad Zaki Yamani, said that he was seeking a substantial rearrangement of Saudi Arabia's contract with the Arabian American Oil Company (ARAMCO). On 22 November he warned that Saudi Arabia would cut oil production by 80 per cent if the US, Western Europe and Japan took any action to counter the Arab oil embargo. Nevertheless, on 7 November at their meeting in Cairo, Kissinger and Egypt's President Sadat surprised the Arab world by announcing that the US and Egypt had agreed to resume diplomatic relations which had been broken off since the start of the 1967 Arab-Israeli war.

5 December After meeting the US secretary of state, Henry Kissinger, in Washington, the Saudi petroleum minister, Ahmad Zaki Yamani, announces that Saudi Arabia is prepared to lift its oil embargo on the US as soon as the Israelis begin withdrawing from occupied Arab lands. However, on 9 December the oil ministers of nine Arab states, meeting in Kuwait, agreed to curtail oil production by 5 per cent or 750,000 barrels a day beginning on 1 January 1974. On 14 December Kissinger again met King Faisal in Riyadh in an effort to persuade him to lift the embargo.

6 December A new constitution comes into force in Bahrain. It was produced by a Constituent Assembly for which elections had been held in December 1972. The constitution was liberal and farsighted and provided for a National Assembly.

11 December The Iranian government reveals that it has sold more than 80 million barrels of its crude oil to unidentified US, European and Japanese firms at $14–$17.40 a barrel, $11–12 a barrel higher than posted prices. On the following day in London, the US secretary of state, Henry Kissinger, called for a joint effort by the US, Europe, Canada and Japan to develop long-term solutions to the world energy crisis exacerbated by the Arab oil embargo.

On 17 December Kissinger completed a five-day tour of Algeria, Egypt, Saudi Arabia, Syria, Jordan, Lebanon and Israel (Jerusalem) to discuss last-minute details of the UN Geneva Middle East conference. However, on 18 December this was postponed until 21 December.

18 December Iraq announces its plans to increase oil production from a current daily level of 2.1 million barrels a day to 3.5 million barrels a day.

23 December At the end of a two-day meeting in Tehran, six Gulf states announce that they will double the price of oil, effective from 1 January 1974, to $11.65 a barrel.

23 December Kuwait announces that five Palestinian air hijackers will be turned over to the Palestine Liberation Organization (PLO) for trial.

In a separate incident on 28 November, three Palestinian hijackers had released a Royal Dutch 747 jet airliner in Dubai following four days of erratic flying to various locations in an unsuccessful effort to force the Netherlands' government to alter its pro-Israeli policy.

25 December Arab petroleum producers in Kuwait announce that, as of 1 January 1974, they will ease their oil embargo while maintaining a total ban against the US and the Netherlands. However, on 27 December the US *Washington Post* pointed out that the Arab countries, with the exception of Saudi Arabia and Kuwait, were not holding to the oil embargo because they needed funds to finance the Soviet sale of arms to Egypt.

29 December Egypt and four Middle East oil-producing countries reach an agreement with the US-owned Bechtel Inc. for the construction of an oil pipeline between the Red Sea and the Mediterranean.

December The separate Abu Dhabi government is disbanded to give way to the federal UAE system. In a ministerial re-shuffle, some of Abu Dhabi's members became federal ministers. One was Dr Mana ibn Said al-Otaiba who became the first federal minister of petroleum and mineral resources.

1 9 7 4

1 January Organization of Petroleum Exporting Countries (OPEC) oil prices are not raised as planned by the December conference in Tehran. As a result of Saudi opposition to a price increase, prices were held at current levels for the first quarter (and subsequently for the remainder of the year). OPEC's thirty-sixth conference had ruled that the posted price of OPEC oil should be increased by almost 130 per cent, from $5.11 to $11.65 a barrel.

9 January US President Nixon calls for the foreign ministers of eight oil-consuming countries to meet in Washington on 11 February to discuss world energy problems. On 15 January the nine European Economic Community (EEC) members accepted the invitation. On 10 January the US secretary of state, Henry Kissinger, had called on oil-producing and oil-consuming countries to reach a long-term agreement on energy issues. He was speaking on the eve of his Middle East mission aimed at gaining Egyptian and Israeli withdrawals along the Suez Canal. On 12 January the Saudi petroleum minister, Ahmad Zaki Yamani, warned that any counter-action by the oil-consuming nations to break the Arab oil embargo would result in international economic disaster.

9 January France announces the signature of an agreement with Saudi Arabia for 27 million tons of crude oil over the next three years. On 10 January the French government announced a 30–45 per cent increase in the price of petrol and home and industrial fuel oil.

21 January The Kuwaiti foreign minister, Shaikh Sabah al-Ahmad al-Jaber, says that it is premature to speculate on lifting the Arab oil embargo against the US despite Egyptian-Israeli troop withdrawals from the Suez area. On 17 January a Suez Canal military buffer zone agreement between Israel and Egypt was announced simultaneously in Jerusalem, Cairo and Washington. On 18 January Egypt and Israel signed an agreement to separate their forces alongside the canal as a result of US Secretary of State Kissinger's shuttle diplomacy. On 20 January, in Damascus, Kissinger ended his Middle East mission after urging the Syrians to enter into peace negotiations with the Israelis. On 21 January Britain lifted its arms embargo in the Middle East imposed during the October 1973 war.

25 January Iran agrees to supply Britain with five million additional tons of crude oil in exchange for $240 million worth of industrial goods. On 9 February France and Iran agreed to exchange oil for industrial and energy development projects worth $3,000–5,000 million.

5 February The Saudi petroleum minister, Ahmad Zaki Yamani, says he has no knowledge of any Arab country promising to lift its oil embargo against the US as President Nixon had suggested in his 30 January State of the Union message. Nixon had attributed his claim to personal reassurances from friendly Middle East leaders. Nevertheless, on 27 January Yamani had said that King Faisal was preparing to take steps towards reducing crude oil prices to avoid harming the world economy.

7 February Five Popular Front for the Liberation of Palestine (PFLP) guerrillas seize the Japanese embassy in Kuwait and threaten to kill 10 hostages including the Japanese ambassador, unless the Singapore government releases four guerrillas captured on 31 January.

13 February At the end of the world energy conference (11–13 February) in Washington, 13 major oil-consuming countries adopt, against French objections, a 17-point proposal to combat the energy crisis. On 10 February Libya, Kuwait and Saudi Arabia had criticized the proposed conference as a futile attempt by the US to force a confrontation with oil-producing nations.

On 21 February the shah proposed the creation of an international development fund for which he promised $1,000 million, to ease the economic problems of poor countries caused by higher oil prices. Iran's wish to portray itself as an important representative of the poorer nations was again demonstrated on 24 February when the shah accused US oil companies of deliberately manipulating petrol shortages to drive up prices. He claimed that the US still imported as much oil as it did before the Arab embargo.

As if to justify his charges, on 28 February the Royal Dutch/Shell Group announced a 153 per cent rise in earnings for 1973 while on 14 March British Petroleum Company Ltd (BP) announced a 332 per cent increase in 1973 profits to a record $760 million.

16 February US Secretary of State Henry Kissinger receives an Israeli-Syrian peace plan from the foreign ministers of Egypt, Syria, Saudi Arabia and Algeria who have ended a two-day summit conference in Algiers on 14 February.

21 February Kuwait rejects as too low bids from 32 US, European and Japanese oil companies for 85 million barrels of oil. On 29 January Kuwait had reached an agreement to immediately purchase 60 per cent of the Kuwait Oil Company, jointly owned by Gulf Oil Corporation and BP.

23 February The Islamic summit conference meeting in Lahore officially declares that the Palestine Liberation Organization (PLO) is the sole, legitimate representative of the Palestinian nation. The three-day conference, which ended on 24 February, discussed the status of Israeli-occupied territories (the West Bank and Gaza, Sinai and the Golan Heights), the future of Jerusalem and the oil crisis.

28 February Iraq announces the resumption of diplomatic relations with West Germany which were severed in 1965 when Bonn recognized Israel. On the same day the US and Egypt announced the resumption of full-scale diplomatic relations which had been severed in the wake of the 1967 Arab-Israeli war. On 4 March the EEC offered to explore long-term economic, technical and cultural co-operation with 20 Arab countries.

6 March Iran reports killing nearly 100 Iraqi soldiers in heavy fighting during the past three days along its common border with Iraq. On 10 February Iran and Iraq had blamed each other for heavy fighting that had erupted along the border. On 15 February Iraq's UN representative, Talib al-Shibib, at a special Security Council meeting accused Iran of starting the hostilities. On 20 February the Iranian chief delegate to the UN, Fereydun Hoveida, accused Iraq of a campaign of border harassment since December 1973 that had now erupted into real fighting.

18 March Seven of the nine Arab oil-producing countries agree at a Vienna meeting to lift the oil embargo imposed on the US in October 1973 after the 1967 Arab-Israeli war. Libya and Syria refused to join their colleagues. However, on 20 March the Saudi petroleum minister, Zaki Yamani, warned Western countries that if no progress was made in the Middle East dispute, the Arabs might re-impose the embargo. Nevertheless, on 25 March Saudi Arabia resumed its shipments of oil to the US.

On 13 March in Tripoli, oil ministers of the nine Arab oil-producing countries had agreed to consider lifting their oil embargo against the US. On the following day, meeting in Brussels, representatives of 12 oil-consuming countries had decided to seek a meeting with the producers to reach an agreement on the stability of oil supply and prices.

18 April President Sadat announces that Egypt will no longer depend on the Soviet Union for military aid and that arms will be sought from other countries.

25 April The US *New York Times* reports that Arab oil money is being invested in Western companies, including some $41,000 million in the US.

9 May The Saudi secretary of state for foreign affairs, Omar Saqqaf, endorses US Secretary of State Henry Kissinger's peace moves after the two meet in the Saudi capital, Riyadh. Kissinger began his fifth Middle East peace mission on 28 April when he met the Soviet foreign minister, Andrei Gromyko, in Geneva in an effort to enlist Moscow's support for a Syrian-Israeli peace accord. On 30 April he had talks with the Algerian president, Houari Boumedienne.

21 May UN Secretary-General Kurt Waldheim announces that Iran and Iraq have agreed to a cease-fire and acceptance of a UN mediation plan to settle their ongoing conflict.

2 June The Organization of Arab Petroleum Exporting Countries (OAPEC) agrees to maintain the total embargo of oil shipments to the Netherlands and continue reduced shipments to Denmark.

7 June In a letter to UN Secretary-General Kurt Waldheim, the leader of the Kurdish Democratic Party (KDP), Mulla Mustafa Barzani, accuses Iraq of conducting a war of genocide against the Kurds. War had been resumed in April after Barzani rejected Baghdad's autonomy package. On 13 June Kurdish tribesmen fought Iraqi troops in northern Iraq following the Baghdad rejection of Kurdish demands. On 26 June the Iraqi president, Ahmad Hasan al-Bakr, decreed 'Kurdish autonomy' despite Kurdish rejection of Baghdad's terms for self-rule. As the KDP was driven up to the Iranian border, it benefited from strong Iranian support.

9 June Iran agrees to purchase 50 US F-14A Navy fighter planes at a cost of about $950 million.

10 June Saudi Arabia increases from 25 per cent to 60 per cent its share of Arabian American Oil Company (ARAMCO) concessions and assets. In line with other Arab oil-producers the Saudi government had taken a 25 per cent share in ARAMCO in January 1973. The government's revenues from petroleum had increased dramatically from $1,214 million in 1970 to $22,573 million in 1974. Huge price increases in October and December 1973 (following the Arab-Israeli war) almost quadrupled the cost per barrel. Moreover, production had risen from 1,387 million barrels (3.8 million barrels a day) in 1970 to 3,095 million barrels (8.5 million barrels a day) in 1974.

Having pressed for the resumption of oil supplied to the US in March, Saudi Arabia resisted any move by radical OPEC members to increase oil prices further and was even reported to have threatened to leave OPEC unless it had its way.

13 June Colonel Ibrahim al-Hamdi leads a bloodless coup, ousting the North Yemeni government and establishing a military junta.

15 June US President Nixon ends two days of talks with Saudi officials in Jeddah where he is told by King Faisal that there will never be a Middle East peace until Jerusalem is returned to Arab sovereignty.

On 16 June in Damascus, Nixon and the Syrian president, Hafez al-Asad, announced the resumption of US-Syrian relations which had been severed after the 1967 Arab-Israeli war. From Damascus, Nixon went to Israel where he pledged long-term military and economic assistance. He ended his Middle East tour in Amman where he announced a joint commission to review co-operation with Jordan on a regular basis.

25 June The Sudanese president, Muhammad Ga'afar Nimeiry, frees eight Palestinians convicted for the murder in 1973 of three diplomats in Saudi Arabia. However, when the freed commandos arrived later in the day in Egypt they were immediately imprisoned by the Egyptian authorities.

11 July A meeting in Cairo of OAPEC delegates agrees to establish an Arab Energy Institute for solar and nuclear energy research. Based in Kuwait, OAPEC had been founded in 1968.

17 July Iran announces the purchase of 25.04 per cent in the steel and engineering division of the German Krupp works in Iran.

21 July The US treasury-secretary, William Simon, ends two days of talks in Saudi Arabia and Kuwait on economic relations between the US and the two countries.

31 July The EEC and the Arab League agree to establish a permanent joint commission to plan long-term economic co-operation.

4 August The Shah of Iran announces a revised five-year plan totalling $69.6 million and providing for an annual 25.9 per cent growth rate. On 19 August Iran raised the price of natural gas to the Soviet Union by 85 per cent to 57 cents per 1,000 cubic feet.

7 August King Faisal of Saudi Arabia ends a week of discussions with Egypt's President Sadat in Cairo where the focus of attention was the Jordanian-Palestinian dispute over the future of the West Bank.

25 August Kuwait gains 60 per cent control of the Japanese-owned Arabian Oil Company. On 14 May the Kuwaiti parliament and cabinet had ratified an agreement whereby the government gained 60 per cent control of the Kuwait Oil Company, jointly owned by Gulf Oil Corporation and BP. On 29 January it had reached an agreement to immediately purchase 60 per cent of the Kuwait Oil Company.

On 21 February Kuwait had rejected as too low bids from 32 US, European and Japanese oil companies for 85 million barrels of oil.

3 September Abu Dhabi emirate in the form of the Abu Dhabi National Oil Company (ADNOC) reaches an agreement to receive a 60 per cent share of the Abu Dhabi Petroleum Company owned by six western oil companies. The agreement was back-dated to 1 January 1974. ADNOC now had a monopoly over distribution and was responsible for all petroleum installations and oil-based industries in Abu Dhabi Emirate. ADNOC had been founded in 1971.

13 September OPEC ministers end a two-day meeting in Vienna after agreeing to raise by 3.5 per cent taxes and royalties paid by foreign oil companies to the oil-producing states. On the same day the Organization of Economic Co-operation and Development (OECD) said that the inflation rate for non-Communist industrial nations was a record 13.3 per cent for the 12-month period ending 31 July, but declined to 12 per cent rated annually during May–June.

On 29 September the foreign and finance ministers of the US, Britain, West Germany, France and Japan ended two days of discussions in Washington on efforts that could be taken to meet the oil price crisis.

On 30 September the Kuwaiti foreign minister, Shaikh Sabah al-Ahmad al-Jaber, speaking to the UN General Assembly, accused the industrial nations rather than Arab policies of being responsible for their own inflation, because of their mismanagement of their own domestic affairs.

23 September Iraqi forces claim to capture every city and town in Kurdistan, threatening to cut in half the area of Kurdistan held by Kurdish rebels.

2 October The Saudi petroleum minister, Zaki Yamani, takes a more conciliatory line on oil prices, saying that they would decline if there was a political solution to the Arab-Israeli conflict. On 13 October in Riyadh, King Faisal went further, telling the US secretary of state, Henry Kissinger, that he would do what he could to lower high oil prices before the world economy was ruined. Kissinger had started a seven-nation Middle East peace mission on 9 October.

3 October It is announced that the US navy will be allowed to keep its port facilities in Bahrain as a result of a shift in Bahraini government policy.

28 October Twenty Arab heads of state meeting in Morocco approve a resolution recognizing the PLO as the sole legitimate representative of the Palestinian people. On 13 November in the opening UN debate on the Palestine question the PLO chairman, Yasser Arafat, declared that the goal of the organization was a secular state in Palestine. The UN's Israeli delegate, Yosef Tekoah, promptly replied that this would mean the destruction of Israel.

1 November The International Monetary Fund reports that OPEC's reserves rose 8.95 per cent in September to $34,700 million, with Saudi Arabia advancing from thirteenth to fourth place in total reserves during the past year.

13 November The PLO chairman, Yasser Arafat, gives his famous speech to the UN General Assembly in New York in which he tells his audience 'I carry an olive branch in one hand and a machine gun in the other. Do not let the olive branch fall from my hands.' The speech was a turning-point for Palestinian diplomacy.

22 November Palestinian extremists who consider the PLO policies towards Israel as too lenient, hijack a British Airways passenger jet in Dubai and force it to land in Tunis. On the same day the UN General Assembly had approved two resolutions declaring Palestinian sovereignty rights and granting the PLO observer-status in the UN. On 25 November the four Palestinan commandos, after killing one passenger, surrendered to Libyan officials after Egypt had partially met their demands and freed five terrorists held in connection with the December 1973 attack on Rome airport. On 27 November the PLO itself announced the arrest of 26 people in Beirut and other Arab cities for their alleged involvement in the 22 November hijacking.

12 December The British £ sterling drops to its lowest level ever recorded in the wake of Saudi Arabia's decision not to accept British currency as payment for oil. In Vienna on 13 December OPEC ministers agreed to increase oil prices by 38 cents a barrel on 1 January 1975 and to increase the government share of oil marketed through their foreign companies to a maximum of $10.12 a barrel.

16 December Iraq reports that Iranians using US-made Hawk missiles have shot down two Iraqi planes in the northern part of Iraq near Iran. On 13 August Iran's Islamic Republic News Agency (IRNA) had reported that three Iranians were killed by Iraqi shelling around Qasr during the previous week.

1 9 7 5

4 January The Iranian prime minister, Amir Abbas Hoveida, warns that the use of force against one oil-producing state by a superpower will cause a world catastrophe. The Egyptian president, Anwar Sadat, echoed this sentiment on 9 January when he said that the Arabs would blow up their oil wells if the US tried to take the wells over by force. On 8 January the shah met King Husayn of Jordan in Amman where they agreed to seek a just peace in the Middle East, the key issue in the region's oil politics. In Cairo on 12 January he and President Sadat issued a joint communiqué calling for the resumption of the Geneva Middle East peace conference, support for the Palestine Liberation Organization (PLO) as sole representative of the Palestinians, the withdrawal of Israel from occupied Arab territories and the end to changes being made in Jerusalem by the Israelis.

19 January The Iranian foreign minister, Abbas Khalatbari, and the Iraqi foreign minister, Sa'doun Hammadi, fail to reach an agreement on their dispute over the Shatt al-Arab waterway dividing Iran and Iraq in the south. A delegation led by the under-secretary of the Iraqi Irrigation Ministry, Afif Rawi, had arrived in Abu Dhabi on 8 January to 'inform the United Arab Emirates of the grave situation resulting from Iranian troop concentrations on the Iraqi border'.

The Arab League had reportedly asked King Husayn of Jordan to persuade the Shah of Iran, during his visit to Jordan, to reduce Iran's military pressure on Iraq so that Iraqi armoured brigades might occupy positions on the Syrian-Israeli border. These brigades were currently in Iraqi Kurdistan fighting Iranian-backed Kurdish rebels. The shah had arrived in Amman on 6 January on his first visit to Jordan for ten years. During his discussions with King Husayn, it was widely reported that the king had agreed to mediation in the Iran-Iraq border dispute.

The shah's visits to Egypt and Jordan were indicative of Iran's desire for better relations with the Arab world. President Sadat of Egypt greeted him as a 'dear brother' and called his visit a 'turning point in the history of the region'. The shah was accompanied by his foreign minister, Khalatbari. The shah and Sadat were understood to have discussed agreements reached in May 1974 under which Iran pledged loans and investments of £360 million, although little progress had been made on these.

20 January King Faisal of Saudi Arabia ends a week-long visit to Syria, Jordan and Egypt in a new bid to unify Arab strategy against Israel. Closer economic ties were discussed in Damascus although Syrian officials confirmed that Saudi Arabia had already given Syria its share of the sum allotted to frontline (with Israel) states by the Rabat (Arab League) summit conference.

2 February The British commander of Oman's defence forces, Major-General Creasey, says that the shah has guaranteed air support against foreign intrusion of Oman's air space as requested. On 2 January the *International Herald Tribune* had reported that Iran had extended its naval presence in Oman under an agreement with it for joint naval operations in the crucial Strait of Hormuz. The Omani minister of state for foreign affairs, Qais Abd al-Moneim al-Zawawi, said that Iran would have the major responsiblity for implementing the agreement which was aimed at keeping the waters on both sides of the Strait 'secure and free'. He denied that the operations were a threat to Iraq, saying 'We are committed to a policy of free passage . . . There is no reason for Iraq to be concerned that Oman or Iran will hinder its use of the strait.'

About 20 million barrels of oil a day were carried by tankers through the strait. The agreement followed a July 1974 agreement between Oman and Iran on their continental shelf.

8 February The Beirut newspaper *Al-Anwar* reports the Iraqi discovery of a major oilfield on the western fringe of Baghdad.

9 February The US agrees to sell Iran six new DD-963 destroyers containing new anti-aircraft weapons at a cost of at least $700 million.

Iran's expenditure on US armaments was to reach $10,400 million between 1972 and 1976. In 1973 alone it bought $2,200 million worth of US weaponry, in 1974 $4,400 million and in 1975 $3,000 million. Its defence budget had soared from $880 million in 1970 to $6,325 million in 1975. During their May 1972 meeting with the shah in Tehran, Nixon and Kissinger had promised the shah that Iran might purchase any US non-nuclear weapons systems in quantities which the shah could specify. The agreement was part of their strategy for making Iran the West's 'policeman of the Gulf'. After the quintupling of oil prices following the 1967 Arab-Israeli war, the shah had the financial means to fulfil his military dream. By 1973 Iran had become the largest single purchaser of US arms in the world.

10 February The US Defence Department confirms that the Vinnell Corporation of Los Angeles will recruit former special forces to train Saudi Arabian troops to protect its oilfields in the kingdom.

12 February Iran announces that the riyal will no longer be linked directly to the US dollar but rather to the International Monetary Fund's special drawing rights of 16 nations. On 14 March Saudi Arabia, Kuwait and Qatar followed Iran's example.

23 February The seventeen-nation Arab Boycott Office meets in Cairo to consider changes in the list of firms it has banned from operating in Arab countries in retaliation for their dealings with Israel. When it ended its meeting on 5 March, it had removed eight businesses and 35 subsidiaries from its blacklist.

2 March The shah decrees the dissolution of Iran's two-party political system for at least the next two years. In its place he announced the formation of a single-party system based on the Iran National Resurgence Party (Rastakhiz) with Prime Minister Amir Abbas Hoveida as secretary-general. The move reflected his dissatisfaction with the present structure of party politics and his desire to unify those who supported the principles of his White Revolution policy (later to be called the 'Revolution of the Shah and the People').

6 March At OPEC's first summit conference in Algiers the shah and Saddam Husayn, vice-president of Iraq's Revolutionary Command Council (RCC), sign an agreement which 'completely eliminated the conflict between the two countries'. The agreement, which Iraq saw as favouring the militarily stronger Iran, settled their border differences and deprived the Kurds in Iraq of help from Iran in their struggle against the Iraqi government, thus effectively ending the Kurdish rebellion in Iraq.

Nevertheless, the price Iraq paid was the abandonment of its claims to full sovereignty over the whole Shatt al-Arab waterway dividing Iran and Iraq, and an agreement that the Thalweg (the median line of the deepest channel) should from then on constitute their boundary, allowing both countries to share the waterway. Nevertheless, the agreement, which was signed into a treaty on 15 June, was to remain a fragile one.

9 March The International Monetary Fund reports that the Organization of Petroleum Exporting Countries' (OPEC) trade surplus totalled a massive $97,000 million in 1974, compared with $22,000 million in 1973. Earlier the US treasury had released some rough estimates showing a much lower OPEC surplus for the first eight months of 1974, $25,000–28,000 million divided as follows: the US $7,000 million, Britain $3,000 million, Europe $2,000 million, the Third World $3,000 million and the Euro-markets (chiefly London) $10,000–13,000 million.

On 6 March OPEC ministers had ended their meeting in Algiers with a proposal to negotiate oil price stabilization with the industrialized nations. On 19 February London oil industry sources had reported a drop in oil production in January in Kuwait, Iran, Saudi Arabia and other Middle East countries because of the decline in global economic activity. Production for February was 10 per cent down from its 1974 level to 26 million barrels a day.

On 7 April representatives of oil-consuming and oil-producing nations were to hold preliminary talks in Paris although on 15 April the date of the proposed conference was set back when the negotiators failed to agree on an agenda.

13 March At the request of the shah, Iraq declares a two-week truce in its fight against Kurdish rebels. However, the Algiers agreement involving Iraq's acceptance of the Thalweg demarcation line in the Shatt al-Arab waterway was followed by Iran's cutting off supplies to Mulla Mustafa Barzani's Kurdish Democratic Party (KDP). Within a week the Kurdish revolt had collapsed. However, on 16 March Barzani said that the Kurds would continue their struggle for autonomy and rejected recent Iraqi peace proposals. His attitude may have been justified since at the end of the two-week cease-fire on 31 March, Iraqi forces moved against the remaining Kurdish troops in north-eastern Iraq. By 2 April they had completed their takeover of former Kurdish strongholds. On 4 July Damascus radio reported the formation of a new Kurdish nationalist movement in Iraq.

25 March King Faisal of Saudi Arabia is shot dead at his open *majlis* (assembly which any subject could attend) at the Royal Palace in Riyadh by his nephew, the 28-year-old Prince Faisal ibn Musaid ibn Abd al-Aziz al-Saud. It was the Prophet Muhammad's birthday.

According to Holden and Johns in *The House of Saud*, Prince Faisal entered his uncle's *raisa* (headquarters) unannounced, following the figure of the Kuwaiti oil minister, Abd al-Mutaleb Kazimi, whom he had known at the University of Colorado. As Kazimi was being introduced to the king by his Saudi counterpart, Zaki Yamani, the young prince aimed a .38 calibre pistol round the Kuwaiti's shoulder and fired three shots at the king. The first struck the king's throat, the others grazed his head and shattered an ear. The chief of royal protocol, Ahmad Abd al-Wahhab, fought the assassin to the ground. The king was raced to the Central Hospital of Riyadh but he could not be revived.

According to Holden and Johns, when, as a student at the University of Colorado in 1970, Prince Faisal had pleaded guilty of conspiracy to selling the drug LSD, King Faisal had apparently refused to intervene on his nephew's behalf. The prince was released on probation, remaining at the university until 1971. Once back in Saudi Arabia, the king insisted his nephew remain at home.

In 1965 the prince's brother Khaled had been shot dead by Saudi police after leading an abortive attempt to destroy a new radio transmitter (considered decadent by the puritan traditionalists) in Riyadh. This may have been Prince Faisal's instigation to murder.

At the University of Colorado he had, in addition, been influenced in half-baked radical ideas by his American girlfriend. He had expressed his desire to kill the king while in Beirut and was close to former King Saud whom King Faisal had ousted, and had recently become engaged to one of Saud's daughters, Sitta bint Saud. Moreover, he was from the Rashid clan of Hail whom the Al Saud had fought for over a century.

Despite fears of discord, the king was succeeded without fuss by his half brother Prince Khaled ibn Abd al-Aziz al-Saud after the senior princes had consulted with the *ulema* (clergy). The proclamation naming Khaled as king and his brother Fahd as crown prince was made a little over three hours after the killing.

The king was buried just over 24 hours later, with the funeral attended by a magnificant display of heads of state. The princes followed the bier from the *raisa* to a small mosque nearby where a crowd of about 100,000 had congregated. The body was then taken in a white ambulance to a bleak cemetery outside Riyadh and laid with the head to the north, the feet to the south and the face turned towards Mecca. The grave was unmarked as is the custom among the puritan 'Wahhabis' (more correctly *Muwahhidun*, or Unitarians). The crowd went mad with intense grief, engulfing the senior princes who stood about the grave.

Arab suspicions fell on the US Central Intelligence Agency (CIA), arguing that Faisal's intransigence over Jerusalem made him a natural target. The US *Washington Post* wrote: 'Faisal probably did more damage to the West than any other single man since Adolf Hitler.' According to Holden and Johns, however, no credence was given by the Saudis to widespread rumours that the CIA had been involved on Kissinger's instructions following the US secretary of state's last frosty interview with the king. Holden and Johns suggest that Arab radicals were more likely to have been behind the killing.

13 April Christian Phalangist gunmen ambush a bus at Ain el-Roumaneh, Lebanon, killing 27 of its Palestinian passengers. Many regarded the incident as the starting-point of the Lebanese civil war.

18 May Egypt's President Sadat ends a week-long visit to Kuwait, Iraq, Jordan and Syria where he discussed a possible joint position towards the US during the next stages of the Arab-Israeli negotiations.

21 May Three Iranian terrorists shoot dead US Colonel Paul Shaffer and Lieutenant-Colonel John Turner as they are being driven to their offices in Tehran. Only 10 days later, on 31 May, the US State Department disclosed that the Rockwell International Corporation had contracted with Iran to build a communications intelligence base in Iran capable of intercepting military and civilian communications throughout the Gulf region. It was not known whether the killings were connected with the project.

5 June The Suez Canal is reopened after being closed for eight years.

7 June Islamic militants stage demonstrations in Iran's holy shrine city of Qom to protest the social reforms introduced by the shah.

18 June Prince Faisal ibn Musaid, the assassin of King Faisal of Saudi Arabia, is beheaded before a 20,000-strong crowd. The initial Saudi government announcement had said that he was 'deranged' but it was eventually concluded that the killing had been an act of 'wilful and premeditated murder'. When at first the interrogators had told the prince that the king was merely wounded, he responded in great agitation, repeating his determination to kill the king. When they later changed tack and informed him of the truth – that King Faisal was dead – he suddenly became completely serene.

On 29 June King Khaled appointed a new Council of Ministers to replace the government of the late king.

10 July Dubai announces the nationalization of the five foreign oil companies that produce and market Dubai's 250,000 barrels of oil a day. The firms were to receive $110 million for their lost assets.

10 July UN officials in Beirut announce that Saudi Arabia will donate more than $11 million to the UN Relief and Works Agency for Palestinian Refugees (UNRWA). On the following day the US made a $6-million contribution to UNRWA.

16 July In Jeddah, 40 Islamic nations adopt a resolution calling for the expulsion of Israel from the UN.

7 August The Iranian government purchases a 25 per cent share of Deutsche Babcock and Wilcox AG of Oberhausen, making it the largest single shareholder in one of West Germany's top 50 companies.

1 September Middle East broker for several US firms, Adnan Khashogji, admits to pocketing $250,000 of a bribe intended for Saudi General Hashim Hashim, former commander of the Saudi Royal Air Force, given by the US Northrop Corporation. The revelation followed the hearings of the US Senate Foreign Relations Subcommittee on Multinational Corporations, and the publication of Northrop and Lockheed papers related to it. The fees were to have been paid to Khashogji for two contracts, worth $2,600 million, to supply Saudi Arabia with 60 Northrop F-5 fighters and five years of F-5 training and spares. Khashogji was later alleged to have said 'I pocketed it myself to save Northrop making a dreadful mistake.'

10 September During the week up to 10 September, over 100 people are reported killed in fighting between Muslims and Christians in Beirut. On 23 September Maronite Christian religious and political leaders in Lebanon issued a warning against any attempts to alter the country's long-standing balance between the Muslim and Christian communities. Inter-ethnic fighting was to continue throughout the year. On one day, 1 November, 100 people were reported to have been killed.

19 September A group of Arab countries pledges $25 million to UN Educational, Scientific and Cultural Organization (UNESCO) to replace funds withheld by the US because of the organization's alleged anti-Israeli actions.

1 October Saudi Arabia reports August oil production at 8.2 million barrels a day, up 1.2 million over July, while Abu Dhabi reduces its production to 1.35 million barrels a day.

10 November A UN General Assembly resolution declares that 'Zionism is a form of racism'.

18 November Kuwait, Saudi Arabia, Bahrain, Oman and the United Arab Emirates (UAE) agree to establish an investment bank to channel their wealth into development projects.

23 November The British foreign secretary, James Callaghan, meets Saudi Arabian officials in Riyadh and signs an agreement promising cultural and technical co-operation.

1 December Gulf Oil and British Petroleum Company Ltd (BP) sign an agreement with Kuwait finalizing the agreement for a 100-per cent takeover of the Kuwait oil industry by the Kuwaiti government. The agreement involved compensation to BP and Gulf of $66 million, a discount on the 93 per cent of postings third party selling price of 15 cents a barrel reflecting BP's and Gulf's continuing provision of technical services and personnel, the large size of their purchases and their undertakings to buy Kuwaiti bunker fuel and use Kuwaiti tankers. It also involved a BP commitment to take an average of 450,000 barrels a day between 1 January 1976 and 1 April 1980 and a Gulf Oil commitment to take 500,000 barrels a day over the same period.

8 December Iraq announces the takeover of the remaining 23.75 per cent of French, British and Dutch assets in the Basrah Petroleum Company, completing Iraq's nationalization of its oil wealth. The way had been opened for Iraq's decision by Kuwait's full takeover of its oil industry on 1 December.

11 December The Oman government claims to have successfully ended its 10-year war against rebels in the southern Dhofar province. On 17 October Iranian troops had attacked the rebels in Dhofar while the Omani air force struck at rebel positions in South Yemen. Although the Popular Front for the Liberation of Oman (PFLO) continued to issue aggressive communiqués from Aden, active guerrillas had been reduced to a handful of men based in South Yemen (the PDRY). PFLOAG had become PFLO in July 1974.

21 December Pro-Palestinian guerrillas, led by Iilich Ramirez Sanchez – alias 'Carlos' – break into the OPEC ministers conference in Vienna, kill three people and wound seven others. Two of those killed were gunned down by Gabrielle Krocher-Tiederman of the Baader-Meinhof gang. Carlos operated for Dr George Habash's Popular front for the Liberation of Palestine (PFLP).

The group took 81 hostages, including 11 OPEC ministers. In particular they threatened the Saudi petroleum minister, Zaki Yamani, and the Iranian petroleum minister, Jamshid Amouzegar, if their demands were not met. On 22 December the guerrillas flew some of the hostages on a comandeered Austrian plane to Algeria. On the same day a group calling itself the Arm of the Arab Revolution claimed credit for the attack as Palestinian groups in Beirut, including the PLO, disclaimed any responsibility. On 23 December, after a stop-over in Tripoli, Libya, the guerrillas returned to Algiers where they set the remaining hostages free and surrendered to the Algerian authorities. In exchange they had been granted safe passage and a ransom paid by the Saudis and Iranians which was rumoured to be anything from $5 million to $50 million. Algeria gave Carlos temporary refuge but he was later said to have been given political asylum in Libya which he described as his 'Boss'.

1 9 7 6

2 January A British magazine article shows that the sultan of Oman's survival depends on British military support. 'Officially', wrote Fred Halliday in the British weekly magazine *The New Statesman*, 'the British admit to only 600 military personnel in Oman; but there are, in fact, over 2,000 – some working as combat officers and pilots, some as training operatives, and some as servicing and communications experts at the two British air-force bases of Salalah (in Dhofar) and Masira. A key branch of the British apparatus is made up of the estimate of 100 members of the Special Air Service (SAS), a counter-insurgence unit used on behind-the-scenes missions and on training local forces'.

Halliday described the Dhofar province as 'an ideal setting for counter-insurgency operations' because the combat area was relatively small, the population limited and the guerrillas' supply lines ran through mountains less than 20 miles (32 kilometres) wide. Moreover, 'there are no troublesome observers to report British actions'. One British tactic was 'food control' which could more accurately be described as starvation and forced resettlement. The British firm, Sir William Halcrow, had built nine resettlement centres as part of an £8-million counter-insurgency project and the mountain population was being forced to concentrate in these or in newly-built centres around the capital, Salalah, according to Halliday.

He said that the resettlement programme was supported by a policy of 'systematic bombardment of the guerrilla-held areas by the sultan's air force, navy and artillery detachments. All animals and crops outside government areas are attacked, as are wells and mountain paths used by inhabitants.' The population had the choice of 'either to starve, get shelled to death, or to take refuge in government centres'.

On 13 January the US *New York Times* reported that 'Despite Oman's contention that it has crushed its southern rebels, Iranian forces will remain . . . for at least the near future.' Iran had some 3,000 troops in Oman, according to the Iranian Foreign Ministry.

14 January Some 3,000–4,000 Cuban military personnel are stationed in South Yemen, according to the *Christian Science Monitor* quoting 'Western intelligence sources'. However, on 15 January *United Press International* said that 'an official Washington source' had confirmed the Cuban presence, which was estimated to be 'only a few hundred strong.'

15 January The Kuwaiti finance minister, Abd al-Rahman Salem Atiqi, tells a press conference that Kuwait has ordered weapons from the Soviet Union as part of a programme to diversify its sources of arms. He was quoted as saying that it was 'essential for the USA to grasp the significance of the deal'. The US had to realize that by selling arms to Israel, it was forcing the Arab states to look elsewhere for weapons, he said. Kuwait's foreign minister, Shaikh Sabah al-Ahmad al-Jaber, had visited the Soviet Union in December 1985. Apart from Iraq, Kuwait was the only Arab state known to have ordered arms from the Soviet Union – its sources of arms to date being Britain, France and the US.

20 January In an interview published in the Kuwaiti newspaper *As-Siyasa*, the Shah of Iran again protests against the 'childish renaming' by the Arabs of the Persian Gulf as the Arabian Gulf. He said that this was 'a fabricated name which does not exist on world maps and atlases' and which did not have any historic basis.

On 7 January Iran had recalled its ambassadors from the seven Gulf countries after reports that they were forming the agency, indicating their intention to rename the Gulf. On 9 January the Iraqi foreign minister, Sa'doun Hammadi, arrived in Kuwait for talks with the Kuwaiti foreign minister, Shaikh Sabah al-Ahmad al-Jaber, on the situation in the Gulf, 'especially in the wake of Iranian anger over the setting up of an Arab Gulf News Agency.'

21 January British Airways' Concorde aircraft begins a twice-weekly supersonic service from London to Bahrain. It completed the 3,515-mile, (5,656-kilometre) journey in 3 hours 38 minutes, 15 minutes ahead of schedule.

26 January The UN Security Council's debate on the Middle East ends with the defeat of a pro-Palestinian resolution by a US veto on a 9-1 vote. However, on 27 January the Palestine Liberation Organization (PLO) was accepted as a new member of the Group of 77 developing nations of UN Conference on Trade and Development (UNCTAD). On 12 January the Security Council had begun its debate on the Middle East by voting to permit the PLO to participate in the debate with the rights of a member nation.

31 January The offices of two newspapers, one pro-Iraqi and one pro-Libyan in a Beirut suburb are attacked by Saiqa, a pro-Syrian Palestinian guerrilla group, killing seven newsmen, wounding another seven and kidnapping five. The pro-Iraqi *Beirut* and the pro-Libyan *Al-Muharrer* both supported the Rejection Front Palestinian groups who opposed a negotiated settlement with Israel. Iraq was critical of Syria's role in the developing Lebanese civil war.

On 18 January any hopes for a cease-fire in Lebanon were shattered when Phalangist and other right-wing forces attacked the port slum areas of Qarantina and Maslakh in an attempt to secure supply lines to their positions in Beirut's centre and to 'liberate' remaining non-Christian pockets in Beirut's eastern sector. Qarantina was virtually destroyed by rocket- and mortar-fire and its mainly Shi'i Muslim, Kurdish and Sunni Muslim Palestinian inhabitants were rounded up and transported to Muslim areas.

3 February The Iranian government reports that a sharp reduction in oil revenue has slowed the country's growth rate by 60 per cent since the spring of 1975.

18 February Saudi Arabia and Iraq sign an agreement in its final form on the demarcation of their borders, according to a Riyadh Radio report. The two countries had reached an agreement on the delineation of their borders in the shared Neutral Zone in July 1975.

23 February The Northrop Corporation says it paid Iran $2.1 million as an apparent repayment for the use of a third party as an agent in Northrop's sales of military aircraft to Iran. On 19 January Saudi Arabia was reported to have blocked the payment of $68 million in agent's fees to the Saudi businessman Adnan Khashogji who was accused in 1975 of bribing two Saudi generals on behalf of the US Northrop aircraft company. The fees were allegedly to have been paid to Khashogji for two contracts, worth $2,600 million, to supply Saudi Arabia with 60 Northrop F-5 fighters and five years of F-5 training and spares.

On 11 March The US *Wall Street Journal* reported that the US Defence Department had awarded Northrop a $1,500-million contract to provide support facilities and training for the Saudi air force. Under the Foreign Military Sales Act the US would act as an agent between the foreign government and the contractor providing the services.

24 February Associated Press-Dow Jones quotes a Kuwaiti oil ministry announcement that Kuwait has begun negotiations with the American Independent Oil Company (Aminoil) to take over Aminoil's operations in the Saudi-Kuwaiti partitioned zone.

26 February The Popular Front for the Liberation of Oman (PFLO) condemns Sadat's visit to Oman. Claiming that he was mediating in the dispute between Oman and South Yemen, the PFLO said that South Yemen was not involved and that the Arab League fact-finding committee on Dhofar had conducted its talks with the PFLO as a principal party in the dispute, not with South Yemen.

29 February The Egyptian president, Anwar Sadat, ending a visit to the Arab oil-producing states that resulted in pledges of aid, announces that he has made a three-point 'secret agreement' on the Middle East with the US as part of the 1975 Sinai accords. His visit, accompanied by a delegation which included the Egyptian premier, Mamdouh Salem, the foreign minister, Ismail Fahmy, the finance minister, Ahmad Abu Ismail (who returned to Egypt after the visit to Saudi Arabia), the housing and reconstruction minister, Othman Ahmad Othman, and the planning minister, Ibrahim Hilmi Abd al-Rahman, was aimed at seeking financial support for Egypt's flagging economy and enlisting support for Egypt's policies on the Arab-Israeli question. He visited Saudi Arabia from 21 to 26 February, before making brief visits to Oman, Abu Dhabi, Bahrain and Qatar, arriving in Kuwait on 28 February.

Although Sadat declared himself completely satisfied with agreements on economic and political questions, the amount of aid promised to Egypt was thought to have been about $700 million, disastrously short of the $4,000 million he had said Egypt needed to keep the economy afloat over the next two years. Saudi Arabia granted $300 million and the United Arab Emirates (UAE) $150 million, while Qatar promised an undisclosed amount. Kuwait was believed to have agreed to give $150–$200 million.

Aid from Saudi Arabia and the Gulf states virtually ceased after Egypt signed the second disengagement agreement with Israel (the Sinai Accords) in 1975. Before the second agreement, in July 1975 Saudi Arabia had lent Egypt $600 million. The last stage in the implementation of the second disengagement agreement began on 15 February when UN emergency force troops entered the northern sector of the new UN buffer zone.

7 March The national executive of the Australian Labour Party finds the former Australian premier, Gough Whitlam, guilty of 'grave errors of judgement' for his part in seeking Iraqi funds for the party's election campaign, according to a Reuter report. However, it stressed that the party 'at no time officially engaged in any negotiations . . . to receive Arab funds' and that no money had been received.

On 27 February the Australian government had investigated a report that Iraq had offered $A500,000 to the election funds of the Australian Labour Party. According to an article in the Sydney newspaper *The Australian*, two armed Iraqi officials, 'one of them the head of the secret police', met Whitlam at a Sydney flat five days before the 13 December 1975 election in which he was heavily defeated. Whitlam had told them that 'only Zionist pressure in Australia prevented him from being pro-Arab' and had been assured that money would be made available (although none had arrived). The newspaper alleged that Whitlam had initiated the appeal for Iraqi funds at the start of his political campaign in November. Although a 'left-wing and pro-Arab' member of the party executive (William Hartley) had offered to act as an intermediary, negotiations had been conducted through a businessman, Henri Fischer, who was described as right wing and anti-semitic.

Whitlam claimed that he had met the 'unarmed members of the [Iraqi] Ba'th Party' at a social gathering on 10 December. He insisted that neither the subject of raising funds to cover his party's $A400,000-campaign debt nor his neutral stand on the Arab-Israeli question had been raised at the meeting. According to the report, Whitlam had issued a writ for $A500,000 against the newspaper's publishers, News Limited.

8 March Kuwait's population is 995,000, according to a recent survey reported by the weekly *Middle East Money*. According to the survey, of the total population only 472,000 were Kuwaiti nationals.

10 March Diplomatic relations between Saudi Arabia and Marxist South Yemen (the Popular Democratic Republic of Yemen – PDRY) are established. Aden radio welcomed the move as a 'victory for the two fraternal peoples', denying 'poisonous rumours' that South Yemen had received $400 million from Saudi Arabia and accusing 'hired pens' of attempting to 'rouse public opinion by portraying the relationship as one of expedience'. Riyadh Radio stressed that the two countries were seeking to guarantee the 'security and stability of the Arabian peninsula and the interests of the Arab nation, away from foreign influence'.

Nevertheless, on 29 March Saudi Arabia was reported to have given South Yemen $100 million in aid. On 31 March the kingdom was reported to have agreed to sponsor a scheme to build an oil terminal on South Yemen's Hadramaut coast linked by pipeline to Saudi and other Gulf ports. The line would provide an alternative outlet should a dispute block the entrance to the Gulf.

On 7 April Iran strongly condemned the planned pipeline. An editorial in the ruling Iranian Rastakhiz Party newspaper said the scheme would allow the Gulf emirates to export their oil without using the strategic Gulf waterway which Iran was defending with 'arms costing thousands of millions of dollars'. Iran had first been invited to dispatch troops by Sultan Qaboos of Oman in 1972.

Since South Yemen gained independence from Britain in November 1967, Oman had been its bitter ideological enemy. In November 1969 there had been a serious border clash at Wadiah, involving tanks, armoured cars and aircraft. However both countries were worried about Iran's influence in the Gulf and it was thought that South Yemen might be prepared to end its support for the PFLO guerrillas in return for Saudi pressure on Sultan Qaboos of Oman to bring about the withdrawal of Iranian forces.

Détente between Saudi Arabia and Aden boded well for prospects of eventual Yemeni unity since it would discourage pro-Saudi monarchists in North Yemen from harassing the South Yemeni regime. According to a report on 11 March by the Beirut weekly *Al-Hawadeth*, the announcement of diplomatic relations had been the result of a secret visit to Saudi Arabia by the North Yemeni foreign minister, Muhammad Saleh Mouti, during President Sadat of Egypt's visit to Saudi Arabia in February 1976.

Oman announced on 10 March that it welcomed the development and announced on the same day a two-month amnesty for 'all Omani citizens who have been misled by the false propaganda'. The amnesty was aimed at members of the PFLO. On the following day Oman and South Yemen agreed to a cease-fire although later in the month Omani defence spokesmen claimed that South Yemen was still shelling Omani coastal towns.

Furthermore, in a commentary broadcast on 14 March by the Voice of Oman Revolution (Aden) the PFLO said the 'Omani masses and our audacious revolutionaries will not throw away their weapons and will not bow at the feet of the British colonialists and the Iranian invaders'. However, on 18 April Oman's Defence Ministry claimed that 332 members of the PFLO had surrendered to the government since the sultan had announced the end of the revolt in December and that all had been pardoned under the terms of the amnesty.

Later in the month, the Soviet ambassador to Aden, Vladimir Koboshkin, was declared *persona non grata*.

11 March The *Washington Post* says that Central Intelligence Agency (CIA) officials have told members of the American Institute of Aeronautics and Astronautics that it estimates that Israel has 10–20 nuclear weapons available for use. On 5 April Israel denied a *Time* magazine report that it had assembled 13 atomic bombs at the start of the 1973 Arab-Israeli war and then stored them when the war turned in Israel's favour.

14 March Egypt's President Sadat ends the 1971 Soviet-Egyptian treaty.

16 March According to a Reuter report, the Netherlands' Foreign Ministry has just been informed of the execution in Baghdad three months ago of Holenbert Leon Aronson on charges of spying for Israel. Aronson had been tried by a revolutionary court in October 1975 and on 3 November the Iraqi news agency reported that he had been executed. However, the Netherlands' Foreign Ministry was later informed that he was still alive but under sentence of death. The prime minister of the Netherlands, Joop den Uyl, told a press conference that Iraq had executed Aronson 'without a form of trial, contrary to the most elementary human rights'. He said that the Iraqi authorities 'had never told the truth' to the chargé d'affaires, Gerben Meihuizen. Meihuizen was immediately recalled to Amsterdam for consultations. The Netherlands' foreign minister, Max van der Stoel, described the execution as 'a revolting business'. Nevertheless, the Foreign Ministry indicated that it did not intend to break links with Iraq.

On 24 March the Israeli foreign minister, Yigal Allon, was quoted as saying that the allegation that Aronson had worked for Israel was 'a tissue of lies'. For its part, on 22 March the Baghdad daily newspaper *Al-Jumhuriya* accused the Netherlands of conducting 'a campaign of lies and provocations against Iraq' over the execution, and harbouring 'a deeply-rooted imperialist rancour' against Iraq because of the 'revolution's blow to the oil monopolies, which included Dutch shares'. Den Uyl and der Stoel had 'failed to give any justification for the spy's presence in the northern part of our country', the newspaper said, adding that 'agents and spies' would be 'punished by the revolution and the masses, regardless of any considerations'.

19 March In 1975 the Arabian American Oil Company (ARAMCO) discovered three oilfields in Saudi Arabia with total proven reserves of 7,000 million barrels, ARAMCO's chairman, Frank Jungers, is quoted as saying. The three fields were: Ribyan, some 30 miles (48 kilometres) offshore in the Gulf and 65 miles (105 kilometres) from the neutral zone; Lawada, also offshore and 30 miles (48 kilometres) east of Ribyan; and an onshore field, Dibdiba, 85 miles (137 kilometres) inland and 75 miles (121 kilometres) south of the neutral zone border. At the time, the Saudi government owned 60 per cent of ARAMCO, a consortium of Standard Oil of California (Socal – 30 per cent), Exxon (30 per cent), Texaco (30 per cent) and Mobil (10 per cent).

According to the March edition of the *Petroleum Economist*, Saudi Arabian oil revenues increased by 420 per cent to $22,573 million in 1974 as a result of higher posted prices, production growth and the gradual increase in the royalty and income-tax rate. Average daily crude-oil production was 8.5 million barrels in 1974, compared with 7.6 million barrels in 1973. Saudi oil production represented 14.4 per cent of the world total in 1974, and about 27.7 per cent of OPEC production.

27 April The UAE president, Shaikh Zayed, opens the UAE's first oil refinery at Umm al-Nar, a small island east of Abu Dhabi. The 15,000-barrel-a-day refinery had been built by Kellogg International of Britain in three years at a cost of $50 million.

4 May Iranian police shoot and kill two alleged terrorists in Tehran, bringing to 31 the number of guerrillas executed or killed by police in shoot-outs since January. On 22 May the newspaper of Iran's ruling Rastakhiz Party said that Libya had supplied arms and money to Iranian terrorists. Also in May guerrillas killed two colonels in the US air force. Other US citizens had been killed in 1972 and 1973.

6 May The seven member emirates of the UAE agree in principle to merge their armed forces under the operational command of the chief-of-staff, Major-General Awad Khaledi. The son of the UAE president, Shaikh Zayed, Shaikh Khalifa, would be appointed deputy supreme commander of the new federal defence force under his father.

12 June All Iraqi reservists are ordered to report to their units as Iraqi troops mass near the Syrian border.

11 July Kamal Jumblatt, head of the Muslim-Lebanese leftist alliance and leader of Lebanon's Druze community, asks Saudi Arabia, Algeria, Libya, Iraq and Egypt for military and political intervention against the Syrian forces who have entered Lebanon.

7 August The US secretary of state, Henry Kissinger, signs an agreement whereby Iran will buy $10,000 million in arms from the US as part of a 1975–80 trade arrangement that will total about $50,000 million. He defended the size of the transaction as being in the best interest of the US. Total US military sales to Iran for 1975 were to be worth $3,021 million while Iran's defence budget was to increase from $3,680 million in 1974 to $6,325 million in 1975, a 72 per cent increase.

12 August Christian Maronite forces capture a Palestinian quarter of Beirut, Tel al-Zaatar, and massacre over 1,000 men, women and children.

27 August Iran and the US-based Occidental Petroleum Corporation cancel a $125-million transaction to develop Caspian Sea oil and to process and market other Iranian petroleum. Iran had announced plans on 20 June to buy $125 million worth of shares in Occidental in a series of joint ventures with the company.

29 August The Kuwaiti premier, Shaikh Jaber al-Ahmad al-Sabah, and his cabinet resign, the Kuwaiti National Assembly is dissolved and constitutional provisions on press freedom and elections are suspended following tensions arising from the large Palestinian population in Kuwait and the government's pro-Syrian policy in the Lebanese civil war. However, on 6 September Shaikh Jaber formed a new 18-member cabinet, retaining all members of his previous cabinet.

6 September In a move sponsored by Egypt, the Arab League unanimously raises the status of the PLO from a non-voting member to the League's twenty-first full voting member.

18 October A truce to end the Lebanese civil war is signed in Riyadh after a two-day meeting attended by the heads of state of Saudi Arabia, Kuwait, Egypt, Syria and Lebanon and the PLO leader, Yasser Arafat. The agreement allowed for the expansion of the Arab League peace-keeping force in Lebanon, the withdrawal of all combatants to pre-April 1975 positions, and Palestinian adherence to the 1969 Cairo agreement which confined Palestinian guerrilla forces in Lebanon to refugee camps and to the Arkub region of the south-east. By 21 October fighting slowed down as the peace negotiated by the six Arab leaders took effect. On 26 October the Arab League summit in Cairo approved the proposals of the six leaders. Three weeks later Syrian troops, technically part of the Arab League force, entered Beirut and the Lebanese civil war was officially declared over (although it was to be a deceptive end).

15 November Syrian peace-keeping troops move out of the eastern sector of Beirut and enter the centre of the capital, completing their occupation of the city. By 21 November Syrian troops, accompanied by contingents of other Arab peace-keeping forces, had complete control of Lebanon except for a 15-mile (24-kilometre) strip along the Israeli border.

16 November Iranian security police shoot and kill three 'terrorists' and capture seven others in Tehran in an intensified drive to rid the city of guerrillas.

24 November The US and Iran sign a contract providing for US civilian experts to train Iranian air-force personnel to handle the logistics of the aircraft Iran is buying from the US.

25 November Damascus reports that Iraq and Syria have withdrawn most of the troops massed along their border since June following an agreement negotiated by Egypt.

25 November South Yemen claims that its ground forces have shot down 1 of 10 Iranian F-4 Phantom jets that violated its airspace on a spy mission after taking off from Oman.

28 November Amnesty International says that Iran's secret police, the Organization of National Security and Intelligence (SAVAK), has imprisoned 25,000–100,000 of its citizens for political reasons and has frequently tortured them. In its annual report for 1974–5, Amnesty International's secretary-general said 'No country in the world has a worse record in human rights than Iran.' SAVAK was set up with US help in 1953 by General Bakhtiar following the shah's return from exile after the Iran oil crisis.

On 28 May the International Commission of Jurists had also accused SAVAK of torturing political prisoners.

29 November Shaikh Zayed is elected president of the UAE for a second five-year term. He had been elected president on the UAE's formation in December 1971.

2 December The International Committee of the Red Cross says that the Lebanese civil war has left more than 300,000 destitute, most of them Palestinians who represent 12 per cent of the population.

14 December A bomb blast at Baghdad's international airport kills three, injures more than 230 and causes heavy damage to the building.

17 December The Organization of Petroleum Exporting Countries (OPEC) meeting in Qatar from 15 to 17 December sets varying oil prices. Saudi Arabia and the UAE said they would raise oil prices by only 5 per cent for the first six months of 1977 while OPEC's 11 other members said that they would increase prices by 10 per cent, and by another 5 per cent after 1 July. On 20 December Iraq and Iran both criticized Saudi Arabia for not agreeing with other members to raise its oil prices by 15 per cent over 1976.

1 9 7 7

9 January The founder of the militant Palestinian Black September group, Abu Daoud, is arrested in Paris. Black September had been responsible for the killing of 11 Israeli athletes at the 1972 Munich Olympics. However, on 12 January a Paris court found no grounds for holding Abu Daoud and he was expelled to Algiers.

18/19 January Serious rioting in Egypt over food prices demonstrates the country's urgent need for economic support from its oil-rich Gulf neighbours.

1–12 February The UN secretary-general, Kurt Waldheim, visits Egypt, Syria, Saudi Arabia, Lebanon, Jordan and Israel. From 15 to 21 February the US secretary of state, Cyrus Vance, visited Israel, Egypt, Lebanon, Jordan, Saudi Arabia and Syria.

2 February The agreement establishing the Arab Monetary Fund comes into force. Its members comprised 19 Arab countries and the Palestine Liberation Organization (PLO). The agreement establishing the Fund had been approved by the Economic Council of Arab States in Rabat, Morocco, in April 1976. Of the total 12,000 shares in the Fund, Saudi Arabia was the single largest holder with 1,800, followed by Kuwait with 1,200 (as of 31 December 1985).

6 February Saudi Arabia rejects a compromise plan proposed by Qatar to end the Organization of Petroleum Exporting Countries' (OPEC) two-tier pricing system.

16 March Kamal Jumblatt, leader of Lebanon's Druze community, is assassinated. It was widely believed that the Syrians had killed him.

17 March The US president, Jimmy Carter, in Clinton, Massachusetts, calls for the establishment of a Palestinian homeland.

18 May In Israel, the right-wing Likud Party wins the election. A new government formed by Menachem Begin was expected to take a hardline stand against Arab demands for the return of the Occupied Territories. Begin was the former leader of the Jewish terror group, Irgun Zvai Leumi, which fought against the British prior to the declaration of the state of Israel in 1948.

19 May A summit conference is held in Riyadh between Saudi Arabia's King Khaled, the Egyptian president, Anwar Sadat, and the Syrian president, Hafez Asad.

25 May In talks in Washington from 23 to 27 May, Crown Prince Fahd of Saudi Arabia assures President Carter that the Saudis will not impose another oil embargo on the US to force concessions from Israel to achieve a Middle East peace settlement. On 10 May Fahd repeated a proposal, reportedly also submitted by Syria's President Asad, that the creation of a Palestinian state in the Israeli-occupied West Bank and Gaza Strip be part of an overall peace settlement.

16 June Iran is hit by a nationwide energy shortage attributed to contractual problems, a sharp drop in water levels and an underestimation of energy demand.

29 June European Economic Community (EEC) heads of state issue a declaration on the Middle East, including a call for a Palestinian homeland.

4 July Syria accuses Iraq of responsibility for a car bomb which exploded in Damascus on 4 July, killing 1 person and injuring 12. Documents found in the car showed that it had entered Syria from Iraq on 28 June and evidence pointed to Baghdad's involvement. Damascus radio concluded that 'this new crime is a link in a chain of malicious acts by the tribal Takriti regime' whose purpose was to weaken Syria. 'Takriti regime' was a reference to the fact that both the president, Ahmad Hasan al-Bakr, and the deputy chairman of Iraq's Revolutionary Command Council (RCC), Saddam Husayn, were from the town of Takrit, in northern Iraq.

On 10 July another bomb exploded in Damascus, killing 2 and wounding 53. Meanwhile, Iraq accused Syria of the explosion at Baghdad airport in December 1976. Also in December the Syrians arrested various people, allegedly directed from, and financed by Baghdad, in connection with the attempted assassination of the Syrian deputy premier and foreign minister, Abd al-Halim Khaddam.

In February Iraq announced that an alleged Syrian agent had been arrested with a suitcase of explosives in the shrine of Imam Husayn in the holy Shi'i city of Kerbela in Iraq which was then full of pilgrims. In June two men were hanged in Syria after the assassination of the rector of Damascus University in February, allegedly under instructions from Iraq.

6 July The Iraqi information minister, Tariq Aziz, describes the recent talks in Baghdad with the Kuwaiti minister of interior and defence, Shaikh Sa'd Abdullah Salem al-Sabah, as 'one of the most important contacts ever held between Kuwait and Iraqi leaders', according to Kuwait's *Arab Times*. Shaikh Sa'd visited Iraq from 27 June to 3 July and his talks with Iraq's interior minister, Izzat Ibrahim, the deputy chairman of the RCC, Saddam Husayn, and the minister of state, Sa'doun Shaker, had been concerned mainly with Kuwait's disputed border with Iraq. Despite the polite protocol, observers agreed that the highly sensitive border issue was by no means settled.

Iraq had claimed sovereignty over Kuwait shortly after the country became independent in 1961. Although Iraq recognized Kuwait in October 1963, it still had an outstanding claim to the strategic Warba and Bubiyan islands off Kuwait's coast. Iraqi troops were reported to have crossed into Kuwait in late 1974 and again in September 1976. A high-level Iraqi delegation had visited Kuwait in April 1977 to discuss the border problem.

13 July Saudi and Iranian delegates to the OPEC Stockholm meeting say they might consider an oil-price freeze through 1978, but other OPEC members oppose or refuse to commit themselves on the subject. On 3 July Saudi Arabia and the UAE had announced a 5 per cent increase in the price of their oil to $12.70 a barrel, the price charged since 1 January by the 11 other members of OPEC. However, on 4 May the Saudi finance minister, Muhammad Ali Aba al-Khail, had expressed Saudi reluctance at contributing $4,000 million to the International Monetary Fund's temporary lending facility, the figure expected to make the plan a success. He contended that Saudi Arabia, the richest OPEC nation, was really poor given that its assets were merely money rather than wealth derived from a developed economy.

On 28 April Saudi Arabia had said that it would not raise its oil prices to conform with those of other OPEC members and on 8 January it had published a statement that it would require US companies to submit reports to prove that they were passing on to consumers the benefits of the lower Saudi oil-price increases.

16 July Egyptian President Sadat announces that the Soviets have cancelled their military contracts with Egypt and that Saudi Arabia has agreed to finance the development of the Egyptian armed forces.

July At the end of July Princess Misha'il bint Fahd ibn Muhammad, the granddaughter of King Abd al-Aziz's eldest surviving son, and her lover Khaled Muhalhal, a nephew of General Ali Shaeir, the Saudi ambassador to Lebanon, are executed. They were executed for adultery although the story was not to be known abroad until January 1978. The executions took place in a parking lot off Jeddah's King Abd al-Aziz Street instead of in the Midan Bab al-Sharif where executions were normally carried out. It also broke convention by being held on a Saturday rather than on a Friday. The princess was shot in the head six times and Khaled Muhallal was clumsily decapitated with a sword. It was clear that the execution had not been carried out according to due process of the law but was ordered by her uncle Muhammad as his tribal right (in Islamic law four male witnesses must attest to have seen actual penetration). The incident was to highlight the widening gap between Saudi modernists and traditionalists.

July AMIO has decided to manufacture anti-tank missiles, helicopters and military jeeps, according to an article in the London-published Middle East magazine. The Cairo-based AMIO was set up by Egypt, Saudi Arabia, Qatar and the UAE in May 1975 with a capital of $1,040 million to offset the Soviet refusal to replace arms lost by Egypt during the Arab-Israeli war of 1973.

1 August US Secretary of State Cyrus Vance begins a 12-day tour of the Middle East to promote US efforts to reconvene the Geneva peace conference. However, on 9 August he encountered strong Israeli opposition to returning the West Bank and the Gaza Strip, to the creation of a Palestinian state in the Occupied Territories or to dealing with the PLO, even if it accepted UN resolution 242 (which involved the recognition of Israel). On 14 August the Israeli government announced plans to grant equal rights to Arabs in the West Bank and Gaza, covering social services such as health care, national insurance and free education. Nevertheless, on 2 September Israel disclosed a settlement plan for two million Jews in a region stretching from the Golan Heights to the tip of the Sinai Peninsula by the end of the century as a security buffer.

7 August Jamshid Amouzegar replaces Amir Abbas Hoveida as Iranian premier after the latter resigns on 6 August at the request of the shah. The shah appointed Hoveida, a loyal, personal friend, as minister of the Imperial Court.

13 September Princess Ashraf, the shah's twin sister, narrowly escapes assassination while she is driving on a narrow road near the French Riviera resort, Juan les Pins.

18 October West German commandos, led by two British Special Air Service (SAS) commandos, force their way onto a hijacked Lufthansa airliner in Mogadishu, Somalia, killing three of the four Palestinian terrorists and freeing the 86 passengers and crew held captive since 13 October.

Soon afterwards the suicides of some of the Baader-Meinhof Gang leaders was announced and some hours after that West German industrialist Hanns-Martin Schleyer, kidnapped on 5 September, was murdered. On 19 October Schleyer's body was found with three bullets in the head and a slashed throat in a car boot in Alsace after what West German officials described as the largest man-hunt in West German history.

The bloody saga began on 13 October when a West German group calling itself the Struggle Against World Imperialism seized the jet as it took off from the Spanish island of Majorca for Frankfurt. Having made refuelling stops in Rome, Cyprus and Bahrain the jet landed at Dubai on 15 October. It then took off for Aden where it landed despite the South Yemeni government's decision to block off the airport runways.

On 16 October the hijackers shot the pilot, Captain Jurgen Schumann, in the head in full view of the passengers and left his body lying on the floor of the plane for hours. On 17 October the jet left Aden and landed in Mogadishu where the terrorists pushed the body of the dead pilot onto the runway.

On the same day the German chancellor, Helmut Schmidt, arrived in Mogadishu and began negotiations with the Somali government to permit West German armed commandos to attempt a rescue. His effort was backed by Britain, France and the US.

15 November The Israeli prime minister, Menachem Begin, formally invites Egypt's President Anwar Sadat to meet him in Israel for discussions on a Middle East settlement. On 9 November Sadat shocked Egypt's People's Assembly, saying 'Israel will be astonished when it hears me saying now, before you, that I am ready to go to their own house, to the Knesset itself, to talk to them.' After four wars with Israel and almost 30 years of ferocious anti-Israeli propaganda throughout the Arab world, his offer was greeted in the Arab world with amazement.

On 16 November he arrived in Damascus where he vainly hoped to persuade Syrian President Asad to support his visit. On 17 November he accepted Begin's invitation, a decision which led to the immediate resignation of his foreign minister, Ismail Fahmy, followed hours later by the resignation of his replacement, Mahmoud Riad. Meanwhile, Libya, Iraq and radical Palestinian groups strongly denounced his decision. Only Morocco, Oman and Sudan were prepared to endorse it.

The initial Saudi response was reserved. The Saudis announced that a peace initiative 'must emanate from a unified Arab stand'. The Saudi leadership was irked that Sadat had not mentioned his intention when he visited Riyadh on 2 November.

16 November The shah announces that Iran will strive to prevent an increase in OPEC oil prices in 1978, a change from his previous statement that Iran would be neutral during forthcoming OPEC price discussions.

20 November Making his dramatic address to the Israeli Knesset (parliament), Egypt's President Sadat promises Arab recognition of the state of Israel but warns that there cannot be a peace settlement without the Palestinians. He stressed that he wanted a permanent peace arrangement in the Middle East, not a separate agreement between Israel and Egypt.

Earlier in the day he had toured Jerusalem's holy sites, implying his acknowledgement of Israel's sovereignty over Jerusalem which the Palestinians regarded as an integral part of Palestine.

On arrival at Ben-Gurion Airport on 19 November he had been greeted by a 21-gun salute, a red carpet and a guard of honour. It was the first visit by an Arab head of state since the creation of Israel in 1948.

On his return to Cairo on 21 November, he received a triumphal welcome in Cairo whose streets were lined with crowds chanting his praise.

5 December Egypt severs relations with Iraq, Syria, Libya, Algeria and South Yemen in the wake of their efforts to sabotage President Sadat's peace efforts. At the end of the

Arab summit (2–5 December) in Tripoli, Libya, called by Libyan President Qadhafi on the same day, the five Arab hardline states – Syria, Iraq, Libya, Algeria and South Yemen as well as the PLO – issued the Tripoli Declaration calling for a new Arab front to resist Egypt's peace initiatives. Saudi Arabia and the other conservative Gulf states stayed away from the summit.

6 December The UAE oil minister calls for the replacement of the US dollar with an OPEC dollar as the authorized unit of payment in oil sales.

10 December Saudi Arabia extends its economic boycott against Israel, adding 16 foreign vessels to its blacklist.

15 December The Grumman Corporation settles a dispute with Iran over commissions claimed by Iran in connection with the 1974 sale of 80 F-14 aircraft and agrees to provide $24 million worth of spare parts and equipment for the F-14s free of charge.

25 December Israeli Prime Minister Begin and Egyptian President Sadat begin a summit meeting at Ismailiyya on the Suez Canal. However, when the meeting ended on the following day they had failed to agree on basic issues such as the terms for Israel's withdrawal from Sinai, the West Bank, the Gaza Strip and East Jerusalem. On 28 December Begin publicized the plan he had submitted to Sadat. The plan barred the establishment of a Palestinian state in the West Bank and Gaza Strip, reaffirmed Israel's claim to sovereignty over the two territories, and gave greater autonomy to the Arabs living in the territories. He also proposed guaranteed access to Jerusalem's holy shrines for Jews, Christians and Muslims. On 31 December the Egyptian foreign minister, Muhammad Ibrahim Kamil, disclosed a counter-proposal, stating that Israel must accept the principle of total withdrawal from the West Bank and Gaza and must recognize the right to self-determination for Palestinians in the region.

31 December Shaikh Sabah al-Ahmad al-Sabah, the ruler of Kuwait since 1965, dies of a heart attack and is succeeded by Crown Prince Shaikh Jaber al-Ahmad al-Sabah.

31 December US President Carter arrives in Tehran for talks with the Shah of Iran and King Husayn of Jordan.

1 9 7 8

3/4 January The US president, Jimmy Carter, visits Riyadh where he has difficult talks with Crown Prince Fahd of Saudi Arabia, the defence minister, Prince Sultan, and the foreign minister, Prince Saud al-Faisal. The Saudis were not prepared to give Carter any backing for Egypt's peace talks with Israel. After Carter had left the kingdom, Saud al-Faisal issued a statement to the effect that a Middle East settlement must be based upon a complete Israeli withdrawal from the occupied territories, including Arab (East) Jerusalem, and the fulfilment of the legitimate rights of the Palestinians.

9 January Between 10 and 72 people are killed in anti-shah riots in Iran's holy city of

Qom where 4,000 religious students demand the restoration of freedom for Muslims in the mosques. They were provoked by an unsigned article published in the newspaper *Ittilaat* entitled 'Iran, and the Black and Red Reactionaries' in which insulting references were made to a religious leader who was clearly meant to be Khomeini. According to Dilip Hiro (*Iran under the Ayatollahs*), the author was the shah's information minister, Dariush Humayun, and the article was believed to have the shah's personal approval.

4 February Arab radical states – Syria, Libya, Algeria, South Yemen and the Palestine Liberation Organization (PLO) – end a three-day summit in Algiers where they map their strategy against Egyptian President Sadat's peace moves. Iraq boycotted the meeting. Meanwhile, US President Carter and Sadat began two days of private meetings at the presidential summer retreat at Camp David, Maryland.

14 February The US announces plans to sell $4,800 million worth of jet war-planes to Egypt, Saudi Arabia and Israel, subject to congressional approval. The package included six McDonnell-Douglas F-15 combat aircraft to Saudi Arabia and F-5Es to Egypt. It also included 15 extra F-15s to Israel in addition to 25 already ordered and 75 of the cheaper General Dynamics F-16s. On 15 February the Israeli prime minister, Menachem Begin, deplored the US administration's decision to sell the planes to Egypt and Saudi Arabia. The project was to see a powerful Zionist lobby campaign against the Saudi part of the deal, and a well-financed Saudi counter-campaign led by Prince Bandar ibn Sultan, the Saudi ambassador to Washington and the articulate son of the Saudi defence minister.

A motion to prevent the Saudi sale was eventually defeated by the US Senate on 15 May and the date for delivery of the F-15s was set for 1982.

18 February Anti-government riots in Tabriz, Iran's second biggest city, kill at least six people and injure 125.

19 February An aircraft comandeered by Palestinian commandos carrying 11 hostages, three of whom are PLO members, returns to Larnaca airfield, Cyprus, after being refused permission to land in Kuwait, Somalia, Ethiopia, Greece and finally, South Yemen. Later in the day a force of 74 Egyptian commandos landed at Larnaca Airport. In a clumsy attempt to rescue the hijacked plane, the commandos exchanged fire with Cypriot National Guard troops, leaving 15 dead and 22 wounded. The hijackers quickly freed their hostages and surrendered, but the Egyptian operation had been at a terrible cost which repelled international opinion. To the bemusement of many, on 22 February Egypt took the initiative by severing diplomatic relations with Cyprus for its handling of the affair.

26 May Iraq's Ba'thist-dominated government is reported to have executed 14 members of the pro-Soviet Iraqi Communist Party in April as the result of a growing dispute between the two factions of the Communist Party, both of which belong to the National Progressive Front. According to the London-based Committee Against Repression and for Democratic Rights in Iraq (CARDRI), between 24 and 27 May 38 Iraqis were executed in Iraqi army camps. The majority were members of the armed forces and all were accused of political activity inside the Iraqi army. CARDRI alleged that the death sentences were imposed by special court martials whose decisions were not subject to any review or appeal.

31 May Some 2,500 rioting students at Tehran University cause about $1 million worth of damage. The riots erupted after two groups of orthodox Muslim male students opposed the integration of the sexes at the university, a policy instituted by the shah at the beginning of the year. On the following day several hundred women students at the university conducted peaceful demonstrations against the presence of special guards in their dormitories. On 9 May anti-government riots fomented by Muslim religious leaders had swept several Iranian cities, with the worst rioting occurring in the Holy city of Qom, the home of Iran's leading clergy and the site of previous violence. By 11 May violence had spread to Tehran for the first time.

6 June In an attempt to counter increasing violence in Iran, the shah dismisses the hated, hardline General Nemotollah Nassiri who had been head of the Iranian Organization of National Security and Intelligence (SAVAK) since 1965 and appoints him ambassador to Pakistan. On 7 June General Nasser Moghadam replaced Nassiri as SAVAK chief.

In order to prevent violence due on the next fortieth-day mourning processions expected on 19 June, the shah had visited religious buildings such as the Imam Ali Reza shrine in Mashhad, banned pornographic films and called off his anti-inflation campaign.

15 June The chief PLO representative in Kuwait, Ali Yasi, is shot dead at his home by unidentified gunmen.

19 June The Organization of Petroleum Exporting Countries (OPEC) announces that it will leave the price of oil unchanged at $12.70 a barrel throughout 1978.

26 June A rival faction of the pro-Soviet ruling front deposes and executes the South Yemeni president, Salem Rubaya Ali, after 12 hours of heavy fighting in Aden, the South Yemeni capital. On 2 July a shocked Arab League froze political and diplomatic relations with South Yemen and suspended economic and cultural ties. This followed the bloody events of the previous days. On 24 June the North Yemeni president, Ahmad Husayn al-Ghashmi, had been killed by a bomb that exploded in the suitcase of a visiting envoy sent by Rubaya Ali. Ghashmi was replaced on 25 June by a three-man Military Command Council. On 17 July North Yemen's People's Council elected Colonel Ali Abdullah Saleh as president.

17 July Two British workers who had been publicly flogged for breaking Saudi Arabia's alcohol laws are dismissed from their jobs.

27 July Ayatollah Khomeini claims for Iran's religious establishment the exclusive leadership of the anti-shah campaign. He was thought to be responding to Mehdi Bazargan's call for 'gradualism' and advice against the clerical monopoly of leadership in the struggle against the shah.

31 July An armed Arab terrorist shoots his way into the Iraqi embassy in Paris and holds eight people hostage before surrendering to the French police. Increasingly frequent clashes between Iraqi and other Arab groups in Paris and London were believed to be linked to the growing dispute between hardline Iraq, which opposed peace negotiations with Israel, and PLO factions which favoured a milder response to negotiations. On 9 July the former Iraqi premier, Abd al-Razzak al-Naif, was shot twice in the head in London as he walked out of his hotel towards a taxi. He died the following day. On 27 July Britain expelled 11 Iraqis because they allegedly posed terrorist threats. Iraq promptly retaliated by expelling the British ambassador, Alexander Stirling, on the same day. The communal violence continued into the next month when on 3 August two Arab gunmen believed to have links with Iraq broke into the Paris offices of the Arab League and the PLO and killed two PLO officials and wounded three others.

10 August In a wave of protests against the Iranian government – in particular against its promotion of the liberation of women and of land redistribution – crowds stage violent demonstrations in Isfahan to protest against the arrest of a local religious leader. On 17 August they took control of the city. The shah declared martial law and it took the army two days to regain control of the city. From 7 to 16 August bloody riots took place in various towns. Over 100 people died in army shootings.

19 August A fire sweeps through a packed cinema in the southern Iranian city of Abadan, killing 477 people. The government declared its suspicion that the fire was deliberately caused by Muslim extremists opposed to its liberalization policies but militants accused SAVAK of responsibility. They argued that the Iranian-made film showing, *The Deer*, would not have offended anti-shah elements and that the cinema exit doors had been locked from 'the outside'. On 21 August Ayatollah Khomeini accused the government of responsibility for the fire. On 23 August the army moved into Abadan to control riots that broke out during mourning ceremonies for the victims. On 25 August further violence erupted in Abadan with demonstrators chanting 'Death to the Shah'.

On 27 August, in an effort to defuse the escalating violence, the shah replaced Prime Minister Jamshid Amouzegar with a reconciliation cabinet led by the 68-year-old Ja'far Sharif Emami, an old and faithful friend who was to prepare Iran for 'free' elections in June 1979. Sharif Emami had briefly been prime minister from August 1960 to May 1961. Amouzegar had been prime minister since 1977 as well as secretary-general of the Rastakhiz Party sponsored by the shah. He had also been Iran's principal negotiator at OPEC meetings.

6 September The Iranian government bans all unauthorized demonstrations following a machine-gun attack on a Tehran police station. This led to a demonstration on 7 September of an estimated half a million demonstrators, marching through north Tehran to the Majlis (lower house) building, protesting the ban and calling for the return of Ayatollah Khomeini and the replacement of the monarchy with an Islamic regime. Khomeini called the marches a 'referendum' that the shah should go.

8 September The Jaleh Square massacre (known as 'Black Friday'): the Iranian government imposes martial law in Tehran after troops had fired at several thousand anti-government demonstrators in the capital. The massacre left between 95 and 3,000 dead, depending on widely varying estimates. The massacre was to be a crucial turning-point in the revolution.

10 September US President Carter telephones the shah to assure him of continued US support although he also calls for more political liberalization in Iran. In a US television interview on 11 September the shah confessed that the impact of the increasingly violent and widespread riots had been unexpected. On 12 September the government served, or issued arrest warrants for Muslim radicals and other anti-shah activists. On 14 September Khomeini called from Najaf on Muslims in Iran to practise passive resistance and urged troops to rebel if the shah showed any signs of surviving the rapidly developing struggle against him.

16 September A huge earthquake destroys the ancient north Iranian caravan town of Tabas on the edge of the Kavir desert in the province of Khorasan. By 21 September it was estimated that 15,200 had been killed in the epicentre and 10,000 in surrounding villages. The shah immediately ordered the army and the Red Lion Society to fly in medical and other supplies. However, the clergy operated a simultaneous operation, with

Ayatollah Shariatmadari calling for international help. Although visits to the disaster area were made by the Empress Farah on 18 September and by the shah on 20 September, the latter remained at Tabas airport, lavishly dressed as a field marshal, while the empress was criticized for having placed a conservation order on Tabas which prevented renovation work being carried out on the old houses. While the government operation was criticized as inefficient, the clerical operation was praised by local Iranians. Khomeini warned the people not to let the government use the earthquake to divert their attention from revolution.

17 September Concluding the US-sponsored Middle East summit at President Carter's retreat at Camp David, Maryland, Israeli Premier Begin and Egyptian President Sadat agree to a framework for a peace treaty between their two countries. They also signed a settlement for the broader Arab-Israeli issue of the West Bank and Gaza. President Carter, who conducted the summit, signed as a witness.

On 18 September the major points in the agreement were revealed. These included the progressive Israeli withdrawal in stages from and the return to Egypt of the entire Sinai Peninsula and the establishment of normal Egyptian-Israeli relations. The final Israeli withdrawal would occur within two to three years after a peace agreement was signed, according to the settlement.

On 19 September the PLO leader, Yasser Arafat, denounced the agreement as 'a dirty deal' while Saudi Arabia and Jordan were 'cautiously' critical. On 20 September the Syrian president, Hafez Asad, accused Sadat of defecting to the enemy. Lebanon complained that the Camp David summit made no provisions for a Palestinian homeland. Begin, meanwhile, conceded that Israel and the US held different interpretations about Israeli settlements on the West Bank.

Nevertheless, when Sadat returned to Cairo on 23 September he received a tumultuous welcome from a war-weary nation.

24 September Four Arab hardline states – Syria, South Yemen, Algeria and Libya – and the PLO end a four-day meeting in Damascus with the announcement that they are severing all economic and political relations with Egypt following its signature of the Camp David Accords with Israel. Meanwhile the US secretary of state, Cyrus Vance, had arrived in Saudi Arabia on 21 September after stopping off in Jordan to gain support for the agreement. Having also visited Syria, he returned to Washington on 25 September. On 28 September the Israeli Knesset (parliament) approved the accords and the removal of Jewish settlements in Sinai, thus clearing one procedural obstacle to Egyptian-Israeli peace negotiations. On 1 October 100 West Bank Arab leaders rejected the accords, calling for an independent Palestinian state governed by the PLO.

Iran: Countdown to Revolution

26 September In a move which many felt was closing the stable door after the horse had bolted, a now embattled shah bars members of the royal family from financial dealings with the government. More importantly, perhaps, on 2 October he granted an amnesty to exiled anti-government activists, including Iran's charismatic, exiled cleric, Ayatollah Khomeini. In late September he dissolved the Rastakhiz Party.

6 October Khomeini is expelled by Iraq, where he has lived in exile in Najaf since 1965. After an unsuccessful attempt to cross into Kuwait by road, he flew to Paris on 23 October and was offered asylum by the French president, Giscard d'Estaing, in the village of Neauphle-le-Chateau near Paris.

Nevertheless, the shah seemed to be giving out ambiguous signals on 6 October when he promised to continue with his reform programme despite the unrest. On 10 October President Carter had, for the second time in a month, expressed his support for him. On 11 October the Iranian government imposed a press ban after a protest strike by newspaper employees but lifted it two days later.

On 22 October the British foreign secretary, Dr David Owen, said that it would not be in the best interest of the West for the shah to be toppled. While conceding that the shah had a poor human rights record, he pointed out that if the fanatical Muslim element came to power it would deny women all rights.

On 25 October some of the 1,126 political prisoners – who had been released under an Iranian government amnesty to mark the shah's fifty-ninth birthday – claimed that they had been tortured. On 29 October some 34 SAVAK officials were dismissed or forcibly retired in a further attempt by the government to stem the spiralling unrest.

20 October Saudi Arabian troops of the Arab League force in Lebanon replace Syrian soldiers in key positions in Christian East Beirut. Christian militia leaders hailed the Syrian withdrawal as a tactical victory.

31 October An estimated 40,000 Iranian oil workers strike in one of the most serious anti-government actions yet to face the shah. Prime Minister Ja'far Sharif Emami called the strike an act of treason.

On 12 November Iran Air employees returned to work but teachers began to stage a nationwide strike. However, on 13 November most Iranian oil workers were forced back to their jobs by troops and on 14 November oil production rose to 3.3 million barrels a day compared to a low of 1.1 million barrels a day during the strike.

1 November The Iranian government reports that 23 people have been killed and 56 injured in clashes with troops. On 5 November troops took over Tehran's major newspapers and national radio and television networks. On the same day the government announced that a specially appointed commission would investigate the finances of the shah's family, many of whom had by now left the country.

5 November The Arab League concludes a four-day summit meeting in Baghdad by issuing a communiqué asking Egypt not to sign a peace treaty with Israel. On 18 November the Iraqi capital was to host a visit by the Empress Farah, the first such visit by a member of the Iranian royal family.

5 November Huge demonstrations leave Tehran's banks, cinemas, some hotels and US and British airline offices burning. In the evening the shah announced that 'I have heard your revolutionary message'. There were unconfirmed reports of mutinies in regional garrisons.

On 6 November the shah replaced Prime Minister Sharif-Emami with General Gholam Reza Azhari, and asked the new prime minister to form a military government to end the 'violence and unrest' of the previous day.

8 November The former Iranian prime minister, Amir Abbas Hoveida, former SAVAK chief, General Nemotollah Nassiri, and Dariush Humayun, the alleged author of the anonymous anti-Khomeini article in *Ittilaat*, are among more than 15 government officials arrested by the government. On 19 November the government freed a further 210 political prisoners in a further and now desperate attempt to appease the opposition. However, the violence continued and on 3 December Premier Gholam Reza Azhari blamed it on the Tudeh (Communist) Party.

26 November Employees on strike at Iran's Bank Markazi (Central Bank) reveal that between 100 and 200 prominent Iranians have recently redirected large sums of money abroad through personal and commercial transfers. Estimates of the amount sent out between August and late September ranged between $2,000 million and $10,000 million. The list of those accused included members of the royal family and military and political leaders already facing corruption charges. The names included the ambassador to the US, Ardeshir Zahedi, former prime minister Jamshid Amouzegar and the Tehran military law administrator, General Oveissi. The government dismissed the list as 'total fabrication' while senior bank officials denied its authenticity, pointing out that some of the signatures belonged to dead people.

10 December In a low-key ceremony the Nobel Peace Prize is presented in Oslo to President Sadat of Egypt and Prime Minister Begin of Israel. Only Begin attended the ceremony – Sadat remained in Egypt – which reflected the extent to which the spirit of the Camp David peace talks had soured since Egypt and Israel agreed to make peace in September.

10/11 December A peaceful march of between 300,000 and one million people is led through Tehran by Ayatollah Taleqani and the National Front leader, Karim Sanjabi, on 10 December. The two men led a second march to Tehran's Shahyad Square on 11 December which consisted of almost two million people.

11 December Amnesty International accuses the Iranian government of the continued torture of political prisoners despite government assurances that it had stopped the practice.

12 December At least 50 people are reported killed and 500 wounded in anti-government rioting that erupted on 11 December in Isfahan, Iran's second biggest city. On 12 December striking oil workers refused to return to work at the end of the Ashura holiday, forcing oil production back down to 1.2 million barrels.

By 31 December anti-government strikes were to push oil production down to a record low of 250,000 barrels a day. On 4 December thousands of anti-government workers had struck again, reducing oil production by 30 per cent.

13 December Ayatollah Khomeini, speaking from his exile in the village of Neauphle-le-Château near Paris, announces that he has warned foreign governments that their support for the shah will deprive their countries of Iranian oil and that all treaties with them will be annulled if the regime is replaced by an Islamic one.

At Neauphle-le-Chateau Khomeini had set up an effective headquarters with a good telephone link. Leading Iranian revolutionary personalities such as Muhammad Beheshti, Hussein Ali Montazeri, Mehdi Bazargan (leader of the Iran Freedom Movement) and Karim Sanjabi visited him there.

According to Shaul Bakhash in *The Reign of the Ayatollahs*, Khomeini had already designated a nucleus of clerical leaders such as Motahhari, Beheshti, Hashemi Rafsanjani, Mousavi-Ardabili and Bahonar to act on his behalf in Tehran.

17 December The shah appoints Gholam Hussein Sadiqi to form a civilian government in face of the mounting tension in the country. However, despite his impeccable record of opposition to the shah which included three years in prison, Sadiqi failed to win National Front co-operation.

On 29 December the shah appointed the 63-year-old French-educated lawyer, Shahpour Bakhtiar, a National Front member, to form a new civilian government to replace the military government established on 6 November. On 30 November, however, although he was considered Sanjabi's number two in the National Front, the NF tried to oust Bakhtiar on the grounds that his appointment did not satisfy their minimum demands for the shah's abdication. At a Tehran rally attended by 4,000 of his supporters, the National Front leader, Karim Sanjabi, had declared that the shah must go.

23 December Iranian terrorists shoot and kill two oil company executives including an American in separate attacks near Ahwaz, the oil industry's operational centre in south-west Iran. In the face of increasing violence hundreds of American dependants had left Iran on 6 December. On 31 December the US urged all American dependants to leave, in the wake of anti-government rioting in Mashhad, Lar and Khurramabad and claimed that government troops had killed hundreds of civilians.

27 December Abd al-Fattah Ismail is elected president of South Yemen.

---

1 9 7 9

Iran: Countdown to Revolution: January

2 January A spokesman for Ayatollah Khomeini denies allegations by US and West European intelligence officials that the Islamic opposition in Iran has received financial and military aid from Libya and the Palestine Liberation Organization (PLO).

2 January Some 500 Iranians and US students attack the Beverley Hills, California, home of the shah's elder sister Princess Shams. The princess was accompanied by the elderly and ill queen mother (the shah's mother) Taj al-Moluk who had left Iran a few weeks earlier.

3 January The Iranian premier-designate, Dr Shahpour Bakhtiar, says he opposes the sale of oil to Israel and South Africa as well as the shah's policy of guarding the security of the Gulf, a US strategy. This was clearly a last-ditch attempt to conciliate the fast-gathering forces of revolution. The shah had asked Bakhtiar to form a new government on 29 December.

On the same day a British royal visit by Queen Elizabeth and Prince Philip was cancelled in response to a statement by the shah and the Empress Farah that 'in the present circumstances' they would be unable to entertain the queen as they would have wished to in Iran.

4 January The shah signs a decree formally appointing Dr Bakhtiar premier. Soon afterwards the National Front, of which Bakhtiar had been considered number two to Karim Sanjabi, issued a statement saying that Bakhtiar's agreement to form a government under the shah was 'a betrayal of our cause'. On 6 January a crowd of 100,000 demonstrated against Bakhtiar in Qom. Although on the same day Bakhtiar ended censorship and eased martial law by reducing the hours of curfew, Khomeini announced that obedience to the new administration was tantamount to 'obedience to Satan'.

8 January The day sees some of the worst rioting in Iran so far. In Tabriz demonstrators set fire to buildings and others clashed with security forces in Tehran. Just south of Tehran, two Afghans were accused of theft and hanged by the mob. Vast protest rallies were held in cities such as Qazvin and Isfahan, the latter witnessing a procession of an estimated half million.

On 7 January mobs had rioted in Tehran where troops opened fire. On 11/12 January in Shiraz, crowds set fire to the Organization of National Security and Intelligence (SAVAK) buildings and at least 14 people, including SAVAK officials, were killed. In contrast, on 13 January peaceful rallies saw fraternization when demonstrators placed flowers in the barrels of the soldiers' guns.

10 January The Bakhtiari tribe in south-west Iran, to which Dr Shahpour Bakhtiar belongs, throws its weight behind Khomeini.

13 January The Iranian government announces the formation of a nine-member regency council under Sayyid Jalaleddin Tehrani, a former cabinet minister noted for his loyalty to the shah, to carry out the duties of the shah who is leaving the country on 'vacation'.

On the same day Khomeini announced that he had formed a Council of the Islamic Revolution which would pave the way for a transitional government to replace the administration of Dr Bakhtiar. Khomeini said that he would not take part in the government but would give 'general guidance'.

14 January A US citizen, Martin Berkowitz, a former US colonel and currently head of the office of a US construction company in Iran, is found stabbed to death at his home in Kerman. A slogan on the wall read: 'Go home to your country'.

16 January The shah, accompanied by the Empress Farah, leaves Iran for Aswan in Upper Egypt, en route for the US. The shah went ostensibly on 'vacation' and for 'medical treatment', although their departure was recognized by most as exile. They were greeted in Aswan by President Sadat and accorded full ceremonial honours. The couple's three youngest children had flown to the US on 15 January. In Egypt the couple cruised on the Nile with President Sadat. According to Mrs Jehan Sadat, the shah told the president that the US had forced him to leave.

Before leaving, the shah said that he hoped that Dr Bakhtiar's government 'will be able to make up for the past and also lay the foundations for the future'.

From Paris Khomeini congratulated his followers for forcing the shah's departure, appealed to the armed forces to prevent the US from dismantling sophisticated military equipment, said that an Islamic government would take legal action to recover money transferred abroad by the royal family and called for the resumption of university lectures.

On 17 January he demanded that the shah be brought back to face trial and punishment because he had 'fled with the blood of the people on his hands and his pockets filled with stolen money'.

18 January The US Central Intelligence Agency (CIA) reports the closing of a monitoring facility in Iran because of political turmoil, but says that a second more important one is still functioning. It added that the equipment was only intended for tracking the flights of Soviet missiles.

20 January Khomeini announces definite plans to return to Iran following massive, countrywide demonstrations on the previous day in his support.

On 22 January Sayyid Jalaleddin Tehrani, previously known for his loyalty to the shah, submitted his resignation as head of Iran's Regency Council to Khomeini in Paris.

22 January The shah and the Empress Farah leave Egypt for Morocco. King Hasan met the couple at Marrakesh Airport but offered them none of the honours accorded by Sadat. They were housed at Marrakesh's Jinan al-Kabir palace. On 23 January the shah postponed plans to continue to the US. Although the US State Department confirmed that he was welcome, the ambassador to Morocco, Richard Parker, advised him to continue at once, warning him that if the situation in Iran changed, his presence in the US might no longer be welcome.

24 January Khomeini insists on returning to Iran and rejects an offer by Dr Bakhtiar to resign and let the people decide in a plebiscite on whether they want a monarchy or a republic. On the same day, in order to prevent Khomeini's return, the Iranian National Security Council ordered all airports in the country closed until 28 January.

On 25 January Khomeini announced that he would fly into Iran on 28 January (although the date was again put back to 1 February).

26 January Defying an Iranian government ban on public rallies and angered over the closure of airports, over 100,000 supporters of Khomeini take to the streets of Tehran, initiating one of the worst confrontations between demonstrators and the army.

30 January The US orders the evacuation of all dependants and non-essential US citizens in Iran and urges all others to leave in the wake of new outbursts of anti-US demonstrations.

Iran: Countdown to Revolution: February

1 February Khomeini returns in triumph from France to Tehran where some three million people greet him. Premier Shahpour Bakhtiar, meanwhile, promised strong measures to prevent the ayatollah from proclaiming a provisional Islamic government. From the airport, Khomeini made a brief speech in which he denounced foreign intervention in Iran. He then travelled to Tehran's Behesht-e Zahra cemetery where many demonstrators had been buried. So massive were the crowds that he had to be borne by helicopter for the last part of the journey.

At the cemetery he denounced the shah's regime and that of his father, Reza Shah, as illegal, warned that he would 'shut the mouths' of Dr Bakhtiar and his cabinet if they did not resign and said that he would not allow the US to bring the shah back. He appealed to the army to join the revolution.

4 February The US Defence Department announces that Iran has cancelled about $7,000 million of the $11,560 million of weapons it had ordered from the US during the shah's reign.

5 February Khomeini announces that he has appointed Mehdi Bazargan as premier to head a provisional government. On the following day, the US re-stated its support for the Bakhtiar government but on 7 February the US ambassador to the UN praised Khomeini, calling Islam 'a vibrant cultural force in today's world'. He was going further than any other Carter administration official in supporting the Iranian revolution.

9 February Homafar (air force technicians) at the Doshan Tappeh air base, east of Tehran, rebel in support of Khomeini. Imperial guards (the Javidan) raced from the palace but failed to quash the rebellion. On 10 February, when the guards returned, civilians had joined the homafar, erecting barricades and preparing molotov cocktails (fire-bombs). Also on 10 February the army declared a curfew but Khomeini ordered the people to ignore it. Armed with weapons obtained from the Doshan Tappeh base, the rebels then started attacking army bases and police stations in and around Tehran. By noon on 11 February they had taken most of the police stations and army bases. Similar battles were being fought in other cities. Late that morning, senior military commanders agreed that the only way of preserving the army was to declare neutrality and recall all soldiers back to their barracks. It was, however, too late. The airport was taken and subsequently closed.

The revolutionaries continued in their victorious drive, capturing the shah's palace by noon on 12 February.

On 12 February Dr Bazargan appointed General Muhammad Vali Qarani chief-of-staff in place of General Gharabaqi, as well as making him interim defence minister. At the same time he dismissed General Rabi'i, the air-force commander who had himself resigned and who was subsequently arrested, and appointed General Mahdeyoun to the post. After a few hours however, Rabi'i was himself replaced by his own deputy, General Shahpour Azarbarzin. By 13 February most senior officers appear to have accepted the departure of the shah and rallied to Dr Bazargan and the new chief-of-staff.

On 13 February a rare calm had descended on Tehran and most other Iranian cities. Members of the shah's regime, such as the former SAVAK chief, Nemotollah Nassiri, and the former court minister, Amir Abbas Hoveida, were taken to Khomeini's headquarters, a converted school, to await trial. (See Petrossian: *The Cambridge Encyclopedia of the Middle East and North Africa*).

14 February The US embassy in Tehran is attacked, apparently by left-wing gunmen. They fought their way into the building which they ransacked before leading the embassy staff out at gunpoint and reportedly putting a knife to the throat of the US ambassador, William Sullivan.

During the night, new bouts of shooting were heard in Tehran. Revolutionaries rushed to the besieged television station and to threatened power plants and other vital installations. Some thought the gunfire came from extremists, others thought it was the work of SAVAK and counter-revolutionaries (see Petrossian).

On 15 February Nassiri and three others became the first victims of what was to be a series of summary trials followed by execution. It was later revealed that the executions were aimed at bringing home to the counter-revolutionaries the reality of the revolution. The executions were to total about 600 – not all political – in the first six months of the year. Their summary nature instilled fear in people and brought calls from moderates in Iran and from around the world for a halt. However, the people's desire for vengeance was too strong to be curbed easily. (See Petrossian, above.)

1 March Mulla Mustafa Barzani, who has led the Kurds of Iraq for about 30 years, dies in a US hospital, aged 76. In mid-July several hundred members of the Kurdish Democratic Party (KDP) returned to Iraq after four years of refuge in Iran where they had lived since the collapse in 1975 of the Kurdish rebellion. They were headed by Barzani's 35-year-old son, Masoud Barzani.

According to Kurdish sources, several thousand Kurds were forcibly removed from their home in northern Iraq during the first few months of 1979 and resettled in special camps guarded by the army. Pesh Merga (Forward to Death) guerrillas continued, nevertheless, to undertake guerrilla operations against government troops in the mountains. Heavy aerial bombardments on Kurdish Iranian villages in early June and attacks on Kurdish rebels in northern Iraq were aimed at preventing the Kurds from co-operating with the KDP and Jamal Talabani's Patriotic Union of Kurdistan.

5 March Khomeini orders the formation of the Revolutionary Guards (Pasdaran) which he said would combine the functions of the army, a police force and the mosque and have the power to support liberation movements and to 'spread Iran's Islamic revolution throughout the world'. By May the Pasdaran were said to have 10,000 permanent members and some 100,000 reservists.

26 March On the lawn of the White House in Washington, Egypt and Israel sign the peace accords initiated at Camp David in the previous year. The accords, signed in the presence of US President Carter, were promptly denounced by the Arab League as a capitulation. Arab states cut diplomatic ties with Egypt, the Arab League headquarters was moved from Cairo to Tunis and Arab aid to Egypt was cut off.

30 March The former shah and the Empress Farah leave Morocco for the Bahamas. They had become less than welcome by Morocco's King Hasan who was facing protests from his own people.

1 April Iran's referendum sanctions the declaration of the Islamic Republic of Iran based on the Islamic Constitution agreed upon in December, the latter modelled on the western and principally French presidential parliamentary system. A key difference was the provision granting ultimate authority to a collegially elected spiritual leader or guide (Vali-e Faqih – the Trustee and Jurisconsult). This referred to Khomeini until his death or incapacitation. The concept was based on the Shi'i belief that in the absence of the Twelfth Imam, it was the duty of the clergy to establish a just system to implement Islamic laws.

25 April The United Arab Emirates (UAE) government resigns in an effort to prevent discord among the seven emirates. The government had been formed in January 1977 by the crown prince of Dubai and since December 1973 the UAE prime minister, Shaikh Maktoum ibn Rashid. However, disagreement had arisen between the largest and by far the richest of the emirates, Abu Dhabi, and the second largest and richest, Dubai. Dubai's ruler, Shaikh Rashid ibn Said al-Maktoum, feared that closer unity of the emirates would destroy the independence of the individual shaikhdoms and increase the dominance of Abu Dhabi. In early April, the Kuwaiti foreign minister, Shaikh Sabah al-Ahmad al-Jaber al-Sabah, had started talks with the UAE leaders at Shaikh Zayed's request.

May Arabs in Iran's Khuzestan province call for autonomy in street marches and fight with government troops in Khoramshahr. Meanwhile, the month saw border clashes in Kurdish areas of Iran.

10 June The former shah and the Empress Farah arrive in Mexico from the Bahamas after the Mexican government had granted them an entry visa for six months. In Washington it was officially announced on 19 April that the Carter administration had indicated to the shah during March that he was not welcome in the US at that time because of the delicacy of US-Iranian relations. On 2 May the then Iranian foreign minister, Dr Ibrahim Yazi, warned the US not to give the shah sanctuary.

11 June Ayatollah Muhammad Baqr al-Sadr, the spiritual leader of the Iraqi Shi'is, is placed under house arrest in Iraq. Sadr had been a powerful critic of Iraq's Ba'thist regime. Since the Iranian revolution, which Sadr had ardently supported, there had been considerable Shi'i disturbances in Iraq, particularly in the holy Shi'i cities of Najaf and Kerbala. Sadr was believed to have decided to leave for Iran at the end of May but was supposedly persuaded by Ayatollah Khomeini to remain in Iraq and continue his leadership of Iraq's Shi'i community.

13 June The Popular Front for the Liberation of Oman (PFLO) claims that on 10 June it attacked a base of the Omani armed forces in Aram, Dhofar province, killing seven soldiers, including a British officer. The resurgence of PFLO operations was generally attributed to the ending of Iranian military support for Sultan Qaboos's regime in Muscat. Under the shah, Iranian troops had played a major role in quelling the ongoing Dhofar-based rebellion. The new revolutionary regime in Tehran had decided to withdraw the remaining 200 Iranian troops in Oman. On 25 February the Omani leadership denied Western press reports that Iranian troops in Oman were being replaced by an Egyptian force of a possible 7,000 men.

16 July Saddam Husayn becomes president of Iraq, chairman of the Revolutionary Command Council (RCC) and commander-in-chief of the armed forces. Husayn's swearing-in followed the resignation of fellow Takriti, President Ahmad Hasan al-Bakr. The transfer of power had been meticulously planned by Husayn and was widely expected. Izzat Ibrahim al-Douri, a loyal associate of Husayn, was appointed vice-president. Some days before Bakr's resignation it was announced that the RCC secretary, Muhi al-Din Abd al-Husayn Mashhadi, was to be replaced by Tariq Hamad al-Abdullah.

28 July Following the appointment of Saddam Husayn as president of Iraq, a Syrian-backed 'plot' to overthrow the regime is uncovered. A Ba'th Party court of seven RCC members was promptly established under Na'im Haddad. Within a few days, 22 people had been executed, including the RCC secretary-general, Mashhadi, a close friend of Saddam Husayn and five of his colleagues, Adnan Hamdani, Muhammad Ayish, Muhammad Mahjub, Ghanim Abd al-Jalil and Abd al-Khaliq al-Samarra'i. Mashhadi was reportedly shot along with his entire family.

The executions, which Haddad described as 'democratic', were reportedly carried out by Saddam Husayn and the remaining members of the RCC 'in person', and a video film of the trial was circulated among inner circles of the Ba'th Party as a warning.

According to Farouk-Sluglett and Sluglett (*Iraq since 1958*), Mashhadi had voiced concern over Saddam Husayn's 'dynastic power base' and Ayish had objected to his claim to have been elected unanimously, since he himself had not voted for him. Farouk-Sluglett and Sluglett point out that since most of the remaining RCC members were implicated in the 1979 executions, they were bound together by the knowledge that if Saddam Husayn fell, they fell with him.

Some claimed that up to 500 Ba'th members were executed. Meanwhile, July saw general repression in which whole families were said to have 'disappeared' and mass deportations of Shi'i Muslims taken place.

Observers suggested that there had not actually been a conspiracy but that before President Bakr's resignation, opposition had been expressed against both Bakr and Husayn and that the latter, having assumed the presidency, had decided to eliminate all possible rivals. The regime's opponents were thought to have been motivated by resentment of the political dominance of Husayn's family and fellow Takritis, desire for unity with Syria and revulsion over the violent suppression of dissident members of Iraq's majority Shi'i population. (Saddam Husayn is a Sunni as are most of his colleagues. Between 60 and 70 per cent of the population of Iraq is Shi'i and 15 per cent Sunni Kurdish.)

At an RCC meeting in early July, Mashhadi, a Shi'i, was thought to have condemned the intolerable manner in which the Shi'is had been treated. The meeting had been convened to discuss the violent quelling of a Shi'i demonstration in mid-June which had been staged as a protest against the arrest on 11 June of their spiritual leader, Ayatollah Muhammad Bakr al-Sadr. At a further meeting on 12 July, the RCC stripped Mashhadi of his post and membership and he confessed to a Syrian-backed 'conspiracy' to overthrow the regime. He named his co-conspirators whom he said had united after the failed Nadim Kazar coup attempt in 1973. The events led to a marked deterioration in relations with Syria.

9 August A government spokesman, Sadeq Tabatabai, states that the Iranian government has cancelled some $9,000 million worth of US arms ordered by the shah's regime. These were F-16 aircraft, AWACS and units for the navy.

13 August The Iraqi ambassador to Lebanon, Abd al-Husayn Muslim Hasan, escapes a machine-gun attack in Beirut. The attack followed a verbal onslaught by the PLO on the Iraqi regime.

On 15 May at the Old Bailey in London 18-year-old Mrs Khouloud Moghrabi was sentenced to 12 years' imprisonment for conspiring to murder the Iraqi ambassador to England, Taha Ahmad al-Dawood, on 28 July, 1978.

23 October The exiled shah flies from Mexico to the US for an operation to remove his gall bladder. It was admitted that he had cancer of the lymph gland. In Tehran Iran's so-called 'hanging judge', Ayatollah Khalkhali, called on Muslims to drag him from his hospital bed and dismember him.

26 October In a communiqué published in Stockholm, the Patriotic Union of Kurdistan (PUK) claims that the KDP had executed three of its members in October 1978. In January 1979, in what appeared to be a further result of inter-Kurdish rivalry, an attempt had been made on the life of the KDP leader, Masoud Barzani, in Vienna.

30 October Iraq demands the revision of the Algiers agreement of 1975 which regulates the Iran-Iraq border on land and through the Shatt al-Arab waterway. Iraq also said that Iran must give up three Gulf islands and provide self-rule for Iran's Arab, Kurdish and Baluch minorities. The agreement divided the Shatt al-Arab between Iraq and Iran at the *thalweg* or deep point in the middle of the waterway.

4 November Iranian students storm and occupy the US embassy in Tehran, taking about 62 US citizens and 36 citizens of other nationalities hostage. This was the signal for Iran's so-called Second Revolution. Ostensibly the seizure was in response to US interference and its decision in October to admit the shah for medical treatment. According to Vahe Petrossian (see *The Cambridge Encyclopedia of the Middle East and North Africa*), it was in fact aimed mainly at pro-Western forces in Iran that were hostile to the religious and cultural aspirations of the Iranian people and who were intent on renewing the old dependencies on the US. This, he points out, had been symbolized by the meeting in Algiers on 2 November between the Iranian president, Bazargan, and President Carter's national security adviser, Zbigniew Brzezinski, a former hardline supporter of the shah and an advocate of forceful measures against the revolutionary movement.

Images of Bazargan and Iran's foreign minister, Ibrahim Yazdi, shaking hands with representives of the US, the Iranian revolution's biggest symbolic enemy, brought the revulsion of Muslim radicals to a head. Unable to strike back directly at Bazargan, who enjoyed Khomeini's support, they struck at the next most convenient target, the US embassy.

On 17 November Khomeini ordered the release of all women and black hostages.

5 November Iran cancels the 1957 Military Co-operation treaty with the US.

6 November Iran's Prime Minister Bazargan and his cabinet of liberal ministers resign and hand over power to the Islamic Revolutionary Council which had been operating as a parallel government since February.

9 November The US halts the shipment of $300 million worth of spare parts bought by Iran.

14 November The US freezes over $10,000 million in Iranian assets abroad in retaliation for the seizure of the US embassy in Tehran.

20 November Islamic militants seize the Great Mosque in Mecca, Saudi Arabia. At 5.20am as the imam of the Mosque began the dawn prayer he was rudely pushed aside by a young man who cried into the microphone that he, 'the Mahdi', and his men sought shelter from persecution in this, Islam's holiest mosque. He was Muhammad ibn Abdullah al-Qahtani. Three shots were fired and a mosque servant fell dead. The killer was Juhaiman ibn Muhammad al-Otaibi, the organizer of the uprising.

The next two weeks were to see a ferocious battle within the Great Mosque between the diehards, encouraged by the recent revolution in Iran, who wanted Saudi Arabia to become a purist Islamic state shorn of corruption and extravagance, and the security forces, advised by foreign experts. When the rebellion ended two weeks later the bodies of 75 rebels and 25 pilgrims (*hajjis*) were found in the cellars of the mosque.

On the morning of 5 December Juhaiman led out into the open the last 170 of his group; on 9 January he and 63 of his followers were taken into the squares of various Saudi towns and beheaded.

The Mecca siege had taken place to a background of regional instability, with the Iranian clerics (*ulema*) threatening to 'export Islamic revolution' to Saudi Arabia's minority Shi'is in the oil-rich Hasa province who were showing signs of discontent. Warnings had reached the police that during the two-million strong pilgrimage (*hajj*), riots were to be anticipated in the Hasa villages of Qatif, Safwa and Seihat, while Iranian pilgrims were expected to demonstrate in Mecca itself.

In fact the *hajj* itself passed off with little more than a few chanting walkabouts, insignificant against the bloody riots that were to take place in 1987. The taking of the mosque and the siege which followed, however, were to be extremely violent. Juhaiman had given his followers two weeks to gather their weapons and had himself come to the mosque five days before the month-long *hajj* ended. Somehow they managed to smuggle an impressive armoury into the mosque where it was hidden in the huge cellars in which the rebels were to spend much of the ensuing battle.

The government's initial response was confused, with so many forces and services being flown into Mecca that there was little central command. Attempts to winch troops into the mosque by helicopter by daylight resulted in appalling loss of life. By the end of the first week the government was in control of the mosque itself with the rebels now isolated in its steaming cellars. However, riots were sparked off in the eastern towns although they were to be quickly put down with a mixture of promises and threats. The end to the siege on 5 December represented a turning-point for the kingdom. Princes were no longer to be seen in foreign casinos or similar places, nor would overt extravagance be tolerated within the ruling family.

26 November In Saudi Arabia 160 people die when an airliner carrying pilgrims to Mecca explodes.

2 December Iran's new Islamic Constitution is approved by a referendum.

7 December The shah's nephew (Princess Ashraf's second son) Shahriar Mustafa Shafiq, is murdered in Paris's Rue de la Villa Dupont in the sixteenth *arrondissement*. In Tehran Sadeq Khalkhali, head of the Islamic Revolutionary Tribunal, claimed credit for the murder. He said that such murders would continue 'until all these dirty pawns of the decadent system have been purged'.

14 December Tehran radio announces that Iraqi forces have entered Iranian territory but have been repulsed.

15 December After being refused re-entry into Mexico, the former shah and the Empress Farah leave the US for exile in Panama at the invitation of Panama's effective leader and former chief-of state, General Omar Torrijos.

On 18 November Khomeini had declared that the 52 US hostages remaining in the US embassy would be tried as spies by revolutionary courts unless the US extradited the shah to Iran.

22 December A state of emergency is declared in the Iranian province of Baluchistan following a local rebellion against Tehran's central government.

December The Muslim People's Republican Party (MPRP), created with the blessing of Iran's moderate Ayatollah Shariatmadari, briefly takes over Tabriz. They seized the radio and television stations and other key buildings but overplayed their hand by trying to spark off a revolt in Qom itself where Khomeini, Shariatmadari and most of the religious hierarchy were based. Khomeini's supporters responded by executing four of the leaders of the revolt. Khomeini himself visited Shariatmadari whom he apparently presented with evidence that counter-revolutionaries were using him to overthrow the whole religious leadership. Consequently, Shariatmadari ordered the MPRP's offices to be closed and the revolt collapsed.

1 9 8 0

Sayings of the Year

'After all this, Khomeini comes and calls on the Iraqi people ... to go out on the rooftops and protest against the government. He said the Shah had gone and someone else had come. It turned out that it was another Shah, but this time wearing a turban.' Saddam Husayn, Nineveh, 15 April.

'Iraq is once again to assume its leading Arab role . . . Iraq is destined once again to face the concerted machinations of the forces of darkness . . .' Saddam Husayn, Nineveh, 15 April.

'An Iraqi ruler who bows to Khomeini or to anyone else will be trampled upon by the Iraqis . . .' Saddam Husayn, Baghdad, 20 July.

'We are now forced to fight for peace and to bring the rulers of Iran back to their senses, so that they will establish relations of good-neighbourliness between Iran and the countries of the region.' Tariq Aziz, Paris, 25 September.

'It is not a question of a fight between one government and another; it is a question of an invasion by an Iraqi non-Muslim Ba'thist against an Islamic country, and this is a rebellion by blasphemy against Islam.' Khomeini, Tehran, 20 October.

[War cannot be fought] 'with sandals and prayer beads, cane and staff, fist and slogan . . . We cannot go to war on donkeys and frighten those armed with MiGs and Mirages.' Shahab al-Din Eshraqi, Khomeini's son-in-law, November (supporting Iran's professional army against the hardline clergy).

4 January The UN secretary-general, Kurt Waldheim, cuts short a mission to Iran when Ayatollah Khomeini refuses his request to see the US hostages.

9 January A total of 63 of the Islamic militants who seized the Great Mosque at Mecca in November 1979 are decapitated.

11 January Revolutionary Guards reportedly raid the headquarters of the Muslim People's Republican Party (MPRP) in Tabriz, claiming that it served as a 'base for rioters'. In the ensuing battle, four people died and 25 MPRP members were taken to Tabriz prison. On 12 January 11 were executed, unleashing renewed violence in the province. Despite Ayatollah Shariatmadari's alleged disassociation from the MPRP on 6 January, rioting by his followers continued. Shariatmadari had disagreed with Khomeini on the question of the Velayat-e Faqih (the Guardianship of the Jurisconsult), which gave Khomeini effective supreme authority in Iran, and he also believed that the clergy should not run the country.

25 January Abul Hasan Bani Sadr becomes Iran's president. A previously obscure Islamic economist who had spent the 15 years preceding the revolution in exile in France, Bani Sadr was considered to be Khomeini's favourite candidate for the post and won a popular mandate with a 75 per cent majority. A modernist, educated in the Western tradition, the 46-year-old president started his term of office with the high expectations of many.

Bani Sadr's support was from the middle classes, the modernists, the secular forces and, above all, the Mujahedeen-e Khalq Organization, a Muslim guerrilla movement that had been fighting the shah since the late 1960s. The Mujahedeen was led by Masoud Rajavi.

Since first meeting Khomeini in 1972, Bani Sadr had regarded him as a father, a sentiment that Khomeini reciprocated. Well versed in Islamic jurisprudence, Bani Sadr had for years published his political beliefs which centred on the concept of *ta'min-e imamat* (generalized imamate) in which all Muslims share the religious leadership. He believed that the clergy should be subject to the state.

In November 1979 he had served briefly as foreign minister and finance minister.

On 29 January Khomeini described support for Bani Sadr's presidency as incumbent on the people. However, the Islamic Republican Party (IRP) leader, Ayatollah Beheshti, was to claim that Bani Sadr represented the danger of 'liberalism'.

7 February Bani Sadr is named as head of Iran's ruling Islamic Revolution Council (IRC). He took over the council with full executive powers. Khomeini approved the move, resolving in his favour, at least temporarily, a power struggle with the right-wing clergy and the hardliners. Bani Sadr quickly became the focus for those who believed that the religious leaders should return to the mosques and leave the running of the country to professional politicians and Western-educated technocrats. Bani Sadr had already won the agreement of the IRC to deny the students, who were holding the US embassy hostages, free access to radio and television.

On 19 February Khomeini delegated to Bani Sadr his powers as commander-in-chief of the armed forces. As such, in May Bani Sadr confirmed Abu Sharif as commander of the Revolutionary Guard, but within a month Abu Sharif, officially known as Abbas Zamani, was forced to resign by the IRP hardliners and replaced by the IRP loyalist Morteza Reza'i.

11 February Ayatollah Khomeini's message on 11 February, marking the revolution's first anniversary, raises the prospect of an eventual normalization of relations with the US. This was indicated by a shift of emphasis away from the strong attack he made on the US shortly after the seizure of the US embassy on 4 November 1979. Khomeini made no mention of the extradition of the shah, wrongly, it now seemed, supposed to be his main demand.

In an interview in the French newspaper *Le Monde* on 12 February, Bani Sadr said that the shah's extradition was not linked to the fate of the hostages. The US merely had to admit publicly to crimes committed in Iran since 1953 when a CIA-backed coup had put the shah back on the throne; to promise not to interfere again in Iran's internal affairs; and to recognize Iran's right to seek the extradition of the shah and the return of his fortune. He added that Iran was so convinced of its case that it agreed in advance to accept the conclusions of an international inquiry commission.

On 12 February the US State Department announced that it was imposing a temporary news blackout on its efforts to end the hostage crisis. Although the State Department appeared to be taking Bani Sadr's suggestions seriously, it was not prepared to humiliate itself by admitting guilt, particularly since it felt that there were no guarantees that such a move would secure the release of the hostages.

Secret documents, released by the students holding the embassy, failed to prove US interference in Iran after the shah's fall and indeed appeared to support the US claims that it had tried to co-operate with the new regime. However, the US role in the 1953 coup and in creating the Iranian Organization of National Security and Intelligence (SAVAK) were well known and many observers felt that apologizing for these would win the US considerable sympathy in Iran. Contrary to reports at the time, very few of these documents were actually shredded.

Observers believed that the release of the hostages would be guaranteed if the following conditions were met with: US public acknowledgement of 'certain historical facts' in the two countries' relations; restating support for an international commission of enquiry into the shah's rule; reaffirmation of Iran's right to take action in the US courts to freeze the shah's assets; a promise to free Iranian assets frozen by President Carter on 14 November 1979.

23 February Khomeini states that he will let parliament decide the fate of the US hostages, taking the question almost entirely out of the hands of the students and allowing Bani Sadr to concentrate on consolidating his administration before March's parliamentary elections.

Meanwhile, on 24 February the UN-sponsored commission of enquiry started hearings in Tehran into Iran's allegations against the exiled shah and the US. The commission was made up of five international jurists. However, it suffered from the discrepancy between the Iranian and the US interpretaion of its mandate – the US seeking a direct link between its findings and the release of the hostages.

26 February The shah is given the go-ahead to sell a stud farm in Britain, but is told he cannot touch the proceeds of £800,000, pending a claim on them by the Iranian Horse Society.

14 March–9 May Iran's IRP captures some 60 seats in the two-round Majlis (lower house) elections. According to Vahe Petrossian, although the IRP had failed to create a popular base, it had exploited President Bani Sadr's miscalculations and gained Khomeini's ear, thus enhancing its popularity with the voters. The remaining members of the 270-seat Majlis were potential Bani Sadr supporters but his tactics were so provocative that even his sympathizers sided with the IRP on key votes. Bani Sadr, Petrossian says, further burnt his bridges with the Majlis by staying away after members did not rise from their seats to honour him on his first visit.

20 March Khomeini's Iranian New Year's Eve message urges Iranians to make the new year 'the year for a restoration of order and security'. Among other things he called for the revolutionary courts to be gradually merged with the regular judicial system. As a result, even hardliners such as Ayatollah Muhammad Beheshti, chief justice of the supreme court and Ayatollah Mousavi-Ardabili, the prosecutor general, demonstrated support for such integration. However, the guidelines were to have little effect and were only briefly to slow down the waves of executions. Observers were becoming aware of Khomeini's tendency to oscillate between moderate and hardline positions which reflected the myriad and sometimes mutually hostile groups who spoke in his name.

23 March The exiled shah leaves Panama for Cairo just 24 hours before Iran was due to serve the Panamanian authorities, through the Panamanian *caudillo* Omar Torijjos, with a request for his extradition. He had moved to Panama after leaving the US in December 1979. Bani Sadr and Sadeq Qotbzadeh had attempted the extradition through the services of the French lawyer, Christian Bourget, and an Argentinian businessman, Hector Villalon. Observers felt that Bani Sadr and Qotbzadeh believed that if extradition proceedings were at least seen to be initiated, they could persuade the hardliners to release the hostages.

1 April A hand-grenade attack is made at Baghdad's Mustansiriyah University by an 'Iraqi of Iranian origin' on Iraq's deputy prime minister, Tariq Aziz, one of President Saddam Husayn's 'inner circle'.

Following the attack, on 8 or 9 April Iraq's leading Shi'i intellectual Muhammad Baqr al-Sadr, and his sister, Amina Bint al-Huda, were secretly and summarily executed. Al-Sadr had been a mainstay of the Shi'i Al-Da'wa al-Islamiyya Party (literally meaning The Islamic Call) and had long been considered an ideological threat to the regime.

Saddam Husayn had pressurized Al-Sadr to reverse his religious judgement that Baghdad's Ba'thist regime was 'un-Islamic'. After the Iranian revolution in February 1979, Al-Sadr had sent a congratulatory telegram to Khomeini in which he expressed the opinion that 'other tyrants have yet to see their day of reckoning'. Tehran radio had called Al-Sadr 'the Khomeini of Iraq' and encouraged Iraq's 65 per cent Shi'is to seek his spiritual guidance.

In addition, up to 40,000 Iranians were deported from Iraq to Iran, members of the Al-Da'wa party were arrested and membership of it was made retroactively punishable by death.

Husayn spoke of Iraq's refusal to be intimidated even if it meant 'dancing on the wings of death'.

7 April US President Carter announces further punitive measures against Iran, following Ayatollah Khomeini's refusal on 7 April to approve the transfer of the US hostages from the control of the militant students holding them to Iran's ruling Revolutionary Command Council (RCC) headed by the moderate President Bani Sadr. Carter's measures included the breaking of diplomatic relations, the prohibition of exports (excepting food and medicines) to Iran, a study of Iranian assets frozen in the US with a view to their confiscation, and the invalidation of visas issued to Iranians for future entry into the US. Official Iranian reaction to the measures was one of jubilation and triumph.

9 April Relations between Britain and Saudi Arabia deteriorate after the transmission on the British independent television network of a dramatized documentary called 'Death of a Princess'. The programme, which was co-produced by Associated Television (ATV), dealt with the events leading up to the execution for adultery of a Saudi princess and a Saudi student in Jeddah, 1977. It was considered by the Saudi authorities to be highly offensive to both Islam and the Saudi royal family. However, the execution itself had, at the time, horrified many countries.

In January 1978 the British press had reported that Princess Misha'il, the granddaughter of Prince Muhammad ibn Abd al-Aziz (King Khaled's elder brother) had been publicly executed by firing squad. Khaled Muhalhal, a nephew of General Ali Shaeir, the Saudi ambassador to Lebanon, was described as her lover and was beheaded immediately afterwards. The Saudi embassy in London had confirmed the reports on 1 February 1978, adding that the couple had been convicted by a *shari'a* (Islamic) court. A scene in which Saudi princesses made 'trysts' with young men from their cars in the desert had particularly upset the Saudis.

On 5 April the British foreign minister, Lord Carrington, expressed his 'deep regret' at the ATV decision to show the film. This, however, had little effect on the Saudi authorities who, on 23 April, asked the British ambassador, James Craig, to leave the kingdom and postponed the posting to London of their own new ambassador. Saudi officials also implied that trade links with Britain would suffer. The British government deplored the showing of the film but explained to Saudi Arabia that it could not override the British right to freedom of speech.

17 April US President Carter says that military action will be his only choice if Iran fails to free the US hostages.

18 April Ayatollah Khomeini attacks Iran's universities, giving the go-ahead for more widespread attacks on them. This gave hardline fundamentalists the excuse to purge left-wing elements in the universities. Following a march on Tehran University campus led by President Bani Sadr on 22 April, the universities closed down altogether and were not to reopen for two years.

23 April Iran and South Yemen establish diplomatic relations.

24 April The US launches an abortive military strike to free the 53 embassy hostages held in Tehran. Six C-130 transport aircraft and eight Sikorsky RH-53D helicopters landed in the Iranian desert west of Tabas on a covert mission to rescue the hostages from the embassy building in Tehran. However, with three of the helicopters failing to function, the mission was a fiasco. As the US commander tried to abort the mission, one helicopter and one C-130 aircraft crashed and eight US airmen were burnt to death.

On 27 April Hojatolislam Sadeq Khalkali gave a press conference in the US embassy compound at which he mockingly identified the dismembered bodies from body-bags. On 29 April Carter denounced the treatment as a 'horrible exhibition of inhumanity'.

Suspicions that Iranian agents in the armed forces had helped the US mission led to a purge of the military. The rescue operation was fiercely denounced in Iran whose leaders claimed that God had inflicted a defeat on the US. On 25 April President Carter appeared on US television to accept full responsibility for the operation.

By the end of May the hostages were said to have been dispersed among 16 towns throughout Iran in order to forestall a new rescue attempt.

30 April Three gunmen seize 20 hostages at the Iranian embassy in London and demand freedom for 91 Arabs in Iran. On 5 May Britain's Special Air Service (SAS) commandos made a spectacular assault on the building in London's Knightsbridge, killing four of the five gunmen and rescuing the 19 surviving hostages. The only terrorist not to die was protected by women hostages who pleaded for his life.

14 May Iran's President Bani Sadr announces that 96 US citizens have landed in the Bakhtiari mountains in western Iran and are about to launch a campaign of sabotage and assassination. According to Shaul Bakhash, in *The Reign of the Ayatollahs*, this and other similar claims reflected an atmosphere of paranoia in Iran after the 25 April US attempt to rescue the hostages.

20 May Within days of his appointment to head Iran's anti-narcotics campaign, Hojatolislam Sadiq Khalkali orders the execution of 20 people found guilty of drug trafficking. Although as an Islamic judge he had become notorious for sending hundreds of Iranians to their deaths, he had supported the moderate President Bani Sadr and was popular with the masses. By the end of August, says Shaul Bakhash in *The Reign of the Ayatollahs*, some 200 people had been executed 'often on the flimsiest of evidence'. Bakhash points out that Khalkali's executions led to another spate of killings for various crimes.

2–5 June On the initiative of Iran's President Bani Sadr an international conference is held in Tehran to examine 'US crimes in Iran' since 1953. The conference was attended by about 300 delegates from 54 countries. Among them, at Iran's invitation, was a 10-man US delegation headed by Ramsey Clark. Clark had been US attorney-general under President Lyndon Johnson. Clark told the delegates that it was essential to release the hostages at once, given the increasing threat of US intervention, and he offered to take the place of one of the hostages.

19 June Iraqi police in Baghdad kill three 'terrorists' in the British embassy compound.

20 June Elections to Iraq's National Assembly take place, the first since the revolution of 1958. Although some 840 candidates contested 250 seats, it was believed that ultimate control of the Assembly was in the hands of the Ba'th Party. At the opening sesion Na'im Haddad was elected speaker.

30 June Ending three days of talks in Saudi Arabia, South Yemen's President Muhammad describes the meeting as 'brotherly, frank and cordial'. Observers believed that the visit was intended to allay fears that Communist South Yemen's treaty with the Soviet Union threatened Saudi Arabia. After leaving the kingdom, Ali Nasser Muhammad visited the United Arab Emirates (UAE) and Kuwait.

In addition to seeking improved relations with the more conservative Gulf states, it was also speculated that South Yemen might seek better relations with Iraq. In the first part of 1980, hostility between Iraq and South Yemen had been underlined by the formation in Iraq of a South Yemeni opposition front, the sentencing of alleged Iraqi spies in South Yemen and the reported expulsion of South Yemeni students from Iraq.

3 July In Kerman, Iran, two middle-aged women found guilty of prostitution and two men charged with sexual offences are stoned to death. They were dressed in white robes and buried up to their chests in the ground. According to Shaul Bakhash, in *The Reign of the Ayatollahs*, the judge of the Islamic court who passed the sentences threw the first stone. On 8 July Hojatolislam Sadeq Khalkhali ordered seven alleged drug offenders to be shot by firing squad in full public view of a Tehran street.

4 July Tens of thousands of representatives of the IRP, the Mujahedeen, the Pasdaran, the Crusade for Reconstruction, the 'students of the Imam's line' (holding the US hostages), the Seminary Teachers of Qom, the Combatant Clerics of Tehran and others hold a rally in Tehran in support of Khomeini's call for a new bureaucratic order. Among other things they called for the purge of 'agents of East and West' and the imposition of Islamic dress on all women in government offices.

4 July Douglas Hurd, minister of state at Britain's Foreign and Commonwealth Office, states that there is no question of Britain agreeing to exchange the Briton, Christopher Sparkes, who had been accused by the Iraqis of 'subversive activities' and 'industrial espionage', for an Iraqi who was currently serving a life sentence in London for the murder of Colonel Abd al-Razzak al-Nayef.

10 July Ayatollah Khomeini personally authorizes the release of one of the US hostages, the 28-year-old vice-consul at the US embassy, Richard Queen, for medical treatment outside Iran. Following his release, he was diagnosed as having multiple sclerosis.

20 July Hashemi Rafsanjani is elected speaker of Iran's Majlis (lower house).

21–29 July Two generals, former air-force commander Said Mahdiyun, and Ahmad Mohaqqeqi, a former gendarmerie commander, and 300 other army and air-force officers are arrested in Iran for plotting to overthrow the government. According to Shaul Bakhash in *The Reign of the Ayatollahs*, when Muhammadi-Reyshahri's military revolutionary tribunal had completed its work, as many as 140 people had been executed. The government claimed that the plot aimed to bomb Khomeini's home and restore Prime Minister Bakhtiar to power. Centred on the Hor air-force base in Hamadan, it highlighted the power struggle between President Bani Sadr and the professional army on the one hand, and the IRP and the Revolutionary Guards on the other. Khomeini told Bani Sadr that 'The military have the Shah in their blood.'

27 July The shah dies of cancer in Cairo. On 29 July he was buried in the mausoleum of Cairo's Al-Rifa'i Mosque (where the shah's father had been buried) after a full state funeral. Egypt's President Sadat's decision not to invite any world leaders provided a diplomatic exit for countries reluctant to antagonize the revolutionary regime in Tehran. Sadat described the shah as a 'personal friend and Muslim brother'. In contrast, Tehran Radio announced that 'the bloodsucker of the century' had died. The US administration expressed sympathy for the shah's family but made no mention of his long and loyal alliance with the US.

31 July Two Iraqi diplomats are expelled from Austria for trying to deliver explosive devices to the Iranian embassy in Vienna. On 1 August the First Secretary at the Iraqi embassy in East Berlin, and a technical officer at the embassy, were arrested in West Berlin for allegedly trying to hand over a suitcase containing a small amount of explosives for use against Kurdish students. On 13 July Egypt had expelled 18 Iraqi diplomats while on 18 August Iraq ordered Syria to withdraw and replace all its diplomatic personnel at its embassy in Baghdad following the discovery there of arms and other materials.

8 August The IRP candidate Muhammad Ali Raja'i is imposed as Iranian prime minister on President Bani Sadr. A street vendor and then a teacher, Raja'i had joined Bazargan's Iran Freedom Movement in the 1960s. In prison for his activities he had met Ayatollah Muhammad-Javad Bahonar, one of the founders of the IRP. Bani Sadr publicly described Raja'i as 'incompetent' and refused to acknowledge his presence. He then refused to approve Raja'i's cabinet list, leaving half the government departments leaderless.

8 August In Saudi Arabia, British surgeon Richard Arnot and his wife, Penelope, are freed and allowed to return to Britain. On 28 August the British Foreign Office denied a cover-up in the case of the British nurse Helen Smith who had died together with her lover at a party given by the Arnots in Jeddah in 1979.

19 August In Saudi Arabia 301 people die when a Lockheed Tristar lands in flames at Riyadh Airport.

24 August The amir of Kuwait, Shaikh Jaber al-Ahmad al-Jaber al-Sabah, issues a decree providing for the holding of elections to a new National Assembly (parliament) which would meet 'within a period not exceeding the end of February 1981' on the basis of a revised constitution. During the government crisis of 1976, the late Amir Shaikh Sabah al-Salem al-Sabah had suspended four articles of the 1962 constitution relating to the press and the National Assembly which he had dissolved. There had, since then, been a growing demand in Kuwait for the restoration of parliament with even Shaikh Jaber warning, on 24 August, of the 'negative aspects' of the absence of a parliament over the previous four years.

4 September Iraq claims that the Iranians have shelled the Iraqi towns of Khanaqin and Mandali. However, on 9/10 September Iraq claimed to 'liberate' two pockets of territory between Qasr-e Shirin and Naft-e Shah.

9 September The British embassy in Tehran is closed. Douglas Hurd, a Foreign Office minister, said that the risk of the four remaining British diplomats being taken hostage was too great. On the same day two Iranian students were deported from Britain after taking part in a violent demonstration outside the US embassy in London in August. Both had to be forced onto the plane bound for Tehran. They shouted anti-US slogans as they were pushed aboard.

9 September Sadeq Tabataba'i, a Khomeini aide, indicates to the US via West German intermediaries that Iran is prepared to settle the US hostage issue. Of the four conditions which Khomeini laid down on 12 September, one, a US apology for its past 'crimes' in Iran, was dropped. On 14 September a US team led by the US deputy secretary of state, Warren Christopher, flew to West Germany for talks with Tabataba'i.

20 September Iran's President Bani Sadr orders the call-up of military reservists to defend 'the integrity of the country' (against Iraq).

22 September Iraq invades Iran at eight different points and bombs 10 Iranian airfields, thus starting the eight-year Gulf war. Iran retaliated in the Shatt al-Arab. On 17 September Iraq's President Saddam Husayn had announced Iraq's unilateral abrogation of the 1975 Algiers agreement. His goal seems to have been to defeat the Islamic revolution in Iran (and therefore stem the threat of Iran's perceived wish to export its 'Islamic Revolution'), to win territorial concessions from Iran and to establish himself as the Arab world's leading figure.
On 23 September Iran retaliated by bombing Iraqi military and economic targets.
The 1975 Algiers agreement included Iraq's recognition that the *thalweg* or deep-water line of the Shatt al-Arab waterway was the frontier between Iraq and Iran. Until 1975 navigation had been governed by an agreement concluded between the two countries in 1937.

28 September UN Security Council resolution 479 urges the end of hostilities between Iraq and Iran. Iraq announced its readiness for a cease-fire on condition that Iran accepted Iraq's full rights over the Shatt al-Arab. Tehran rejected the UN resolution.

30 September The US sends AWACs reconnaissance planes to Saudi Arabia.

5 October Kuwait decrees general mobilization of the Kuwaiti armed forces in the wake of the continuing hostilities between Iraq and Iran.

12 October Khomeini names President Bani Sadr chairman of the Supreme Defence Council, but, outmanoeuvred by his enemies, Bani Sadr fails to use the council to reassert his flagging authority in Iran. He was consistently blocked by Prime Minister Raja'i who took every opportunity of snubbing him. Later in the month Bani Sadr asked Khomeini to rid him of the Raja'i government which he said would lead the country to 'the greatest abyss in its history'. However, Khomeini did not act.

24 October Iraq captures a vital bridgehead at Iran's key port of Khoramshahr but fails to take Susangird during the campaign of 14–17 November, despite heavy shelling of Khuzestan. The war had started in Iraq's favour, Iran's situation appearing desperate after a series of army purges. However, after Iran's initial setbacks, both sides settled down to a long war of attrition.

2 November Iran's parliament approves four conditions laid down by Khomeini for the release of the US hostages.

7 November Sadeq Qotbzadeh, Iran's former foreign minister who essentially represents the moderates, is arrested but released three days later on Khomeini's orders.

10 November Iraq captures Iran's port of Khoramshahr.

19 November Iran's President Bani Sadr, speaking to a huge meeting to mark the Shi'i mourning month of Ashura, asks why torture taking place in Iranian prisons is not investigated. 'How is it that in the Islamic regime, it is possible to condemn a man to death as easily as one takes a drink of water . . . ?' he asked.

In December merchants of the Tehran bazaar called for the resignation of Prime Minister Raja'i's government, warning that its incompetence was leading to the country's 'complete annihilation'.

November Iraq sees the setting up of the opposition Democratic Patriotic Front which includes the Iraqi Communist Party, the Kurdistan Democratic Party and the Kurdistan Socialist Party.

25 December Iran opens up a third front in Kurdistan in its war with Iraq.

30 December Iraq's President Saddam Husayn declares that 'We signed it [the 1975 agreement with Iraq] but the Iranians gained legal rights under unnatural circumstances and under conditions we could not control . . . the Iranians used military force against us.' By December both Iran and Iraq were stalemated by a wet winter.

1 9 8 1

1 January Iran's Basij-e Mustazafin (the Mobilization of the Oppressed), an auxilary volunteer force founded in 1980, is merged with the Pasdaran (Islamic Revolution Guards Corps).

1 January Several detainees in Bahrain, including former National Assembly member Muhsin Marhnoun, are freed in an amnesty to mark National Day. Marhnoun belonged to the People's Block in the assembly, which was dissolved on 29 August 1975. He had been arrested in December 1975 on his return from a visit to Kuwait.

The Soviet president, Leonid Brezhnev, sent the amir, Shaikh Isa, a friendly message to mark National Day despite the fact that Bahrain had no diplomatic relations with Moscow.

5–10 January Iran's counter-offensive in the Dezful-Susangird area fails. However, Iran claimed to have launched a major counterattack against Iraq and captured hundreds of prisoners. In support of its claims it put on public show nearly 500 Iraqi prisoners of war in Tehran on 7 January. In January Prime Minister Muhammad Ali Raja'i said that the Gulf war had created 1.5 million refugees.

19 January According to a Council of Arab Economic Unity report, Kuwait, Saudi Arabia and Libya employed more than 3.5 million foreign workers in 1980.

20 January At 5.15 pm (Greenwich Mean Time) the US hostage crisis ends in Tehran as all 52 hostages out of the 80 or so diplomatic staff originally taken prisoner in 1979 are released. However, it became clear that Iran had waited too long and compromised itself in its deal with the US. Since mid-1980 Iranian public opinion had favoured releasing the hostages as long as Iran's frozen assets were returned in full, and some kind of understanding was reached on the late shah's and the royal family's allegedly misappropriated funds.

However, according to the deal, Iran was only to get back about one-quarter of its national assets held abroad. Meanwhile, US President Reagan threatened to go back on the agreement worked out by the Carter administration. According to US officials Iran suddenly softened its demands for the full return of its assets in the final days of negotiations.

Total assets held by Iran in the US were about $11,100 million but of these $3,700 million were disposed of to repay syndicated loans, $1,400 million to repay non-syndicated loans and $3,200 million to be settled by arbitration. This left only about $2,880 million that Iran could draw upon immediately. US officials speculated that the sudden change in attitude was caused both by Iran's need for immediate cash as well as fears that the new Reagan administration might take a tougher line. More important, however, may have been the Iranian regime's feeling of urgency to rid itself of a problem that it would have liked to have solved long ago.

The final negotiations took place in Algiers with the Algerian government acting as go-between. In a carefully planned snub to Carter, the hostages were not put onto an aircraft until literally minutes after Carter had been replaced by Reagan at the Washington Inauguration Day celebrations.

Bankers in New York and London were also involved, with the Bank of England playing a crucial role in putting together an extremely complicated financial package. The hostages claimed that they had been treated badly, some being held in solitary confinement for long periods and others being put before fake firing squads.

As a result of the hostages' release, the US and other Western countries, including Britain, lifted trade sanctions against Iran. However, Britain said that it would not resume normal ties with Iran until four British citizens held in Iran on spying charges were released. Nevertheless, Britain's exports to Iran had risen in value from $557 million in 1979 to $960 million in 1980. Before the 1979 revolution they had stood at about $1,800 million.

20 January The Swiss government has blocked any attempt to sell the late shah's $5 million villa at St Moritz ski resort, pending a court ruling on the owner's identity. A Swiss official disputed Iran's claim that the villa had been confiscated in Iran's name.

21 January Iraq's President Saddam Husayn declares that Iraqi forces could enter or destroy any Iranian city but he hoped 'the Iranians would return to their senses to prevent such a step'. On the same day the UN peace envoy Olof Palme said that he believed that the time for quiet diplomacy had come. In mid-February he met President Saddam Husayn in Baghdad to discuss the possibility of negotiations with Iran. Comments made by Saddam Husayn shortly before Palme's visit suggested that Iraq no longer had the military initiative against Iran.

During January Iran had failed to retake Susangird from the Iraqis.

25–28 January The Islamic Conference Organization summit at Taif in Saudi Arabia repudiates UN resolution 242 (the formula for an Arab-Israeli peace settlement), advocates a *jihad* (holy struggle) to win back Jerusalem and make it the capital of Palestine, and extends the Arab boycott of Israel.

1 February The Iranian executive affairs minister, Behzad Nabavi, announces that diplomatic relations with Jordan and Morocco have been broken off because of their 'full support for the Iraqi regime and their enmity to the Islamic revolution in Iran'.

Meanwhile, Iran's official Islamic Republic News Agency reported that the life of the Iranian oil minister, Javad Tondguyan, captured by the Iraqis in October 1980, was in grave danger because of ill-treatment by the Iraqis.

12 February The US Defence Department says that about 250 army and air force troops are going to Oman to conduct communications exercises and set up a temporary communications centre. This was the first time that US forces had been stationed in the Arabian peninsula. The US Army Corps of Engineers had already commissioned Stanley Consultants of the US to do a survey of improvements to the base facilities of Oman's Masirah Island.

15 February Iran's Ayatollah Khomeini tells Iranian oil workers that economic sanctions are 'a gift to our country', adding that if they continued for 10 or 15 years 'we should by then have fully discovered our potential and our capability'. He said that Japan, which had started from scratch, was a model for Iran's development.

19 February In Iran 133 writers, journalists and academics issue an open letter to protest illegal trials, the suppression of basic freedoms, the muzzling of the press, the burning of books and bookstores and other violations of the constitution, according to a London *Financial Times* report.

In early February Khomeini had tried to mediate between Iran's two warring factions: the clerical party and revolutionary organizations ranged against President Bani Sadr on the one hand and the moderate and left-of-centre groups that Bani Sadr repesented on the other. On 5 February *Kayhan* reported Khomeini as saying: 'Don't bite each other like snakes and scorpions . . .'

Also in February the former US embassy in Tehran was handed over to the Shahid (martyrs) Foundation, to be used by war refugees and casualties of the revolution of 1979.

20 February According to the London-based Middle East Economic Digest (MEED) Kuwait's financial assets at the end of 1979 were officially said to total $48,700 million of which two-thirds was held abroad.

23 February Kuwait's five radical candidates fail to win any seats in Kuwait's parliamentary elections. The results reassured Shaikh Jaber, the ruler, in his August 1980 decision to revive parliamentary rule after a four-year gap. Kuwait's conservative tribal leaders increased their representation in the National Assembly (parliament) to about half its 50 seats. The Assembly was to become the most democratic in the Arab world, with the right to vote on all laws. A new cabinet was formed on 4 March by the prime minister, Crown Prince Shaikh Sa'd al-Abdullah al-Salem al-Sabah.

1–7 March Mediation attempts in the Iran-Iraq war by the Islamic Conference Organization fail. On 6 March Iran's President Bani-Sadr told the Islamic Conference Organization team that its proposed cease-fire from 12 March and a gradual Iraqi withdrawal starting a week later were not sufficient. He said that the 1975 Algiers agreement on the Shatt al-Arab waterway and 'punishment' of Iraq's President Saddam Husayn would have to be included in any cease-fire agreement.

5 March Hecklers at a rally held by President Bani Sadr at Tehran University are discovered to belong to revolutionary and Islamic committees – backing the Islamic Republican Party (IRP) – opposed to the president. However, on 6 March the IRP accused Bani Sadr, via the Friday sermon in mosques, of provoking the violence. Prime Minister Raja'i called Bani Sadr a liar for attributing the violence to government supporters while Hojatolislam Sadeq Khalkali called for the president's dismissal and trial. Chief Justice Muhammad Beheshti confirmed that Bani Sadr could be brought to trial while the prosecutor-general, Ayatollah Mousavi-Ardabili, confirmed that an investigation of the incident on 5 March would go ahead. Iran's most powerful forces were now united against Bani Sadr.

14 March The former US president, Gerald Ford, arrives in Oman on an unofficial visit. His visit followed the US agreement, subject to Congress approval, to give Oman $155 million in economic and military aid in 1982.

15 March Khomeini calls a meeting of Iran's leaders to try to reconcile President Bani Sadr with those who oppose him in the IRP and the government. The president came alone. The IRP and the government were represented by Chief Justice Beheshti, Speaker Rafsanjani, Prime Minister Raja'i, Prosecutor-Generel Mousavi-Ardabili and the former defence minister, Khamene'i. Former Prime Minister Mehdi Bazargan came as mediator and Khomeini's son, Ahmad, was also present. The meeting was acrimonious and reached no agreement but on 16 March Khomeini issued guidelines for both sides.

March The head of Iran's official Islamic Republic News Agency, Kamal Kharazi, accuses Kuwait of letting its ports be used for the transfer of weapons to Iraq.

8 April Iran's state radio announces a ten-point programme granting legal recognition to groups that have waged an armed struggle against the Islamic Republic provided they lay down their weapons and change their attitude. The offer appeared to be aimed mainly at the Kurdish Democratic Party (KDP) which had been fighting government forces in Kurdistan. Nevertheless, the amnesty coincided with a new clampdown on press freedom in Iran.

21 April The White House announces that President Reagan has decided to sell five airborne warning and control systems (AWACS) aircraft to Saudi Arabia, subject to congressional approval, as part of a package. The package would include equipment designed to boost the range and firepower of the 62 McDonnell Douglas F-15 fighters to be sold to the Saudi air force. The decision was to be opposed by America's pro-Israeli lobby.

22 April Iran plans to double oil exports from 1.4 million barrels a day to 2.5 million for 1981/82, according to budget revenue details published on 22 April. Iran was faced with a $17,000 million deficit if current revenue levels persisted.

30 April Iran seizes an oil survey vessel chartered by the Kuwait Oil Company. Iran claimed that the vessel was in waters designated as a war zone. However, on 8 May the vessel was released.

7 May Tehran's Homayun Street (behind the British embassy) is renamed Bobby Sands Street following the attendance of Bobby Sands' funeral in Belfast by the Iranian ambassador to Sweden. Later in the month the Revolutionary Guards' Organization invited the families of Irish republican prisoners to visit Iran, according to Iran's official Islamic Republic News Agency.

18 May The Iran/US arbitration tribunal – to decide the fate of about $4,000 million of Iranian assets still held in the US – begins work in The Hague.

23 May Eighteen people are arrested in connection with an alleged plot to restore the Iranian monarchy, armed forces revolutionary judge Muhammad Gilani Reyshahri announces. On 22 May 14 people were reported to have been arrested for alleged responsibility for recent bomb explosions in Tehran. They were said to be members of the Oveisi Group, a group named after the shah's late 1978 martial law administrator, General Gholamali Oveisi, now living in Western Europe.

25 May The Co-operation Council for the Arab States of the Gulf, better known as the Gulf Co-operation Council (GCC), is established by Bahrain, Kuwait, Oman, Qatar, Saudi Arabia and the United Arab Emirates (UAE). The GCC's Supreme Council comprises heads of member states and meets annually. The president is a member of each state, according to an alphabetical rota system. The Supreme Council appoints the secretary-general on the recommendation of the Ministerial Council for a renewable three-year term. Each member state contributes in equal proportions towards the budget of the secretariat. The secretary-general in 1986 was the Kuwaiti Abdullah Yaqoub Bishara. The Ministerial Council, consisting of foreign ministers of member states, meets every three months.

The GCC provides for co-operation among member states in the fields of economics, industry, agriculture, transport and communications, energy, defence and external relations. In 1983 the GCC founded the Gulf Investment Corporation. The implications of the Iran-Iraq war had prompted the creation of the GCC.

27 May For the first time Khomeini indirectly attacks President Bani Sadr, noting that Islam is 'hostile to the cult of personality'. In a clear reference to Bani Sadr, he said that the disconcerted 'can go back to Europe, the United States or wherever else they like'. When newspapers supporting Bani Sadr were banned on 7 June, Bani Sadr printed leaflets calling on the people to resist dictatorship. Khomeini responded, saying: 'The day I feel danger to the Islamic Republic, I will cut everybody's hand off. I will do to you what I did to Muhammad Reza [the shah]'. Bani Sadr responded in a letter, saying that Khomeini was 'committing suicide' and entrusting power to his 'power-hungry' enemies. (See Shaul Bakhash, *The Reign of the Ayatollahs*.)

31 May A report on Kuwaiti holdings of US securities has ignited US fears of dangerous levels of Arab economic control in US, according the US *Chicago Tribune*. The report claimed that total Kuwaiti holdings of about $7,000 million in November 1980 were to be raised to $8,000 million by the end of 1981. However, observers believed these fears to be exaggerated.

7 June Israel makes a lightening attack on Iraq's Osirak nuclear research centre at Tuwaitha near Baghdad, arguing that it would be used as the basis for the production of nuclear weapons which could be used against Israel. Israel's US-made General Dynamics F-16s and McDonnell Douglas F-15s aircraft totally destroyed the larger of the two French-built reactors – Tammuz 1, a 70-MW Osiris-type reactor. Following the attack, the former Israeli defence minister, Moshe Dayan, claimed that Israel already had the capacity to make nuclear bombs. Israel announced that it would destroy the Tuwaitha centre again if it was rebuilt.

Iraq's nuclear programme began in 1968 when it was supplied with a two-MW Soviet-made research reactor. However, since then most equipment had been supplied by France who built the research centre at Tuwaitha, some 20 miles (32 kilometres) east of Baghdad, and supplied two experimental reactors as well as 72 kilos of uranium fuel.

Attempts to block Iraqi progress in nuclear development had included the sabotage of French-made reactor cores awaiting shipment in the French port of Toulon and the assassination of the head of the Tuwaitha research centre, Yahya al-Meshad.

The attack was the subject of an emergency foreign affairs ministers' meeting in Baghdad which started on 11 June.

On 10 June the US had taken the unprecedented decision to suspend the delivery of military aircraft to Israel.

9 June Saudi Arabia's King Khaled ibn abd al-Aziz arrives in London for a state visit to Britain until 12 June. He was given a welcoming banquet by Queen Elizabeth on 9 June and started discussions with Prime Minister Margaret Thatcher on 10 June. British military and commercial contracts with Saudi Arabia were high on Britain's agenda and the subject of discussions between the Saudi defence minister, Prince Sultan, and the British foreign secretary, Lord Carrington.

10 June Ayatollah Khomeini strips President Bani Sadr of his title as supreme commander of the Iranian armed forces, in an angry response to Bani Sadr's letter of late May. Also on 10 June the Central Bank governor, Ali Reza Nobari, resigned, anticipating legislation transferring authority over the bank from President Bani Sadr's office to the prime minister's office. Nobari, a Bani Sadr appointee, was replaced by the deputy finance and economics minister, Mohsen Nourbakhsh.

On 11 June Bani Sadr returned from the battle-front, where he was wont to escape the squabbling in Tehran, to Tehran. On 12/13 June he issued yet another 'message to the people' in which he defended his record as president. On 15 June, fearing the consequences, he went into hiding.

The Majlis, meanwhile, made moves to impeach him. With the war with Iraq at an apparent stand-still, in addition to food shortages and general economic problems, Bani Sadr had become the focus, as Ayatollah Shariatmadari had done, of the regime's critics. According to Vahe Petrossian (see Bibliography), his final fatal move was a speech he gave at the Shiraz air-force base calling for resistance against dictatorship. This was tantamount to threatening a military coup against the regime, and therefore against Khomeini himself.

13 June King Khaled of Saudi Arabia is the first foreign head of state to visit France's Elysée Palace since the mid-May election of Socialist President Mitterrand. The visit encouraged trade relations which had concentrated on French weapons sales, public works contracts and telecommunications. According to Crown Prince Fahd, the king told Mitterrand that Saudi Arabia would finance the rebuilding of Iraq's French-built nuclear reactor destroyed by Israel on 7 June.

15 June At the first Arab nuclear power conference which opens at Damascus, the UAE says it intends to have nuclear power stations in operation by 1991. The conference forecast nuclear power stations being built in Iraq (whose nuclear research centre had been bombed by the Israelis on 7 June), Saudi Arabia, Tunisia and Morocco.

15 June The National Front mobilizes a huge rally in Tehran in which it accuses Khomeini directly of responsibility for a reign of terror. Calling the meeting an invitation to revolt, Khomeini called on Bazargan's Iran Freedom Movement and on Bani Sadr to disassociate themselves from the rally. Bazargan promptly complied in a radio broadcast while Bani Sadr issued no statement of support for the rally.

On 20 June, the day of the Majlis's impeachment vote, the Mujahedeen rallied to Bani Sadr's support by calling on its supporters to take to the streets. Serious fighting ensued between guerrillas and Revolutionary Guards in which up to 20 people died. Some of the Mujahedeen were summarily executed.

19 June The Kuwaiti minister for finance and planning, Abd al-Latif al Hamad, warns that of Kuwait's population, only 41.5 per cent is Kuwaiti and even this figure is expected to drop to 25 per cent by the year 2000 if the present trend of employing expatriate workers continues.

21 June The Iranian Majlis (lower house) votes to impeach the former Iranian president, Bani Sadr. The vote was 177 to 1, with 11 abstentions and 20 others absent. Speaking of Bani Sadr's supporters, Hashemi Rafsanjani said that 'these people have made war against God' while the Majlis deputy Sadeq Khalkhali said that 'the revolutionary prosecutor and the revolutionary tribunals must today execute at least 50 of them.'

On 22 June Ayatollah Khomeini dismissed Bani Sadr from office. From a secret hideout, Bani Sadr now called for a mass uprising. The regime responded with unprecedented violence, including summary executions in the streets. Over 50 opponents of the regime were killed in the streets and in the prisons. According to Petrossian, although the chances of the Mujahedeen overthrowing Khomeini were slight it seemed that the IRP leaders, having never commanded the popularity which Bani Sadr and the Mujahedeen enjoyed, became so nervous that they over-reacted to the challenge.

28 June Ayatollah Muhammad Husseini Beheshti and 72 colleagues are killed when a bomb destroys the IRP headquarters in Tehran. Beheshti was in the chair addressing the IRP faithful when the explosion from 66 pounds (30 kilograms) of dynamite ripped through the building. Those killed included Beheshti, four cabinet ministers, 10 deputy ministers and 27 Majlis deputies. Prime Minister Raja'i and the Majlis speaker, Hashemi Rafsanjani, had left the assembly only minutes before the explosion which killed many of Iran's moderates. According to Dilip Hiro in *Iran Under the Ayatollahs*, Beheshti's death deprived the governing party of its most astute and pragmatic figure (see Biographies). Khomeini accused the Mujahedeen of the explosion although according to Hiro a monarchist group in Paris called the Military Organization for National Equality claimed credit for it.

30 June The ruling Likud Party, led by Menachem Begin, wins the Israeli election. On 22 June US President Reagan's administration issued its first public criticism of Begin's hardline policies. The US defence secretary, Caspar Weinberger, said that Israel's attack on the Iraqi nuclear research centre on 7 June and Iraq's raids on Israel had 'set . . . peace back quite a way'.

June Iran rejects Iraq's offer of a Ramadan cease-fire. In June Bandar Khomeini Port was said to have closed after an Iraqi aircraft sunk a ship near the harbour.

13 July Two Tehran businessmen are executed for opposing the Islamic Republic and supporting the leftist-Islamic Mujahedeen-e Khalq. Since the ousting of President Bani

Sadr in June, some 150 people had been executed or arrested, according to Vahe Petrossian in the London-based MEED.

15 July The Saudi information minister, Muhammad Abdou Yamani, says that Saudi Arabia has agreed to pay all the costs of rebuilding the French-built Iraqi nuclear reactor destroyed by the Israelis on 7 June. Meanwhile, the French foreign minister, Claude Cheysson, told the Beirut newspaper, *Al-Nahar*, that France was willing to supply a new reactor to Iraq, under the same conditions as to other buyers. He also said that France was willing to sell weapons to Iraq, the Gulf states and Egypt but not to 'totalitarian despotic regimes'.

On 20 July Iraq's President Saddam Husayn said in Baghdad that Iraq intended to build 'two, five, ten nuclear reactors, according to its needs', despite the attack on its nuclear reactor on 7 June. He thanked Saudi Arabia for its offer of 15 July to rebuild the reactor and cautioned France to take a firmer stand in condemning the Israeli attack. On 16 July Portugal had announced that it would supply 130 tons of enriched uranium to Iraq, its main oil supplier, in 1981.

17 July President Saddam Husayn is quoted as saying that Iraq wants to build a naval base on Kuwait's Bubiyan Island and has asked Kuwait for a 99-year lease on part of the island. He told the Kuwait daily newspaper, *Al-Anba'a*, that the base would be for the 'defence of Iraq and Kuwait [against Iran]'. He reminded the Kuwaitis, in referring to what was a long-standing border dispute between Iraq and Kuwait, that Iraq had only an 8-mile (13-kilometre) shelf on the Gulf 'which is our sole outlet to the sea'.

Meanwhile, Saddam Husayn, in an implicit warning to Saudi Arabia, called on oil producers to 'put an end to the surplus and restore a state of balance in this field'.

17 July The Muscat-based newspaper *Oman* reports that the Soviet Union has established missile bases in South Yemen along the borders with Saudi Arabia, North Yemen and Oman.

24 July Muhammad Ali Raja'i is elected president of Iran's Islamic Republic with 88 per cent of the vote. He replaced Bani Sadr whom Khomeini had dismissed on 22 June. Officials figures showed that 14.6 million voters turned up for the election.

Meanwhile, one of the leading members of the Mujahedeen-e Khalq guerrilla organization, Muhammad Saadati, was executed after being sentenced to death for the alleged complicity in the 29 June murder of the Evin prison governor, Muhammad Kachoui.

On 15 July Hashemi Rafsanjani was re-elected speaker of the Majlis.

29 July The ousted Iranian president, Bani Sadr, flees into exile in Paris with Mujahedeen-e Khalq leader Mas'ud Rajavi. Both men were granted political asylum in France. Although Tehran called for Bani Sadr's extradition, observers felt that the government welcomed his departure since he was still popular in Iran and might present a threat to the regime.

Bani Sadr had been in hiding in Iran with Mujahedeen protection since mid-June. He formed an alliance with the Mujahedeen in July, only days after the group had described Khomeini as the enemy of the people. Given that both Bani Sadr and the Mujahedeen owed their popularity to their presumed loyalty to Khomeini, they were certain to lose popular support by cutting themselves away from him so radically.

5 August Hojatolislam Muhammad Javad Bahonar is confirmed as Iran's new prime minister by parliament.

7 August Iraq will spend $133,377 million in its 1981–85 five-year plan, despite the continuing war with Iran, the London-based MEED quotes Iraq's planning minister, Taha Ibrahim, as saying.

8 August King Fahd of Saudi Arabia's eight-point plan for peace in the Middle East is revealed. Its key points were the creation of an independent Palestinian state, a guarantee for all states in the region to live in peace, and complete Israeli withdrawal from the territories occupied since 1967.

12 August A protocol defining the Iraq-Turkey border is signed.

15 August In Kuwait, seven Jordanians are sentenced to life imprisonment after being convicted of planting five bombs in Kuwait in June.

17 August The Federal Reserve Bank of New York transfers control of $2,050 million in Iranian financial assets, completing the US's side of the agreement for the release of the hostages in January.

On 17 August Iran's Majlis approved all but one of the 22-member cabinet submitted by Prime Minister Bahonar.

19 August France's President Mitterrand confirms to Iraq's visiting foreign minister, Tariq Aziz, that France is prepared to rebuild Iraq's nuclear reactor destroyed by Israel on 7 June.

24 August Seventy-two people are executed in Iran, bringing to 815 the number of executions officially reported since 20 June. According to the London-based MEED, of these, 417 were members of the Mujahedeen-e Khalq.

26 August Muscat radio announces that an agreement had been reached on the formation of a joint Soviet-controlled military command based in Aden.

30 August The new Iranian president, Muhammed Ali Raja'i, as well as the man who replaced him as prime minister, Javad Bahonar, are killed in a bomb explosion at Bahonar's office. The bomb was reported to have killed six others and injured 23, among them Colonel Vahid Dastgerdi, head of the national police force, and General Sharafskha, acting commander of the ground forces. The killings were widely attributed to the Mujahedeen, struggling against what they considered the clerical dictatorship of Khomeini. 'The terrorists are trying to force us to act severely and so lose popular support', said the Majlis speaker, Hashemi Rafsanjani. In revenge, hundreds of Mujahedeen were shot, despite Khomeini's call for moderation.

On 1 September the interior minister, Ayatollah Reza Mahdavi-Kani, was appointed interim prime minister. The general-secretaryship of the IRP, formerly held by Bahonar, was given to Hojatolislam Ali Khamenei, one of the three surviving IRP founders.

6 September The ruler of Ajman, the smallest of the seven UAE emirates, Shaikh Rashid ibn-Humaid al-Nuaimi, dies after a short illness at the age of 78. He was succeeded by his second son, Shaikh Humaid ibn-Rashid al-Nuaimi who was born in 1930. During his father's later years, Shaikh Humaid had been largely responsible for Ajman's day-to-day affairs.

7 September Iran's London consulate is briefly occupied by Iranian students supporting the left-wing Islamic Mujahedeen-e Khalq, Iran's main opposition group. In late August there had been similar incidents at Iran's embassies in Brussels, The Hague and Stockholm.

8 September The Kuwaiti ruler, Amir Shaikh Jaber, arrives in Ankara on the first leg of a 12-day tour which would take him to Bulgaria, Hungary, Rumania and Yugoslavia. The tour was part of Kuwait's aim to diversify away from the US and Western Europe in which two-thirds of its investments were officially placed. It wanted to challenge sensational stories about 'the Arabs buying America'.

11 September The Iranian oil ministry cancels all contracts and other agreements made with foreign oil companies during the shah's reign according to the official Islamic Republican News Agency. Many companies had reduced purchases from Iran because of the high price of its crude oil, at $37 a barrel.

12 September Mohsen Rez'ai is appointed commander of Iran's Pasdaran (Revolutionary Guards).

14 September A New York state judge refuses to hear a $50,000-million lawsuit brought by Iran against the shah and Empress Farah.

19 September One hundred and forty-nine people are executed in Iran, according to Shaul Bakhash in *The Reign of the Ayatollahs*. The government called them 'leftist militants'. A week later 110 were executed in one day. The executions had begun immediately after President Bani Sadr's impeachment, and had intensified after the bombing attacks on the IRP headquarters and Prime Minister Bahonar's office. Reflecting the regime's fear and its need for vengeance, Bakhash says that executions of 50 people a day had become routine. In September even a 13-year-old girl was shot by firing squad, while in Kerman two Mujahedeen members were hanged from a city bridge and in Tehran four teachers were shot in the school playground in view of their children.

19 September The US State Department defended its freezing in US banks of about $2 million of Iranian assets. The action was aimed at making Iran release $1 million in US funds frozen in Tehran. It was also holding on to Iran's embassy and consular offices in Washington until Iran handed the US embassy in Tehran to the Swiss.

27–29 September Iraqi forces are pushed back across the Karun River and break off their siege of the Iranian port of Abadan.

29 September Four of Iran's military chiefs are killed in a plane crash. On 1 October General Ali Zahirnejad was appointed joint chief-of-staff, Colonel Ali Sayyid Shirazi commander of the ground forces, and Colonel Muhammad Hasan Moinpur air-force chief.

29 September A man described as the virtual ruler of Iran's Khorasan province, Hojatolislam Abdolkarim Hashemi-Nejad, is assassinated in Mashhad. A Majlis deputy and prominent IRP member, his assassins were thought to belong to the Mujahedeen.

1 October Three Iranian aircraft attack a crude-oil gathering centre in Kuwait according to a Kuwaiti government spokesman. The attack, in the Umm al-Aish region about 24 miles (40 kilometres) south of the Iraqi border, was the fourth by Iranian aircraft on Kuwaiti border areas since the Iran-Iraq war began.

By the week ending 2 October – a week of bloody fighting – Iran had lifted Iraq's siege of Abadan, ruining any chances Iraq might have had to impose its full control over the Shatt al-Arab waterway dividing Iran and Iraq. On 28 September Iraq had admitted that its army had withdrawn to the left bank of the Qarun River because of heavy Iranian air attacks.

2 October In Iran's presidential election, the Interior Ministry says that Hojatolislam Ali Khamenei has won 1 million of the 1.1 million votes counted in Tehran and 13.8 million of the 14.4 million votes cast in the rest of Iran. The electorate was said to number 22 million. The new prime minister, Ayatollah Muhammad Reza Mahdavi-Kani, resigned suddenly on 15 October and was succeeded by Ali Akbar Velayati, an Islamic fundamentalist trained in the US as a doctor. However, the Majlis rejected Velayati's nomination as well as that of the oil minister, Muhammad Gharazi, and it was not until 29 October that it endorsed Khamenei's third choice, the foreign minister, Hussein Mousavi, by 115 votes to 39 with 48 abstentions. The 40-year-old Mousavi was an architect and publisher who had studied in Tehran.

3 October Iranian government forces recapture the northern town of Bukan from Kurdish guerrillas after five days' fighting, according to Tehran Radio.

6 October Egyptian President Sadat is assassinated by Islamic militants. On 14 November he was formally replaced by Vice-President Hosni Mubarak, who had been vice-president of Egypt's ruling National Democratic Party since 1978.

6 October Israel's Defence Ministry confirms that an Israeli missile ship which ran aground at Ras Sabil off the Saudi coast was subsequently released in a salvage operation.

6 October More than 3,000 firms from 73 countries attend Baghdad's International Trade Fair, despite the Gulf war.

7 October The former Iranian prime minister, Mehdi Bazargan, attacks the government's severity towards the opposition and condemns the daily executions of leftist Islamic militants whom he describes as 'dedicated' Iranians. IRP supporters responded by calling for his execution.

8 October North Yemen's former president, Abdullah Sallal, returns to San'a from exile in Cairo at the invitation of President Ali Abdullah Saleh. Earlier in October Abd al-Rahamn al-Iriani, who overthrew Sallal in January 1974, accepted an invitation to return.

19 October London's *Financial Times* is told by Oman's minister of state for foreign affairs, Qais abd al-Moneim, that the US may have to spend $1,000–1,500 million on military facilities in Oman over the coming decade.   Also on 19 October Oman's ruler, Sultan Qaboos, issued three decrees setting up a 45-member state advisory council to fulfil his November 1980 promise to allow more public participation in government.

28 October The US Senate upholds the sale of AWACS to Saudi Arabia. The Senate voted 52 to 48 in favour of an $8,500 million armaments sale to the kingdom, ending a fierce political debate. Israel strongly condemned the move. The package included five E-3A Sentry airborne warning and control systems (AWACS) aircraft. Although it would not receive these before 1985, four US AWACS were already based near Riyadh.

29 October Iran's Majlis confirms Foreign Affairs Minister Hussein Mousavi's nomination as prime minister. Mousavi, a 40-year-old architect, was President Khamenei's third nomination for the premiership in less than a week. The Iranian interim prime minister, Ayatollah Mahdavi-Kani, and his entire cabinet had resigned on 15 October. The Majlis member for Tehran, Ali Akbar Velayati, was nominated by President Khamenei to succeed him but on 22 October the Majlis rejected his nomination because of insufficient evidence of his part in the struggle to overthrow the shah's regime. The second unsuccessful candidate was the oil minister, Muhammad Gharazi.

Shortly after taking office, Mousavi assured the private sector of the continuation of a mixed economy.

30 October The long-standing border dispute between Dubai and Sharjah is settled after an international arbitration tribunal had been set up in 1978.

October Amnesty International says that more than 3,500 people are known to have been executed in Iran since the 1979 revolution, although the true number may be higher. Its latest figures stated that 1,800 people had been executed since President Bani Sadr was deposed on 20 June. According to the Mujahedeen-e Khalq, almost 200 children, wounded in demonstrations in Tehran, were taken from their hospital beds to the notorious Evin prison and executed in October.

Meanwhile, two British prisoners, Andrew Pyke and Frank Skinner, were moved from Evin in September to a prison in Karaj.

1 November Kuwait's National Assembly's financial and economic committee passes a bill involving a 'secret' KD 2,000 million ($7,000 million) to Iraq. According to the committee's chairman, Jassem al-Kharafi, the loan had been approved by government decree before the National Assembly's revival in March, preceding an interest-free $2,000-million loan to Iraq approved on 21 April by the Assembly. According to the London-based MEED, the April loan was reported to be part of a $14,000-million financial package Iraq had been seeking from Kuwait, Saudi Arabia, the UAE and Qatar. Iran had already sent threatening signals to Kuwait for giving Iraq financial aid.

7 November Shaikh Zayed is re-elected for a further five years as president of the UAE. Despite his long illness which prevented him from attending the Supreme Council of Rulers' meeting, Shaikh Rashid, the ruler of Dubai, was re-elected prime minister of the federation. He was represented by his son, Crown Prince and Deputy Prime Minister Shaikh Maktoum.

18 November The US State Department says that it has filed a claim against Iran for at least $180 million on behalf of about 3,000 US citizens and companies which suffered losses as a result of the 1979 revolution.

19 November After a visit to Aden, the secretary-general of the Council of Arab Economic Unity, Fakhri Kaddori, announces that South Yemen will become the sixth member of the Arab Common Market (ACM) during the first half of 1982. North Yemen was also negotiating to join. Other members of the ACM, set up in 1964, were Iraq, Jordan, Libya, Mauritania and Syria.

24 November According to Adeni sources, Sultan Ahmad Omar, leader of the South Yemeni-supported National Democratic Front (NDF) has agreed to a cease-fire with North Yemeni President Saleh in Kuwait. On 23 November Saleh and South Yemen's President Muhammad had talks in Kuwait on the proposed union of the two Yemens. On 2 December Saleh and the NDF signed an agreement in Aden aimed at ending their war which had caused some 3,000 casualties in 1981.

25 November The Arab summit meeting at Fez in Morocco rejects King Fahd of Saudi Arabia's 8 August peace plan for the Middle East although on 11 November the GCC's two-day summit in Riyadh had endorsed it. On 1 November Egypt's President Mubarak had told US businessmen that the plan 'could lead to more normal relations throughout the area'.

27 November The UAE will contribute Dh 750 million ($204 million) to a 10-year Arab development plan approved at the Amman Arab summit in November 1980, according to the London-based MEED. The plan was aimed at improving the living standards of the poorer of the Arab League member states.

29 November In an offensive which began on 29 November, Iran is said to have re-taken the town of Bustan in Khuzestan from the Iraqis. Between September and December successful Iranian counter-offensives had succeeded in recapturing much territory, including areas such as Abadan, Bostan and Gilan-e Gharb.

2 December Representatives of the European Space Agency sign a $23-million agreement in Riyadh to launch the Arab Satellite Communications Organization's (Arabsat's) first satellite, which will be put into a stationary earth orbit in 1984.

6/7 December The US Rapid Deployment Force carries out its Bright Star 82 military manoeuvres in Oman. Meanwhile, British air-force Phantom jets conducted three weeks of joint exercises with Omani forces. The US *Washington Post* had recently reported that Saudi Arabia and other Gulf states had offered Oman $1,200 million to cancel agreements giving the US access to Oman's military facilities.

13 December Two Iranians die when a bomb they are carrying explodes near London's Marble Arch.

15 December Iran's Majlis approves the appointment of Ali Akbar Velayati as foreign affairs minister and Hojatolislam Ali Akbar Nateq Nuri as interior minister. Velayati had been President Khamenei's first choice as prime minister. Nuri was Khomeini's representative in the Reconstruction Jihad.

16 December The Bahraini government arrests 73 people for plotting to overthrow the government on Bahrain's National Day. They were 58 Bahrainis, 11 Saudis, one Omani and one Kuwaiti. All were Shi'is and all were believed to be members of the Islamic Front for the Liberation of Bahrain, trained in and encouraged by Iran.

1 9 8 2

Sayings of the Year

'Khomeini is not a man of religion. Whoever describes him as such is fanatical, stupid and understands nothing of politics. Khomeini is a politician. When he realizes he is losing more than he is gaining, he will establish peace'. Saddam Husayn, Baghdad, 10 November.

9 January A draft constitution uniting North and South Yemen is agreed in Aden. It provided for the capital of the new state to be San'a and the religion Islam. Coming soon after a Kuwait-sponsored cease-fire agreement, the constitution came within the framework of the November 1972 Tripoli communiqué calling for Yemeni unity. Since the December cease-fire there had been no major incidents of fighting between North Yemeni forces and guerrillas of the Aden-backed National Democratic Front (NDF).

15 January British businessman, John Allen Bowden, has been held in jail in Iran on unspecified charges since November 1981, according to Britain's Foreign Office. He was the third British businessman to be held in Iran. Andrew Pyke was being held at Karaj, 25 miles (40 kilometres) from Tehran and Frank Skinner in Tehran's Qasr prison.

Meanwhile, the authorities at Tehran's Evin prison confirmed that Shokrallah Paknejad, a leading socialist politician who had opposed both the shah and the present regime, had been executed in late December 1981. Paknejad had been a founder of the NDF set up shortly after the revolution.

25 January The United Arab Emirates (UAE) announces that it is following Jordan and Kuwait's boycott of France's state-owned vehicle manufacturer Renault. The boycott was imposed on 17 December by the Damascus-based Arab Boycott of Israel Office.

27 January The six member states of the Gulf Co-operation Council (GCC) agree in Riyadh to establish a $3,000-million Gulf Investment Corporation as a first step to setting up a Gulf common market. GCC defence ministers also discussed the establishment of an armaments industry, defence help for Oman and a joint air-defence system based on Saudi Arabia's US-supplied airborne warning and control systems (AWACS) aircraft. GCC ministers may also have agreed to form a 'rapid deployment force' for the Gulf to avoid the need for superpower intervention.

During their January meeting the GCC petroleum ministers gave Oman top priority for investment in revenue-earning projects, agreeing to establish a committee of advisers from Saudi Arabia's Petromin, the Kuwait National Petroleum Company and the Abu Dhabi National Oil Company, to survey the potential for petrochemical, petroleum refining and pipeline projects in Oman. On 1 February they discussed the possibility of building a pipeline through Oman to bypass the Strait of Hormuz, securing the flow from Iranian attack.

28 January King Husayn of Jordan announces the establishment of the Yarmouk volunteer force to fight with the Iraqis against Iran. He said that he would spend as much time as possible at the battle-front.

28 January British businessman Andrew Pyke is released from Iran's Karaj prison in Tehran after being held for 17 months without trial. He left Iran on 5 February. On the same day the US State Department said that at least six US nationals were being held in Iranian prisons.

On 8 February the West German ambassador, Jens Peterson, escaped serious injury when he was attacked in his car by unidentified gunmen in Tehran. He was recalled to Bonn soon after the attack.

January The Bahraini interior minister, Shaikh Muhammad al-Khalifa, calls for a Gulf 'rapid deployment force' to counter regional emergencies following the recent coup attempt in Bahrain, according to the Saudi newspaper *al-Jazirah*.

January Kurdish guerrillas in Iraq sabotage the oil pipeline carrying Iraqi oil to Turkey.

6–9 February One hundred delegates from African and Asian socialist organizations, parties and liberation movements attend a world peace conference in Aden to discuss Israeli military aggression and the US military buildup in the region. Oman claimed that the conference aimed to destabilize the region.

8 February The operational commander of Iran's leftist-Islamic Mujahedeen-e Khalq movement, Mousa Khiabani, is killed in a gunfight with Revolutionary Guards in Tehran. Khiabani was running the Mujahedeen in the absence of its leader, Masoud Rajavi, who had fled to France with the former Iranian president, Bani Sadr, in July 1981.

In mid-February Iran's President Khamenei told the US magazine *Newsweek* that an 'assembly of experts' would soon choose a council of three to five members to succeed Khomeini as Iran's spiritual leader.

12 February Agreement has been reached in principle for France to supply Iraq with $667 million of self-propelled guns, according to the London-based Middle East Economic Digest (MEED). In 1981 an agreement was reached for France to supply Iraq with Roland ground-to-air missiles mounted on an armoured chassis.

15 March Ayatollah Khomeini encourages the de-politicization of the Iranian army and the Iranian Revolutionary Guards Corps (the Pasdaran).

19–30 March Iraqi forces are obliged to withdraw from the Shush-Dezful region. Their failure to take Susangard on 19/20 March was considered a turning-point in the war. On 1 March Khomeini had asked the visiting Islamic Conference Organization (ICO) delegation to 'sit in judgement on Iraq' but both Iraq and Iran rejected the ICO peace plan of 5 March. After Iran had destroyed over 40 Iraqi aircraft on 4 April, Iraq's deputy premier told the US *Washington Post* that 'We don't care if Iran is dismembered', while Iran's Majlis speaker, Hashemi Rafsanjani, said that the removal of Saddam Husayn was Iran's 'strategic goal'.

7 April Sadeq Qotbzadeh is arrested on charges of plotting with military officers and clerics to bomb Khomeini's home and to overhrow the state. The announcement was made by Hojatolislam Muhammadi-Reyshahri, prosecutor of the military revolutionary court. Qotbzadeh denied any intention on Khomeini's life and claimed that he had sought to change the government, not to overthrow the Islamic Republic. According to the *Iran*

Times, he implicated Ayatollah Shariatmadari whom he claimed had been informed of the plan and had promised funds and backing if the plot succeeded.

10 April Syria halts the transit of Iraqi oil through the Banias (Mediterranean) pipeline. As a result of losing this lifeline, Saddam Husayn responded by making his first call to the Iraqi people for austerity.

12 April Saddam Husayn announces that Iraq will withdraw from all Iranian territory if it can be assured that this would end the war. However, Iran ignored the offer, taking heart from serious unrest that had broken out in Iraqi Kurdistan.

25 April Israel completes its withdrawal from the Sinai Peninsula, which has now been fully restored to Egypt according to the 1979 peace agreement.

29 April Iran stages a major offensive against Iraq in the south. The offensive was code-named Bait al-Muqaddas (Jerusalem, literally meaning 'The Sacred House').

23 May The Iranian cabinet approves a $6-million budget to 'meet the needs of' Iraqi prisoners of war. Iran claimed to have captured over 40,000 Iraqis during the war so far.

24 May In a campaign lasting from 29 April to 24 May Iran retakes Khoramshahr from the Iraqis in its Bait al-Muqaddas offensive. Because of its destruction, the Iranians renamed the city Khuninshahr ('City of Blood'). The Iraqis were driven back to the international border, their morale severely damaged. The *Christian Science Monitor* reported on 27 May that Hashemi Rafsanjani had ruled out a cease-fire until Saddam Husayn had been punished as a war criminal and Iraq had paid $150,000 million in reparations.

26 May North Yemen's former foreign affairs minister and presidential counsellor, Abdullah al-Asnag, is sentenced to 10 years' imprisonment by North Yemen's State Supreme Security Court. Facing a possible death sentence, he had pleaded guilty and begged forgiveness at a public trial in June 1981.

28 May Despite US appeals to Israel to remain neutral in the Iran-Iraq war, Israel has sold some $27 million worth of military equipment to Iran, says the US State Department spokesman, Dean Fischer. Israel's defence minister, Ariel Sharon, responded by saying that Israel and the US had agreed to keep Israeli arms sales to Iran secret. He suspected that the US had now revealed them to justify its own sales of weapons to Iraq and Jordan.

On 1 June Iran's President Khamenei called the claims 'ridiculous propaganda' and Khomeini called them an attempt 'to defame Islam'.

30 May Anti-government riots take place in southern Iraqi cities such as Kerbala, Basra, Hilleh and Nasiriyah with majority-Shi'i populations. According to Dilip Hiro in *The Longest War*, these had been set off by Iran's recent victories.

2 June GCC foreign ministers meeting in Riyadh formulate a peace plan in the Iran-Iraq war, but it is aborted by Israel's invasion of Lebanon on 6 June.

4 June The proportion of Kuwaiti nationals has dropped to 38.9 per cent, compared with 41.5 per cent recorded in the 1980 census, according to the London-based MEED. Planning Ministry experts estimated that Kuwait's population had reached 1,562,000, a 15.2 per cent increase on 1980 figures.

6 June Israel invades Lebanon in what it calls 'Operation Peace for Galilee'. On 31 August it drove the Palestine Liberation Organization (PLO) out of Beirut. The PLO chairman, Yasser Arafat, subsequently set up his new headquarters in Tunis as his followers were dispersed to various Arab countries.

9 June Responding to an ICO appeal to end the Iran-Iraq war and to direct weapons against Israel's invasion of Lebanon, Iraq's Revolutionary Command Council (RCC) agrees to cease-fire terms in the absence of President Saddam Husayn, but these are rejected by Iran.

13 June Crown Prince Fahd ibn Abd al-Aziz becomes king of Saudi Arabia on the death of his half brother, Khaled. Fahd was a dominant influence behind his brother when Khaled succeeded King Faisal in 1975. Born in 1923, Fahd is the eldest son of the seven sons (the 'Sudairi Seven') of King Abd al-Aziz's favourite wife, Hassa bint Ahmad al-Sudairi. He also became prime minister and appointed his half brother, Abdullah, as crown prince and First Deputy Prime Minister. It is thought that opposition to the Sudairi Seven has tended to gather around Abdullah. Abdullah befriended his younger half brothers who defected from King Saud to Nasser's Egypt in the 1960s. Abdullah's politics are more radical than Fahd's and he is more critical of US and Western influences.

Fahd's full brothers include the second deputy premier and defence and aviation minister, Prince Sultan, the Riyadh governor, Prince Salman, and the deputy interior minister, Prince Ahmad. Since 1975 he had played a key role in many aspects of the kingdom's modernization and industrialization programme. He was a prime mover behind the creation of the GCC in 1981. In February 1985 he visited Washington in an attempt to persuade the US to put pressure on Israel to make peace efforts acceptable to the Arabs.

Since the revolution in Iran in 1979 and the Mecca siege of Islamic fundamentalists in the same year, King Fahd had made efforts to neutralize the militants who accused the regime of decadence. Responsibility for various bomb attacks in the kingdom in 1985 was claimed by the Iran-based Islamic Jihad Organization. His substitution of the title 'Custodian of the Two Holy Cities' for 'king' in the following year was clearly aimed at inoculating the Saudi regime from further militant anger.

24–27 June At the ninth Regional Congress of the Ba'th Party, Iraq's President Saddam Husayn re-asserts complete control and carries out a major reshuffle and dismissals from the RCC, the Regional Command of the Ba'th and the cabinet. He halved the size of the RCC, restricting it to his close allies: Izzat Ibrahim (al-Douri), Taha Yasin Ramadan, Tariq Aziz, Adnan Khairalla, Sadoun Shakir, Hasan Ali Amiri, Naim Haddad and Taha Muhyi al-Din Maruf.

30 June Iraq announces its withdrawal from remaining positions in Iranian territory, although some pockets are retained. On 20 June President Saddam Husayn had announced that Iraq would withdraw voluntarily from Iranian territory by 30 June.

June Vladimir Kuzichkin, a Soviet diplomat who had served as vice-consul in Tehran, defects to Britain. He reportedly provided information on 400 Soviet agents operating in Iran which the British passed on to the Iranian authorities.

June According to the Stockholm International Peace Research Institute (SIPRI), Saudi Arabia, the biggest Middle East arms spender, spent $22,450 million on arms in 1981, compared with $18,470 million in 1980, and Oman doubled its defence spending over the same period to $1,440 million. SIPRI said that Iraq had financed much of its arms supplies with a $2,000-million loan from Kuwait and other Arab states.

4 July Three Iranians go missing at a Christian Lebanese forces militia checkpoint north of Beirut. They were the Iranian chargé d'affaires, Hussein Mousavi, a Revolutionary Guards official, Ahmad Mostavaselian and a photographer, Kazem Akhavan. In June Israel had made its fateful decision to invade Lebanon, intending to destroy the PLO. Unfortunately 'Operation Peace for Galilee', as the Israelis dubbed the invasion, was to become a bloody three-year occupation during which the mainstream Amal movement, founded to give the Shi'is a real status in Lebanon, played a leading role in resisting the Israelis.

An even more radical group, the Hizbullah (Hizb Allah, party of God), was founded in Beirut in the wake of the Israeli invasion. Headed by a council of 12 clerics led by Shaikh Muhammad Hussein Fadl Allah, the Hizbullah were soon to be involved in the kidnapping of Western and Israeli hostages. Ali Akbar Mohtashami, the Iranian ambassador to Syria, encouraged it, seeing it as a means of promoting an Islamic revolution in Lebanon. Its symbol became a blue and blood-red image of the globe, with a raised arm holding a rifle with the Qur'anic words 'Indeed, the party of God, they are victorious.'

In the wake of the Israeli invasion, Iran had sent a contingent of 300–500 Revolutionary Guards to Lebanon via Syria. An apparently reluctant Syria allowed them to install themselves at Baalbek.

11 July An assassination attempt at the Iraqi town of Dujayal against Iraq's President Saddam Husayn fails. In the ambush, 10 of his bodyguards were killed but he was unharmed. The assassination attempt was made by soldiers belonging to the militant Islamic Al Da'wa organization.

13 July Iran rejects the UN Security Council resolution 514 appealing for a cease-fire and the withdrawal of both sides to the international border, and orders the advance on Baghdad to 'rid the Iraqi people of the Ba'th' [Party]. On 9 July Rafsanjani had listed the conditions for a cease-fire: retaining the 1975 border treaty, repatriation of over 100,000 Iraqis from Iran, payment of $100,000 million to Iran in reparations and the punishment of Saddam Husayn as a war criminal.

However, Iran's 13–28 July campaign to capture Basra was to fail. According to Dilip Hiro in *The Longest War*, Iran was no longer fighting off Iraqi aggression but was the invader, making this the fourth stage of the war. The earlier phases, he says, had been the Iraqi advance into Iran (until late March 1981), the stalemate (until mid-March 1982) and the Iraqi retreat from Iran (until the end of June 1982).

15 August Iraq announces a total maritime exclusion zone around Iran's oil terminal at Kharg Island, implying that it would attack any vessel approaching Kharg. Repeated Iraqi threats of air strikes against the Kharg Island export terminal were to push up crude-oil quotas in spot markets and lead to considerable fluctuations in hull premiums. However, the Islamic Republic News Agency (formerly the Pars news agency) said on 15 September that there had been no interruption in the flow to tankers carrying Iranian crude oil. On 14 September the Iranian oil minister, Muhammad Gharazi, said that Iran's crude exports were running at 1.7 million barrels a day.

25 August US marines arrive in the port of Beirut followed by French and Italian troops. They were to leave on 10 September.

1 September US President Reagan reveals his Middle East (Arab-Israeli) peace plan.

5–8 September A new Middle East peace plan is proposed at the Arab summit meeting in Fez. With the exception of Libya, all the members of the 'Steadfastness Front' (Syria, Algeria, South Yemen and the PLO) agreed to the plan which implicitly recognized the state of Israel. However, Israel rejected the plan.

The conferees, including Saddam Husayn, also adopted King Fahd's proposals for ending the Iran-Iraq war: a cease-fire during the coming *hajj* (pilgrimage to Mecca), complete evacuation by Iraq of Iranian territory and $70,000 million in compensation to Iran through the Islamic Reconstruction Fund, financed by the Gulf states. Iran, confident of victory and determined to oust Saddam Husayn, rejected the proposal.

11 September Futures traded on both Kuwait's official and Souk al-Manakh 'unofficial' stock market, are temporarily banned by the government in a further attempt to relieve the crisis faced by the markets, says MEED. Dealers had agreed to restrict interest on post-dated cheques already outstanding, to 20 per cent a year. Until recently these had carried interest at up to 300 per cent, reflecting expectations of rising share prices during a dangerous speculative boom.

14 September South Yemen's President Ali Nasser Muhammad makes an official visit to Moscow shortly after an attempted coup against him in favour of former President Abd al-Fattah Ismail who lives in exile in Moscow. According to the London-based newspaper, *Al-Sharq al-Awsat*, President Muhammad had been called away early from the Arab summit in Fez to challenge the plotters whose mastermind, former state security minister Muhammad Said Abdullah, was executed in early September.

14 September Bashir Gemayel, Lebanon's president-elect, is assassinated.

15 September In Tehran, Sadeq Qotbzadeh is executed at the end of a lengthy trial. Although he had been condemned to death it was widely believed that Khomeini had, via his son Ahmad, offered to spare him, and that the execution had been carried out on the authority of the special military prosecutor, Hojatolislam Reyshahri. Ayatollah Shariatmadari was then placed under house arrest and a campaign was taken up against him. Documents were produced to suggest that, in negotiations with the shah's government in 1978, he had approved of martial law and had even described himself as an opponent of Khomeini. He was then stripped of his coveted title of Marja-e Taqlid or spiritual 'Source of Emulation'.

16–18 September Christian Phalangist militias carry out massacres in the refugee camps of Sabra and Chatila in West Beirut. Israel was accused of allowing the militiamen to enter the camps, and of using searchlights to facilitate the massacre. On 25 September some 300,000 people protested in Israel against the government's apparent implicit involvement in the massacre.

On 27 September and in the wake of the Sabra and Chatila massacres, French, Italian and, on 29 September, US troops returned to Beirut.

September Iraqi planes attack ships in the maritime exclusion zone in the Gulf.

1–10 October Iran's attempts to capture Mandali, some 56 miles (90 kilometres) from Baghdad, from the Iraqis are unsuccessful. On 1 October Iran had mounted its Muslim ibn Aqil offensive in hills overlooking Mandali. Later in the month Iraq fired surface-to-surface missiles at Dezful, and raided Kharg Island as well as Iranian tankers.

30 October Iran's Revolutionary Guards announce their intention of organizing naval units.

1–11 November Iran occupies Iraqi territory in the Musian region of the southern war front.

3 November The US *Washington Post* reports the execution in Baghdad in June of the Iraqi minister of health, Riyadh Ibrahim Husayn. He had reportedly suggested that Saddam Husayn might relinquish the presidency in order to comply with Iran's major condition for ending the Iran-Iraq war. According to some sources, Saddam Husayn had invited him into a neighbouring room and shot him dead with a revolver.

13 November There are huge demonstrations in Baghdad with participants shouting 'Yes, yes Saddam; this is the referendum!' On 9 November Saddam Husayn had called for referenda in Iraq and Iran to test his popularity in Iraq, and Khomeini's in Iran.

16 November Following Ayatollah Montazeri's suggestion about the need for the active presence of the clergy on the battlefield, 350 clerics from Qom are sent to the front.
After Iraq had checked Iran's 'human wave' offensive, the front began to stabilize into a kind of trench warfare.

17 November The Supreme Council for the Islamic Revolution in Iraq is established in Tehran as an umbrella organization for Islamic groups opposed to the Iraqi regime. The council was chaired by Hojatolislam Sayyid Muhammad Baqir al-Hakim.

21 November According to a *New York Times* report, Mehdi Bazargan has addressed an open letter to Hashemi Rafsanjani, accusing the government of creating an 'atmosphere of terror, fear, revenge and national disintegration . . . What has the ruling elite done in nearly four years, besides bringing death and destruction, packing the prisons and the cemeteries in every city, creating long queues, shortages, high prices, unemployment, poverty, homeless people, repetitious slogans and a dark future?'

15 December In his eight-point liberalization decree, Khomeini curbs the reign of terror that had followed the Islamic Republic Party (IRP) headquarters explosion in June 1981. It appeared to be aimed at repudiating the hardliners who had broken the back of the political opposition with at least 2,500 executions since mid-1981.

December An Assembly of Experts is elected to address the question of succession to the Iranian leader, Ayatollah Khomeini.

1 9 8 3

Sayings of the Year

'We think that in the future, when an Islamic or people's government is set up in Iraq
... that will be more useful for the people of Iraq who remain.' (Rafsanjani on Iran's
desire to limit Iraqi casualties), Tehran, 15 March.

'... the need to influence the relationship between the rulers of Iran and their
supporters, by creating differences between them on the question of war and peace,
is a matter of paramount importance'. Saddam Husayn, 26 March.

'... if you execute the orders of Khomeini's regime ... your death will be certain
because this time we will use a weapon that will destroy any moving creature on the
fronts'. (The Iraqi High Command, threatening the use of chemical weapons), 14
April.

'I warn the governments of the Gulf ... to stop opposing Iran and helping Saddam
... An Islamic government is better for all the shaikhs of the region than the flimsy
American power.' Khomeini, Tehran, 16 August.

5 January The US Central Command, created almost exclusively for intervention in the
Middle East, is reactivated by the US joint chiefs' chairman, General John Vessey.

9 January The Iranian Mujahedeen-e Khalq leader, Masoud Rajavi, has a public meeting
with the Iraqi deputy premier and foreign minister, Tariq Aziz, in Paris. The Tehran
regime was to use such meetings to show that the Mujahedeen and other groups opposed
to it were unpatriotic.

15 January Some 60 dealers on Kuwait's unofficial Souk al-Manakh stock market are
confined to their homes. Earlier reports suggested that 17 dealers faced bankruptcy while
54 others were suffering serious financial problems.

15 January During his visit to Saudi Arabia, Iraq's President Saddam Husayn discusses
with King Fahd the possibility of building a pipeline to carry Iraqi oil across the kingdom.
In February, in an interview with the US *Wall Street Journal*, the Iraqi deputy premier and
foreign minister, Tariq Aziz, confirmed that Iraq's plans to build the pipeline across Saudi
Arabia to Yanbu on the Red Sea had been approved.

The line, to be financed by Western oil companies rather than by the Saudis as originally
planned, would be completed in 1989. Aziz confirmed Iraq's current severe financial
difficulties, adding that Saudi Arabia and Kuwait had started giving Iraq 300,000 barrels
a day of crude oil as a contribution to the war effort.

25 January About 22 guerrillas belonging to the Union of Iranian Communists are
executed in the Caspian Sea resort of Amol, in the wake of a widely publicized trial at
Tehran's Evin prison. They were accused of killing about 50 people, including members
of the Revolutionary Guards (Pasdaran). Although the Iranian leader, Ayatollah Khomeini,
had called for judicial reforms in December, he had not ruled out execution for people
convicted of violent crimes.

30 January Khomeini tells Tehran's bazaaris (merchants) that they have a religious duty to contribute to the war effort against Iraq.

On 29 January six Revolutionary Guards commanders were killed while visiting the southern war front.

Meanwhile, the prize for the first 200 winners of a literary competition organized by the Revolutionary Guards in the northern resort town of Sari, was to be sent to the battle front.

1 February Iraq has lost 117 warplanes in the war with Iran, according to the US *Washington Post*. On 18 January Iraq reported 66 bombing missions in the southern battle-front. However, according to Dilip Hiro in *The Longest War*, aircraft supplies from France and Egypt had maintained Iraq's total combat aircraft at about its pre-war strength of 332, while Iran's air-worthy military aircraft had been reduced to about one-quarter of its pre-war strength of about 440 planes.

On 21 January intelligence sources in the Far East said that China was supplying tanks to Iraq. Meanwhile, a Soviet decision to resume weapon supplies to Iraq was believed to have been taken during a December visit to Moscow by a delegation led by Iraq's First Deputy Premier Taha Yasin Ramadan, and Deputy Premier and Foreign Minister Tariq Aziz.

1 February The first troops of a British contingent for the multi-national peace force in Lebanon arrives in Beirut.

1 February Kuwait Petroleum Corporation (KPC), Kuwait's umbrella organization, signs an agreement with the US Gulf Oil Corporation (GOC) to buy GOC's main downstream operations in the Netherlands, Belgium and Luxembourg. In January the US Getty Oil Company had filed a suit in New York against Kuwait and Kuwait Oil Company for lifting more than its 50 per cent share in the jointly-operated oilfield in the neutral zone shared by Kuwait and Saudi Arabia.

7 February The Iranians cross into Iraq. However, they were to fail in their Wa al-Fajr (By Dawn) offensive in the Fakeh region of Khuzestan aimed at capturing the Basra-Baghdad road near Amara.

In January figures showed that Iraqi prisoners of war registered by the International Committee of the Red Cross in Iran totalled 28,423 while only 5,285 Iranian prisoners of war were registered in Iraq. On 12 February Iraq claimed that its air force and navy had attacked Iran's crucial Kharg Island export terminal. However, the Iranian oil minister, Muhammad Gharazi, said the terminal was operating normally.

7–10 March At the Non-Aligned Summit in New Delhi, Iran rejects an Iraqi blanket peace offer. Baghdad had already been slighted when the date of the summit had been put back from September 1982 and its venue moved from Baghdad, increasingly threatened by Iran, to the safety of New Delhi. On 9 March Iraq proposed that the non-aligned heads of state should arbitrate in the war with Iran and pledged to abide by the results. However, Iran's prime minister, Hussein Mousavi, demanded a complete Iraqi withdrawal from Iranian territory, war reparations and international condemnation and punishment of the Iraqi regime.

14 March Organization of Petroleum Exporting Countries (OPEC) ministers in London agree on a production ceiling of 17.5 million barrels of oil a day, with Saudi Arabia as 'swing' producer.

According to an OPEC publication in April, Saudi Arabia had more reserves than any other member with 167,850 million barrels, followed by Iran with 57,000 million barrels. Of OPEC's gas reserves, Iran had 47 per cent and Saudi Arabia 12 per cent.

10–17 April Iran stages an offensive in the Ein-Khosh area in order to reach the Basra-Baghdad highway, but fails. On 20/21 April Iraq fired surface-to-surface missiles at Dezful. In March it had struck Iran's small Nowruz oilfield in the Gulf.

11 April Sultan Qaboos of Oman starts a four-day state visit to the US. A US State Department official confirmed during the visit that Oman had given the US access, under certain circumstances, to military facilities being developed by the US Army Corps of Engineers in Oman. On 27 April a $300-million Eurodollar loan was signed for Oman.

13 April Saudi Arabia's 1983/84 spending programme represents a substantial reduction from the previous year. Nevertheless, it was still set to record a large budget deficit as it tried to reconcile the demands of its development programme and the severe drop in oil revenues.

16 April Women in Iran who violate Islamic standards of dress will face imprisonment of between one month and one year, the government announces. Women had to cover their hair with scarves and were forbidden to wear tight-fitting clothing. At the same time the religious leadership gave its official blessing to women working outside the home but stressed that they must safeguard their purity and bring up their children well. The Majlis (lower house) had recently approved a bill allowing women to initiate divorce proceedings.

18 April The British secretary of state for foreign and commonwealth affairs, Francis Pym, visits Saudi Arabia and the United Arab Emirates (UAE). He had cancelled a visit to Saudi Arabia, Qatar, the UAE and Oman scheduled for 5 January, following Britain's refusal in December to receive an Arab League delegation which included a representative of the Palestine Liberation Organization (PLO).

18 April A bomb blast wrecks the US embassy in Beirut, killing more than 50 people and injuring 120. The Shi'i organization, Al-Jihad al-Islami, claimed full responsibility for the attack.

28 April Iraq celebrates Saddam Husayn's forty-sixth birthday with demonstrations and feasts. Observers saw them as an attempt to divert attention away from the war. In May Iran's official Islamic Republic News Agency (IRNA) reported that so far the war had cost Iran over $136,000 million in lost output and public-sector assets. One of Iran's conditions for ending the war was the payment by Iraq of $150,000 million in war reparations.

2–5 May A contract for six Aerospatiale Super-Puma helicopters armed with Exocet air-to-surface missiles is signed in Paris during the 2–5 May visit of the Kuwaiti defence minister, Shaikh Salem al-Sabah al-Salem.

4 May Iran expels 18 Soviet diplomats and bans Iran's Tudeh (Communist, literally 'masses') Party. In February it arrested the 73-year-old Nureddin Kianuri, secretary-general of the party, members of the Tudeh central committee and other party leaders. The party was proscribed and its offices closed down. Over 1,000 party members were arrested. In April 18 Soviet diplomats were expelled from Iran. On television on 30 April Kianuri confessed to 'espionage, deceit and treason', having acted on Moscow's direction and having supplied the Soviets with secret military and other information. The crackdown against the Tudeh may have been precipitated by the defection of a Soviet diplomat to Britain in June 1982.

7 May The US secretary of state, George Shultz, flies to Riyadh to discuss with King Fahd the Lebanese-Israeli agreement he had helped to negotiate. The US wanted Saudi Arabia, Syria's main financial backer, to pressurize Syria to withdraw from Lebanon.

13 May The Iranian government has impounded foreign property belonging to the shah and members of his family, says the deputy prime minister, Manuchehr Muhammadi, according to the London-based Middle East Economic Digest (MEED). The property included Rolls-Royce cars, a stable in England and a villa in St Moritz.

22 May US President Reagan appeals to Khomeini to spare the lives of 22 prominent Baha'is reportedly facing execution. There were some 300,000 Baha'is in Iran. In March the UN secretary-general, Perez de Cuellar, had sought information about the reported executions of Baha'is in Iran. More than 100 of their leaders were said to have been executed since the revolution. Baha'ism, founded in Iran in 1844 as an offshoot of Islam, is condemned by the Islamic regime as a corruption of Islam rather than being protected as a separate religion.

In June the Paris-based National Council of Resistance claimed that 30,000 opponents of the Tehran regime had been executed and 100,000 imprisoned since June 1981. The council was led by the Mujahedeen-e Khalq Organization and former President Bani Sadr.

24 May A French External Relations Ministry official announces that France has agreed on ways of helping Iraq meet its debts, thought to amount to as much as $2,000 million. On 28 March a $500-million Eurodollar loan for Iraq's Rafidain Bank had been signed in Paris.

27 May The National Iranian Oil Company (NIOC) has paid $57 million to two oil firms, says MEED, as part of an eventual $300 million to compensate nine Western companies that had run Iran's oil industry before the 1979 revolution.

On 3 June MEED quoted a National Energy Committee member, Ali Larijani, as saying that Iran's oil reserves were sufficient to last at least 100 years at present production levels.

May In Iraq, six members of the family of Hojatolislam Sayyid Muhammad Baqir al-Hakim, the chairman of the Supreme Council of the Islamic Revolution in Iraq (SCIRI), are executed. Iranian officials referred to Hakim as the leader of Iraq's future Islamic state.

21 June Iran claims that between 22 May and 21 June about three tons of heroin and opium have been seized and about 1,300 smugglers and addicts arrested, according to MEED. In June eight Iranians were arrested by Sharjah police for trying to smuggle in 53 kilos of heroin.

23 June A UN report, issued by a team that had visited war-damaged civilian areas in Iraq and Iran, favours Iran. The report said that Iranian border towns had been heavily damaged while human losses and damage to property in Iraq were negligible. The report noted that retreating Iraqi troops had adopted a scorched-earth policy.

Nevertheless, Tehran scorned the team's refusal to condemn Iraq outright. Iran took pride in its claim to have intentionally spared Iraqi civilian areas. In a Tehran Home Service broadcast on 16 March, the Iranian Majlis speaker, Hashemi Rafsanjani, had said that it is 'in Iranian interests to spare enemy [Iraqi] soldiers who are to serve the future Islamic Republic of Iraq'.

24 June The PLO chairman and Fatah leader, Yasser Arafat, is expelled from Syria and flies to Tunis. He accused Syria of lying about its alliance with mutinous Palestinian elements led by Abu Musa (Mousa Said) who had initiated a revolt against his leadership on 7 May.

3 July The Iraqi deputy premier and foreign minister, Tariq Aziz, arrives in Egypt for talks with President Mubarak. This was the first visit to Egypt by an Arab minister since Arab states broke their ties over Egypt's peace agreement with Israel in 1979. Iraq had been Egypt's sternest critic at the time but was now dependent on Egyptian weaponry.

6 July Britain is giving the Kuwaiti-owned St Martins Property Corporation planning permission for a major property development at Hay's Wharf in London's docklands, says MEED. The development was to be one of Kuwait's biggest developments in Britain.

6 July An Iran Air jumbo jet on an internal flight from Shiraz to Tehran is hijacked and flown to Kuwait. On 7 July it flew on to Paris where the hijackers surrendered. Accusing France and Kuwait of collaborating with the six hijackers, Iran closed down the French consulate in Isfahan. France rejected Iran's call for the extradition of the hijackers.

On 7 July an Iranian helicopter was said to have been hijacked in Bahrain. Two similar incidents had been reported in June.

9 July Two ministers are dismissed and six new ministers sworn in in the UAE's first major cabinet re-shuffle since 1980. Observers linked the reorganization with an attempt to streamline ministerial procedure at a time of depressed spending and budget cuts.

13 July Iran announces that 13 profiteers and hoarders have been fined a total of $540,000, says MEED. This followed Prime Minister Hussein Mousavi's tough speech on 10 July in which he referred to 'power-seeking dark gangs and economic terrorists' in the bazaar. The campaign against dishonest profit-makers had been inspired by a series of warnings by Khomeini.

On 25 May Khomeini had warned a group of clerics led by President Khamenei: 'If one day the standard of your life rises above that of the common people, then you should realize that you will be despised by them'.

14 July Iran's Assembly of Experts meets to plan Khomeini's succession as Vali-e Faqih (Guardian and Jurisconsult – Iran's spiritual leader) . The Assembly of 83 clerics had been elected in December 1982.

On 11 July Hashemi Rafsanjani had been re-elected for a fourth one-year term as speaker of Iran's Majlis (lower house).

20 July The Iraqi deputy premier and foreign minister, Tariq Aziz, calls for austerity, telling journalists that Iraq's priorities are now industry, petrochemicals, and transport and communications. 'What is connected with luxury will stop' he added. Similarly, in a speech on 17 July to mark the fifteenth anniversary of the 1968 revolution, President Saddam Husayn had said that Iraq was able to overcome its present economic difficulties through reducing exependiture, postponing projects, increasing production and improving performance. On 16 July First Deputy Premier Taha Yasin Ramadan had warned foreign companies not to treat Iraq 'negatively' during the 'current financial situation'.

According to MEED, Iraq's export earnings had dropped from $26,278 million in 1980 to $10,250 million in 1982.

22 July Robert McFarlane replaces Philip Habib as President Reagan's roving envoy in the Middle East.

22 July The Islamic Republic of Iran's first five-year development plan (1983–88) envisages spending $167,000 million, with priority given to agriculture, says MEED.

22–29 July Following its offensive in Kurdistan, Iran takes the garrison town of Hajj Umran in its Wa al-Fajr (By Dawn) Two offensive. According to Dilip Hiro in *The Longest War*, the support of Kurdish Democratic Party (KDP) units, intimate with the region, was a great asset to the Iranians. On 30 July Iran staged its Wa al-Fajr Three offensive west of Mehran in the central sector of the war.

5 August Elections are held to the Legislative Council of the Kurdish autonomous region of Iraq, in an Iraqi government attempt to neutralize Kurdish dissidence during its troubled deadlock with Iran. On the same day banks in France reached a $1,600-million agreement to cover Iraq's payments to French contractors.

10 August Syria refuses to reopen the pipeline from Kirkuk to its Mediterranean export terminal at Banias. An Organization of Arab Petroleum Exporting Countries (OAPEC) ministerial meeting at Taif in Saudi Arabia failed to persuade Syria, who supported Iran, to allow Iraqi oil to flow through the line. The meeting was opened by the Saudi Arabian petroleum and minerals minister, Ahmad Zaki Yamani. The closure left Iraq with only one outlet through Turkey.

14 August Baghdad Radio announces the replacement of Iraq's finance minister, Tamer Razzouli, by Hisham Hasan Tewfiq. Razzouli was described as not being 'a member of the inner circle'. Neither a member of the Revolutionary Command Council (RCC), nor of the Ba'th Party Regional Council, he was thought to be a scapegoat for Iraq's poor financial standing.

15 August Mehdi Bazargan, leader of the Freedom Movement, Iran's only remaining recognized opposition group, criticizes the government for calling those who disagree with it heretics.

Also on 15 August Iran's state radio called Western talk of a Soviet threat to the Gulf a myth aimed at disguising moves by 'resurgent Islam' against Western interests.

15 August The UAE's 1983 federal budget projects a $1,499-million deficit, the biggest in its history. According to the August edition of *International Finance*, a publication of the Chase Manhattan Bank's economics group, Saudi Arabia, Kuwait, the UAE and Qatar would have a combined total deficit of $10,000 million in 1984 of which Saudi Arabia would account for the largest share.

25 August The Iranian prime minister, Hussein Mousavi, reorganizes his cabinet, appointing five hardline radical Islamic Republican Party (IRP) members.

8 September A total of 7,746 people in Iran have lost their lives through execution, street battles or under torture since June 1981, according to the Mujahedeen-e Khalq's journal *Mojahed*. According to Shaul Bakhash in *The Reign of the Ayatollahs*, the list did not include 140 Baha'is executed since the revolution. Meanwhile, Amnesty International had documented 2,946 executions in the 12 months following President Bani Sadr's impeachment in 1980.

16 September The Kuwaiti finance minister, Abd al-Latif al-Hamad, resigns after disagreements over the Souk al-Manakh (unofficial stock market) crisis.

19 September Speaking on Tehran radio, Khomeini warns the world powers that if they support Saddam Husayn 'their hands will be cut off from oil resources'. Meanwhile, the foreign affairs minister, Ali Akbar Velayati, reassured Iran's Arab neighbours, saying that Iran's offensives against Iraq were 'like a surgical operation for removing a cancerous tumour in the region, that is Saddam Husayn's regime'.

10 October Yitzhak Shamir is confirmed as Israeli prime minister by the Knesset (parliament). Premier Menachem Begin had resigned on 15 September.

20 October Iran mounts its Wa al-Fajr Four offensive in Kurdistan near Panjwin. Saddam Husayn responded by sending in his Republican Guard and using mustard gas, but failed to move the Iranians who had by now marched some 25 miles (40 kilometres) into Iraq.

23 October The dismissal of one of Saddam Husayn's half brothers, Watban al-Takriti, the governor of Salahaddin province, is announced in Baghdad. He and two other half brothers, Barzan al-Takriti, head of the secret police (the Mukhabarat) and San'awi al-Takriti, assistant police chief, were reported to be under house arrest. They were thought to have been arrested because of their failure to pre-empt a coup attempt against the president. Like Saddam Husayn they were from Takrit but unlike him they had retained the family name of Takriti.

23 October A suicide lorry bomb attack kills 239 US marines and 58 French servicemen in Beirut. The US accused a Shi'i splinter group inspired from Iran. On 23 November the Lebanese government severed relations with Iran.

27 October Oman and South Yemen agree to establish full diplomatic relations following Gulf Co-operation Council (GCC) mediation. Kuwait and the UAE were prime movers in bringing together the two sides. The GCC was motivated by the perceived threat to the region by Iran.

30 October The Japanese deputy foreign affairs minister, Toshijiro Nakajima, visits Baghdad and meets Iraq's First Deputy Premier Taha Yasin Ramadan to urge Iraq not to bomb Iran's Bandar Khomeini petrochemicals plant being built by Japan. Desperate to put pressure on Iran to end the war, on 23 October Iraq had warned Japan that it might attack the complex.

31 October Iran rejects a UN Security Council resolution calling for an immediate cease-fire in the Iran-Iraq war. It was the fourth since the war started on 22 September 1980. Iran had dismissed each resolution as being biased and insisted that the war could not end without the overthrow of Saddam Husayn.

31 October The Kuwaiti defence minister, Shaikh Salem al-Sabah al-Salem, signs an agreement with British Aerospace for the purchase of 12 Hawk-64 fighter-trainer jets.

2 November France says it has delivered to Iraq five Super-Etendard fighter aircraft capable of firing Exocet anti-ship missiles. Given the potential of such weapons to hit Iran's oil installations, France's decision sparked off fears that Iran would close the Strait of Tiran to shipping but Iran denied that it would ever do so.

3 November Tehran Radio says that Iran has captured Iraqi territory near the Iraqi border town of Panjwin in the war's northern sector. It also claimed to have surrounded the headquarters of Iraq's 602nd brigade in an area west of Panjwin. The report added that the assault had coincided with Iraqi attempts to recapture territory taken in Iran's 20 October offensive which began in Kurdistan.

In November Egypt announced that it was buying 200 Rumanian tanks for delivery to Iraq, once its sternest critic. In 1982 Iraq accounted for almost all Egypt's exports of military spare parts, weapons and ammunition.

7–9 November The GCC summit is held in Doha, the Qatari capital. A peace initiative in the Iran-Iraq war was the key agenda.

27 November Iran claims that Iraqi dissidents in Baghdad have carried out suicide bomb attacks on a military building near the Defence Ministry and on the public security directorate building. Meanwhile, in November Ayatollah Montazeri said that Iran's main purpose was to 'bring the entire mass of the Iraqi people under an Islamic government'. He said that the 70,000 or so Iraqi prisoners of war should be encouraged to join the armed forces of a new Islamic regime in Baghdad.

30 November Saudi Arabia's ambassador in the US, Prince Bandar ibn-Sultan, says that the new US-Israeli agreements are 'not helpful to peace' and that Israel is a 'strategic liability to America, rather than a strategic asset'. The US and Israel had agreed on an unprecedented level of military, economic and political co-operation in Washington on 29 November.

12 December Kuwait is rocked by five bomb explosions which kill six people and wound 80. The bombs, aimed at the US and French embassies and vital Kuwaiti installations, were believed to have been set off by Iraqi and Lebanese members of the militant Shi'i Islamic Jihad organization. Iran denied complicity in the bombings. Observers feared that the attacks would lead to a clampdown on Kuwait's reasonably democratic institutions.

20 December The PLO chairman, Yasser Arafat, evacuates Lebanon for the second time, this time from Tripoli. From Tripoli Arafat went to Cairo where his reconciliation with Egypt's President Mubarak was to presage the return of Egypt from the isolation its Arab neighbours had imposed on it since its 1979 peace agreement with Israel.

1 9 8 4

Saying of the year

'If you gave me a pesticide to throw at these swarms of insects ... then I'd use it.' Major-General Mahir Abd al-Rashid, commander of Iraq's Basra-based Third Army Corps. (Quoted in *Newsweek*, 19 March and in Dilip Hiro, *The Longest War*.)

10 January The Iranian embassy in London strongly denies a *Sunday Times* allegation that embassy officials are recruiting terrorists for suicide missions in Europe. The newspaper had named Hadi Khosrowshahi, Iran's ambassador to the Vatican, as one of the main organizers. Lawyers for Iran in London were considering a libel suit.

Meanwhile, Iran issued a statement through its embassies, saying that reports that 20,000 political opponents in Iran had been executed were 'sheer lies'. On 13 January the speaker of Iran's Majlis (lower house), Hashemi Rafsanjani, said that 'We are not terrorists and we don't believe terrorism to be successful'. Accusations of Iranian terrorists being discovered showed that 'our enemies have lost their balance because of their extreme terror ... their fear of the message [of Islam] ... In fact a frightful nightmare has engulfed our enemies, whereby they attribute everything to Iran.'

On 23 January the US State Department confirmed that Iran had been officially designated as a state supporting international terrorism, thus restricting bilateral trade.

11 January Rafsanjani says that it is 'most useful' for Iran that the US has finally been obliged to admit that it will not accept an Iraqi defeat in the Iran-Iraq war. Rafsanjani was referring to statements by US officials that the US had dropped its neutrality and wanted to help Iraq.

Meanwhile, Britain denied Iranian charges that it was selling chemical weapons to Iraq. Iran's official Islamic Republic News Agency referred to bottles of toxic silver nitrate washed up on the French coast and traced to an Iraqi vessel loaded at Liverpool port in England. On 15 January Iran's semi-official newspaper, *Islamic Republic*, described Britain as 'a senile hyena of colonialism'.

11 January France signs a weapons deal with Saudi Arabia valued at about $4,000 million, the biggest such deal France has ever signed. Meanwhile, during his visit to Israel between 24 and 29 January West Germany's Chancellor Kohl came under pressure to abandon plans for weapon sales to Saudi Arabia.

15 January Britain's weekly *Observer* alleges the involvement of Prime Minister Margaret Thatcher's son Mark in the 1981 negotiations leading to the award of a contract in Oman. This was a £300-million contract awarded to Britain's Cementation International to build Oman's Sultan Qaboos University.

18 January Gunmen murder the head of the American University in Beirut, Malcolm Kerr.

19 January Iraq plays a key role at the 45-member Islamic Conference Organization (ICO) summit in Casablanca in inviting Egypt to rejoin the ICO. Iraq had been among the original sponsors of the move to expel Egypt from the ICO and from the Arab League after its peace treaty with Israel in 1979. However, heavily dependent on Egyptian military aid in its war with Iran, it had now become Egypt's key ally. Saudi Arabia had masterminded the campaign for Egypt's return.

21 January Eighty-seven members of Iran's Tudeh (Communist) Party's military network are given prison sentences ranging from less than one year to life.

1 February The US administration recommends aid to Israel for the 1985 fiscal year of $2,250 million and to Egypt of about $2,170 million. Total foreign aid of $15,217 million was recommended.

7 February General Gholam Ali Oveisi and his brother, Gholam Hussein, are shot dead in a Paris street. In 1978, during the final months of the shah's reign, General Oveisi was appointed Tehran's martial law administrator. According to Vahe Petrossian in the Middle East Economic Digest (MEED), in June 1963 Oveisi's troops saved the shah by killing between 1,500 and 10,000 demonstrators (depending on estimates) demanding the release of Khomeini. According to Petrossian, a group of villagers wearing the martyr's white shroud was machine-gunned to death. Although Tehran denied responsibility, it called the killing a 'revolutionary execution'. Oveisi was called the 'Butcher of Tehran' because of his responsibility for the Jaleh Square massacre in September 1978.

Oveisi was thought to have been one of the key Iranian exiles to convince Saddam Husayn to go to war with Iran, promising a military uprising to coincide with the invasion in September 1980.

7 February The US announces the departure from Beirut of its 1,600 marines. On 8 February the 114-member British contingent was withdrawn. Italy withdrew its contingent on 20 February, and France on 25 March.

9 February The United Arab Emirates' (UAE's) ambassador to France, Khalifa Ahmad Abd al-Aziz al-Mubarak, is shot dead in Paris. A group called the Arab Revolutionary Brigades claimed responsibility. The killing was denounced by Iran's ambassador to the UAE, Mahmoud Sadat Madrashahi, as 'an inhuman act'. Some circles had indicated that the killers were a pro-Iranian group.

10 February With an external debt of about $30,000 million, Iraq is the most indebted Arab country, according to the Bahrain-based United Gulf Bank. On 6 January the bank had forecast a $20,000-million current account deficit for the six Gulf Co-operation Council (GCC) states in 1984.

10–18 February Iraq launches air attacks on Iranian cities and uses chemical weapons. The series of attacks on civilian areas was set off by Iraqi missiles fired at the Iranian town of Dezful, and the Iranian shelling of Basra, Khanaqin and Mandali. These attacks ended with a UN-mediated agreement not to attack each other's centres of population. From 16 to 24 February Iran tried, but failed, to march from Dehlorab into Iraq to cut off the crucial Basra-Baghdad highway.

Meanwhile, reports from Baghdad in January suggested that Saddam Husayn had signed an agreement with Jalal Talabani, leader of the Patriotic Union of Kurdistan (PUK). In return for the formation of a 40,000-strong Kurdish army to 'protect Kurdistan against foreign enemies [i.e. Iran]', elections would be held for a legislative and executive council, 30 per cent of the state budget would be allocated to rehabilitate Kurdish areas affected by the war and the autonomous region of Kurdistan would be extended. Saddam Husayn's need for easy access through Kurdistan had prompted the amnesty he had announced for Kurdish fighters in July 1982.

On 15 January Iraq had called up all 18-year-old males to register for military service in preparation for a new Iranian offensive.

11 February Shaikh Ali al-Khalifa al-Sabah, Kuwait's oil and finance minister, refutes allegations that personal considerations have influenced his decisions in dealing with Kuwait's Souk al-Manakh (unofficial stock market) crisis. Some National Assembly members had claimed that a government report had been censored to protect Shaikh Ali's brother, Shaikh Muhammad al-Khalifa al-Sabah.

12 February Iran's artillery starts shelling Iraqi civilian areas for the first time in the Iran-Iraq war. This ended Iran's previous policy of avoiding civilian areas in an effort to win the hearts of the Iraqi people and facilitate the downfall of Saddam Husayn.

On 11 February Iraqi ground-to-ground missiles had hit the southern war sector town of Dezful, fulfilling Baghdad's threat earlier in February to target a 'hit list' of civilian centres. On 12 February Iraq bombed Iran's Bandar Khomeini petrochemicals complex, being built by Japan. On 15 February Iranian aircraft responded by bombing the outskirts of Baghdad despite Baghdad's 14 February announcement that it would stop striking towns for one week if Iran did the same. According to Vahe Petrossian in MEED, this demonstrated that Iraq was more vulnerable than Iran to attacks on its civilian centres which were within easy reach of Iranian fire-power.

On 16 February Iran launched its Wa al-Fajr (By Dawn) Five offensive, by attacking the central war zone between the towns of Mehran and Dehloran.

14 February Iran's ambassador to Syria, Ali Akbar Mohtashami, is wounded by a letter bomb in Damascus. Responsibility was claimed by the Arab Five May Organization who claimed that Mohtashami had been responsible for recent bomb explosions in Kuwait, Baghdad and elsewhere in the Gulf.

On 11 February the trial had begun in Kuwait of 25 people accused of involvement in the December bombings in Kuwait. A spokesman for the Tehran-based Supreme Council of the Islamic Revolution of Iraq (SCIRI) described the proceedings as a 'kangaroo court'.

22 February Iran launches its major 'Khaibar' offensive in the Haur al-Hawizeh marshlands of southern Iraq. The Iranians crossed the marshes, considered by Iraq a natural barrier against attack, by small boats, and by the end of the offensive on 16 March had driven the Iraqi forces out of the oil-rich Majnoon Islands to the south.

Iraq responded with personal insult. Major-General Mahir Abd al-Rashid, the commander of the Basra-based Third Army Corps, cabled Saddam Husayn on 28 February: 'Great Sir, we gladly inform you of the annihilation of thousands of harmful insects that carried out an abortive offensive late last night' (quoted in Dilip Hiro: *The Longest War*). In contrast with the Iraqis, says Dilip Hiro, Iran focused only on denigrating Saddam Husayn, never abusing the Iraqi people or presenting the conflict in Persian-Arab terms.

February In a statement to the UN Human Rights' Commission, Amnesty International says it has recorded 5,000 executions (excluding secret executions) in Iran since the revolution. Thousands had been imprisoned, including 700 Baha'is, it said.

27 March Iraq uses Super-Etendard aircraft and Exocet missiles in a deadly combination for the first time in its onslaught on shipping in the Gulf. On 30 March the UN Security Council condemned the use of chemical weapons in the Gulf and renewed its appeals for a cease-fire. In March Iran's Majlis (lower house) was obliged to reduce the 1984/85 budget, forcing a 40 per cent cut in development spending.

10–13 April The amir of Bahrain makes a state visit to Britain.

18 April Iraq escalates the tanker war. On 25 April an Iraqi-launched Exocet missile hit the Saudi-owned oil tanker, *Safina al-Arab*, writing it off. On 13 May Iran responded in the Lower Gulf by hitting ships using Saudi and Kuwaiti ports. On 22 May US President Reagan announced that neither the US, 'nor the Western world as such, would stand by and see the straits of the Persian Gulf [Strait of Hormuz] closed to international traffic'. On the same day naval units of Iran's Revolutionary Guards become operational.

27 May In Egypt's first fair elections, the Wafd Party wins 58 seats and becomes a genuine opposition party to the ruling National Democratic Party which takes 390 seats.

28 May Iran's second Majlis (lower house) is opened following elections on 15 April and 17 May. Over half of the seats of the new Majlis were taken by new members. Many of the 1,230 candidates were secular, inspiring hope that the new Majlis would back Prime Minister Mousavi's economic reforms. Dr Mehdi Bazargan's Freedom Movement – Iran's only recognized opposition party – boycotted the elections which it regarded as undemocratic.

1 June The UN Security Council condemns attacks on ships trading with Saudi Arabia and Kuwait, urging all states to respect free navigation in the Gulf. On 12 June a UN-sponsored cease-fire went into effect with regard to attacks on population centres. UN observers were posted to Baghdad and Tehran to monitor breaches in the cease-fire. On 10 June Iran and Iraq declared a provisional moratorium on the bombardment of civilian areas. In May the GCC countries had tried unsuccessfully to secure a general condemnation of Iran's behaviour in the war. They later announced that they would replace any petroleum that was lost as a result of attacks on shipping in the Gulf.

5 June Saudi Arabian F-15 fighters intercept Iranian F-4 Phantom aircraft approaching the kingdom's air space, and shoot down one, or even two. Defence had been one of the few economic sectors to receive an increase (almost 6 per cent) in Iran's 1984/85 budget. On 29 May the US had announced that it had sent Stinger shoulder-launched, anti-aircraft missiles and an additional tanker aircraft to bolster Saudi Arabia's air defences in the wake of recent Iranian attacks. Saudi Arabia also extended its new air defence zone, the 'Fahd Line'.

22 July The West German foreign minister, Hans Dietrich Genscher, becomes the first Western leader to visit Iran since the revolution in 1979. The two countries planned the meeting of the West German-Iranian mixed Economic Commission in September, the first time since the Iranian revolution.

July–August Students and villagers are said to have taken part in a popular uprising in Iraqi Kurdistan.

2 August Kuwait's acceptance of eight West German gunboats completes what the chief-of-staff, General Abdullah Farraj al-Ghanim, calls Kuwait's 'basic equipping of land, air and sea forces'. Kuwait had recently signed weapons contracts with the US and the Soviet Union. The latter had signed a military training agreement with Kuwait in July.

6 August Iraq's First Deputy Premier Taha Yasin Ramadan signs an agreement to build a second crude-oil export pipeline through Iraq with Turkey's Prime Minister Turgut Ozal. According to MEED, Ramadan said that the line would be completed in 18 months and would run parallel to the existing Kirkuk to Yumurtalik line. Ramadan denied that Turkey was being asked to mediate the end of the war with Iran although the Iraqi foreign affairs minister, Tariq Aziz, had visited Turkey at the end of July. Turkey had tried to maintain good trade links with Iran and Iraq.

7 August In Tehran, 25 drug traffickers are put to death, bringing the total executed since May to more than 100.

10 August Kuwait's acting minister of state for cabinet affairs, Abd al-Rahman al-Awadi, firmly denies reports that Iraq has asked to lease parts of Warba and Bubiyan islands from Kuwait in exchange for the demarcation of the Iraq-Kuwait border.

10 August By mid-August at least 15 international freighters have been damaged by explosions caused by mines in the Suez Canal, the Gulf of Suez and the southern Red Sea. A group calling itself Islamic Jihad claimed responsibility for the attacks as part of a campaign against Western interests. There was widespread suspicion that Iran was involved as a means of expanding the war with Iraq. Egypt asked the US and Britain for help in removing the mines and a multinational minesweeping force was assembled.

31 August President Reagan's national security adviser, Robert McFarlane, asks government agencies to re-assess US policy towards Iran. Earlier in the month it was announced that, because of loopholes in US law and commitments made in the 1981 agreement that freed the US hostages, the Reagan adminstration was allowing the US to supply Iran with goods that could be used in its war effort.

11 September Iraq renews attacks on commercial shipping in the Gulf, inflicting missile damage on the German-owned tanker, *St Tobias*. In August, in response to Iraq's continuous air raids on Kharg Island and Iranian tankers, Iran had set up a tanker shuttle between Kharg and the Sirri Island oil terminal in the Lower Gulf.

19 September A meeting of GCC foreign affairs and defence ministers calls for increased defence spending to prevent foreign intervention in the region. The GCC was particularly concerned about offers from the US to police the Gulf. In November member states agreed to form a joint defence force for rapid deployment against external aggression. This would comprise units from the armed forces of each country under a central command.

27 September A consortium led by Italy's Saipem signs a contract to build a 500,000 barrel-a-day oil export pipeline from Zubair in Iraq's southern oilfields to a pump station on Saudi Arabia's east-west pipeline, Petroline.

10 October The North Yemeni president, Ali Abdullah Saleh, signs a 20-year treaty of friendship and co-operation in Moscow. However, North Yemen's new oil finds lessened its need for foreign aid. In December President Saleh announced that North Yemen could begin exporting oil in two years.

18–25 October Iran takes back some of the disputed border territory in the war's central sector.

20 October Backed by a more secular, more reform-minded second Majlis, reconstituted in the April–May elections, Iran's Prime Minister Mousavi starts moving against corrupt officials and inefficient bureaucrats.

29 October Khomeini calls for diplomatic relations with all governments except 'a few'. Meanwhile, in August he had taken the initiative by calling for more freedom for Iran's private sector, both because that was morally right and because the private sector would do a better job than direct government intervention in the economy.

1 November The UAE and China establish diplomatic relations.

26 November Washington and Baghdad resume diplomatic relations after a break of 17 years. Iraq had broken ties after the Arab-Israeli war of 1967. In November Iraq's deputy premier and minister of foreign affairs, Tariq Aziz, said that Iraq was 'strong enough to repel any Iranian attack, now or in the future'. Following the supply to Iraq of Soviet and French military equipment, a US report had said that the military balance had shifted in Iraq's favour. The US was assisting Iraq in its financing of oil export pipeline projects and increasing its allocation of commodity credits, while the Soviet Union was supplying Iraq with about two-thirds of its armaments and much of its ammunition. Iran's strong anti-Soviet position had led to further improvements in Soviet-Iraqi relations in March. Nevertheless, by the end of the year Iraq had lost an estimated 220,000 men.

30 November The fifth GCC summit meeting ends in Kuwait.

3 December Peter Kilburn, a 62-year-old US librarian at the American University in Beirut, disappears in West Beirut. On 16 March William Buckley, the 57-year-old US Central Intelligence Agency (CIA) chief in Beirut, had been kidnapped, presumably by Islamic Jihad.

18 December Iran's public prosecutor, Mir-Emadi, says that the four men who hijacked a Kuwait Airways aircraft on its way to Mehrabad airport on 9 December and a group who flew an Air France Boeing 737 to Tehran in August will be put on trial. Two American staff of the US Agency for International Development were killed on board the Kuwaiti Airways plane before Iranian forces stormed the aircraft and captured the hijackers. The Iranians denied US allegations that they had colluded with the hijackers.

1 9 8 5

Sayings of the Year

'The day we put, with the grace of God, a victorious end to the imposed war, no other country would dare attack us'. Hashemi Rafsanjani, Tehran, 1 February.

'They want to force us to compromise so that tomorrow the reactionaries in the region can speak out against Islam and call it an unsuccessful experiment. They aim to erode the Islamic revolution through an imposed peace and drive it towards destruction'. Prime Minister Hussein Mousavi, Tehran, 5 June.

11 February The Palestine Liberation Organization (PLO) chairman, Yasser Arafat, and King Husayn of Jordan reach an agreement on the basis of a joint Middle East peace initiative. The agreement called for total Israeli withdrawal from Arab territories occupied in 1967 as part of a comprehensive settlement, the right of self-determination for the Palestinian people, a settlement of the Palestinian refugee problem according to UN resolutions, a resolution of the Palestinian problem in all its aspects and peace negotiations to be conducted under the auspices of all parties to the conflict, including the PLO – as sole legitimate representative of the Palestinian people, and the five permanent members of the UN Security Council.

However, the agreement was to be aborted by Arab dissensions. It was bitterly opposed by the Palestinian factions based in Damascus, including the Popular Front for the Liberation of Palestine (PFLP) and the Democratic Front for the Liberation of Palestine (DFLP). On 25 February Syria rejected the agreement as an attempt to 'liquidate the Palestinian cause'. Nor did the agreement satisfy the Americans whose preconditions for recognizing the PLO included the PLO's recognition of Israel, its acceptance of UN resolution 242, its renunciation of terrorism and its commitment to direct negotiations with Israel.

5 March The Iran-Iraq war escalates as Iran accuses Iraq of using chemical weapons and poisonous gases against it. The war had entered a dangerous phase with both sides launching heavy bombardments of civilian centres on 5 March. Iran sustained severe casualties as its push north of Basra was repulsed. From 11 to 20 March Iran launched an offensive in the Haur al-Hawizeh marshes to seize the crucial Basra-Baghdad road – an Iranian brigade actually reaching the road on 17 March. However, ferocious Iraqi counter-attacks soon drove the Iranians back.

11 March Mikhail Gorbachev becomes head of the Soviet Communist Party on the death of Konstantin Chernenko. Gorbachev, aged 54, was seen as a potential reformer.

14 March From March to September a spate of kidnappings and killings of Westerners and others by Islamic fundamentalist groups rocks Beirut. On 14 March Nicolas Kluiters, a Dutch Roman Catholic priest, disappeared in Beirut. On 1 April he was found strangled to death. On 16 March Terry Anderson, the 41-year-old Middle East bureau chief of the Associated Press in Lebanon was kidnapped in Beirut by the Islamic Jihad, the original pro-Iranian kidnap group. On 21 March the first Briton, Alec Collett, a 66-year-old New York-based journalist on assignment with the UN Relief and Works Agency (UNRWA), was taken.

On 22 May Michel Seurat, a 37-year-old French academic researcher, was kidnapped by Islamic Jihad. On 27 May Denis Hill, a British teacher at the American University in Beirut went missing and was found shot dead two days later (the head of the university, Malcolm Kerr, had been murdered on 18 January 1984). Also in May, Florence Raad, a 35-year-old Lebanese-French journalist was seized by an unknown group. On 9 June the 58-year-old Scottish-born US national, Thomas Sutherland, the dean of agriculture at the American University of Beirut, was taken by Islamic Jihad. On 29 June a 65-year-old businessman with US nationality but of Syrian origin was reported missing and on 11 September a 65-year-old Italian insurance businessman, Alberto Molinari, was seized although no group claimed responsibility.

On 30 September Arkady Katkov, the 32-year-old attaché at Beirut's Soviet embassy, was abducted with three other diplomats. He was found dead on 2 October but the other diplomats were freed. On 4 October Islamic Jihad claimed that it had executed the 57-year-old Beirut Central Intelligence Agency (CIA) bureau chief, William Buckley, whom they had kidnapped on 16 March 1984.

Islamic Jihad was one of the organizations apparently operating under the Hizbullah umbrella. The Hizbullah (Hizb Allah, meaning Party of God) is a shadowy organization of radical Shi'is with links with Iran. It is led by Shaikh Muhammad Hussein Fadl Allah and Shaikh Ibrahim al-Amin. Another prominent leader of the movement in southern Lebanon is Shaikh Abd al-Karim Obeid. Hizbullah's stronghold is South Beirut but it gained strength over the years in southern Lebanon and has retained a power base in the Biqa' Valley. Although the Hizbullah is a Shi'i organization which aims at setting up an Iran-style Islamic Republic in Lebanon, there was evidence in the mid-1980s that it had formed a joint front with Sunnis in Tripoli, Sidon and Beirut.

The Iranian interior minister, Hojatolislam Ali Akbar Mohtashami, helped to develop Hizbullah when he was Iranian ambassador to Lebanon between 1981 and 1985, encouraging its aggressive tactics which included kidnapping. In 1985 Islamic Jihad's first victim was the CIA Beirut bureau chief, William Buckley, who died under torture in 1985 although his death was announced as an 'execution' (see above).

16 March The National Security Council aide, Oliver North, drafts a plan to support the Contras (the right-wing Nicaraguan rebels against Nicaragua's Sandinista government), with private funds, during the Congress ban on US military assistance to Nicaragua.

4 April Iraq launches rocket attacks on three Iranian towns, and in retaliation Iran fires missiles into the heart of Baghdad. Ali Akbar Velayati, Iran's foreign minister, accused Iraq of having caused the death or injury of about 4,600 Iranians since early March through the use of chemicals and poisonous gases. On 6 April a cease-fire was declared in the 'War of the Cities' and April and May were to see a lull in mutual missile attacks.

18 May The Saudi foreign minister, Prince Saud al-Faisal, visits Tehran in an attempt to arrange a cease-fire during the forthcoming month of Ramadan but fails. This was the first such visit since the Iranian revolution in 1979 and was deeply significant given the antipathy that Iran had frequently declared for Saudi Arabia which it regarded as having corrupted true Islam.

18 May In May Saudi Arabia and Kuwait both suffer bomb attacks from Islamic fundamentalists. On 18 May two explosions took place in Riyadh. The explosions, for which the fundamentalist group Islamic Jihad claimed reponsibility, coincided with the visit to Iran by the Saudi foreign minister, Prince Saud al-Faisal.

On 25 May an attempt on the life of the ruler of Kuwait, Shaikh Jaber, narrowly failed when a car bomb was driven into a motorcade carrying him to Kuwait's Sief Palace. The attack took place ten days after Islamic Jihad's demand that the Kuwaiti authorities release 17 convicted prisoners in exchange for six US and French hostages held by the movement in Beirut. Kuwait's security forces reportedly identified the car bomber as an Iraqi belonging to the Al-Da'wa al-Islamiyya (Islamic Call) organization. Iraq accused Iran of responsibility but Iran denied the allegation.

25 May Hundreds of Palestinian inhabitants of the Sabra and Chatila refugee camps in West Beirut die in a ferocious assault by the Syrian-back Shi'i Amal militia who finally overrun the camp on 31 May. In 1982 the camps had suffered a massacre at the hands of the Christian Phalangist militias.

26 May After a six-week lull Iraq launches missile and air attacks on Iranian cities, resuming the 'War of the Cities'. Iran responded in kind. However, on 15 June Iraq announced a two-week suspension of aerial attacks on Iran's cities and was not to resume them.

May A group of extremist Muslim leaders from throughout the Middle East are reported to have formed a Supreme Council of the Islamic World Revolution in Tehran. The president of the Council, whose aim was to export the Islamic revolution to the rest of the world by whatever means necessary, including terrorism, was said to be Sayyid Muhammad Taqi al-Madrasi, an Iraqi in exile in Iran. Iran was also rumoured to be training suicide squads for terrorist operations abroad. Some observers, however, considered both reports as media invention.

14 June A US Trans World Airlines Boeing 727 is hijacked on a flight from Athens to Rome by two Lebanese Shi'i Muslims who demand the release of over 750 Shi'i prisoners held in Israel, as well as of alleged Shi'i terrorists held in Kuwaiti and Spanish jails. The hijackers were apparently members of a Lebanese group under the control of Hizbullah. The plane was forced to fly to Beirut, to Algiers, back to Beirut, to Algiers again and eventually back to Beirut. At intervals groups of passengers were released but a US navy diver was shot dead. After the final flight to Beirut, the 39 remaining passengers were taken to separate destinations in Beirut. However, mediation by the Shi'i Amal leader in Beirut, Nabih Berri, as well as pressure on the hijackers from Damascus eventually secured their release on 30 June following Israel's release of 331 of its Shi'i detainees.

On 24 June Hojatolislam Hashemi Rafsanjani, the Iranian Majlis (lower house) speaker, denied Iranian involvement in the hijacking at a Damascus press conference. However, he refused to condemn the hijackers saying 'If we wanted to condemn the incident, we have to start with condemning the US and Israel, which persecute Muslims everywhere.'

During the crisis, US President Reagan repeatedly pledged to inflict retribution on the terrorists but few could see how. The US had found itself unable to seek satisfaction when the embassy in Beirut was bombed on two occasions or when more than 240 US troops were killed in the October 1983 explosion that destroyed the US marines' Beirut headquarters.

14 June A pro-government rally of between one and five million people is held in Tehran.

17 June A Saudi prince crews the second orbiter (Arabsat 1B), launched for the Arab

Satellite Communications Organization (Arabsat) from the US space shuttle. Arabsat 1B was launched from low-earth orbit to its work station 22,312 miles (35,900 kilometres) above and shared the shuttle's cargo bay with two other domestic communications satellites, one from Mexico and the other from the US. Saudi Arabia's Prince Sultan ibn Salman ibn Abd al-Aziz accompanied the mission to become the Arab world's first astronaut.

Arabsat 1A had been launched on the night of 8 February 1985 from the Korou space centre in French Guyana aboard a European Ariane rocket. It shared its ride into space with a Brazilian domestic communications satellite and its launch was witnessed by Ali al-Mashat, Arabsat's Iraqi director-general at the time and Alawi Darwish Kayyal, the minister of posts, telegraph and telecommunications of Arabsat's principal shareholder, Saudi Arabia.

Arabsat is a space-based pan-Arab communications network linking all 22 member nations of the Arab League. Both satellites can relay 8,000 telephone calls and seven one-way television transmissions between broadcasting studios or their equivalent in other forms of telecommunications such as radio, telex, fax etc. (source: 'Satellite Communications' by Peter Ryan, published in *The Cambridge Encyclopedia of the Middle East and North Africa*).

26 June Iraq suspends diplomatic relations with Libya after the latter concludes a political and military co-operation agreement with Iran.

13 July Saudi Arabia's current account deficit is forecast to reach $20,000 million by the end of the year, its highest level ever.

14 July Iran warns that it will stop and search ships in the Gulf which it suspects are carrying military goods or contraband to Iraq.

17 July Kuwait passes anti-terrorism laws in the wake of bomb outrages. An anti-terrorism bill calling for the death penalty for acts of terrorism resulting in the loss of life was overwhelmingly passed by the National Assembly (Kuwait's parliament) on 17 July. The bill followed the 11 July bomb explosions at two popular Kuwaiti seaside cafés which killed eight people and injured more than 80. A little-known group in Beirut claimed responsibility for the bombings but most observers believed that they were the work of the dissident Iraqi Da'wa al-Islamiyya (Islamic Call) party. Al-Da'wa had been blamed for a series of incidents in Kuwait starting with the December 1983 bombings and culminating in May 1985 in the attempt on the life of the Amir Shaikh Jaber. The government offered a KD 50,000 ($166,000) reward for information leading to the arrest of those responsible for the attack on 11 July.

28 July Iraq's oil export capacity through Turkey and Saudi Arabia will reach 3.1 million barrels a day in 1988 and Baghdad will continue to seek corresponding increases in its Organization of Petroleum Exporting Countries (OPEC) quota as new outlets become available, says the Iraqi deputy oil minister, Issam Abd al-Rahim al-Shalabi.

31 July The European Economic Community (EEC) Commission decides to impose tariffs of 13.4–14 per cent on imports of Saudi polyethylene.

July Hojatolislam Muhammad Mousavi Kho'eniha is named Iran's new prosecutor-general. Kho'eniha, the leader of the militant students who seized the US embassy in Tehran in November 1979, replaced Yousef Sane'i who had requested the move because of overwork and fatigue. However, the change appeared to indicate differences of opinion between Sane'i, a highly respected religious scholar, and other officials close to Ayatollah Khomeini. Kho'eniha was a radical cleric who had represented Khomeini on the *hajj* to Mecca. His faction stood for the virtual severence of ties with the West and firm government control of the economy.

Addressing members of the association of lecturers and theologians of the prestigious Qom seminary, Khomeini stressed that unity was all important and that people should refrain from unnecessary criticism of the government. He said that religious leaders should constantly remind themselves of the country's achievements rather than concentrate on mistakes. They should, he said, help to guide officials, not try to take revenge, and should ask themselves: 'If we were in their place, what could we have achieved?'

7 August The Arab League summit in the Moroccan city of Casablanca is widely boycotted by Arab states. Disunity among the Arab ranks and failures to make any progress on the issue of Palestine weakened the League's influence. The Arab summit scheduled to be held in Riyadh in November 1983 was postponed until April 1984 but divisions within the PLO and among Arab countries as well as the Iran-Iraq war led to the cancellation of the 1984 summit. The summit that was eventually convened on 7 August 1985, was boycotted by Libya, Syria, South Yemen, Lebanon and Algeria. Saudi Arabia was represented by the deputy prime minister, Crown Prince Abdullah, rather than by King Fahd.

The League was more positive in purely technical affairs and in 1985 two satellites were launched by the Arab Satellite Communications Organization (Arabsat), a League agency based in Riyadh (see 17 June).

15 August Iraqi aircraft begin intense and continuous attacks on Iran's Kharg Island oil export terminal, causing serious damage and disruption but failing to halt shipments. On 2 September Hojatolislam Khamenei, who had been re-elected Iran's president on 17 August, warned that Iran would carry our sorties deep inside Iraq and close the Strait of Hormuz if the attacks continued.

2 September Iraq claims further airstrikes against oil installations on Iran's Kharg Island. On 15 August Iraqi aircraft began serious attacks on Kharg Island's oil export terminal but failed to block shipments of oil from the terminal. President Khamenei warned that if these attacks continued, Iran would carry out sorties deep inside Iraq and close the Strait of Hormuz. Iran mounted an offensive on the Rawandoz region of Kurdistan on 8 September but its intended assault on Basra was repulsed on 11 September by strong Iraqi counterattacks.

13 September Iran receives 508 US-built Tow missiles in a secret arms-for-hostages deal with the US.

26 September Oman and the Soviet Union announce the establishment of diplomatic relations. On 28 November the United Arab Emirates (UAE) followed Oman's example and exchanged ambassadors with Moscow. When the Gulf Co-operation Council (GCC) was formed in May 1981 Kuwait was the only member to have diplomatic relations with the Soviet Union. Soviet support for South Yemen, the backer of the Oman's Dhofari rebels, would have made recognition by Muscat inconceivable then. Indeed, the Soviet invasion of Afghanistan in 1980 was regarded as one of the reasons for the very creation of the GCC. However, the GCC's success in improving relations between Oman and South Yemen helped mitigate some of these fears. By 1983 Saudi Arabia was rumoured to have advised its neighbours to restore relations with Moscow. In August a Saudi soccer team headed by Prince Faisal ibn Fahd travelled to Moscow to play in the World Junior Football Championship in what was a symbolic gesture of goodwill. Kuwait's traditional opinion that a balanced relationship with the superpowers favoured the region was gaining more acceptance.

26 September Britain and Saudi Arabia announce a memorandum of understanding on the sale of 132 military aircraft, including 72 Tornado fighter bombers worth an estimated £3,000–4,000 million.

1 October At least 50 people die in an Israeli air raid on the PLO offices in Tunis.

17 October Hussein Mousavi, the Iranian prime minister since 1981, is reappointed for a further four-year term by President Khamenei, having won a vote of confidence in the Majlis four days previously. Mousavi was thought to have been on the way out until Khomeini offered the 'advice' that change in the midst of war would be unwise and added that there was no-one better suited to the job. Mousavi's continued presence seemed to have halted a movement towards the right, led by Khamenei and prominent conservative clerics. The conservative forces allied with the bazaar had been seeking a 'freer' economy in which the government would restrict itself to a mainly supervisory role.

On 16 August Khamenei had been re-elected president for a further four-year term. On 28 October the Majlis approved the appointments of all but two of Mousavi's nominees for cabinet office.

17 October Bettino Craxi's government in Italy falls after it has agreed to release Muhammad Abbas, the Palestinian who masterminded the hijacking of the Italian cruise liner, *Achille Lauro*, on 7 October. US public opinion was horrified when an elderly and crippled New York Jew was murdered for arguing with the hijackers. The Egyptian government allowed the hijackers safe conduct to Tunis, but US jet fighters forced the plane carrying them to land in Sicily.

October Amnesty International claims that 399 people have been executed in Iran during the year up to the end of October, bringing the total to 6,426 since the revolution in 1979. The Mujahedeen-e Khalq put the number of executions at 40,000 and, in September 1984, published a list of 10,231 political prisoners allegedly killed by the Islamic regime.

23 November Iran's Assembly of Experts, elected on 10 December 1982 to designate a successor to Khomeini as Iran's spiritual leader, choose Ayatollah Hussein Ali Montazeri. On 17 December, however, Montazeri said that the decision went 'against the wishes of my heart' and that he intended to ask the Assembly to withdraw the designation.

25 November Saudi Arabia and the European Economic Community (EEC) reach a confidential agreement on Gulf petrochemical exports.

4 December Robert McFarlane, US national security adviser (National Security Council director) who had been President Reagan's roving envoy in the Middle East since July 1983, resigns for personal reasons and is replaced by his deputy, Rear-Admiral John Poindexter. Marine Corps Lieutenant-Colonel Oliver North, a member of the National Security Council staff, told Poindexter that the Western hostages held in Beirut might die if the US refused Iran more arms. According to Robert McFarlane and Reagan's original testimony in August, the president had approved weapon sales to Iran through Israel. Reagan later said that he 'could not remember'. On 16 March North had drafted a plan to support the Contras (the right-wing Nicaraguan rebels against Nicaragua's Sandinista government) with private funds, during the Congress ban on US military assistance to Nicaragua.

9 December OPEC's decision to defend its 'fair share' of world oil sales plunges the markets into chaos.

17 December Iraqi aircraft penetrate Kharg Island's formidable defences for a series of effective raids. Serious damage was inflicted against facilities although exports continued, mainly via Sirri Island to the south-east. According to Dilip Hiro in *The Longest War*, between 14 August and 5 October Iraq staged 21 air sorties against Kharg. By December, he says Iraq had hit 33 ships in the Gulf that year, and Iran only 14. Nevertheless, Iran seemed to be assured of exporting at least 1 million barrels of oil a day. Iranian specialists were busy planning alternative floating export terminals near Kharg and Kangan to try to keep exports at the preferred level of about 1.6 million barrels a day.

On 28 November the Middle East Economic Digest (MEED) had reported that Iran had invited 11 Far Eastern and European companies to bid for a one-year contract to build a 236-mile (380-kilometre) pipeline from Gurreh, a pumping station serving Iran's Kharg Island, to Asaluyeh, out of range of Iraqi bombers.

1 9 8 6

Sayings of the Year

"You, the glorious people of Islam, have achieved your greatest victory. The explosion you brought to the White House turned it into the Black House. All those who were boycotting you, who cut their relations and promised punishment, are now crawling in front of you, begging your pardon". Ayatollah Khomeini, 20 November (on the Iran-US, arms-for-hostages deal).

2 January The arrest in Tehran is reported of 60 members of the Fedayeen-e Khalq (one of whom committed suicide) and nine members of the Mujahedeen-e Khalq. On 5 January the Iranian Majlis (lower house) approved the final two members of Prime Minister Husayn Mousavi's cabinet.

Later in January the Iranian embassy in Rome was to deny allegations by an official of the Popular Front for the Liberation of Palestine (PFLP) that the guerrilla leader, Abu Nidal, was based in Iran. Nidal was suspected of involvement in recent terrorist attacks at Rome and Vienna airports in which 17 people were killed.

6 January President Reagan signs the authorization for shipment of weapons to Iran. Later in the month, Reagan was to ask the US Congress to approve the sale of more than $1,000 million worth of missiles, helicopters and equipment for fighter aircraft to

Saudi Arabia, despite clear indications that the proposed sale would run into opposition from a group of pro-Israeli statesmen. Plans to buy US-made helicopters seemed likely to be blocked by a proposed amendment to the US Export Administration Act. The move was believed to be aimed specifically at preventing the sale of 45 helicopters to the Transport and Communications Ministry, a deal being discussed by Bell Helicopter Textron. The amendment was introduced by Senator William Proxmire on the grounds that Iraq had aided the escape of Muhammad Abbas, the alleged organizer of the October 1985 hijacking of the Italian cruiser ship *Achille Lauro*.

According to Dilip Hiro in *The Longest War*, on 17 January Reagan authorized the Central Intelligence Agency (CIA) to buy 4,000 Tow missiles from the US Defence Department and sell them to Iran through Israel. A further 1,000 were likewise delivered on 24 February.

13 January The South Yemeni (PDRY) president, Ali Nasser Muhammad, attempts to purge his opponents within the Political Bureau. When six of its members gathered to meet him in Aden he did not appear and his bodyguards opened fire on the assembled members. Several were killed immediately. Others, including the doctrinaire Marxist, Abd al-Fattah Ismail, escaped although the latter subsequently died of his wounds. In Aden rival elements within the armed forces fought for control of Aden City, most of the navy and the air force initially supporting President Muhammad. In a combined operation starting on 17 January more than 6,000 foreign nationals, including about 3,000 Soviet citizens, were evacuated in British, French and Soviet ships. Fighting was soon reported in all of South Yemen's six governorates. The Soviet Union, for whom the Aden and Socotra Island bases were the most important in the Middle East, tried to mediate but with little success.

Towards the end of the month, President Muhammad was reported to be gathering a 40,000-strong force of supporters in Abyan governorate who began marching on Aden. However, reports that they had started massacres seemed to have turned the army to the rebel side. The prime minister, Haidar abu Bakr al-Attas, who was in India when the troubles began and flew on to Moscow, was named on 24 January as interim head of government and Muhammad was stripped of all party and state posts. On the same day the Soviet Union recognized the new regime. The end of resistance by President Muhammad's faction was reported on 28 January and he was believed to have fled to Addis Ababa. The number of casualties in the conflict was thought to include about 2,000 dead. A new government was formed on 8 February with al-Attas confirmed as president, chairman of the presidium of the Supreme People's Council and secretary-general of the ruling Yemen Socialist Party's political bureau. The former deputy prime minister, Dr Yasin Said Nu'man, was named as prime minister.

The new government committed itself to pursuing the unification of the two Yemens. The government announced on 10 February that Abd al-Fattah Ismail, head of state between 1978 and 1980, had been killed on 13 January in the factional fighting between the rival wings of the Yemen Socialist Party.

4 February The visit to Tehran of the Soviet deputy foreign minister, Georgi Kornienko, ends without producing any improvement in relations. On the day that Kornienko began his talks, Tehran Radio revealed that an Iranian delegation had just returned from talks in Afghanistan aimed at co-ordinating the 'activities of the Afghan Islamic Liberation Front fighting the atheist invaders'. The delegation had made the visit on instructions from Khomeini's designated successor, Ayatollah Hussein Ali Montazeri.

Iran had for long condemned the Soviet invasion of Afghanistan as well as the Kremlin's supply of weapons, particularly ground-to-ground missiles and advanced warplanes, to

Iraq. Moscow, meanwhile, accused a reactionary faction of Iranian clerics of playing into the hands of imperialists and Zionists. Moreover, Iran's Tudeh (Communist) leaders had been in Iranian jails since 1983. Tehran maintained that they, including their leader Nur ad-Din Kianouri, had confessed to spying for the Soviet Union.

Another bone of contention was the 500–1,000 Soviet experts who were pulled out of Iran in the spring of 1985 at the height of the 'War of the cities' (between Iran and Iraq). The industrial plants they were helping to build at Ahwaz and Isfahan had both come under attack from Iraqi bombers.

At a conference in Sheffield, England at the end of January, Tehran's mayor claimed that about 6,500 civilians had been killed and 26,000 wounded in the war so far and more than 50 towns and 2,000 villages had been damaged or destroyed.

9 February Iran launches the Wa al-Fajr (By Dawn) Eight offensive against Iraq. 85,000 Iranian troops crossed the Shatt al-Arab waterway and occupied the Iraqi port of Fao on 19 February, threatening Iraq's only access to the Gulf. At the start of the offensive an Iranian envoy was sent to Kuwait to demand that the Kuwaitis forbid Iraqi troops to land on Kuwait's strategic Bubiyan Island, an obvious temptation. On one occasion Iraqi soldiers had forced their way onto the island.

Meanwhile, Iran began operations along the Fao-Basra road to divert Iraqi forces. Later in the month Iraq countered by extending its exclusion area for Iran to the Kuwaiti coast. Both sides, meanwhile, increased their attacks on tankers and other commercial vessels. Iraq continued its attacks on Kharg Island and Iraq launched a counter-offensive on Fao in mid-February. Iran then opened up a second front in Kurdistan with its Wa al-Fajr Nine offensive. At the end of February the UN Security Council called for a cease-fire.

24 February UN Security Council Resolution 582 deplores 'the initial acts which gave rise to the [Iran-Iraq] conflict and the continuation of hostilities', and repeats earlier demands for an immediate cease-fire.

19 March King Husayn of Jordan announces in a television broadcast that he has abandoned efforts to reach an agreement with the Palestine Liberation Organization (PLO) on a joint approach to a Middle East peace settlement, following the breakdown of his talks with the PLO chairman, Yasser Arafat, which concluded on 6 February. A PLO official described the discussions, which were also attended by Jordan's Prime Minister Zaid al-Rifai, as the most important since the 11 February 1985 agreement setting a framework for a peace settlement.

22 March The UN Security Council issues a statement condemning Iraq for violating the 1925 Geneva protocol forbidding the use of chemical weapons. The statement also condemned Iran for failing to agree to an end to hostilities.

4 April Lieutenant-Colonel Oliver North, deputy-director for political-military affairs on the US National Security Council, says in a private memo (revealed later) that $12 million of US arms sales profits are to be used for the Nicaraguan Contras.

15 April US aircraft bomb Tripoli and Benghazi, killing at least 100 people, including President Qadhafi's adopted daughter.

17 April Three British hostages are murdered in Lebanon in retaliation for Britain's role in the US attack on Libya on 15 April. The US claimed that they had struck 'terrorist targets'; in the bombing of President Qadhafi's home, his adopted daughter was killed.

22 April US law enforcement officers arrest 10 Americans, Israelis and West Europeans involved in two arms deals with Iran, says Dilip Hiro in *The Longest War*. The deals, worth $2,380 million, concerned the supply of US-made combat aircraft, transport planes, Tow and Hawk missiles, guided bombs and tanks to Iran, says Hiro.

26 April Qatari troops seize 29 construction workers building a coastguard station for Bahrain on the reclaimed island of Fasht al-Dibal. The island, half-way between Bahrain and Qatar, had been the subject of a longstanding territorial dispute. The Qatari troops withdrew on 15 June prior to the dismantling of the island under the terms of a Saudi-inspired settlement between the two states.

15 May President Reagan approves the North/McFarlane visit to Tehran. On 25 May Robert McFarlane, former US National Security Adviser, and Oliver North (see 4 April) visited Tehran aboard a plane carrying Hawk spare parts and gifts including a kosher chocolate cake baked in Israel. Iran kept the parts, did not deliver the hostages and the airport guards ate the cake. The two men returned in humiliation to the US on 28 May, their attempt to bring about a rapprochement between the US and Iran a disaster.

17 May Iraq makes its first armed incursion into Iran since 1982, occupying Mehran. It also bombed Tehran for the first time since June 1985. On 14 May Iraqi aircraft bombed a passenger train at Haft Tappeh station in Iran. Meanwhile, a meeting of Iraqi and Syrian foreign ministers scheduled for June to discuss a reconciliation between Iran and Iraq was cancelled by Syria's President Hafez Asad.

5 June The way is cleared for a major sale of advanced US missiles to Saudi Arabia's air force and navy after the US Senate fails by one vote to override President Reagan's veto of legislation prohibiting the sale.

1/2 July The presidents of North and South Yemen, Ali Abdullah Saleh and Haidar Abu Bakr al-Attas, hold talks in Libya at the invitation of the Libyan leader, Colonel Mu'ammar Qadhafi. They were the first such high-level meetings since the civil war in South Yemen in January.

2 July The Iranians recapture the Iranian border town of Mehran in the central sector of the Iran-Iraq war. The Iraqis had captured Mehran on 17 May. After the Iranians had occupied the Iraqi port of Fao in February, the Iraqis had suggested an exchange of the two towns but the Iranians refused to consider this. In the 2 July campaign Iranian combined forces in co-ordinated action with the Revolutionary Guards (the Pasdaran) attacked Mehran by night and after a week of heavy fighting announced the capture of more than 1,500 Iraqi prisoners as well as hundreds of Soviet-made tanks.

Following the recapture of the town, Majlis Speaker Hashemi Rafsanjani reiterated Iran's peace conditions: the punishment of Iraq as the aggressor, or alternatively the downfall of Iraq's President Saddam Husayn, and war damage compensation. The victory clearly demoralized Iraq's Arab supporters. Some believed it might discourage the Arab world from supporting Iraq and might even encourage a movement aimed at removing Saddam Husayn. However, a major Iraqi air attack on 12 August on the Iranian oil terminal at Sirri Island was to lead to speculation that the terminal would have to be abandoned.

3 July The ruler of Kuwait, Shaikh Jaber al-Ahmad al-Sabah, dissolves the Kuwaiti parliament, imposes censorship on the press and suspends a system of consultative rule hitherto regarded as a model for the region. Following the June bombing of a Kuwaiti oil depot, Kuwaiti parliamentary deputies wanted to cross-examine the oil and interior ministers, both members of the Al-Sabah family, about possible incompetence. The cabinet, led by the heir apparent Sa'd al-Abdullah, was apparently afraid that such a public interrogation would weaken its attempts to fend off the spill-over dangers of the Iran-Iraq war, and resigned.

Indeed, the speaker of Iran's Majlis (lower house), Hashemi Rafsanjani, promptly linked Kuwait's political problems with Iran's recapture of Mehran on 2 July: 'In our belief, Kuwait's political crisis has nothing to do with the explosions at [Kuwait's] al-Ahmadi oil port, but is linked with the war and the [Kuwaiti] people's growing opposition to support for Iraq', he said. Instead of selecting a cabinet more acceptable to the critics, the amir of Kuwait decided to dissolve the assembly. Many felt that the war was merely being used as an excuse to dissolve the house, arguing that Iran had no popular base in Kuwait.

However, the outspokeness of the deputies and their scrutiny of government affairs had clearly irked the ruling family. Several ministers, angered by apparent financial irregularities, had recently resigned. On 4 July the ruler formed a new 21-portfolio cabinet, reappointing the outgoing government virtually intact. Curiously, many Kuwaitis welcomed the developments, arguing that the elected deputies had offered no real solutions and even that they had intentionally tried to defame the prime minister for their own personal gain. On 13 July the prime minister, Shaikh Sa'd, formed a new government with seven new members.

3/4 July At an extraordinary regional congress (the first since June 1982) of Iraq's Ba'th Socialist Party, President Saddam Husayn re-shuffles the Revolutionary Command Council (RCC), the Ba'th Party Regional Command and the cabinet, greatly increasing his own power. Na'im Haddad, who had been a member of the Regional Command and the ruling RCC since their formation in 1968, was not re-elected to the Regional Command. He was later removed from the RCC and replaced by Sa'adoun Hammadi, the speaker of the National Assembly. By this time all real power in Iraq lay in the presidential palace.

Meanwhile, First Deputy Premier Taha Yasin Ramadan confirmed that there would be no Iraqi pipeline through Syria and that Iraq was concentrating on 'pipeline projects in other countries'. A meeting between Iraqi and Syrian foreign ministers, scheduled for June and aimed at reconciling the two countries, had been cancelled suddenly by Syria's President Asad.

12 August Iraqi air-force jets mount a major attack on Iran's Sirri Island oil export terminal.

1 September The Organization of Petroleum Exporting Countries' (OPEC's) agreement of late July to cut oil production comes into effect, pushing oil prices up to $13 a barrel on the 'spot' market. It was estimated that if prices remained roughly at this level, Saudi Arabia's revenues from petroleum could reach $16,000 million in 1986, compared with $22,000 million in 1985. Following OPEC's decision in December 1985 to secure a greater market share, Saudi production was increased until it reached 5.7 million barrels a day in July. From an all-time high of $34 a barrel in 1981, OPEC's price had fallen to an all-time low of $10 a barrel in July. Saudi Arabia's proven petroleum reserves were estimated in January at 168,800 million barrels which would allow for well over a century's production at 1985 levels of production. However, reflecting OPEC's self-imposed production quotas which followed the world glut, production fell from over 7 million barrels a day in early 1982 to a little over 2 million barrels a day in mid-1985. Since then the policies of the kingdom oscillated.

1–7 September Iraq presents a new peace initiative to the eighth Non-Aligned Summit conference in Harare, Zimbabwe. Ayatollah Khomeini responded by urging his countrymen to 'give one more slap in the face to Saddam Husayn, to force him to either kill himself or give up power.' The ayatollah's speech was seen as a rebuke to Iran's only Arab ally, Syria, who had been under pressure from the Saudis to send two delegations to Tehran, one headed by the Syrian vice-president, Abd al-Halim Khaddam, in an attempt to stop Iran from carrying the war into other Arab states. Majlis Speaker Rafsanjani replied, however: 'It is our right to hit your tankers, it is our right to prevent your ships entering the Persian Gulf, as you are all on the side of Iraq, our enemy.'

Tehran had been instrumental in having Harare chosen as the venue for the conference, having objected to Baghdad as the site. In recent years Iran had been waging a diplomatic offensive in Africa where many countries have large Muslim populations. President Khamenei had made a tour of four left-wing African states in January although his trip to Zimbabwe was marred by the presence of unveiled women and the serving of alcohol at functions he attended.

Meanwhile, it was thought that up to 850,000 Iranian troops were massed along the Iraqi border ready to deal Iraq 'the final blow'.

5 September Four Arabic-speaking gunmen take over a Pan Am 747 airliner on the tarmac of Karachi airport in the morning. Sixteen hours later, 20 of the 380 hostages taken were killed when the hijackers opened fire after the lights of the plane went out – some 15 minutes before a Pakistani commando unit stormed the plane. Sources in Cyprus believed that the operation was designed to discredit the PLO chairman, Yasser Arafat, rather than (as claimed by the hijackers) secure the release of the three men who had killed three Israelis on a boat at Larnaca marina on 25 September 1985. Two groups claimed responsibility for the Karachi hijacking: one was Jundullah (Army of God), a Lebanese pro-Iranian Shi'i fundamentalist group which claimed the attack was carried out by the 'Zulfikar Ali Bhutto squad'.

16 September A Boeing 720 of Air Djibouti on a flight from the Yemen Arab Republic (North Yemen) to Ethiopia was forced by PDRY (South Yemeni) fighter aircraft to land at Aden. The plane was then reportedly searched for supporters of the former PDRY president, Ali Nasser Muhammad, but was later allowed to proceed. In response Djibouti cut air and sea links with the PDRY.

30 September The Syrian president, Hafez al-Asad, tells Jordanian editors that Syria is offering 'total and immediate unity' with Iraq in a move to end the Iran-Iraq war. However, the offer was ignored by Baghdad and not taken seriously by anyone else. Syria had made such offers in 1979 and in April 1986.

21 October The 58-year-old Edward Austin Tracy, a US book salesman and author of children's books, is kidnapped by the militia group calling itself the Revolutionary Justice Organization in Beirut. During 1986 five Westerners had been seized by various groups in Beirut. On 9 September the 57-year-old Frank Herbert Reed, the US director of the Lebanese International School, was kidnapped by Arab Revolutionary Cells-Omar

Moukhtar Forces and on 12 September Joseph James Cicippio, the 58-year-old US deputy comptroller of the American University in Beirut was taken by the Revolutionary Justice Organization.

On 5 March Islamic Jihad claimed that it had executed Michel Seurat, a French academic researcher kidnapped in 1985. On 28 March Leigh Douglas, a 34-year-old British professor at the American University in Beirut, and the 40-year-old British teacher Philip Padfield disappeared. On 11 April Brian Keenan, a 36-year-old Anglo-Irish teacher at the American University in Beirut, was kidnapped. His abducters were unknown. Six days later, on 17 April, John McCarthy, a 31-year-old British journalist-producer with the London-based Worldwide Television News agency was taken, probably by a group calling itself Revolutionary Commando Cells. On 23 April the Revolutionary Organization of Socialist Muslims claimed that a British journalist kidnapped on 16 March 1985, Alec Collett, had been hanged, probably on 17 April, in retaliation for the 15 April US air raid on Libya. A blurred video said to show Collett hanging from a scaffold was released but his body was not found. Also found shot dead in revenge for the US raid were Leigh Douglas, Philip Padfield and the American Peter Kilburn who had disappeared on 3 December 1984.

22 October OPEC oil ministers agree on higher member country output quotas for November and December, particularly for Kuwait, Qatar, Ecuador and Gabon. The quotas did not apply to Iran. According to the new quotas the ceiling for OPEC aggregate output would rise from 16.8 million to 17.0 million barrels of oil a day. Saudi Arabia and the United Arab Emirates (UAE) both agreed to nil increases in their quotas.

24 October Britain breaks off diplomatic relations with Syria after Nizar Hindawi is convicted in London of the April attempt to blow up an El Al airliner.

30 October Shaikh Ahmad Zaki Yamani is removed as Saudi Arabia's charismatic petroleum and mineral resources minister and is replaced as acting minister by Shaikh Hisham Nazer, the planning minister. Yamani had held his post since 1962. He had been a strong advocate of cutting oil prices to win back the energy market share for Saudi Arabia. In contrast, the 54-year-old Hisham Nazer was known to favour lower production and higher prices.

2–5 November The seventh summit meeting of the Gulf Co-operation Council (GCC) heads of state held in Abu Dhabi resolves to defend freedom of navigation to and from GCC ports in the face of disruptions caused by the Iran-Iraq war, and to remove certain trade and economic barriers between the member states.

3 November Details of the visit to Tehran in May of US officials involved in the clandestine delivery of arms to the Iranian regime are published by the Lebanese weekly newspaper, *Ash-Shira'a*. The supporters of Mehdi Hashemi, were widely suspected of leaking the information, opposed as they were to negotiations with the US. They were reported (wrongly) to be behind a bomb attack on the hotel in which the US delegation was staying. Hashemi and his brother Hadi (Ayatollah Montazeri's son-in-law) were arrested in Tehran on 12 October and accused of murder and kidnapping among other crimes.

6 November Haidar abu Bakr al-Attas is elected president of the PDRY (South Yemen) for a five-year term by the Supreme People's Council.

13 November President Reagan defends his 'Irangate' dealings on US television, arguing that he had wanted to renew a relationship with a strategically important country, stop the Iran-Iraq war, end Iran's support for terrorism and win the release of the hostages. On 20 November Khomeini promptly retorted that the restoration of relations with the US was 'out of the question'. On 25 November Reagan called a press conference in which he admitted that profits from arms sales to Iran were used to skirt congressional prohibitions and finance the Contra rebels fighting Nicaragua's Sandinista government. At the same time he announced the resignation of his national security adviser, Vice-Admiral John Poindexter, and the sacking of Poindexter's aide, marine corps Lieutenant-Colonel Oliver North. Reagan claimed that he had not been fully informed of the nature of the activities of his security advisers – it turned out that this meant North who was the operational head of the effort to channel funds to the Contras. Reagan's claims came amid allegations that the arms shipments to Iran were made via Israel and that the proceeds from the sale had been transferred in secret to to the US-backed Contra guerrillas fighting the Nicaraguan government.

In his 2 December television address the president announced that he had appointed Frank Carlucci to head the National Security Council. By mid-December pieces from the 'Irangate' scandal were beginning to fit together. It transpired that the former National Security Council director, Robert McFarlane, had made at least two visits to Tehran and that the bitter reaction that they had produced in Tehran had led to clashes in Tehran between the Revolutionary Guards (the Pasdaran) and Mehdi Hashemi's World Organization of Islamic Liberation Movements militia. Moreover, the editor of the Lebanese weekly *Ash-Shira'a*, Hasan Sabra, which had revealed McFarlane's second trip, announced that two Iranian visitors had come to his Beirut office on 27 October to inform him of the event in his capacity as friend of Montazeri, Khomeini's designated heir.

14 November Abu Dhabi's Abu-Bakush offshore oil platform is bombed, killing 16 people, two of them French. The bombing was assumed to be by Iran since Phantom aircraft were sighted during the attack, but an earlier assault on an offshore field had been admitted as a 'mistake' by Iraq. Iran offered Abu Dhabi compensation without admitting responsibility. The UAE had tried to please both Iran and Iraq, entertaining envoys from the former but giving subsidies to the latter. Some 20 per cent of the UAE population is Shi'i.

Meanwhile, the Iraqi air force attacked Larak Island, some 777 miles (1,250 kilometres) into Iran.

26 November The Saudi-financed King Fahd causeway linking Bahrain and Saudi Arabia is officially opened by King Fahd of Saudi Arabia and the ruler of Bahrain, Shaikh Isa. The causeway had been under construction since 1981 and was originally scheduled for opening in December 1985. Some Saudi clerics were reported to have argued against the causeway on the grounds that a natural link would have existed had God wished it.

More realistically, it was felt by many that defence was the principal rationale for building the 16-mile (26-kilometre) causeway. Should there be a repeat of the attempted coup in 1981 of Bahrain's 70 per cent Shi'i population, Saudi Arabia would be well able to respond, using the causeway's four-lane highway which is wide enough to accommodate tanks. The causeway was expected to lure at least 100,000 Saudis a year to the comparative liberalism of Bahrain.

23–25 December Iran launches its doomed Kerbala-Four offensive against Iraq near Basra but it fails. On 27/28 December a conference on Solidarity with the

Iraqi People, sponsored by the Supreme Council of the Islamic Revolution in Iraq (SCIRI) decided to escalate the armed struggle against Saddam Husayn's regime.

According to Dilip Hiro in *The Longest War*, during 1986 Iraq struck 66 ships in the Gulf, twice its total for 1985 and Iran struck 41, nearly three times the total for 1985.

1 9 8 7

Sayings of the year

'As for what you said, namely that the people now argue with you and take my speeches and statements as evidence in their arguments, I would like to say that I mean it to be this way. In fact, I had intended it to be this way since the early days of the July 1968 revolution.' Saddam Husayn, speaking to provincial mayors, 16 July (quoted in Chubin and Tripp, *Iran and Iraq at War*).

'I come from Iran which has been the birthplace of the most acclaimed and at the same time, the least known revolution of the contemporary period – a revolution based upon the religion of God and in continuation of the path of God's messengers and great divine teachers and a path as long as the whole of human history.' President Ali Khamenei, New York, September 22 (Address to the UN General Assembly).

'The Algerian revolution took one million lives out of fourteen million people. We are fifty million. It is still very early for us to put aside our arms and refrain from the holy defence which is one of our mandatory duties ... We say to the world: we want our rights and justice. Our wish is to see corruption uprooted.' President of the Supreme Judicial Council, Mousavi Ardebili, Tehran, 9 October.

9 January A major offensive is launched by Iran east of Basra in a serious escalation of the Iran-Iraq war. On 10/11 January Iraq claimed to have bombed Qom, Iran's clerical power-base and holy city.

12 January The Archbishop of Canterbury Dr Robert Runcie's personal envoy, the 50-year-old Terry Waite, arrives in Beirut where he enjoys the protection of Walid Jumblatt's Parti Socialiste Progressiste (PSP). He is not to be seen in public again after 20 January. On 31 October 1986, shortly after arriving in Beirut, he had notified the Western press that he was in the city and that progress was being made in freeing the hostages. It was subsequently reported that Waite was at this time involved to some extent in a covert US operation aimed at securing the release of hostages in return for the supply of arms to the Iranian government in what was to become the 'Irangate' scandal.

The day after Waite's visit to Damascus on 1 November 1986, Mr David Jacobsen was released. Waite's visit coincided with the presence in Damascus of the Iranian foreign minister, Dr Ali Akbar Velayati. On 4 November the Majlis (lower house) speaker, Hashemi Rafsanjani, had said that Iran was willing, under certain conditions, to advise groups holding US hostages to release them, but that the US government must prove that it was not hostile to Iran and must support Lebanese Muslim demands for the release of detainees held in Kuwait, Israel and France. On 11 November two French hostages,

M. Camille Sontag and M. Coudari, were released. The French prime minister, Jacques Chirac, thanked the Syrian, Saudi Arabian and Algerian governments for their part in releasing the two men.

Between 13 and 26 January several foreigners were kidnapped in Beirut, including a Frenchman on 13 January, two West Germans on 17 and 21 January, three US citizens and one Indian on 24 January. Altogether 10 Europeans, six Americans, one Saudi and one North Korean were in captivity in Lebanon at the time of Waite's kidnapping.

Although Waite's kidnappers remained unknown it was clear that three US academics at Beirut University College seized on 24 January had been abducted by Islamic Jihad for the Liberation of Palestine. They were the 54-year-old Robert Polhill, the 40-year-old Jesse Turner and the 50-year-old Alan Steen.

26 January Governors of the six Gulf Co-operation Council (GCC) central bank authorities agree in principle to seek a common framework for their currencies. The governor of the Central Bank of Kuwait, Shaikh Salem Abd al-Aziz al-Sabah, stated on 22 February that a currency grid broadly similar to the European Monetary System would be established by the end of the year as the first step towards the creation of a single currency for the Gulf states.

26–29 January The fifth summit meeting of the Islamic Conference Organization is held in Kuwait. Of the 44 states represented, only 23 heads of state attended, making the meeting ineffectual. The three principal items on the agenda of over 30 subjects were the Gulf war, Palestine and Afghanistan. However, Iran's refusal to attend was taken by most Arab states as evidence of its belligerency. The UN secretary-general, Perez de Cuellar, addressed the conference, calling for the establishment of an international panel to decide whether Iran or Iraq was responsible for the war.

A series of bombing attacks took place in Kuwait during the period of the summit and 16 people were charged. Responsibility was claimed by a group called the Followers of the Prophet Muhammad. Bombings in Kuwait had started in December 1983 when there were nine bomb attacks including attempted suicide attacks on the US and French embassies. As a result, 17 members of the pro-Iranian Islamic Jihad were jailed. In May 1985 a suicide car bomb attack on the amir of Kuwait had been blamed on members of a radical Iraqi group. In July bomb attacks on popular cafés had been blamed on the Palestinian renegade Abu Nidal. In June 1986 there were bomb attacks on Kuwait's main Ahmadi oil installation.

27 January US President Reagan, in his State of the Union address, says serious mistakes were made and assumes responsibility for the 'Irangate' scandal.

5 February Iran launches a missile attack on Baghdad, prompting Iraq to retaliate with bombing raids on Iran the following day as part of the continuation of the 'war of the cities'. On 11 February Ayatollah Khomeini said that waging the war should be seen as 'a divine cause', not merely 'a single, final offensive'. Despite a truce on 19 February applied to the bombardment of civilian areas in response to an Iraqi initiative, the fighting in the Gulf continued with little respite.

6 February A British businessman, Roger Cooper, appears on Iranian television to 'confess' to a number of espionage allegations. In his confession he referred to contacts with what he termed 'the BIS – British Intelligence Services', suggesting that such a reference to a non-existent organization nullified the rest of his confession. He was arrested and incarcerated in Tehran's Evin prison in December 1985 although, on British Foreign Office advice, his family chose not to publicize his detention until a year later. On 2 September he was to appear on television again with further 'confessions' of guilt. On 10 December the Iranian authorities announced that Cooper would face trial on spying charges.

26 February The Tower Commission investigating US arms sales to Iran in the so called 'Irangate' scandal criticizes President Reagan for making 'mistakes'. The report also criticized the White House chief-of-staff, Donald Regan, for general 'chaos' and Lieutenant-Colonel Oliver North for concealing information about the plan which involved supplying arms to Iran in exchange for the release of US hostages in Lebanon.

7 March The US informs Kuwait that it will escort its oil tankers once these have been reflagged with the US flag. On 2 March the Soviet Union agreed to lease three of its oil tankers to Kuwait.

21 March Huge, government-sponsored demonstrations take place in Baghdad to celebrate Khomeini's 'failure' to make the past year one of victory. Nevertheless, on 15 March Saddam Husayn had warned against the danger of 'a slow defeat through attrition'.

26 March Tunisia breaks off relations with Iran following the alleged discovery of evidence linking the Iranian embassy in Tunis with terrorism.

9 April An assassination attempt on Saddam Husayn near Mosul fails. His motorcade was ambushed on the city's outskirts by Al-Da'wa militants. According to Hiro in *The Longest War*, six people were reportedly killed, as were 10 presidential bodyguards. The assassination attempt was aimed to commemorate the execution in April 1980 of Ayatollah Baqr al-Sadr, says Hiro.

6 May The freighter *Ivan Korotoyev* is damaged in an attack by Iranian gunboats, making it the first Soviet ship known to have come under fire in the war. On 16 May the *Marshal Chukyov*, one of three Soviet tankers on charter to Kuwait, hit a mine in the Gulf, apparently the first vessel to do so.

On 17 May the US frigate *Stark* was hit in international waters off Bahrain with the loss of 37 of its crew by Exocet missiles fired from an Iraqi warplane. On 18 May an anxious Iraqi President Saddam Husayn described the attack as an 'unintentional accident', an explanation that was promptly (and, to some observers, astonishingly) accepted by the US. On 19 May President Reagan announced that the US had agreed to allow 11 Kuwaiti tankers to sail under the US flag and receive US naval protection.

21 May In the face of congressional opposition, the US abandons plans to sell F-15 fighter aircraft to Saudi Arabia, and on 11 June it withdraws a proposal to sell the kingdom Maverick air-to-ground missiles.

28 May Relations between Britain and Iran deteriorate following the arrest in Manchester of Ahmad Qassemi, an employee at the Iranian consulate in Manchester. Qassemi had originally been arrested on charges of shop-lifting on 9 May, but had claimed diplomatic immunity. When he was arrested on 28 May he attempted to escape, claiming that he believed his pursuers to be agents of the Iranian opposition. After being recaptured he was charged additionally with assaulting a police officer. However, he returned to Iran in early June.

Later the same day, in apparent retaliation for the arrest of Qassemi, the First Secretary at the British interests section of the Swedish embassy in Tehran, Edward Chaplin, was abducted by Revolutionary Guards in Tehran and beaten up. He was released after 12 hours but it was later announced that he would be facing unspecified criminal charges. However, he was subsequently released and left Iran on 9 June.

On 4 June the British authorities announced the closure of the Iranian consulate in Manchester and expelled its five staff, so initiating a tit-for-tat series of diplomatic moves.

2 June The Islamic Republican Party (IRP) is disbanded by Ayatollah Khomeini on the recommendation of Majlis Speaker Hashemi Rafsanjani and President Khamenei. Khomeini commented that the government-sponsored political organization had originally played a valuable role in providing a 'united forum for encountering prevailing problems' but that it had recently become 'an excuse for discord and factionalism.'

6 June At the end of a trial of 16 people in Kuwait charged with sabotaging oil installations and plotting against the government, six Shi'i Kuwaitis are sentenced to death, two of them in absentia, while two defendants are acquitted and the remainder receive prison terms of between two years and life. The charges related mainly to attacks on oil sites in June 1986 and January 1987. Anti-US slogans were shouted by a crowd outside the courtroom after the trial and a statement by the Revolutionary Organization – Forces of the Prophet Muhammad – threatened revenge. Prior to the summit meeting of the Islamic Conference Organization (ICO) in Kuwait in late January, threats against the participants were issued in the name of Al Jihad al-Islami (The Islamic Struggle), the Lebanese-based Shi'i organization, and the Committee for the Defence of Arab Political Prisoners which demanded the release of Al-Jihad al-Islami members in detention in Kuwait. The fundamentalists tended to draw support from poorer, Shi'i and often immigrant sections of the population.

17 June A coup is carried out against Sharjah's ruler, Shaikh Sultan ibn Muhammad al-Qasimi, by his elder brother, Shaikh Abd al-Aziz ibn Muhammad al-Qasimi, but after lengthy negotiations Shaikh Sultan is restored as ruler on 24 June.

27 June Organization of Petroleum Exporting Countries's (OPEC's) eightieth meeting ends in Vienna with an agreement to raise quotas by 5 per cent to 15.06 million barrels a day plus an implicit 1.54 million barrels a day for Iraq, for the remainder of 1987. The agreeement also called upon members to adhere to OPEC's $18-a-barrel pricing regime. On 26 October Saudi Arabia's King Fahd called for OPEC to maintain the regime.

14 July France falls foul of the Tehran regime when Iran declares that the First Secretary in the French embasssy in Tehran, Paul Torri, is wanted for espionage. Two days later the Iranians threatened to break off relations with France unless what they described as the 'siege' of its embassy in Paris was lifted within 24 hours. However, it was to be France who broke off relations with Tehran on 17 July after the Iranian embassy in Paris refused to deliver to the French police Vahid Gordji, an Iranian interpreter wanted for questioning in connection with terrorist attacks. In the weeks beforehand, both embassies in Paris and Tehran had been sealed off.

On 17 July the French government announced the severance of diplomatic relations with Iran, ordering all Iranian diplomats to be confined to the embassy compound until arrangements could be made for their repatriation.

17 July President Reagan's national security adviser, Rear-Admiral John Poindexter, tells the US Congress that he authorized the diversion of money from arms sales to Iran to the Contra rebels in Nicaragua. Earlier, Lieutenant-Colonel Oliver North had said that he assumed, but did not know for certain, that President Reagan was aware of this diversion of funds.

20 July The UN Security Council resolution 598 unanimously demands an immediate cease-fire in the Iran-Iraq war. The Security Council was composed of the five permanent members and 10 elected countries. The 10 paragraphs of the resolution were as follows: a demand for an immediate cease-fire on land, sea and air followed by the withdrawal of all forces to international boundaries; a call for a team of observers to verify the cease-fire under the instructions of the UN secretary-general; a call for the release of all prisoners of war; a call on the two belligerents to co-operate fully with the secretary-general in implementing the resolution and in mediation efforts to achieve a lasting solution to the conflict; a call on all other states to assist in implementing the resolution; a request addressing the Iranian government's demands by asking the secretary-general to explore, in consultation with Iran and Iraq, 'the question of entrusting an impartial body with enquiring into responsibility for the conflict'; a statement of the possibility of international assistance for post-war construction efforts; requests to the secretary-general to explore ways of ensuring lasting security in the region and to report back to the Council on progress on the resolution; and an affirmation that the Council would 'meet again as necessary to consider further steps to ensure compliance with this resolution'. The last paragraph implied willingness to initiate an arms embargo.

The Iraqi government, as expected, welcomed the resolution but stressed that it could only be implemented as a whole. However, Iran described the resolution as unjust on the grounds that it failed to name Iraq as the aggressor in the conflict. In a speech to the UN General Assembly on 22 September, President Khamenei described the resolution as 'an indecent, condemnable position' which had been forced on the Security Council 'by the will of the big powers, particularly the United States'. Although stopping short of rejecting the resolution, he described the Security Council as 'a paper factory for issuing worthless and ineffective orders'.

24 July The Kuwaiti, US-flagged tanker, *The Bridgeton*, the first of such tankers, hits a mine on 24 July, two days after it has been granted US protection. On 29 July four French naval vessels were ordered to sail for the Gulf but on 31 July France joined West Germany, Britain and the Netherlands in declining to participate with the US in an operation to clear mines from the Gulf.

31 July Over 400 Muslim *hajjis* (pilgrims) are killed and 650 injured in fighting in Mecca. Iranian officials were later to maintain that 600 Iranians had been killed and 4,500 injured when Saudi police 'in a pre-arranged joint Saudi-US conspiracy' opened fire on a peaceful march. The Saudis, on the other hand, maintained that the deaths and injuries had been caused by a stampeding crowd in the middle of a political demonstration.

The conflict had its historical roots. During the 1944 *hajj*, a frail old Iranian called Abu Taleb Yazdi began to vomit in the Great Mosque in Mecca. Loathe to sully holy ground, he attempted to catch the vomit in his *litham* (head-dress) but failed to do so entirely. Young Saudi fanatics approached him and accused him of polluting holy ground. They dragged him to the *qadi* (judge) where, with little ado, he was condemned to death and soon after beheaded. The Iranian Reza Shah ordered relations between the two countries to be promptly severed as soon as he heard of the incident. In 1949 Iran's minister of justice, Sadrul Ashraf, was sent to discuss the restoration of relations with King Abd al-Aziz. Presents were exchanged. The shah sent the king a sword encrusted with turquoise in a golden sheath, and a Qur'an. Even during this visit, however, there was an incident. A young Iranian who believed himself to be sterile, was found pouring water over his penis and only the intervention with King Abd al-Aziz by Ashraf saved the man from execution for indecent exposure.

4 August Iran bans all foreign ships from its waters during two days of naval manoeuvres which it calls 'operation martyrdom'.

10 August Iraq mounts air attacks on six Iranian oilfields and refineries. Meanwhile, mines damaged the supertanker *Texas Caribbean* off the Fujairah coast and on 15 August mines destroyed the British-mastered ship *Anita*. On 11 August Britain and France decided to send minesweepers to the Gulf and on 20 and 27 August the Netherlands and Italy respectively announced that they were ready to do likewise. On 21 September US forces attacked and boarded an Iranian vessel, *Al-Ajr*, which they accused of laying mines in international waters. Exactly a week later, on 28 September, British minesweepers entered the Gulf for the first time.

21 September US naval helicopters destroy an Iranian ship, *Al-Ajr*, which they alleged was laying mines in the Gulf waters. On 7 October the US Congress voted to impose an embargo on all imports from Iran. On 8 October the US destroyed three Iranian patrol boats near Farsi Island. The US claimed that the Iranians had fired on a US patrol helicopter.

28 September Mehdi Hashemi is executed after being found guilty of 'waging war against Islam' and being 'corrupt on earth'. Hashemi was the brother of Hadi Hashemi, the son-in-law of Ayatollah Hussein Ali Montazeri, Khomeini's designated successor. Although he was convicted on the basis of his own confessions of murder, torture and abductions, his execution was seen as being related to the political power struggle within Iran between the hardliners and the 'pragmatists'. In Tehran, Hashemi had set up the World Organization of Islamic Liberation Movements, which was closly connected with terrorist movements throughout the world.

Hashemi had been arrested on 12 October 1986 together with Hadi Hashemi and several associates. Among the charges against them were murder, kidnapping, illegal possession of weapons, forging of government documents and carrying out illegal, clandestine operations. More apposite, however, may have been the publication in November of details of the visit of McFarlane and other US officials to Iran in what appeared to be an 'arms-for-hostages' deal which became the so-called 'Irangate' scandal. Hashemi and his associates were thought to have instigated the publication of the scandal in order to embarrass the government and the 'pragmatists'.

2 October Diplomatic relations between Iran and Iraq are formally severed at Iran's request. Since the outbreak of hostilities, each country's interests had been represented by a single chargé d'affaires. In a speech on 27 September Majlis Speaker Rafsanjani reiterated Iran's long-standing demand for the overthrow of President Saddam Husayn.

Following the diplomatic break, Turkey announced that it had agreed to represent both countries' interests. On 11 November a four-day Arab summit conference in Amman ended with a call for Iran to accept the resolution and condemned its occupation of Iraqi territory. The resolution was seen as a compromise between Iraq and Syria, stopping as it did short of calling for Arab or international sanctions against Tehran.

5 October Iraqi planes hit five Iranian crude-oil storage tankers near the Strait of Hormuz.

Iraq responded by launching two surface-to-air missiles against Baghdad and attacked vessels using Arab Gulf ports. On 15 October an Iranian surface-to-surface missile struck a Liberian-registered tanker off Kuwait's Ahmadi port oil terminal, and on 22 October Kuwait's Sea Island oil terminal was hit by an Iranian surface-to-surface missile. On 19 October US naval forces shelled two Iranian offshore oil rigs, and on 26 October the US announced a ban on imports from Iran and tightened restrictions on US exports to Iran as a response to what President Reagan called Tehran's 'increasingly bellicose behaviour'.

10 November The Kuwaiti Interior Ministry announces that 26,898 people have been deported from Kuwait over the past year. On 29 November the trial had ended of five Iraqi nationals charged with involvement in the attempted assassination in May 1985 of the ruler of Kuwait, Shaikh Jaber al-Ahmad al-Sabah. One of the defendants was sentenced to death while of the others, all of whom were being tried in absentia, one was sentenced to life imprisonment and three were acquitted.

11 November Iraq announces plans to restore diplomatic relations with Egypt, following the decision of the Amman summit (8–11 November) to leave the question of ties with Cairo to individual Arab states. The six GCC states, plus Mauritania, Morocco and North Yemen, later announced similar moves.

18 November The US congressional report on the Iran-Contra or 'Irangate' affair lays ultimate responsibility on President Reagan although it does not claim that the president knew that the profits of arms sales to Iran were donated to the Nicaraguan Contras.

21 November The Central Bank of Kuwait floats a combination of treasury bills and government bonds worth the equivalent of $751 million, in the first phase of a rolling programme of medium-term public borrowing that aims to raise up to $50,000 million to help finance the Kuwaiti government deficit.

21 November Oil prices crash to their lowest level for nine months. The London spot markets quoted Dubai Fateh crude at $16.40 a barrel and Brent at $17.20. On 9 December OPEC oil ministers met in Vienna although with little prospect of a rise in prices. Analysts predicted that OPEC's $18-a-barrel pricing regime would continue. The overall quota was expected to be raised to 18.25 million barrels a day in order to accommodate Iraq's increased export capacity following the completion of a second pipeline across Turkey in August.

27 November Two French hostages are released by the pro-Iranian Revolutionary Justice Organization in Beirut. Two days later Vahid Gordji and Paul Torri (see 14 July) were each allowed to fly home after being besieged in their embassies since July. Reports that a deal had been reached between Iran and France were denied in Paris. However, in early December the French government rounded up members of the exiled opposition Mujahedeen-e Khalq guerrilla group, declaring 17 of them, including three Turkish nationals, a serious threat to public order and expelling them to the West African state of Gabon. A further eight Mujahedeen members were placed under house arrest. France denied that a hostage deal had been made but most observers questioned the denial.

8 December The trial opens in Kuwait of five Jordanian nationals accused of café bombings which took place in July 1985. A sixth had already pleaded guilty to involvement in these as well as the attempted assassination of Ahmad Jarallah, editor of *Al-Siyasah* newspaper, in late 1985.

At the end of the trial on 7 January 1988 two of the accused were sentenced to death (one in absentia) while a third was jailed for life and a fourth for three years.

Saboteurs were responsible for explosions which caused major fires in the Ahmadi port petroleum complex in June 1986 and again in May 1987.

9 December North Yemen's President Saleh opens the 150,000 barrel-a-day pipeline from Marib to the Red Sea.

13 December South Yemen's Supreme Court sentences 35 people to death (19 of them in absentia), including former President Ali Nasser Muhammad, for their part in the January 1986 civil war.

14 December OPEC members reach a compromise agreement, keeping total output at 15.06 million barrels a day. The new level still excluded Iraq, which had been producing about 2.5 million barrels a day against its implicit quota of 1.54 million. In what appeared to be a concession to Baghdad which had been demanding a rise of more than $20 a barrel from the existing $18, no mention was made of a reference price. Falling spot prices in Europe and the US showed traders' nervousness about the prospects for discipline within the agreement. Some analysts were already forecasting a drop of prices to as low as $12 a barrel in 1988. Crude-oil prices in early 1986 had fallen from almost $30 a barrel to $9 a barrel before beginning an erratic recovery.

31 December According to Dilip Hiro in *The Longest War*, during 1987 Iraq struck 76 ships in the Gulf; and Iran 87, more than twice the previous year's total.

1 9 8 8

3–31 January The Palestinian Intifada (uprising – literally 'tremor') in the Israeli-occupied West Bank and Gaza escalates. Four Palestinians were deported on 13 January, a move condemned by the UN Security Council. Meanwhile, Israel launched an iron-fist policy which had left 35 Arabs dead and 250 wounded by mid-January. On 21 January the siege of the Palestinian refugee camp of Chatila was lifted by the pro-Syria Amal in solidarity with the Intifada and relations between the Palestine Liberation Organization (PLO) and Syria soon began to improve. A meeting of the Arab League in Tunis on 23/24 January pledged material and political support for the uprising.

On 25 January the US secretary of state, George Shultz, visited Israel to promote a peace plan. Meanwhile, Israel was generally condemned for its handling of the uprising amid reports of atrocities including the burying alive of Palestinian youths (who were rescued) and the killing of children by Israeli troops. Between 20 and 31 March Israel declared that the occupied territories were military zones after the first Israeli soldier was killed. The territories were completely sealed off for the Palestinian Land Day commemoration during which the Palestinians held mass demonstrations and declared an all-out strike.

Following the assassination on 16 April in Tunis of the PLO second-in-command, Khalil al-Wazir (Abu Jihad), the Intifada intensified. At an emergency summit of, the Arab League held in Algiers in June a communiqué was released seeking UN pressure on Israel to alter its response to the uprising. The League pledged to use all possible means to support it and was reported to have arranged $100 million a year in financial support for the PLO.

7 January In a rejoinder letter to the Iranian president, Ali Khamenei, Ayatollah Khomeini announces that Iran's Islamic government 'is a branch of Muhammad's [the Prophet's] absolute vice-regency, and is one of the first precepts of Islam'. According to his enemies, Khomeini was claiming an authority which overrode even the Qur'an. However, his apologists explained that the issue was not theological but was an attempt to assert his authority over the conservative Council of Guardians who had been blocking economic reforms, in particular land reform.

Khomeini's intervention had for long been sought by the government whose legislation on foreign trade and ownership of farmland and industries had been vetoed by the conservative 12-member council of constitutional guardians. The resulting legislative stalemate was holding up economic development and encouraging Iran's enemies to suggest that Islam was unable to cope with modern realities. The prime minister, Hussein Mousavi, responded to Khomeini's ruling by saying that it 'opens the way for the Islamic government to deal with problems and complexities facing . . . society'.

The ruling was the culmination of several decrees since mid-1987. Responding to government requests, Khomeini gave the government the authority to deal with inflation by punishing offenders and hoarders without going to the courts. The punishments imposed were limited to the withdrawal of government services such as electricity supplies and business permits although corporal punishment was also added as at least a theoretical deterrent.

Khomeini added in his letter that Iran's government 'takes precedent over all religious practices such as prayer, fasting or the hajj pilgrimage . . . I openly say that the government can stop any religious law if it feels that it is correct to do so . . . The ruler can close or destroy the mosques whenever he sees fit. The government can prohibit anything having to do with worship or otherwise if [these things] were contrary to the interests of the government . . .'

In the course of a Friday sermon, Khamenei had announced on 1 January that according to Khomeini an Islamic government 'has its authority in the framework of God's religious laws'. However, Khomeini quickly replied that this was a 'misquotation and misinterpretation and completely contradicts my beliefs' – elaborating his reply in the letter. On 13 January, according to one source, students marched through the streets of Tehran shouting 'Khomeini's command is as good as that of the Prophet [Muhammad]'.

However, in a further exchange of letters on 11 January Khomeini expressed his full confidence in Khamenei and the latter announced with apparent sincerity that his sermon on 1 January had been misunderstood and that he agreed with all Khomeini's statements.

22 January The Syrian foreign affairs minister, Farouq al-Shara, during a visit to Riyadh delivers a message to King Fahd asking for Saudi support for Syrian mediation efforts between Iran and the Arab Gulf states.

23 January The commander of Iraq's Fifth Corps, Major-General Abd al-Aziz Ibrahim al-Hadithy, is reported to have been killed in a helicopter crash. Baghdad claimed that the crash, which took place in the northern Tamim governorate, was caused by a technical fault.

26 January Energy ministers from the 13 Organization of Petroleum Exporting Countries (OPEC) member countries meet representatives of seven non-OPEC petroleum exporting countries for the first time but fail to agree on oil export cuts.

26 January The Kuwaiti government is re-shuffled and three new ministerial appointments are made. Most importantly, former defence minister, Shaikh Salem Sabah al-Salem al-Sabah, took over as interior minister, exchanging portfolios with Shaikh Nawwaf al-Ahmad al-Jaber al-Sabah. Observers believed that Shaikh Salem had been brought in to take a tougher line in the wake of bomb attacks in Kuwait, assassination attempts on the ruler and unrest among Kuwait's large Shi'i community. Shaikh Jaber Mubarak al-Hamad al-Sabah, considered by some to be the ruling family's strong-man, took the information portfolio.

6 February The Iranian reformists led by the Majlis (lower house) speaker, Hashemi Rafsanjani, send Ayatollah Khomeini a letter asking for a decree on creating an assembly to arbitrate in practical government decisions. On 7 January Khomeini had decreed that the needs of the Islamic Republic took precedence over all other considerations, including some religious regulations. However, the reformists were concerned that Khomeini had failed to specify what would happen should the conservative Council of Guardians (upper house) continue to veto government legislation it did not like on the grounds of being too un-Islamic.

Khomeini responded to the 6 February letter by announcing the creation of a 13-member assembly of legislative, executive and judicial leaders. The assembly consisted of Rafsanjani, Mousavi, Khamenei, Ardebili, the prosecutor-general, Muhammad Khoe'niha, the head of Khomeini's bureau, Muhammad Tavassoli, and the six theologians appointed by Khomeini to the Council of Guardians. Khomeini's son Ahmad was to attend the assembly sessions to keep his father informed of events. Reformists saw Khomeini's decision as backing government attempts to break a deadlock on legislation considered un-Islamic by the conservative Council of Guardians.

8 February Aden's Supreme People's Council presses the authorities in North Yemen to hand over the former president, Ali Nasser Muhammad, to face execution. The South Yemeni government had sentenced him to death in absentia in December 1987. The demand for Muhammad followed the execution in January of five senior politicians for their role in the January 1986 internal power struggle which led to a civil war that cost an estimated 4,600 lives.

Muhammad was among 35 people sentenced to death, 19 of them in absentia. Others were imprisoned for between 5 and 15 years for high treason after an almost year-long trial in Aden. The South Yemeni regime headed by Haidar Abu Bakr al-Atass, claimed that the trial had been held in public. Pleas for clemency came from North Yemen, whose President Ali Abdullah Saleh declared a period of mourning as a sign of protest, from the PLO, Kuwait, Libya and the Soviet Union. However, all such pleas were ignored.

11 February Iraqi aircraft are reported to have bombed towns deep in Iran, including Shiraz. The attacks were seen as retaliation for the 9 February dogfight over the Gulf in which Iranian fighters shot down three Iraqi Mirage aircraft. The incident suggested that Iran had managed to reactivate its air power despite worldwide sanctions against it.

On 14 February Iran claimed to have bombed a petrochemicals complex near the Iraqi port of Basra. Also on 14 February Oman's minister of state for foreign afairs, Yousef ibn Alawi ibn Abdullah, told Reuter that he supported in principle Soviet proposals for an international peace-keeping force in the Gulf, but added that he opposed a weapons embargo against Iran.

17 February The 44-year-old US Lieutenant-Colonel William Higgins is kidnapped in Lebanon. Higgins, who headed the 76-man UN Truce Supervision Organization, was seized by three gunmen shortly after he left the house of an official of the Shi'i Amal militia in the southern Lebanese city of Tyre. The so-called Organization of the Oppressed of the World (OOW), believed to operate under the umbrella of the pro-hardline Iranian Shi'i Hizbullah, claimed responsibility for the kidnapping. It accused him of being a US spy. The group appeared to have kidnapped Higgins with Tehran's approval. Experts believe that there was no real difference between the movement and Islamic Jihad.

After being dragged from his UN vehicle in Tyre, Higgins was taken north towards the Litani River in a car carrying Iranian diplomatic plates. Higgins was the twentieth American to be kidnapped in Lebanon since 1982. In April UN officials believed Higgins to be dead when his kidnappers released a photograph of him together with a message saying: 'His interrogation is finished. He will be judged for spying for the Americans by the Lebanese and Palestinian people before the tribunal of the oppressed.' According to the Israelis, the kidnapping had been masterminded by a Shi'i cleric from the southern Lebanese village of Jibshit, Shaikh Abd al-Karim Obeid.

According to one newspaper report, the OOW's name was the same as the one which had specialized in kidnapping and murdering members of Beirut's tiny Jewish community in 1985. The newspaper also claimed that in November 1985 the organization said it had abducted four Lebanese Jews in west Beirut and later announced the 'execution' of eight members of the Jewish community. Only three of their bodies were found.

On 17 March 1988 Muhammad Mahmoud el-Jiar, an Egyptian Muslim cleric, was kidnapped in South Lebanon.

27 February The so-called 'war of the cities' is resumed in the Iran-Iraq conflict when Iraq attacks Tehran. From 1 to 31 March both Tehran and Baghdad came under fire from ground-to-ground missiles. Iran captured several towns and villages in north-east Iraq, including the Kurdish town of Halabjeh, ten miles (16 kilometres) from the Iranian border.

15 March In an offensive called Wa al-Fajr (By Dawn) 10 the Iranians capture the Iraqi Kurdish town of Halabja with the assistance of their Kurdish allies. On 16 March Iraq used chemical weapons (probably tabun nerve gas which kills within 15 minutes of contact) against the town, killing up to 6,000 people (some believed 10,000). The Iraqis claimed that the Kurds had attacked their positions from the east and north while the Iranians, having crossed the Darbandikhan reservoir in boats, were attacking from the south. Photographs of men, women and children frozen to death in Halabja were to horrify the world. Iraqi forces had attacked Kurdish villages with mustard gas in April 1987.

At the Islamic Conference Organization (ICO) foreign ministers' conference in Amman between 15 and 21 March, the Iraqi foreign minister, Tariq Aziz, claimed that accusations about the Halabja killings were attempts 'to divert attention from efforts to reach a comprehensive solution on the basis of [resolution] 598'.

So far Khomeini had refused permission for the Iranian use of chemical weapons on the grounds that it would be immoral to use them in a *jihad* (holy struggle).

On 1 April Iran's official Islamic Republic News Agency claimed that Iraqi aircraft had dropped gas bombs on villages in Iraq's north-eastern Qara Dagh region between 21 and 26 March, killing 75 people and making hundreds violently ill.

5 April The reorganization of Saudi Arabia's oil industry is initiated by the election of the acting petroleum and minerals minister, Hisham Nazer, to the chairmanship of the Arabian American Oil Company (ARAMCO).

5–20 April A Kuwaiti airliner is hijacked by a group with links to pro-Iranian Shi'i Muslims in Lebanon. The Kuwaiti jumbo jet, carrying 97 passengers and 15 crew, was hijacked while flying from Bangkok to Kuwait and forced to land at Mashhad in north-eastern Iran. The hijackers demanded the release of 17 Shi'i militants jailed in Kuwait in 1984 for their role in six simultaneous bomb blasts in Kuwait town in 1983, including a suicide attack which devastated the US embassy. The militants were mainly Lebanese and Iraqi members of Iraq's pro-Iranian Al Da'wa (Missionary 'Call') party. Unless their terms were met the hijackers threatened to blow up the plane and its passengers, including three members of Kuwait's Al-Sabah royal family, the brother and two sisters of Kuwait's deputy chief-of-staff. During the first 48 hours of the incident the hijackers released 67 non-Arab passengers and crew, suggesting that they intended a prolonged showdown with the Kuwaiti government.

Kuwait sent a negotiating team to Mashhad where it tried to enlist Iranian mediation. After the airliner eventually landed in Algeria with about 30 hostages on board on 13 April, Kuwaiti officials arrived in Algiers, prepared to talk directly to the hijackers. Through Algerian mediation the release of the hostages was finally negotiated but the hijackers were allowed to go free.

16 April Abu Jihad, military commander of the Palestine Liberation Organization (PLO) and a close friend of Yasser Arafat, is murdered at his villa in Tunisia. The murder was widely believed to have been the work of the Israeli secret service, Mossad. On 26 April Syria allowed Yasser Arafat to reopen the PLO offices in Damascus, following a meeting between Arafat and Syria's President Asad on 25 April.

18–20 April Iran suffers a severe defeat when Iraq recaptures the strategic Fao peninsula. On the same day Iranian naval vessels and oil platforms came under fire from the US naval presence in the Gulf. Nevertheless, on 20 April an Iraqi-proposed cease-fire began in the 'war of the cities'.

4 May Three French hostages are released in Lebanon by Islamic Jihad. The French government denied paying any ransom but began discussions on normalizing Franco-Iranian diplomatic relations and the repayment of $670 million in Iranian loans to France.

13 May The second round of voting in the Iranian Majlis (lower house) seems to confirm the growing strength of the radicals. On 12 September Prime Minister Hussein Mousavi received Majlis approval for 18 ministerial appointments, ending speculation of a serious rift between him and President Khamenei.

14 May Iraqi aircraft attack the Iranian oil terminal at Larak. Meanwhile, Iran began to lose further ground in the land war, claiming on 19 June that this was due to Iraq's heavy reliance on the use of chemical weapons. Iraq, Iran said, had taken Shalamche in the south by using chemical weapons.

15 May Soviet forces officially begin their withdrawal from Afghanistan.

8 June The emergency Arab summit in Algiers pledges all possible support to the Intifada (the Palestinian uprising in the West Bank). The summit was reported to have arranged $100 million a year in financial support to the PLO.

3 July Saudi Arabia orders at least $8,500 million worth of fighter aircraft, helicopters and minesweepers from Britain.

3 July US-Iranian relations reach an all-time low when the US warship *Vincennes* shoots down a civilian Iranian airliner over the Gulf, killing all 290 people aboard. The US pilot apparently mistook the airbus for an F-14 warplane. On 7 July in Tehran mourners shouted anti-US slogans. On 14 August it was announced that the US officer who ordered the shooting of the airbus was to get a 'mild reprimand'.

18 July In an astonishing turnabout Iran suddenly accepts UN Security Council resolution 598 calling for an immediate cease-fire in the Gulf war. The unconditional acceptance of the resolution came in a letter to the UN secretary-general, Perez de Cuellar, from President Khamenei, which was delivered in the early hours of 18 July. He wrote: 'The Islamic Republic of Iran, because of the importance it attaches to the lives of human beings and the establishment of justice and regional and international peace and security, accepts Security Council Resolution 598.'

The cease-fire started on 20 August. Ayatollah Khomeini remarked bitterly that the decision was made 'only on the basis of expediency. I renounced whatever I had said [in the past] only in the hope of God's blessing and satisfaction.' He continued: 'I repeat that accepting this [resolution] was more deadly for me than taking posion. I submit[ted] myself to God's will and drank this drink for His satisfaction.'

Freed from the constraints of war, Iraq was accused on 27 August of launching a week-long assault on Kurdish rebels. More than 50,000 Kurds fled to Turkey, claiming that chemical weapons had been used against them. It was widely felt that Khomeini's decision to end the war was motivated by the fear of further Iraqi chemical attacks.

On 9/10 July Iraq had regained territory in the Panjwin region in the northern sector and on 12 July in the Musian region in the southern sector of the war. On 17 July, the twentieth anniversary of the 1968 Ba'thist coup, Saddam Husayn had repeated his five-point peace plan which included a return by both countries to international borders.

31 July King Husayn of Jordan announces plans to cut legal and administrative ties with the Israeli-occupied West Bank, thereby formally accepting the PLO's aim of establishing an independent state in Palestine.

25 August The first face-to-face meetings between Iranian and Iraqi leaders takes place following the cease-fire of 20 August. The cease-fire followed Iran's agreement on 18 July to end the war. On 1 August a UN investigation had revealed that Iraq had made intensified use of chemical weapons in its military operations in the spring and the summer.

4 October The Kuwait Investment Office is ordered to halve its shareholding in the British Petroleum Company Ltd (BP) by Britain's Monopolies and Mergers Commission. The Kuwaiti government's 22 per cent stake in BP had been referred to the Commission on 4 May.

4 October Dubai's Fateh crude-oil price falls below $10 a barrel. OPEC's secretary-general, Dr Subroto, warned of a price collapse if OPEC quotas were ignored. A meeting of OPEC ministers from 20 to 22 October in Madrid failed to agree to limit production, with Iran and Iraq continuing to dispute quotas. OPEC production in October averaged 21.1 million barrels a day, the highest level for five years. At their Vienna meeting on 28 November OPEC members hammered out an agreement designed to push prices up to an $18-a-barrel target.

10 October The Palestine National Council decides to declare an independent Palestinian state and authorizes the PLO to transform itself into a provisional government. On 31 July King Husayn of Jordan had formally cut legal and administrative ties with the West Bank.

19 October Britain's Armilla Patrol announces that it is to cease escorting merchant ships through the Strait of Hormuz.

15 November In Algiers the Palestine National Council declares the creation of an independent Palestinian state in Gaza and the West Bank. The meeting also endorsed UN Security Council resolution 242 as the basis for a Middle East settlement, thus implicitly recognizing Israel and renouncing terrorism. However, Israel's 1/2 November elections gave a narrow victory to the right-wing parties, led by Yitzhak Shamir's Likud Party, which had promised tougher action against the Intifada. The Likud had gained one seat more than Shimon Peres' Labour Party. The PLO had described the result as 'a fatal blow for peace' and said it expected 'more intransigence, hate and terrorism with a Likud government'.

16 November Saudi Arabia holds England to a 1-1 draw in Riyadh. The result led to calls in England for the resignation of the England football manager, Bobby Robson.

17 November Benazir Bhutto wins the first democratic election in Pakistan for 11 years.

7 December In Stockholm the PLO chairman, Yasser Arafat, says he recognizes the existence of the state of Israel. On 9 December the first anniversary of the Palestinian Intifada was marked in the West Bank by a general strike and continued violence. So far about 329 Palestinians had died in the uprising. Earlier in December the US had refused to grant a visa to allow Arafat to address the UN at its New York headquarters. The UN promptly transferred the session to Geneva in order that he might address it as planned.

14 December In Geneva Yasser Arafat dramatically announces the PLO's recognition of the state of Israel and says that it renounces 'totally and absolutely . . . all forms of terrorism including individual, group and state terrorism.' He also accepted UN resolutions 242 and 338, recognizing Israel's right to exist within secure borders. A spokesman for the Israeli prime minister's office said that the US had been fooled by Arafat's 'cheap words'.

21 December A Pan Am jumbo jet crashes onto the Scottish town of Lockerbie killing all 259 passengers on board as well as at least 11 people on the ground. Early suspicions focused on the Popular Front for the Liberation of Palestine – General Command led by Ahmad Jibril who opposed the recent diplomatic moves of Yasser Arafat.

December Iraq has sent food poisoned with thallium to Kurdistan, affecting over 100 people of whom several died, according to an article in the London-based *Middle East International*. It had been suggested that an outbreak of typhoid fever in Sulaymaniyya in Kurdistan in September had been the result of a biological attack. Iraq was known to be developing biological weapons at Salman Pak south-east of Baghdad, and chemical weapons at Samarra, Baija, Al-Fallujah and Kerbala.

1 9 8 9

1 January A new Organization of Petroleum Exporting Countries (OPEC) agreement comes into force, limiting the output of the 13 member states to 18.5 million barrels a day.

20 January In his inaugural address, US President Bush signals his willingness to improve US relations with Iran if the latter frees the US hostages held in Lebanon.

31 January Eleven people are hanged in Iran: five women for prostitution, five Afghans for robbery and rape and another man for corruption.

In January the London-based Amnesty International published a report in which it claimed that 'thousands of prisoners have been executed since the establishment of the Islamic Republic of Iran in 1979, and political prisoners continue to be executed in secret, often following summary trials'. Amnesty said that other executions had been carried out in public. Among those shot hanged or stoned to death were 'juveniles, the elderly, real or alleged political opponents of the government, members of religious minorities, and prisoners convicted of drug abuse and other criminal offences. Thousands of prisoners have been executed in political cases after trials lasting only a few minutes. These trials contravene Iran's obligation as a party to the International Covenant on Civil and Political Rights to respect minimum international standards for a fair trial.'

Since the end of July 1988 Amnesty International had recorded over 1,000 names of political prisoners who had reportedly been executed. According to Amnesty the majority of the executed victims were supporters of the Iranian opposition groups including the Mujahedeen, the Tudeh (Communist) Party, the People's Fedayeen Organization of Iran, Rah-e Kargar and the Iran Communist Party, as well as the Kurdish opposition groups Komala and the Kurdistan Democratic Party (KDP) of Iran.

25 January A Bahraini steward on the airline Gulf Air is arrested at Bahrain International Airport on his return from Syria. According to the Committee for the Defence of Political Prisoners in Bahrain, he was then kept in Bahrain's al-Qal'a prison and later tortured to death.

5 February The French foreign minister, Roland Dumas, arrives in Tehran. It was the first visit of a French minister to Iran since the revolution in 1979. Dumas met Majlis Speaker Hashemi Rafsanjani, President Khamenei and the Iranian foreign minister, Dr Ali Akbar Velayati, to discuss the expansion of Franco-Iranian ties. Two days later, on 7 February, Velayati was in London meeting the British foreign secretary, Sir Geoffrey Howe. Although discussions centred on Afghanistan, Howe expressed Britain's continuing concern at the imprisonment of British businessman Roger Cooper who had been in Tehran's Evin Prison since 1985.

On 4 February President Mitterrand had met the United Arab Emirates (UAE) defence minister, Muhammad ibn Rashid al-Maktoum, in Dubai.

8 February The US *Los Angeles Times* reports an attempted *coup d'état* against the regime of Iraqi President Saddam Husayn in January. The report, based on intelligence and diplomatic sources as well as reports from Iraqi dissidents, said that the coup had been suppressed with ease.

9 February Kuwait's media receives instructions from the Ministry of Information prohibiting them from publishing or broadcasting any literary work or economic study written by Dr Su'ad al-Sabah or any interview with her, according to the London-based *Index on Censorship*. Dr al-Sabah is a Kuwaiti poet, writer and human rights activist. The ministry advised radio and television authorities against mentioning her name in any report or social or cultural event. The Kuwaiti authorities confiscated a number of Arab newspapers and magazines which contained interviews with her or published her studies or poetry. They gave no reason for the ban.

13 February Under an amnesty to mark the tenth anniversary of the Iranian revolution, 740 prisoners are freed. However, on 14 February 70 alleged drug smugglers were hanged.

14 February Ayatollah Khomeini issues a *fatwa* (edict) calling on Muslims to kill Salman Rushdie and his publishers for insulting Islam in his novel, *The Satanic Verses*, which had been published in London in September 1988. Khomeini called for the banning of the book worldwide and declared Rushdie an apostate. Rushdie and his wife, the American novelist Marianne Wiggins, left their north London house and went into hiding under armed guard. Khomeini appeared to be responding to the death of six people and the wounding of 100 in riots that had taken place in the Pakistani city of Islamabad on 12 February. On 15 February thousands of anti-Salman Rushdie demonstrators stoned the British embassy in Tehran while a senior Iranian cleric put a $1 million price on the novelist's head.

15 February The Iranian premier, Hussein Mousavi, arrives in Ankara for talks aimed at improving Iran's questionable relationship with Turkey. On 2 February Iran and Turkey had signed three border agreements designed primarily to prevent Kurdish guerrilla infiltration and heroin smuggling across their common border.

16 February The leaders of Egypt, Iraq, Jordan and North Yemen sign the agreement in Baghdad which formally brought into being the Arab Co-operation Council (ACC). The rationale of the new community, which was clearly influenced by the structure of the European Community, was that Egypt contained the largest population in the region, Iraq the largest army and Jordan the most dynamic private sector. The Yemen Arab Republic (North Yemen) was included at Iraq's request. Initial goals were to consolidate economic ties, boost trade and tourism, encourage the freer movement of goods and labour, set up joint ventures and encourage investment and regional trade. The council aimed eventually to establish a common customs union. It was hoped that the combination of Iraq's massive, battle-trained army and Egypt's well-developed armaments industry would give the ACC powerful military muscle.

Observers pointed out that the Saudis must have welcomed Iraq's adhesion which eliminated any possibility of its joining the Gulf Co-operation Council (GCC) and posing as a rival. Nevertheless, they remained conscious of Iraq as a competitor for regional power. They cannot have welcomed North Yemen's adhesion and must have seen this as a threat to their influence over their southern neighbour, particularly at a time when it was seeking unity with South Yemen and was making dramatic oil finds.

17 February Iran's President Ali Khamenei suggests that the British writer Salman Rushdie may be pardoned if he repents of his novel, *The Satanic Verses*, which Muslims consider profane and which had earned a death sentence from Ayatollah Khomeini. On 18 February Rushdie expressed 'profound regret' that the book had distressed Muslims. However, the Iranian government said the statement fell short of the public repentence required for a pardon and on 19 February Khomeini renewed his *fatwa* ordering the death sentence and declaring it every Muslim's duty to send Rushdie to Hell.

On 21 February the 12 European Economic Community (EEC) countries recalled their ambassadors and suspended high-level contacts with Iran. Iran responded by recalling its own ambassadors from EEC countries and Britain counter-responded by ordering the Iranian chargé d'affaires out of Britain. On 22 February President Khamenei said that an 'arrow of retribution' had been fired at Rushdie. Meanwhile, President Mitterrand of France denounced the death threats as 'absolute evil'. Several well-known US writers read statements supporting Rushdie and in protest against bookstore chains which had ceased selling the book. Khomeini said that the Rushdie affair was a godsend to Iran and that 'the world of arrogance and barbarism unveiled its true face of chronic enmity against Islam in the Rushdie affair'. He added: 'As long as I am alive, I will not let the government fall to the liberals. I will cut off the influence of American and Soviet agents in all fields.'

On 23 February publishers in France and West Germany reversed the stand they had taken by announcing that they would, after all, go ahead with the publication of *The Satanic Verses*.

On 24 February Indian police shot dead 12 Muslim anti-Rushdie demonstrators in Bombay and on 26 February a bomb attack on the British Council Library in Karachi killed a Pakistani security guard.

On 25 February Iran cancelled a British trade exhibition, planned for Tehran in March, over the Rushdie affair. On 28 February the Iranian Majlis (lower house) voted to break diplomatic relations with Britain if it did not change its stand (by condemning and banning the book) within a week.

26 February A delegation from the Kuwait Fund for Arab Economic Development signs an agreement in Damascus to lend Syria $21.5 million to finance an irrigation dam.

27 February Iraqi President Saddam Husayn receives the Jordanian premier, Zaid al-Rifai, in Baghdad while the Iraqi foreign minister, Tariq Aziz, visits Bahrain. The visits marked the start of a new Iraqi diplomatic offensive aimed at bolstering ties between the newly-formed Arab Co-operation Council (ACC) and other Arab regional blocs. On 28 February Tariq Aziz met King Hasan of Morocco in Marrakash where they discussed the ACC and the Maghreb Union as well as bilateral ties. On the same day Iraq's deputy premier, Taha Yasin Ramadan, arrived in Ankara to discuss the expansion of ties between Iraq and Turkey. The Turkish finance minister told journalists that trade beteen Iraq and Turkey had reached $2,400 million in 1988.

2 March The British foreign secretary, Sir Geoffrey Howe, says that he understands the hurt feelings of Muslims in Britain and that he finds *The Satanic Verses* offensive to British society as well, but Britain would not consider normalizing relations with Iran 'unless the Ayatollah abandons his threat of murder and incitement to violence against Salman Rushdie and his publishers'. He added: 'The only link between the book and the British government is our commitment to the principle of free speech. We don't think that principle can be set aside, and certainly should not be overridden by a threat to murder or incitement to violence.'

On 7 March Iran broke diplomatic relations with Britain over the Rushdie affair, the first time since the Anglo-Iranian oil crisis of 1951–53.

On 8 March *Moscow News* published a petition signed by more than a dozen Soviet intellectuals including Andrei Sakharov, appealing to Khomeini to show 'clemency' towards Salman Rushdie. One of the signatories was Roald Sagdeiev, an adviser to President Gorbachev, who said that such clemency 'would be in accordance with the precept of Jesus and Muhammad'.

On 16 March at its meeting in Riyadh the Islamic Conference Organization (ICO) declared Salman Rushdie an apostate and *The Satanic Verses* blasphemous against Islam. The statement said that the book 'transgresses all norms of civility and decency and is a deliberate attempt to malign Islam and venerated Islamic personalities'.

3 March The former US National Security adviser, Robert McFarlane, becomes the first former Reagan aide sentenced in the Irangate scandal. McFarlane was sentenced to two years probation. The trial of Oliver North had started on 21 February after Attorney-General Richard Thornburgh and independent counsel Lawrence Walsh had reached an agreement on how to handle the disclosure of classified information.

13 March A seven-hour exchange of fire takes places on the southern front between Iraqi and Iranian forces. Each side blamed the other for starting it.

13 March The Iranian Interior Ministry grants official recognition to two more political parties, the Combatant Clergymen's Party and the Women's Society of the Islamic Republic of Iran led by Khomeini's daughter.

15 March Kuwait's state prosecutor charges 33 people with plotting to overthrow the state.
 The UN Human Rights Commission fails to condemn Iraq for chemical weapons abuse. On the first anniversary of the Iraqi army's attack on the village of Halabja in Iraqi Kurdistan in which up to 6,000 civilians are said to have died, the Commission failed to criticize Iraq after India and Yugoslavia had led support for Iraq's successful proposal not to raise the subject at the Commission's annual meeting in Geneva.

20 March European Economic Community (EEC) foreign ministers decide that member states are free to send ambassadors back to Tehran. The 12 EEC countries had pulled their ambassadors out in response to Ayatollah Khomeini's death sentence on the British author Salman Rushdie for his book *The Satanic Verses*.
 On 22 March nine more Iranians were expelled from Britain. Most were students. The order brought to 18 the total number of students compelled to leave Britain since the start of the dispute. Many of those expelled had been in Britain since before the Iranian revolution of February 1979.
 On 27 March the British home secretary (interior minister), Douglas Hurd, began a ten-day tour of the Gulf states in Bahrain. He was also to visit Kuwait, Oman and Saudi Arabia to discuss 'security co-operation and regional developments.'

28 March Ayatollah Hussein Ali Montazeri is forced to resign as Khomeini's designated successor because he is regarded as susceptible to counter-revolutionary influences.

29 March Iraq agrees to pay damages for the deaths of 37 US sailors killed when the frigate USS *Stark* was struck by an Iraqi Exocet missile in the Gulf in May 1987.

30 March Iran orders the Swiss consul in Tehran to leave the country for engaging in 'activities incompatible with diplomatic norms'. Switzerland had maintained normal relations with Iran, where it represented US interests, since the revolution in 1979.

30 March At a meeting in the Omani capital Muscat, Arabsat, the Arab League satellite communications organization, re-admits Egypt. Egypt had been expelled after its peace treaty with Israel in 1979.

1 April Elections to Iraq's third National Assembly are held.

3 April Turkey recalls its ambassador from Tehran in a dispute over what Iran regarded as Turkish interference in its affairs. Iran followed suit later in the day by recalling its ambassador from Ankara.

6 April Eighteen Britons are expelled from Iran in retaliation for the British expulsion of a number of Iranians as a result of the Salman Rushdie dispute. On 25 April a further 18 Britons were expelled.

6 April Sixty-six alleged drug dealers are hanged in Iran. A total of 379 people had been hanged as alleged drug dealers so far in 1989. On 22 May a further 29 were hanged in public in several Iranian towns.

4 May Oliver North is convicted on 3 out of 12 charges connected with the 'Irangate' affair. (See 3 March.)

6 May Baghdad radio announces that Iraq's defence minister, Adnan Khairallah Tulfa, has been killed in a helicopter crash in a sandstorm on 5 May. Khairallah was a key member of Iraq's ruling Ba'thist elite and President Saddam Husayn's maternal cousin and brother-in-law. His wife was the daughter of the former president, Ahmad Hasan al-Bakr, and his sister was Saddam Husayn's wife. Baghdad gossip suggested that he was murdered for taking his sister's side in a quarrel within Husayn's family. Adnan's father, Khairallah Tulfa, was mayor of Baghdad. Adnan was replaced as defence minister by General Abd al-Jabbar Khalil al-Shanshal.

8 May Iran's President Khamenei arrives in Peking on a 'bridge-building mission'. Apart from increased co-operation in various areas of industry and technology, the Chinese agreed to double their imports of Iranian oil to two million tons. China was Iran's sixth biggest trading partner. Mutual trade was worth $600 million.

On 3 March the Chinese vice-premier, Tian Ji Yun, had visited Tehran where he announced China's interest in helping Iran's post-war reconstruction.

10 May A West German magazine claims it has obtained a copy of 'secret minutes' of a meeting in July 1988 at which Ayatollah Khomeini ordered the bombing of Pan Am flight 103 which blew up over the Scottish town of Lockerbie in December 1988. The magazine's claim, reported in the London-based Middle East International, added that the minutes showed that a Palestinian group had been paid £412,000 for planting the bomb. Reliable observers condemned the report as an invention.

22 May UN Reliefs and Works Agency (UNRWA) Commissioner-General Giacomelli, on a visit to Kuwait, warns that the agency is short of funds. Nevertheless Kuwait's total contribution of $6.5 million was the largest of the total Arab states' 1988 contribution of $20 million.

23 May Egypt attends the Arab summit conference at Casablanca. Libya's President Mu'ammar Qadhafi also attended, indicating Libya's acceptance of Egypt, a long-time foe. On 24 May Qadhafi and Egypt's President Mubarak had talks for the first time since 1977. On 13 May Egypt had been re-admitted to the Organization of Arab Petroleum Exporting Countries (OAPEC).

25 May Two Canadians and a Swede are arrested in the US, charged with trying to ship over $600 million worth of arms and munitions to Iran. The shipment was said to have included C-130 aircraft parts, parts for Phantom jets and recoilless rifles. The charges against the three men included violating the US Arms Export Control Act.

3 June Ayatollah (now considered Imam) Khomeini, Iran's supreme spiritual leader, dies of a heart attack in Tehran. President Khamenei was named as his successor, making him both president (until October) and Vali-e Faqih or spiritual leader. He promised to uphold Khomeini's Islamic vision. On 8 June the Iranian Majlis speaker, Hashemi Rafsanjani, announced his candidacy for the 18 August presidential election.

Khomeini's death was officially announced at 7.00am on 4 June, 12 days after he had been admitted to hospital for surgery to stop intestinal bleeding. He was buried on 6 June amid scenes of almost hysterical public grief in Iran. The burial itself had to be delayed because the vehicle carrying the body could not make its way through the millions barring the way to Tehran's Behesht-e Zahra cemetery. The body had been lifted to the burial place by helicopter where mourners tore apart its white shroud. The corpse, which at one stage fell onto the ground, was flown out again to be dressed in a new shroud before being flown back for the final burial on 6 June. At least eight people died and some 500 were injured in the crush that took place at the burial.

11 June Continuing its wide-ranging negotiations for an ever-more sophisticated armoury, Saudi Arabia signs a major arms co-operation deal with France worth an estimated $2,700 million. According to the deal, France would supply frigates and Mistral surface-to-air missiles to Saudi Arabia. On 29 May the Saudi defence minister, Prince Sultan ibn Abd al-Aziz, started a five-day visit to Britain to discuss defence co-operation. He also discussed the outcome of the Casablanca Summit in meetings with Prime Minister Margaret Thatcher and her foreign minister, Sir Geoffrey Howe.

On 3 July Saudi Arabia signed its first commercial loan, worth $660 million, with eight Saudi banks.

17 June The Arab Co-operation Council (ACC) supports Iraq's claim to both banks of the Shatt al-Arab waterway and calls on the UN to clear the waterway of war debris.

19–23 June The Iranian Majlis speaker, Hashemi Rafsanjani, visits the Soviet Union to finalize a massive financial package. The deal involved $2,000 million of Soviet financing for projects worth at least $6,000 million over the next decade, according to the London-based Middle East Economic Digest (MEED). A co-operation pact was also signed whereby the Soviet Union would provide most of Iran's power generation over the coming decade.

On 31 May Iran and Bulgaria had signed trade deals worth over $200 million. Bulgaria had said that it was willing to modernize Iran's defence industries.

23 June Michel Aflaq, founder of the Ba'th Party, dies in Paris, aged 79 (see Biographies). He was to be buried in Baghdad. Born in Syria, Aflaq had fled to Baghdad in 1968.

24 June Kuwait's State Security Court sentences 22 people to up to 15 years' imprisonment for allegedly plotting to overthrow the government. Eleven other defendants were acquitted. The 33 had been charged on 15 March. Those charged, of whom 13 were still free, included 15 foreign nationals and a number of professionals, police and government officials. All were thought to be Shi'is.

25 June A further 14 alleged drug dealers are hanged in the Iranian city of Mashhad, bringing to 858 the total number of people who had been executed so far in Iran during 1989, 690 of them for drugs-related offences. On 17 June Iran had executed 15 alleged drug traffickers in a public execution in Bakhtaran, and on 11 June 34 people had been hanged in public executions in Tehran and Tabriz after being convicted of drug smuggling. On 22 May 29 alleged drug traffickers had been hanged in several Iranian towns in public executions.

On 6 April 66 alleged drug dealers had been hanged in Tehran, bringing to a total of 379 people accused of being drug dealers executed so far in 1989.

On 25 April 15 Iranians were reported to have been stoned to death in the southern port of Bushehr. The victims, of whom 12 were prostitutes, were executed in a public ceremony at a sports stadium. The judge who presided over what had been the biggest public mass execution in Iran since the revolution in 1979, recommended the use of smaller stones to prolong the agony of the victims.

In May a document prepared by Ayatollah Khomeini's son, Ahmad, purported to be correspondence between his father and Ayatollah Hussein Ali Montazeri, formerly Khomeini's spiritual heir and latterly a critic of the government, indicated that Montazeri's followers had been executed for smuggling weapons to the 1986 *hajj* (pilgrimage) to Mecca. The document was entitled *The Book of Sufferings*. Critics of the regime maintained that many of the so-called 'drugs smugglers' recently executed in Iran were followers of Montazeri. In October 1988 Montazeri had given a fiery speech attacking recent spates of execution and torture and attacking the government's economic policies. In 1987 he had interceded for Mehdi Hashemi, the brother of his son-in-law, who was arrested during the 'Irangate scandal' and executed on 28 September 1987. Montazeri's followers were reported, probably wrongly, to have been behind an attack on the US National Security Adviser McFarlane team's hotel in Tehran in 1982 during the team's curious attempt to exchange weapons for US hostages in Beirut. In mid-1986 Montazeri had successfully called for the release of prisoners in Iranian jails not considered a threat to the regime.

28 June Kuwait and the Soviet Union sign a protocol for wide-ranging economic and technical co-operation. In addition to joint oil, gas and electrical projects, the accord prepared the way for Soviet aid to halt Kuwait's desertification. It also involved considerable Kuwaiti investment in the Soviet Union.

On 29 May Kuwait had signed a defence contract with Yugoslavia for the supply of what the two sides called 'sophisticated military equipment'.

5 July A US judge, Gerhard Gesell, imposes a three-year suspended sentence, two years of probation and a $150,000 fine on Oliver North, the ex-marine lieutenant-colonel and former White House aide at the centre of the 'Irangate' arms-for-hostages scandal. The lenient sentence came as a relief to the White House where President Bush would be spared a campaign for a presidential pardon to keep North out of prison by the conservative lobby which claimed that 'his only crime was patriotism'.

10 July Two bombs explode in Mecca during the *hajj* (pilgrimage), killing one Pakistani *hajji* (pilgrim) and wounding 16 others. The Iranian government indicated its suspicions that Saudi Arabia and the US were responsible.

10 July In Qatar's first government reshuffle since 1978, seven ministers are replaced and 11 newcomers are appointed to a 16-member cabinet.

17 July The US offers to pay compensation of up to $200,000 to each of the victims from the Iranian airliner shot down by US forces in the Gulf on 3 July 1988. On 10 May a West

German magazine had 'claimed' that it had obtained a copy of the 'secret minutes' from a meeting in July 1988 at which Ayatollah Khomeini had ordered the bombing of the Pan Am flight 103 which blew up over Scotland in December 1988. According to the so-called minutes, a Palestinian group was paid £412,000 for planting the bomb. Many believed that the bombing had been in revenge for the 3 July tragedy (see 10 May) but others denied this.

18 July The UAE head of state, Shaikh Zayed ibn Sultan al-Nahayan, begins a four-day state visit to Britain. At a dinner at Buckingham Palace, he encouraged a deeper British involvement in solving the problems of Palestine and Lebanon. He was visited at Buckingham Palace by the PLO's Bassam Abu Sharif who had met Jordan's King Husayn in London earlier in the day. Abu Sharif's visit to Queen Elizabeth's palace created some controversy among Zionists in Britain.

20 July According to a statement released by the Committee for the Defence of Human Rights in Saudi Arabia, a Saudi woman was arrested on 20 July and subsequently killed. Zahra Hasan Habib Alnasie, according to the report in the London-based *Index on Censorship*, was arrested at the Jordanian-Saudi border and tortured to death by the Saudi secret police. She had in her possession a book containing Shi'i prayers, according to the report.

24 July Twenty-three alleged drug traffickers are hanged in Iran, bringing the total number of executions in Iran in 1989 to 896, 713 of them for alleged drugs-related offences.

On 17 July 15 senior army and Revolutionary Guard officers were reportedly executed in Iran. They had been accused of plotting to overthrow the Islamic Republic and of collaborating with the US. According to the reports Montazeri's supporters saw the executions as a further step in the campaign to isolate him in the Iranian leadership power struggle.

27 July Britain stops the proposed sale to Iraq by British Aerospace of 60 Hawk jet aircraft. The decision was taken on British Foreign Office advice that Britain should abide by the embargo on arms sales to both Iraq and Iran. The deal was worth £300 million.

28 July The speaker of Iran's Majlis, Hashemi Rafsanjani, is elected Iran's new president as expected. He won 15.5 million of the 16.4 million votes cast. However, contrary to expectations, he did not achieve a land-slide mandate. A third of the electorate did not vote at all. The only other candidate, Dr Abbas Sheybani, unexpectedly won over half a million votes. Every incentive had been made to encourage people to vote, with rumours that anyone whose identity card was not stamped might be considered a 'counter-revolutionary'. Voting had been widely pronounced a religious duty by the government.

In his acceptance speech on 3 August, Rafsanjani reassured the radicals that he would not depart from the late Imam Khomeini's policies but stressed the importance of a healthy economy, thus reassuring the moderates. Rafsanjani also offered to help free the US hostages in Lebanon on condition that the US responded reasonably to his attempts.

On 20 August the Majlis gave blanket approval to all 22 members of Rafsanjani's new cabinet which was dominated by young technocrats, rather than clerics. Pragmatism and economic reform were to be the hallmarks of the new government.

30 July Iran's radical interior minister, Hojatolislam Ali Akbar Mohtashami, tells a press conference that 'Hizbullah groups from all over the world are marching in revenge for Shaikh Obeid's abduction.' Earlier, the Iranian caretaker prime minister, Hussein Mousavi, had urged all Muslim revolutionary forces to strike at US and Israeli interests, pointing out that the Israeli kidnapping of Shaikh Abd al-Karim Obeid 'might endanger the life of US and Western hostages'. However, President Rafsanjani was reported to have been against such threats and favoured a 'wait and see' attitude. The Israelis had kidnapped Shaikh Obeid from the Lebanese Shi'i village of Jibshit on the night of 27/28 July.

On 31 July the Iranian foreign minister, Dr Ali Akbar Velayati, stated that the decision to hang US Marine Lieutenant-Colonel William Higgins in revenge for Shaikh Obeid's abduction was taken by Hizbullah and had 'nothing to do with Iran'. William Higgins, a UN truce observer, had been kidnapped in February 1988 near the Lebanese port of Tyre. Iran's soft line was clearly connected with the visit on 31 July of the Soviet foreign minister, Edward Shevardnadze, the first official visitor to come to Iran since Rafsanjani's election to the presidency.

31 July The Bahraini foreign minister, Shiakh Muhammad al-Khalifa, begins a four-day visit to the US. He discussed arms sales with the defence secretary, Richard Cheney, and was later to meet President Bush and US Secretary of State Baker.

5 August The governor of Jordan's central bank, Said Nabulsi, confirms that the Saudi government has deposited $200 million to boost Jordan's economy. Jordan's foreign debt had recently been estimated at $6,500 million.

15 August Kuwait receives the first of three consignments of armoured personnel carriers manufactured by Egypt's state-owned Arab Organization for Industrialization.

17 August Up to 700 people die in an explosion at a military establishment near Baghdad.

8 September Kurdish guerrillas of the Kurdish Democratic Party of Iran (KDPI) claim to have killed 76 Iranian soldiers in a series of attacks over the previous two days. In a campaign over the previous three weeks the KDPI claimed to have killed a total of 172 Iranian troops. The group relaunched its military campaign after the assassination of its leader Abd al-Rahman Qassemlou by the Iranians in Vienna in July during negotiations with an Iranian official. On 3 August guerrillas of Komala, Iran's Kurdish Communist organization, captured the main road between Sanandaj and Saqqez in Iran's Kurdistan province. They held onto the road for several hours for the second time in seven days.

11 September The French interior minister, Pierre Joxe, ends three days of talks with his Kuwaiti counterpart, Shaikh Salem al-Sabah in Kuwait. They signed a protocol on security co-operation which covered the exchange of information on terrorism and drug-trafficking as well as co-operation on internal security.

18 September Kuwaiti coastguards apprehend 55 people attempting to land at two sites on the coast in order to enter Kuwait illegally.

20 September A foreigners' social club in Baghdad is attacked with grenades which explode, injuring 25 foreigners, one seriously.

21 September Britain's Sunday newspaper *The Observer* reports that one of its correspondents is being held incommunicado in Iraq. Farzad Bazoft, an Iranian with British travel documents, was detained at Baghdad airport on 15 September as he was about to board a plane to London. On 7 October Daphne Parish, a British nurse working in Baghdad, was arrested and denied consular access. No charges were made but the British embassy believed that her detention was connected with the arrest of Bazoft. Both were accused of espionage on 15 October.

7 October Iraq's finance and agriculture ministers are sacked. No explanation was given.

16 October A Saudi diplomat, Abd al-Rahman Shurawi, loses both his legs in a car bomb attack in Ankara. No one claimed responsibility.

16 October In Kuwait, four Kuwaiti actors and a director are indicted for insulting Islam. Abd al-Husayn Abd al-Rida, Sa'd Faraj, Khaled al-Nafisi and Muhammad al-Surayib took part in the play *Hadha Sayf* ('This is a Sword'), directed by Abd al-Amir al-Turki. The play had opened in Kuwait in May 1988 but had been banned by the government after 36 nights.

22 October The EEC outlines its proposals for a free trade deal with the GCC states. However, on 7 November the EEC decided to end duty-free benefits for six Saudi petrochemicals exports.

29 October The UAE football team qualifies for the finals of the 1990 World Cup in Italy at the expense of Saudi Arabia and Qatar. On 12 September Iran and Iraq had agreed to play each other in a football tournament to be held in Kuwait. The tournament was part of the Friendship and Peace Games which involved the 40 member-states of the Islamic Conference Organization (ICO).

1 November Bahrain shows a massive budget deficit, indicating the effects of decreasing oil revenues. The Bahrain Monetary Agency issued its annual report which showed that the country's budget deficit had grown from a 1987 figure of $13,200 million to $225,000 million at the end of 1988.

1 November Iran's Majlis approves a bill allowing the arrest of US citizens abroad for trial in Iran in reaction to a similar measured announced by the US.

3 November Eight people are executed in Saudi Arabia for rape, murder and drug trafficking. Two were Pakistani nationals. According to official sources, 71 people had been executed so far in 1989. On 20 October two people were beheaded in Saudi Arabia after being convicted of murder, and on 30 September 10 people were executed in the kingdom after being convicted of murder, rape, abduction or robbery.

3 November The US and Iran sign an agreement giving Iran early access to a $818-million account held by the Bank of England since 1981, according to MEED.

4 November Four men are hanged in Tehran as spies for the US. The hangings took place at a public ceremony to mark the tenth anniversary of the seizure of the US embassy. On 11 November 20 people were executed publicly in several Iranian cities in Iran after being convicted of alleged drug trafficking.

5 November At a Muscat meeting, GCC information ministers issue a communiqué supporting 'Iraq's historic rights over the Shatt al-Arab' waterway.

8 November In Jordan's first general election since 1967, Islamic fundamentalists win over one-third of the seats in the 80-member parliament.

26 November The amir of Kuwait refuses to accept a petition signed by over 20,000 Kuwaiti citizens calling for the reopening of the National Assembly which had been suspended in 1986.

26 November The Bahraini crown prince and defence minister, Shaikh Hamad ibn Isa al-Khalifa, meets the visiting Iraqi defence minister, Abd al-Jabar Shanshal, to discuss military co-operation.

27 November The British government arranges a bank loan of £2,000 million to finance the continuation of the al-Yamama offset defence contract with Saudi Arabia, says the London-based journal, *Middle East International*. The loan, through British commercial banks backed by Britain's Export Credit Guarantee Department, was to make up for shortfalls in payment by the Saudis. The deal, worth over £15,000 million, involved the sale of 100 Tornado fighter planes by a consortium of British manufacturers to the Saudi government in return for a continuous supply of crude oil. However, the recent fall in oil prices had reduced the cash flow from the sale of Saudi oil to a level which was threatening to halt delivery of the planes to the kingdom.

30 November In Aden an agreement aimed at ultimate unification is signed by the North Yemeni president, Ali Abdullah Saleh, and the South Yemeni president, Ali Salem al-Beidh. In May a series of joint commissions to examine various aspects of integration had been established.

On 4 December the junior minister at the British Foreign Office, William Waldegrave, arrived in Aden for the first visit by a British minister since South Yemen gained its independence from Britain in 1967. He signed an agreement with South Yemen for British technical assistance.

7 December Iraq's minister for civil and military industries, Brigadier Husayn Kamil, announces that Iraq has launched its first space rocket. The missile was named *Tammuz* (July) and was, he said, a three-stage, 48-ton rocket, 25 metres in length. He added that Iraq had also developed a second, long-range surface-to-surface missile called A'bid (worshipper) which had a range of 1,243 miles (2,000 kilometres). In the face of widespread scepticism, US sources confirmed the launch of the Tammuz rocket. Iraq had proved earlier claims of military developments at its April defence exhibition in Baghdad.

12 December Iraq and Bahrain sign a non-aggression pact in Manama. It was thought to be similar to the agreement signed between Iraq and Saudi Arabia in March.

21 December The annual four-day GCC summit ends in Muscat without the expected reconciliatory references to Iran.

23 December Saudi Arabia and Oman have agreed on the demarcation of their border, according to a Saudi Press Agency report. The agreement was signed by King Fahd and Sultan Qaboos in Muscat, following the GCC summit. Tension along the border had come to a head in October, with reports of armed clashes and Saudi support for Omani opposition groups.

1 9 9 0

8 January Police use riot shields and truncheons to break up a pro-democracy meeting at the house of former parliamentarian Ahmad Shraihan in Kuwait's Jahra suburb. It was called by Kuwaitis demanding the restoration of parliament which had been dissolved in July 1986. Witnesses said that 10,000–15,000 people took part. The Kuwaiti information minister, Shaikh Jaber Mubarak al-Hamad al-Sabah, later said: 'The old assembly will not return ... Maybe we can find something that is more appropriate.'

9 January The second stage of the Iraqi crude-oil pipeline across Saudi Arabia is officially opened. Its capacity was to reach 1.65 million barrels a day by the end of January.

11 January Amnesty International publishes a 27-page report on human rights abuses in Saudi Arabia. The report claimed that more than 700 political prisoners had been detained without trial over the past seven years. It listed the names of 66 political prisoners it believed were held in various prisons in the kingdom, pointing out that most of the detainees were Shi'is. Amnesty claimed that the Saudi authorities had never responded to any of its complaints about abuses over the seven-year period until they refuted the present report.

12 January The Iranian president, Hashemi Rafsanjani, defends his plans to encourage foreign investment in Iran and criticizes the 'narrow-mindedness of some government operatives'. One Majlis (lower house) member described foreign capital as a 'poisoned gift'. In early January Ayatollah Hussein Ali Montazeri had attacked over-dependence on foreign finance. On 9 January the Majlis had approved a $394,000 million five-year development and reconstruction plan aimed at reducing the rate of inflation from 28.6 per cent in 1989 to 8.9 per cent, creating two million jobs and achieving an annual growth rate of 8 per cent.

The plan provided for $27,000 million in foreign credits and the gradual privatization of the economy. Hundreds of state-owned enterprises which had been nationalized or confiscated after the revolution were being sold through Tehran's resurrected stock exchange. Observers saw the economy as the key to Rafsanjani's political survival.

17 January Iran's spiritual leader, Ayatollah Khamenei, praises the Soviet leadership for giving Soviet Muslims religious freedom but warns it not to treat them harshly. In December Muslims from Soviet Azerbayjan (Azeris) had torn down border fences and demanded access into Iran. On 15 January Moscow had sent extra troops to prevent clashes between Muslim Azeris and Christian Armenians. Iran had tried to maintain its improving relations with the Soviet Union by playing a low-key role in its support for the Soviet Azeris.

17 January Kuwait's crown prince and prime minister, Shaikh Sa'd al-Abdullah al-Salem al-Sabah, says that the leadership wants popular participation, but in 'a new form'. The government maintained that the parliament dissolved in July 1986 had created factionalism. However, critics pointed out that the 50-member parliament had, in fact, drawn attention to information that the government wanted to remain secret. On 15 January protesters had held a meeting at the house of Faisal al-Sani, a member of the dissolved parliament. A similar meeting in January had been broken up by the police.

20 January The Palestine Liberation Organization (PLO) chairman, Yasser Arafat, arrives in Muscat for a two-day visit to Oman which ends in an announcement that a Palestinian embassy will be established in the sultanate.

20 January At a joint meeting of the councils of ministers of the two Yemens held in San'a, decisions are taken to merge certain government bodies and to set up 33 ministries of the proposed united Yemeni state. On 26 December South Yemen had given a general pardon to political dissidents.

25 January The Organization of Arab Petroleum Exporting Countries (OAPEC) names the senior Saudi civil servant, Abd al-Aziz al-Turaiki, as its new secretary-general. The post had been vacant since the resignation in 1987 of the Libyan Ali Atiqa.

26 January Iraq's 1989 oil revenues are estimated at $15,000 million, higher than expected, says the London-based Middle East Economic Digest (MEED). MEED also quoted the British company Employment Conditions Abroad as saying that it ranked Iraq as the most expensive country in the world.

28 January The French defence minister, Jean-Paul Chevenement, begins a two-day visit to Baghdad. In his talks with President Saddam Husayn and with Iraq's vice-president, its defence minister and its minister for civil and military industry, he discussed co-operation with France in Iraq's development of new industrial projects. Central to the discussions was believed to be Iraq's request to manufacture French Alpha aircraft and AS-30L aerial missiles under licence in Iraq, according to the London-based journal Middle East International.

4 February Sharjah Television announces that the ruler of Sharjah, Shaikh Sultan ibn Muhammad al-Qasimi, has formally removed from office his successor and elder brother, Shaikh Abd al-Aziz. Shaikh Abd al-Aziz had led an unsuccessful attempt to oust the ruler in June 1987 and had only been given his titles when Abu Dhabi and Dubai intervened to end the rift between the two brothers.

7 February Kuwait's crown prince and prime minister, Shaikh Sa'd al-Abdullah al-Salem al-Sabah, meets opposition members of Kuwait's dissolved parliament. It was the first official contact between the two sides since the pro-democracy movement became highly active in December 1989. The speaker of the dissolved parliament, Ahmad Abd al-Aziz al-Sa'doun said that the meeting was positive. The 32 opposition members had asked to meet the amir after he had said in a televised address on 20 January that 'the door of dialogue is open'. Several regular Monday protest meetings called by members of the deposed parliament had been broken up by police. In return for setting a date for new elections, the amir was said to want an increase in his constitutional powers.

11 February The US human rights group Middle East Watch issues a 235-page report on Iraq in which it describes the Iraqi government as 'one of the most brutal and repressive regimes in power today'. The report criticized US and Western governments for failing to denounce Iraqi policies in order to protect their economic relations with Baghdad.

On 5 January the London-based Organization for Human Rights in Iraq had issued a statement that between 10 and 23 January Iraqi forces had moved against 30 towns and villages in Basra, Nasiriyya and Amara governorates in south-eastern Iraq and evicted their populations. Ten thousand people were reported killed or wounded in the operation which was seen as part of Iraq's plan to create a 'cordon sanitaire' 19 miles (31 kilometres) wide along the frontier with Iran. It followed Iraq's major offensive against the Kurdish north in 1989.

7 February The amir of Qatar, Shaikh Khalifa ibn Hamad al-Thani, meets the British prime minister, Margaret Thatcher, during a one-day visit to London.

9 February In London the visiting Iranian cleric Ayatollah Mahdavi-Kani gives the go-ahead to rebuild Iran's embassy in London. The embassy had been badly damaged during the attack on it by the British Special Air Service (SAS) in order to lift a siege in 1980. In June 1988, after a seven-year battle in the courts, Britain had agreed to pay over £1.8 million towards the cost of repairs.

16 February The Iranian government claims to have killed Hajj Baluch Shahbakhsh, the leader of a group of bandits which controls the illicit opium trade in Baluchistan.

21 February A report published by the London-based human rights organization, Amnesty International, says that it fears that 10 Kuwaiti Shi'is may have been tortured after being arrested on 14 and 18 February.

25 February Two Iranian gunboats attack Kuwaiti trawlers in the Gulf and seize two crew members, according to Kuwait's newspaper *al-Watan*. On 14 February Kuwait had arrested a number of Shi'is on charges of involvement in the bomb attacks in Mecca during the 1989 *hajj*, according to the Islamic Revolutionary News Agency. In September 1989 Saudi Arabia had executed 16 Kuwaitis for the bombings.

25 February Following talks in Riyadh between the North Yemeni president, Ali Abdullah Saleh, and Saudi Arabia's King Fahd, the king is quoted as saying that he backs Yemeni unity 'absolutely and without reservation'. On 30 January South Yemen had announced that it had released all its remaining political prisoners, including supporters of the former president, Ali Nasr Muhammad.

27 February A UN human rights commission report moderates its criticisms of Iran's treatment of prisoners which had been based almost entirely on reports by exiled opposition groups. The UN envoy, Reynaldo Galiunco Pohl, issued his report after a ten-day visit to Iran in late January. His requests for visits had been rejected since 1984. He said he had met four people whom opposition contacts had claimed had been executed and said that reports of political prisoners being executed as 'drugs' smugglers' appeared to him to be mere speculation. He strongly denied claims by the leftist-Islamic Mujahedeen-e khalq that he had delivered a mild report in exchange for Iran's help in gaining the release of Western hostages in Beirut. According to MEED, the Baghdad-based Mujahedeen claimed that 90,000 people had been executed and 150,000 imprisoned in Iran since the revolution.

On 16 February an all-party group of 248 British MPs had signed a statement urging the UN to expel Iran for its repression of human rights. Earlier, a petition had been received by the European Parliament in Strasbourg calling for the UN to recognize the Mujahedeen as Iran's legitimate government.

28 February Iraq's Revolutionary Command Council (RCC) issues a decree that men who kill close female blood relatives for committing adultery will not be punished. According to the Baghdad newspaper, *Al-Ittihad*, the amendment to the law, which did not apply to men who killed their wives, was aimed at improving moral standards in Iraq.

3 March Iraq's national football team has withdrawn from the tenth Arab Gulf Cup tournament in Kuwait, the Iraqi Football Association (IFA) says. Iraq had won the cup three times and been expected to retain it. The IFA said that Saudi Arabia – which had already withdrawn from the competition – had warned Iraq not to play because of 'an unhealthy atmosphere' in Kuwait.

7 March The director of the Soviet Foreign Ministry's Middle East department, Vladimar Polyakov, visits Saudi Arabia en route from Cairo to San'a. He was the first senior Soviet official to visit Saudi Arabia since Riyadh suspended relations with the Soviet Union in 1938. Saudi Arabia and Bahrain were the only Arab states not to have diplomatic ties with the Soviet Union. On 3 March Bahrain and Hungary had established full diplomatic relations, Bahrain's first with an East European country. On 21 July Saudi Arabia and China were to establish diplomatic ties during the visit to Riyadh of the Chinese foreign minister, Qian Qichen. In response, Taiwan suspended diplomatic ties with Saudi Arabia.

10 March Iraq's President Saddam Husayn announces an unconditional two-month amnesty for all exiled Kurds. The offer which covered both Jalal Talabani, leader of the Patriotic Union of Kurdistan (PUK) and Masoud Barzani, leader of the Kurdish Democratic Party (KDP), was open to over 20,000 Kurds who had fled to Turkey in August 1988.

15 March Farzad Bazoft, the London *Observer* newspaper journalist sentenced to death in Iraq for spying, is hanged in Baghdad and his body is handed to the British embassy. Iraq ignored an international chorus of revulsion against the execution. The British secretary of state for foreign affairs, Douglas Hurd, called it a 'a barbarous act', The British ambassador, Harold Walker, was temporarily recalled (he was to return on 16 May), ministerial visits were suspended and five Iraqi cadets training in Britain were sent home. Otherwise, Britain's response was considered comparatively mild. Britain explained that it was showing restraint to protect Daphne Parish, the British nurse sentenced to 15 years as Bazoft's accomplice and another Briton in jail in Iraq on corruption charges, Ian Richter.

Bazoft and Parish had been sentenced by a revolutionary court on 10 March. Bazoft had been arrested in September 1989 after trying to check reports about an explosion at a military installation at Hilleh. He had been driven to the site by Parish, a nurse at Baghdad's Ibn al-Bitar Hospital. He had later told the Iraqis that he had been spying for Israel but *The Observer* said that his confession had been fabricated and extracted by force.

Within hours of the execution Britain's House of Commons (lower house) was told that at one stage Bazoft had been jailed for a year in Britain for theft and bomb-hoaxing and that he had volunteered information to the British police four times. While many in Britain questioned the relevance and timing of these revelations, the Iraqi regime saw them as strengthening their case against Bazoft. By 26 March Iraq has secured Arab League condemnation of Britain's and other European Community interference in Iraq's internal affairs.

17 March Iran's President Rafsanjani tells a press conference that the question of the Western hostages in Lebanon is 'moving towards a solution'. He referred to a statement made by the Lebanese Shi'i leader, Shaikh Mahmoud Fadlallah, condemning terrorism and hostage-taking. Shaikh Fadlallah had visited Tehran in February.

18 March A meeting between Iraq's RCC and the Arab Ba'th Socialist Party suggests that Iraq may be heading for a freer political system. On 13 February Iraq's President Saddam Husayn had said he wanted to encourage 'freedom of speech', adding that unless people were allowed to air their complaints they would be 'speaking in the darkness'. In a gesture of self-confidence, on 17 January the Iraqi government had lifted restrictions on foreign travel for Iraqis after almost eight years. In November Saddam Husayn had told Iraqi jurists that 'after deep thought, pluralism has been adopted as part of our party's trend'. However, moves towards democracy were greeted with intense scepticism by many observers.

29 March Britain and the US say that they have uncovered a plot to smuggle electronic capacitors, used to trigger nuclear explosions, from the US to Iraq via London's Heathrow Airport. On 31 March an Iraqi Airways employee was expelled from Britain and three people were charged with violating export restrictions. Iraq denied that it had tried to buy triggers, arguing that the devices had many other uses. In May Saddam Husayn was to show a capacitor on Iraqi television. The Foreign Ministry maintained that it had been imported legally from the US in 1988 and that Iraq did not intend to use its capacitors for nuclear purposes, only for scientific research.

2 April Iraq's President Saddam Husayn threatens Israel with the words: 'Let them [Western nations] cease such attempts to give Israel a pretext to strike ... I swear by God we will let our fire consume half of Israel if it tries to wage anything against Iraq.' He explained that '[a] sophisticated binary chemical weapon' was available in Iraq and that Iraq did not need nuclear weapons because it possessed chemical ones. He contrasted the outcry over the execution of Farzad Bazoft with the West's silence over the murder of the Canadian Scientist Gerald Bull in Brussels on 22 March. Bull had helped Iraq develop its long-range artillery. Bull's son, Michael, claimed that his father had received death threats from the Israeli secret service, Mossad, for helping develop Iraq's military machine.

On 9 April the Second Secretary at the US embassy in Baghdad, Zachary White, was expelled from Iraq. The expulsion was in retaliation for the US expulsion from Iraq's Washington embassy of Hamid al-Amiry for his role in an alleged asassination plot aimed at two members of the Iraqi opposition. On 31 March an Iraqi Airways official in London, Omar Latif, had been deported for his alleged compliance in a plot to smuggle to Iraq appliances which could be used as triggers for nuclear weapons.

From 7 to 12 April two technicians from the Vienna-based International Atomic Energy Agency visited the Tammuz reactor at Tuwaitha outside Baghdad, within the framework of regular inspections that began in 1972.

11 April British customs officials seize eight pieces of piping; a week later the British government claims that they are part of a giant gun to be built in Iraq. According to the manufacturers, Sheffield Engineering, the pipes were for a petrochemical project and had been ordered in June 1988 by Iraq's former Minerals and Industry Ministry. After Britain's Royal Armament Research Development Establishment was consulted, however, customs officials confirmed that the pipes were part of a gun with a range of up to 622 miles (1,000 kilometres) which could fire nuclear or chemical weapons. On 15 April British newspapers revealed that a blueprint for making a similar gun existed in a book co-written by Gerald Bull, the scientist who had been shot dead in Brussels on 22 March.

21 April The Soviet Union is to organize direct flights to Saudi Arabia for the *hajj* (starting in late June) by direct Aeroflot flights from Moscow, Kazan, Tashkent and Baku, according to a Soviet government spokesman.

22 April Kazem Rajavi, the brother of the Mujahedeen leader Masoud Rajavi, is shot dead by gunmen outside his home in Switzerland. The assassins were assumed to be Iranian government agents.

30 April The US hostage, Frank Reed, is released by his kidnappers in Beirut. On 22 April another US hostage, Robert Polhill, had been released by the Islamic Jihad for the Liberation of Palestine and handed over to US officials in Damascus. The release of Western hostages had long been called for by the 'pragmatists' in Tehran led by President Rafsanjani but rejected by the hardliners such as the former interior minister, Hojatolislam Ali Akbar Mohtashami. At the same time Rafsanjani had tried to distance Iran from the hostages issue, saying that both the kidnappers and the Western countries were ready to solve the issue which 'does not concern us at all'.

On 2 May Iran's spiritual leader, Ayatollah Khamenei, criticized those in Iran who called for direct talks with the US, but said that Iran was ready to help free the hostages 'as a humanitarian duty'.

3 May Iran's UN mission calls 'absurd and ironic' a US *Washington Post* allegation that in March 1988 Iran had used chemical weapons on the Kurdish town of Halabja in the belief that it was occupied by Iraqi forces. Iraq had itself earned international revulsion by using chemical weapons against the town.

12 May Ten Kuwaiti pro-democracy activists, including one of the movement's leaders, Ahmad al-Khatib, are released on bail. However, on 13 May Ahmad al-Rabe'i and Ali Buarki were detained and on 15 May Abd al-Aziz al-Qatami and Abdullah Fahd al-Nafisi were detained. The pro-democracy movement had called for a boycott of the June poll to decide on an interim national council.

14 May Pakistan's prime minister, Benazir Bhutto, arrives in Tehran at the start of a Middle East tour aimed at winning support for Pakistan's position in its dispute with India over Kashmir. The first half of her tour took in Syria, Jordan, North Yemen, Egypt, Libya and Tunisia. In June she planned to visit Qatar, Iraq, Kuwait, Bahrain, Morocco, Somalia and Algeria.

20 May Iran's minister for culture and Islamic guidance, Muhammad Khatami, confirms that Iran has failed to enable Iranian pilgrims to perform the *hajj* to Mecca in June. On 14 and 15 May Iran's deputy foreign minister held talks in Riyadh with his Saudi counterpart. They were the first talks since relations were cut following violent clashes between Iranian pilgrims and Saudi police in Mecca in 1988 and in which over 400 people were killed.

22 May The new Republic of Yemen comes into being, following the dissolution and union of South Yemen (The People's Democratic Republic of Yemen – PDRY) and North Yemen (the Yemen Arab Republic). The republic's combined population (North Yemen 9.5 million; South Yemen 2.5 million) made it the most populous state in the Arabian peninsula. Although the concept of unity had been discussed since South Yemen's independence in 1967, the reality had been friction between the two states.

On 29 May the new republic was admitted as a member of the Arab Co-operation Council at a meeting in Baghdad attended by the heads of state of the four member countries and

Yemen's new vice-president Ali Salem al-Beidh. On 16 June President Saddam Husayn of Iraq was the first head of state to visit the new republic. The visit was aimed at congratulating President Ali Abdullah Saleh on establishing unity. Saleh asked Aden's former president, Haider Abu Bakr al-Attas, the prime minister of the new republic, to form a government. The cabinet formed on 24 May included 20 North Yemenis and 19 South Yemenis.

27 May Iraq's President Saddam Husayn tells an Arab summit meeting in Baghdad that he hopes that an exchange of letters with Iran will lead to 'direct and profound dialogue', followed by a comprehensive peace. The summit condemned 'threats, campaigns and hostile measures [against Iraq]'. Saddam Husayn was eager to maintain Arab support against what he described as a campaign by the US, Britain and Israel to obstruct Iraq's technological development.

May New figures show that Kuwaitis account for only 27.3 per cent of Kuwait's population, according to the Planning Ministry. The population stood at 2,014,135 of whom 550,181 were Kuwaitis. Some 46 per cent of the population were Asians and 39 per cent non-Kuwaiti Arabs.

4 June Before huge crowds gathered at Ayatollah Khomeini's tomb south of Tehran to commemorate the first anniversary of his death, Iran's spiritual leader, Ayatollah Khamenei, re-states Khomeini's ideas. Khamenei's repetition of the *fatwa* (edict) made by Khomeini against the British author Salman Rushdie in March 1989 caused anxiety in London. On 6 June, however, President Rafsanjani told the press: 'If Mrs Thatcher condemns Rushdie's novel, there will remain no problem on the way to the resumption of ties'.

6 June The US Pentagon announces plans for a $4,000-million arms sale to Saudi Arabia. The package was to include armoured cars, anti-tank missiles and launchers, artillery and the modernization of the AWACS surveillance aircraft the Saudis had bought from the US in 1987. On 9 July Saudi Arabia signed a $3,000 million deal to buy 315 M-1 battle tanks from the US company General Dynamics. Congress had approved the sale in 1989.

On 2 June Britain's foreign secretary, Douglas Hurd, had discussed Saudi-British trade in Riyadh with the Saudi foreign minister, Prince Saud al-Faisal.

10 June Elections lead to the appointment of 50 deputies to Kuwait's new National Council. However, only 20 had belonged to the former National Assembly which the amir, Shaikh Jaber, had dissolved in 1986 on grounds of security problems and increasing factionalism. Calling the proposed council 'toothless' and unconstitutional, pro-democracy activists had called on voters to boycott the election. Nevertheless, some 62 per cent of Kuwait's 62,000 eligible male voters turned out (women did not have the right to vote in Kuwait). On 11 June the government resigned and on 13 June the amir reappointed Crown Prince Shaikh Sa'd al-Abdullah al-Salem al-Sabah as prime minister.

On 18 June Kuwait's state security court acquitted four Kuwaiti Shi'is accused of having plotted to overthrow the government in 1986. On 20 May the amir had pardoned 17 pro-democracy campaigners who had been detained since 8 May.

On 25 May two Kuwaiti human rights campaigners had been deported from Britain for reasons of 'national security'. Their request for political asylum had been rejected. Together with three Bahrainis and another Kuwaiti, they had been arrested by British Special Branch police on 23 May in connection with a plot to murder the author Salman Rushdie. One of the Bahrainis was Sa'id Shihabi, editor of the Shi'i weekly *al-Alam*.

20 June After four days of fighting between Revolutionary Guards and Kurdish Democratic Party of Iran (KDPI) guerrillas in and around the towns of Saqqez and Oshnoiviyeh in Kurdistan province, the Iranian government claims to have killed 18 guerrillas with no casualties while the KDPI claims to have killed 40 Iranian troops and lost two. On 1 June a rebel Kurdish radio station claimed that 17 people had been executed in Sanandaj, the capital of the province. They had been arrested during demonstrations on May Day.

Meanwhile, on 23 June Kurdish Democratic Party (KDP) guerrillas relaunched their offensive against the Iraqi army with two days of raids against army positions in Iraq's Sulaymaniyya province near the Iranian border. Iran claimed that 34 Iraqi troops were killed and 16 captured in the fighting.

21 June A massive earthquake hits north-west Iran, killing about 50,000, injuring 60,000 and leaving half a million homeless. Generous Western help was welcomed by the 'pragmatists' led by President Rafsanjani while the hardliners at first said that support from the US and countries that had supported Iraq in the war should be rejected. On 29 June Rafsanjani called the international response 'very beautiful'. 'I was very touched', he added, describing critical hardliners as 'pestering flies'. Damage to the worst-hit province, Gilan, was thought to be worth about $7,000 million.

26 June Speaking in Kuwait after a meeting with the amir, Shaikh Jaber, Iraq's deputy premier Sa'doun Hammadi identifies Kuwait and the United Arab Emirates (UAE) as the Organization of Petroleum Exporting Countries' (OPEC's) main over-producers. 'I believe that prices will go up to $18 [a barrel] if there is a cut of 1.5 million barrels [a day] by Kuwait and the emirates', he said. Ominously, he added that Iraq was losing $1,000 million a year for every $1 drop in the price of a barrel of oil. On 30 June Iran's oil minister, Gholamreza Aqazadeh, joined the debate, saying that OPEC had not been firm enough with over-producers, in particular with the UAE. Iran, like Iraq, wanted higher oil prices to finance post-war reconstruction. On 1 July the OPEC president, Sadeq Boussena, said that demands by two unnamed Gulf members (clearly the UAE and Kuwait) for quota increases would create problems at the 25 July Geneva OPEC conference.

On 25 June Boussena had met Kuwait's new oil minister, Rashid al-Amiri, who was later quoted as saying that Boussena had accepted Kuwait's demand for a quota higher than its present level of 1.5 million barrels a day. In an important cabinet reshuffle on 20 June the Kuwaiti oil minister, Shaikh Ali al-Khalifah al-Sabah, had been appointed finance minister, replacing Jassim Muhammad al-Kharafi. According to MEED, Shaikh Ali had been OPEC'S leading moderate, calling for oil prices to be held constant in nominal terms during the early 1990s. Consequently, Kuwait's oil production levels had been persistently above its OPEC quota. The appointment to the oil ministry of al-Amiri, a little-known academic, was significant.

1 July The amir of Kuwait, Shaikh Jaber, approves the new budget in which public expenditure is $12,400 million, 13 per cent up on 1989. Revenue was estimated at $8,200 million of which 83 per cent was accounted for by oil exports. Kuwait's record budget deficit was expected to be covered by income from the state's massive foreign investment portfolio.

3 July The Iraqi and Iranian foreign ministers sit down in Geneva for their first direct talks since the Iran-Iraq war cease-fire in August 1988 brought about by UN Security Council resolution 598. Iran's foreign minister, Ali Akbar Velayati, and his Iraqi counterpart, Tariq Aziz, agreed that the talks had been friendly. Resolution 598's second step was the exchange of prisoners of war but Iraq had not withdrawn its troops from all Iranian territory and Iran still held 50,000 Iraqi prisoners.

11 July Iran's foreign minister, Ali Akbar Velayati, ends a trip to Kuwait with the assurance that 'all the differences accumulated in the past years between the two countries have been removed'. Relations had been damaged by Kuwait's firm financial and logistic support for Iraq in its eight-year war with Iran. In response Tehran at times had sought to overthrow the Kuwaiti regime, had been behind attacks in Kuwait and had tried to incite Kuwait's large Shi'i community against the government. Following Iranian air attacks on Kuwaiti oil tankers, Kuwait had managed to re-register its merchant fleet under US flags.

16 July Iraq's National Assembly begins a series of emergency sessions aimed at organizing 'the life of the Iraqis on a clear democratic basis', says the Assembly's speaker, Sa'di Mehdi Saleh. The sessions followed approval on 7 July by the RCC and the ruling Arab Ba'th Socialist Party's Regional Command of a draft constitution. The constitution, to be approved by a plebiscite later in the year, would allow for a multi-party system. Once the constitution had been validated, presidential elections would take place.

16 July The British nurse, Daphne Parish, is released from a Baghdad prison after the Zambian President Kaunda had appealed to Iraq's President Saddam Husayn. In March both Parish and Farzad Bazoft had been found guilty of spying. Bazoft was executed and Parish was given a 15-year prison sentence.

18 July Iraq accuses Kuwait of 'theft tantamount to military aggression' and deliberate border violations, in a letter from Iraq's foreign minister, Tariq Aziz, to the secretary-general of the Arab League, Chadli Klibi. He called on Kuwait to cancel Iraq's war debts and organize an 'Arab Marshall Plan to compensate Iraq for what it had lost in the war' with Iran. He said that the Kuwaiti government had committed 'an aggression on the land and steals the wealth of those who protected Kuwait's soil, honour and wealth'. The letter also said that Kuwait had established oil installations in the southern sector of the Rumaileh (which Iraq shared with Kuwait) oilfield in 1980, 'thus flooding the world oil market partly with oil stolen from that field'.

In early July President Saddam Husayn, followed by his oil minister, Issam al-Shalabi, and his deputy prime minister, Sa'doun Hammadi, began a campaign of diatribe against both Kuwait and the UAE, accusing them of sabotaging Iraq's economy by greatly exceeding their OPEC oil output quotas. In subsequent correspondence both states were accused of being US stooges. Shortly after the 18 July letter, 30,000 Iraqi troops were moved to the Kuwaiti border. (Iraq's entire armed forces were about one million men against Kuwait's of about 17,000 men). In his 17 July televised attack on Kuwait and the UAE, Saddam Husayn said that the fall in oil prices in the first half of the year had cost Iraq $14,000 million, adding immediately: 'Iraqis will not forget the maxim that cutting necks is better than cutting the means of living.'

On 18 July Kuwait's foreign affairs minister, Shaikh Sabah al-Ahmad al-Jaber al-Sabah, began an emergency tour of Gulf Co-operation Council (GCC) states, starting in Riyadh.

25 July The Kuwaiti crown prince and prime minister, Shaikh Sa'd al-Abdullah al-Salem al-Sabah, is quoted as saying that he is prepared to enter into talks with Iraq and that the 'good ties between Kuwait and Iraq will return'. However, he said that Kuwait would not submit to blackmail. Iraq was demanding $2,400 million in compensation for oil it claimed Kuwait had stolen from the Rumaileh oilfield. It also wanted to discuss disputed territory, including Kuwait's strategic Bubiyan and Warba islands close to Iraq's Umm Qasr port.

27 July The OPEC ministers' meeting in Geneva decides that the price of oil will be increased by $3 to $21 a barrel until the end of 1990 and fixes a production ceiling of 22.491 million barrels a day for its members. This ceiling represented OPEC's endorsement of the 10–11 Jeddah agreement when Saudi Arabia, Iraq, Kuwait and Qatar met to tighten up the organization's production discipline. The decision was reached in the wake of Iraq's angry challenges to Kuwait and the UAE for exceeding their quotas. Iraq, supported by Libya, wanted a minimum price of $25 a barrel, Iran argued for a compromise of $23 but Saudi Arabia eventually persuaded the cartel to adopt $21 a barrel.

Iraq's bullying was seen as the main factor in Saudi Arabia's agreement to push up the price to this figure. Iraq's oil minister, Issam al-Shalabi, said that he was happy with the meeting and denied that Iraq would enforce quota discipline. 'We do not want to act as policemen', he said. On 27 July Iran's President Rafsanjani, speaking in Tehran at Friday prayers, called on the Soviet Union to co-operate with the Iraqis, Libyans amd Algerians to say 'we will not sell oil at less than $30'.

July The naturalized Swedish interpreter, Jalil al-Nu'aimi, is hanged in Baghdad. Accused of spying, Nu'aimi had been arrested as he landed in Baghdad with an official delegation.

1 August A meeting between Kuwait's prime minister, Crown Prince Shaikh Sa'd and President Saddam Husayn's deputy on the RCC, Izzat Ibrahim Douri, ends acrimoniously. It had been postponed from its original date of 28 July, to 31 July. Iraq was demanding that Kuwait commit itself to abiding by OPEC rules, that it cede to Iraq the southern part of the shared Rumaileh oilfield, that Kuwait pay Iraq $2,400 million for oil extracted from the field by Kuwait and that it write off the war debt owed to it by Iraq.

2 August Iraq launches a full-scale invasion of Kuwait, its tiny southern neighbour. Iraqi forces crossed the border at 2am local time and quickly gained control of the whole country. The amir and most of his extended family fled to Saudi Arabia in limousines. Iraq, claiming that it had been invited to help Kuwaiti revolutionaries attempt to overthrow the amir, established a new Kuwaiti 'Provisional Free Government' which was widely believed to be made up of Iraqi officers in Kuwaiti dress. The new 'government' closed all ports and airports, banned foreign travel, imposed a curfew and attempted to cut off telecommunications with the outside world. Iraq said it would leave Kuwait as soon as the new government was in place. US President Bush condemned Iraq's 'naked aggression', froze Iraqi and Kuwaiti assets in the US and sent extra warships to the Gulf. However, he told reporters that the US did not contemplate any military intervention. Kuwaiti assets in Britain, worth thousands of millions of dollars, were frozen by the government. The Iraqi army announced the mobilization of all reserves. The UN Security Council, summoned by Kuwait, passed resolution 660 calling for an immediate Iraqi withdrawal. Iran and Syria joined in the condemnation, with Syria calling for an emergency Arab League summit. From the rest of the Arab world there was at first a stunned, heartbroken silence.

THE 1991 GULF WAR

At midnight GMT on 16 January 1991 US and allied forces started bombing raids on strategic sites in Baghdad and elsewhere in Iraq as a White House spokesman declared that 'The liberation of Kuwait has begun.' The 15 January UN deadline set for Iraq's withdrawal from Kuwait had expired without any sign of Iraq's willingness to comply. The deadline was based on UN Resolution 678 of 29 November 1990 which allowed all necessary means to restore international peace and security in the area after 15 January. The resolution also called for Iraq's compliance with the previous 10 UN resolutions. The first, Resolution 660 of 2 August 1990, condemned Iraq's invasion of Kuwait and called for its immediate, unconditional withdrawal followed by negotiations for the resolution of differences between Iraq and Kuwait. On 30 November Iraq had rejected Resolution 678, claiming that it was 'illegal and invalid' and insisting that Kuwait was and would remain an integral part of Iraq.

As US and allied troop concentrations had built up in Saudi Arabia and other Gulf states between September and December, intensive international efforts were being made to prevent what increasingly appeared to be inevitable war. Given the turbulent history of the region since the Second World War (see Introduction), many feared that the war would unleash years of violent chaos throughout the region, with a worst-case scenario of the breakup of Iraq and territorial claims on it made by Turkey, Syria and Iran. Saddam Husayn had successfully widened the implications of such a war by calling for 'linkeage' between Iraq's withdrawal from Kuwait and a US agreement to establish an international conference to resolve the Arab-Israeli conflict. The US refused to contemplate linkeage although many believed that such a conference was, in the long run, inevitable. When asked whether Iraq would attack Israel if war broke out, the Iraqi foreign minister, Tariq Aziz, replied, 'Yes, absolutely yes.' Iraq was as good as its word. When the first Iraqi Scud missiles landed on Tel Aviv, even Arabs opposed to Saddam cheered, so deep-rooted had Arab hostility to an apparently implacable Israel become.

On 6 January Saddam said that Iraq was ready for the 'mother of battles between triumphant good and doomed evil'. As last-minute Geneva talks between Aziz and US Secretary of State James Baker on 9 January failed, Iraq's First Deputy Prime Minister, Taha Yasin Ramadan, was hosting an international conference of Muslim clerics in Baghdad. They responded eagerly to his call for support for Iraq against the wicked 'infidels' who had taken over the holy places (referring to the Saudi cities of Mecca and Medina, Islam's holiest cities). While some Iraqi opposition leaders believed that by attacking Iraq the US had helped Saddam heal internal wounds and widen Arab popular support, Saddam's critics, remembering his secularist past and the anti-Islamic image painted of him by Khomeini's Iran, marvelled at his opportunism.

Massive demonstrations in support of Saddam in Algeria, Jordan, Lebanon and Tunisia, and mounting waves of anger in Egypt and Syria – both members of the alliance – against the allied attack on Iraq, proved that Saddam had judged correctly. The allies had stressed that they were concentrating on high-technology 'surgical' air-strikes against Iraq's communications network and its military, nuclear, chemical and biological installations and would avoid civilian areas and Islamic shrines. Nevertheless, soon after the war began Saddam gave further encouragement to Islamic solidarity by claiming that the holy Shi'i shrines of Kerbela and Najaf had been bombed. Followers of Iran's hard-line cleric, Hojatolislam Ali Akbar Mohtashami, although unable to support Saddam, until so recently considered Iran's number one enemy, demonstrated in Tehran against the US's presence on Iran's doorstep. Iran's spiritual leader, Ayatollah Ali Khamenei, announced that anyone who fought America's 'greed and its plans has engaged in the *jihad* [holy struggle] in the cause of God'. Even Shi'i clerics in Iraq, long persecuted by Saddam, were stirred to fury. In a communiqué on 18 January the Tehran-based Hojatolislam Muhammad Baqir al-Hakim, the leader of the Supreme Council of the Islamic Revolution in Iraq, ordered his followers to stand against 'United States aggression'. In May 1983 six members of his family had been executed by Saddam.

After the end of the Iran-Iraq war in 1988 Iraq appeared to be on the point of social and economic breakdown. In order to placate an impatient population, Saddam offered it a package of reforms which included economic liberalization, political pluralism, freedom of the press and a new constitution. His invasion of Kuwait may have been a further attempt to divert attention away from troubles at home. The invasion was accompanied by the slogans of Arab unity, a just distribution of wealth and the liberation of Palestine. In the ideal, pan-Arab world idealized by the Ba'th Party, the oil wealth of Kuwait and the other Gulf states would be equally distributed among the region. The Ba'th party slogan 'One Arab Nation with one eternal mission' would thus be fulfilled, if cynically so. The support Saddam inspired showed just how envious the poor Arab states had been of the rich ones.

After the invasion, Saddam tried to alter Kuwait's demography by seizing records of Kuwaiti citizenship and urging Kuwaitis to flee into Saudi Arabia. Iraqis from Basra province were encouraged to settle in Kuwait. Iraq held foreign nationals against their wills as so-called 'human shields' until Saddam decided that their purpose – to ward off attack – had been served and released them in December. Meanwhile, his troops entered foreign embassies that had refused to relocate to Baghdad and seized their occupants. There were reports of widespread looting, rape and executions by the Iraqi army in Kuwait.

Observers believed that the greatest dangers existed in the war's aftermath when popular support for Saddam might blow the lid off autocratic regimes in the region. They also believed that any attempt by the US to establish a friendly regime in Baghdad would fail. In addition, fighting in the largely Shi'i areas of southern Iraq would make Iranian involvement inevitable. While Western leaders, horrified by the parading of bruised Western pilots on Iraqi television, called for Saddam's downfall, Arabs opposed to Iraq's occupation of Kuwait were cautious on this subject, maintaining that the Iraqis must themselves decide on his future.

As the massive build-up of US, European, Egyptian, Syrian and other forces continued throughout the summer and autumn of 1990, the debate continued on how and why the invasion had ever taken place (the background to Iraq's claims on Iraq is covered in the Introduction to this book and in the text). Some critics maintained that the US should have known that Iraq would invade. In an audience with Saddam a week before the invasion, the US ambassador to Iraq, Ms April Glaspie, had sympathized with his complaint that Kuwait had been driving down oil prices, adding: 'I know you need funds. We understand that and our opinion is that you should have the opportunity to rebuild your country. But we have no opinion on the Arab-Arab conflicts, such as your border agreement with Kuwait.' Saddam is believed to have inferred from her statement that the US would not respond militarily to an invasion of Kuwait.

Events leading up to Iraq's invasion of Kuwait

On 3 August, the day after the invasion, the US imposed a trade and travel ban on Iraq while the Soviet Union – Iraq's main arms supplier – suspended all arms sales. The crisis was to demonstrate an astonishing degree of US-Soviet harmony. In September Presidents Bush and Gorbachev met at Helsinki where they reached a joint resolution condemning Iraq.

The Arab League Council meeting in Tunis condemned the invasion although six members voted against the condemnation. Jordan's King Husayn and PLO Chairman Yasser Arafat flew to various capitals in attempts to mediate. Iraq itself promised to withdraw its forces as soon as the situation in Kuwait was 'stable'. On 4 August the US warned Saddam Husayn not to attack Saudi Arabia whose integrity was one of the US's vital interests while European Community (EC) leaders agreed to impose trade sanctions against Iraq. Japan, among many other countries, announced a trade and aid embargo on Iraq.

On 6 August Iraqi troops began rounding up British and US citizens from Kuwaiti hotels and transferring them to Iraq. In Kuwait demonstrations and some night-time resistance were reported. Iraq threatened to invade Saudi Arabia if the Saudis cut off the pipeline which carried Iraqi oil to the Saudi port of Yanbu as the US was asking it to do. At the same time the UN Security Council passed Resolution 661 which involved wide-ranging sanctions against Iraq, including a complete trade boycott.

On 7 August the Saudis closed down the Yanbu pipeline as 15,000 US troops moved into the kingdom, backed up with armoured units and warplanes. Turkey closed down the pipeline running from Iraq to the Mediterranean. The Iraqis devalued the Kuwaiti dinar to parity with the Iraqi dinar which had previously been worth one-tenth of the value of the Kuwaiti dinar. On 8 August Iraq formally annexed Kuwait.

On 9 August Arab leaders met in Cairo and on the following day voted to send a pan-Arab force to defend Saudi Arabia. Only Iraq and Libya voted against, the PLO, Algeria and Yemen abstaining. Also on 10 August Iraq asked all diplomatic missions in Kuwait to relocate to Baghdad by 24 August, on the grounds that Kuwait was now merely an Iraqi province. On 11 August Egypt, Morocco and Syria agreed to send troops to Saudi Arabia. Meanwhile, in the (Palestinian) West Bank, Jordan and elsewhere large demonstrations supported Saddam.

On 12 August he responded by playing his trump card, 'linkeage', suggesting that Iraq would withdraw from Kuwait if Israel withdrew from the Occupied Territories and both Syria and Israel pulled their forces out of Lebanon. Meanwhile, President Bush called for Saddam's overthrow. On 13 August Britain and the US implemented a naval blockade of Iraq without UN sanction. On 14 August King Husayn met Saddam in Bagdad before flying to Washington to meet Bush. As Syrian and Moroccan troops arrived in Saudi Arabia, Syria declared its support for the US – an ironic development given long US-Syrian hostility.

On 15 August Saddam astonished the world by accepting in full Iran's terms for a Gulf peace, although his hopes that Iran might allow supplies through its border in exchange were fruitless. On 16 August Iraq ordered all Britons and Americans in Kuwait to assemble at two hotels but there were no Iraqis to receive them when they arrived. On 17 August the Iraqis said they would detain Westerners in Kuwait at civil and military installations. On 18 August 40 Britons and over 20 US, German and French citizens were moved to Iraq.

On 19 August the US called up reserves for the first time since the Vietnam War. By now the crisis had boosted the price of oil to $28 a barrel as Saudi Arabia announced that it was willing to raise its own production to two million barrels a day (b/d). Britain and the US dismissed an offer by Saddam to free all foreigners in Kuwait and Iraq in exchange for the withdrawal of US troops and an end to the naval blockade, emphasizing that nothing could be discussed until Iraq withdrew from Kuwait. On 20 August the Soviet Union agreed to support the naval blockade of Iraq as long as US and British forces were under UN command, but neither Washington nor London were willing to agree to this. Meanwhile, more foreigners were rounded up in Kuwait by the Iraqis on 20 and 21 August. All vital installations in Kuwait were by now reportedly mined. All Iraqi troops had by now withdrawn from Iranian territory. On 22 August the UK agreed to deploy ground troops in the Gulf as the Saudis prepared their people to protect themselves from Iraq's chemical warfare arsenal.

On 23 August Saddam was televised meeting a group of British hostages (clearly with a view to a worldwide audience), patting the head of a little boy called Stuart and explaining that his expression of 'human shield' for the 'guests' as he described the hostages had been a mistranslation. British politicians described their revulsion at the broadcast. On 24 August Iraqi troops surrounded diplomatic missions in Kuwait that had refused to close. On 25 August the UN Security Council passed Resolution 665 which endorsed the use of minimum force in the naval blockade; Iraq promised it would retaliate if any of its ships were attacked. On 26 August the PLO called for a UN or Arab League force to replace US troops in Saudi Arabia and Kuwait while Iran opened its borders to refugees from Iraq and Kuwait.

On 28 August Iraq announced that it would release all women and children held in Iraq and Kuwait. On the same day Iraq declared that Kuwait was now Iraq's 19th *liwa* or governorate. Iraqi troops forcibly entered the Moroccan embassy in Kuwait. Meanwhile, the PLO and Jordan suggested that Kuwait become a semi-autonomous principality on the basis of Monaco's relationship with France. Iraq is said to have accepted the proposal. On 29 August the US announced a $6,000 million arms deal with Saudi Arabia. On the same day Syria crushed pro-Iraqi demonstrations in eastern Syria.

On 12 September the last remaining members of the Swiss and Austrian embassies in Kuwait moved to Baghdad. On 13 September 400 mostly US and British women and children arrived in London from Baghdad. On 14 September Japan agreed to boost its contribution to the military intervention in the Gulf to $2,000 million. On 15 September France's defence minister, Jean-Pierre Chevènement, arrived in Jeddah, then visited French troops stationed at Yanbu and met the Saudi defence minister, Prince Sultan ibn Abd al-Aziz and King Fahd. On the same day the Olympic Council of Asia voted 27 to 3 to suspend Iraq from the Asian games in Beijing. On 26 September the Iraqis were reported to have rounded up seven more Americans, bringing the total to at least 100. On 25 September the US Pentagon had put the number of Iraqi soldiers in Kuwait and southern Iraq at 430,000, an increase of 165,000 over the previous two weeks.

On 27 September Britain and Iran announced that they were restoring diplomatic ties which had been broken off in March 1989 in the wake of *The Satanic Verses* affair. Nevertheless, the three grievances separating the two countries still needed to be settled. They were the *fatwa* (Islamic edict) against Salman Rushdie, the fate of the British hostages in Lebanon and the plight of the British businessman, Roger Cooper, who had been in Tehran's Evin Prison since December 1985.

In the autumn of 1990 Saddam Husayn struck a conciliatory note, announcing that he was exploring French President Mitterand's recent peace plan. The plan had proposed that Iraq's announcement of intent to withdraw would be the first step towards a solution and that the aspirations of the Palestinians should be resolved by the Arabs and the international community. In response, even Britain's Prime Minister Margaret Thatcher urged President Bush to show restraint rather than to yield to growing pressure from some of his advisers and from the amir of Kuwait to go to war. For a moment Bush appeared to be softening his line when he said that he believed that there may be opportunities for Iraq and Kuwait to settle their differences permanently, for the states of the Gulf to build new 'arrangements for stability and for all the states and peoples of the region to settle the conflict that divides the Arabs from Israel'.

However, stories told by Sri Lankan workers in Jordan who had fled Kuwait, of starvation, shootings, beatings and rape by Iraqi soldiers in Kuwait affected Western public opinion. Amnesty International reported that Iraqi forces had executed and tortured scores of people in Kuwait and that hundreds more were being detained. It said that the testimony 'builds up a horrifying picture of widespread arrests, torture under interrogation, summary executions and mass extra-judicial killings'. The policy of exemplary terror in Kuwait was reported to be the responsibility of Ali Majid, Saddam Husayn's cousin and the former governor of Kurdistan who was placed in charge of Iraq's '19th province'.

Meanwhile the statues of Saddam Husayn going up all over the city showed just how far Kuwait's absorption had gone as did the fact that half Kuwait's ethnic Kuwaiti population of 750,000 had left within three months of the invasion; Iraqis and Palestinians were being encouraged to settle in their place. The demographic changes taking place in Kuwait as well as the removal to Iraq of virtually anything that could be moved (even including traffic lights) seemed to presage a *fait à compli* which would not easily be reversed even if Kuwait were retaken and the Iraqis forces driven out.

During November and December the UN coalition continued to mobilize in Saudi Arabia. The spread of nationalities was astonishing with even Syria, traditionally hostile to the US, on the allied side. By January there were almost 700,000 allied troops in Saudi Arabia and neighbouring Gulf states. The US was fielding 430,000 troops, Britain 35,000, Saudi Arabia 40,000, Kuwait and the other GCC countries 10,000, Egypt 20,000, Syria 19,000, and France 10,000. Other members of the alliance were Pakistan, Bangladesh, Morocco, Senegal, Niger, Czechoslovakia, Honduras and Argentina.

In an apparent attempt to win international sympathy, on 6 December Saddam Husayn suddenly announced that all foreigners held in Iraq and Kuwait were to be released 'with our apologies for all harm'. Nevertheless, later in the month he confirmed that Israel would be Iraq's first target if war broke out. January saw the peace mission of the UN Secretary-General, Perez de Cuellar. But he confessed his failure on 13 January when he told reporters: 'You need two for tango. I wanted to dance but I didn't find any nice lady for dancing with.'

On 14 January France launched a last-minute bid to avert war. The proposals, endorsed by Germany, explicitly linked an Iraqi withdrawal to an international conference on wider Middle East issues. The French foreign minister, Roland Dumas, was to go to Baghdad to present Saddam with the plan. However, the US opposed the trip while Iraq would not agree to concrete negotiations. With this last chance for peace aborted, the streets of Baghdad began to empty as its population braced itself for the war which would inevitably follow.

BIOGRAPHIES

Abdullah: Crown Prince Abdullah ibn Abd al-Aziz
Born 1923

Born in Riyadh, Crown Prince Abdullah is the leading conservative within Saudi Arabia's Al-Saud, the ruling family. A half brother of King Fahd, he is the thirteenth son of King Abd al-Aziz by Princess Hasa bint Asi al-Shuraim of the Shammar tribal confederation. He has headed Saudi Arabia's elite, 40,000-strong national guard since 1963. Its recruits come exclusively from the great Saudi tribes and represent a counterweight to the army. Abdullah does not appear to have had a formal education, official sources claiming that he was trained by 'noted scholars and intellectuals'. Most of his early years were spent in the desert, and he remains popular with the Bedouin tribes, enjoying strong ties with their leaders. After King Faisal's assassination in 1975 he was appointed Second Deputy Prime Minister.

Aflaq, Michel
Born 1910 – Died 23 June 1989

A Syrian Christian writer, Michel Aflaq elaborated the basic ideology of Ba'thism and its slogans – 'Unity, Freedom, Socialism' and 'One Arab Nation with an Eternal Mission' – in Damascus in the 1940s and 1950s. Aflaq believed that the Arabs are one people who have been divided by imperialism and Zionism; only when they are united can they achieve a rebirth (*ba'th* in Arabic). During the 1930s he declared his admiration for Nazi Germany as the model synthesis of nationalism and socialism rather than through any love for its racial philosophy. Aflaq's own ideology was to be partly responsible for the creation of the United Arab Republic in 1958, the Iraqi Ba'th regime of 1963 and the rise to power of Saddam Husayn, the present dictator of Iraq.

A Greek Orthodox Christian, born in Damascus and educated in Bab Tuma, Damascus's Christian quarter, Aflaq won a scholarship to the Sorbonne in Paris in 1929. There he met Salah ad-Din al-Bitar who collaborated with him on creating the Ba'th Party shortly afterwards. The Iraqi Ba'th claim descent from Aflaq and Bitar while the Syrian Ba'th claim descent from Zaki al-Arsuzi.

By the 1950s the Ba'th Party had gained a considerable following in Syria and branches had been started in Iraq. In 1966 there was an intra-Ba'th coup in Syria which ousted Aflaq and Bitar, leading to an open split between the Syrian and Iraqi Ba'thists, the latter supporting Aflaq. Aflaq went to Baghdad in 1968 and remained there as a guest of the government for most of the rest of his life. The last political leader to whom he gave support was Saddam Husayn, the president of Iraq whose regime is a far cry from the Ba'th Party's ideals of unity, freedom and socialism. Aflaq was to die in Paris.

Ali: Shaikh Ali al-Khalifa al-Adhbi al-Sabah
Born 1945

Kuwait's finance minister, Shaikh Ali was born in Kuwait and educated in Cairo, San Francisco and London. He held various important posts before becoming Kuwait's oil minister (1978–83), finance minister (1984–85), oil and industry minister (1985–90) and, in June 1990, finance minister and chairman of the Kuwait Investment Authority, replacing Jassem Muhammad al-Kharafi in both posts. He was replaced by Rashid Salem al-Amiri as oil minister. Shaikh Ali was a leading advocate of keeping world oil prices low to heighten demand, a key factor in encouraging Iraq to invade Kuwait in August 1990.

BIOGRAPHIES

Aqazadeh, Gholamreza
Born 1948
Born in Khoy, Aqazadeh has been Iran's oil minister since October 1985. A graduate in mathematics and computer technology, he worked for the Bandar Abbas steel industry before the revolution. Since 1979 he has held the posts of internal manager of the daily *Jomhuri Islami* newspaper and deputy foreign minister for adminstration and finance. He has been deputy prime minister for executive affairs since 1982.

Arafat, Yasser
Born 1929
Born in Cairo, in 1946 Arafat was involved in gun-running from Egypt to Palestine. In 1950 he studied civil engineering in Cairo and became a student activist and in 1952 was elected president of the Palestinian Students Union in Cairo. In 1957 he started work as an engineer. He formally established Fatah, the Palestinian commando group, in 1965 and in 1968 he joined the Palestine Liberation Organization (PLO). In 1969 he was elected chairman of the PLO executive committee. In 1971 he was expelled with his forces from Jordan and in 1983 from Lebanon. Since then he has been based at the PLO headquarters in Tunis although he spends much time in Baghdad.

The Intifada or Palestinian uprising in the West Bank in 1988 paved the way for his dramatic recognition of Israel and renunciation of terrorism in December 1988. Since then he has enjoyed a respected diplomatic status. Visiting France's President Mitterrand and former US President Carter in Paris in mid-1990, he echoed de Gaulle's eloquent plea for a 'peace of the brave'. However, his support for Saddam Husayn after Iraq's invasion of Kuwait in August 1990 showed the intense pressure he is under from Palestinian radicals who claim that his path to peace has brought the Palestinians no concrete gains.

Asad, Hafez al–
Born 1928
Born in Qardaha in north-west Syria, Asad has been president of Syria since 1971. He belongs to the minority, quasi-Shi'i Alawi sect of Islam. Following the 1973 Arab-Israeli war he negotiated a partial withdrawal of Israeli troops from Syria with Henry Kissinger. In 1976 he sent Syrian troops into Lebanon and did so again in early 1987. He put down an Islamic fundamentalist uprising in Hama in 1982 at the cost of up to 10,000 lives.

By 1989 he had imposed Syrian control over the greater part of Lebanon. He has for long enjoyed Soviet support and was one of the few Arab states to support Iran in its eight-year war with Iraq. Generally regarded as a radical within the Arab world, Asad supported the Palestinian radicals against Yasser Arafat's mainstream Palestine Liberation Organization (PLO). In Lebanon, Syria operates through Amal, a Shi'i organization which it equipped in 1986 with tanks and armoured personnel carriers. By 1989 Asad had mended fences with some of the Arab moderates and did not block Egypt's re-admission to the Arab League in May of that year. A *quid pro quo* appears to have been that he would be allowed a free hand to impose a *pax Syriana* in Lebanon. He brought Syria on to the side of the multinational alliance before it launched its attack on Iraq on 17 January 1991.

Attas, Haider Abu Bakr al–
A former minister of construction, Attas was South Yemen's prime minister from 1985 to 1986 and, following the overthrow of the government of Ali Nasser Muhammad, president since February 1986. When the two Yemens united in May 1990 Attas became prime minister of the new republic.

BIOGRAPHIES

Aziz, Abd al (family name of the House of Saud). See under first names.

Tariq Aziz
Born 1936

Born in Mosul, Iraq, the Chaldean Christian Tariq Aziz studied at Baghdad University before starting a career in journalism. He first worked on *Al-Jumhuriyah* newspaper, before becoming chief editor of *Al-Jamaheer* in 1963. He held various journalistic and government posts until be became information minister in 1974, a member of the Ba'th regional leadership in 1977 and deputy prime minister in 1979. In 1983 he became foreign minister, the post he still holds. In February 1989 Aziz said that reports that there had been a coup against Saddam Husayn in January 1989 were 'baseless'. At the end of the Arab Co-operation Council meeting in April 1990, he said that Iraq was ready to destroy chemical weapons and sign the nuclear non-proliferation treaty if Israel did likewise. However, Aziz led Iraq's sabre-rattling campaign against its erstwhile Arab allies in the summer of 1990 when he accused Kuwait of setting up military missions on Iraqi territory and called on Kuwait and the UAE to cancel all Iraq's war debts, urging that these be considered part of 'an Arab Marshall plan'. He also accused his vulnerable neighbours of deliberately lowering oil prices at Iraq's expense. Aziz represents Saddam Husayn's campaign to become the strongman of the region in the wake of its advantageous cease-fire with Iran. The failure of his peace talks on 9 January 1991 in Geneva with US Secretary of State Baker made the 17 January multinational attack on Iraq inevitable.

Bazargan, Mehdi
Born 1907

Born in Tehran, Bazargan took his doctorate in mechanical engineering in France. He was a deputy minister in Dr Musaddiq's government from 1951 to 1953 and co-founded the Freedom Movement of Iran (FMI) in 1961. Arrested and imprisoned several times before the revolution in 1979, he co-founded the Human Rights Association in 1977 and was appointed by Ayatollah Khomeini to control the anti-shah strike of oil industry workers. He was appointed Iran's first post-revolutionary prime minister by Khomeini, assuming office on 11 February 1979 after the overthrow of Dr Shahpour Bakhtiar's government. A moderate who wished to control revolutionary violence, he resigned on 6 November over his opposition to the student takeover of the US embassy in Tehran and over the increasing clerical interference in political affairs which culminated in the takeover. After the hostages were released in 1981 official propaganda accused him of following 'the American line'.

A member of parliament for Tehran from 1980 until 1984, he opposed the continuation of the Iran-Iraq war and did not seek re-election in 1984. He co-founded the Association for the Defence of the Freedom and Sovereignty of the Iranian Nation (ADFSIN) and currently concentrates on the activities of FMI and ADFSIN. In May 1990 he led the opposition to the government by writing a critical open letter with 89 other people to President Rafsanjani, accusing the regime of corruption, cruelty and incompetence. He still leads the liberal internal opposition.

Beheshti, Ayatollah Muhammad Husseini
Born 1928

Born into a religious family in Isfahan, Beheshti went to study theology at Qom when he was eighteen. Two years later he joined the faculty of theology at Tehran University. There he became involved in the oil nationalization movement headed by Muhammad Musaddiq. After graduating in 1951, he taught at a high school in Qom while continuing his theological studies in the evenings. In 1959 he gained a doctorate of philosophy at Tehran University. During the heady period of 1962–63 he helped to form the Qom Students' Association. He was suspected by SAVAK of association with those who had assassinated Prime Minister Mansur in January 1965. Friends arranged to send him to Hamburg, out of danger, where he supervised the building of a mosque with the blessing of Ayatollah Borujirdi. During his five year sojourn in Germany he founded the Muslim Student Union in Europe. In 1969 he visited Khomeini in Najaf.

On his return to Iran he took to publishing Muslim texts. In 1971 he began a weekly Qur'anic commentary session in Tehran. In 1975 he was briefly imprisoned as a result of this. In 1976 he was involved in setting up the nucleus for the Organization of Militant Clergy (OMC) which was intended by its founders to become a semi-secret Islamic political party. The OMC became increasingly adaptive as the revolutionary movement developed in the late 1970s and Beheshti himself played a key role in smuggling tapes of Khomeini's speeches into Iran.

When Khomeini was forced to move from his exile in Najaf to Paris, Beheshti visited him there. He was one of the founder members of the Islamic Revolutionary Council (IRC) and played an important role in talks with Iran's military leaders before the revolution. He was chairman of the IRC from September 1979 to February 1980. He would almost certainly have aimed for the presidency had Khomeini not ruled out the clergy for the role. Beheshti was killed with seventy-two others when a bomb exploded in the Islamic Republican Party (IRP) headquarters where he was chairing a meeting of over ninety party leaders on 28 June 1981. As the second most important person in Iran to Khomeini, Beheshti was deeply mourned. On 30 June up to one million mourners marched in the cortège to the Behesht-e Zahra cemetery where he was buried. Khomeini persuaded the nation's most senior cleric, Ayatollah Golpaygani, to join the procession. The IRP central committee appointed Hojatolislam Muhammad Javed Bahonar to replace Beheshti as party general secretary.

Beidh, Ali Salem al-

When the new united state of Yemen was declared on 22 May 1990, the former South Yemeni politician Ali Salem al-Beidh became vice-president and Ali Abdullah Salih, former president of North Yemen, became president. Although the former secretary-general of Aden's Yemen Socialist Party, Beidh is considered today a moderate who has struggled to unite the moderates and the hardliners of the South during the period leading up to unity.

Berri, Nabi
Born 1939
Born in the Lebanese town of Tibnin, Nabi Berri was a lawyer before becoming leader of the Movement of the Deprived, better known as Amal (Hope) when its founder, Musa Sadr, disappeared (presumed killed) in 1978 during a trip to Libya. Although under Berri it became the mainstream Shi'i organization, it has lost considerable support to the more militant Hizbullah because of its compromising stand towards Syria and the Lebanese Christians. Equipped in Syria in 1986, Amal's forces are estimated at 4,000 paid militia.

Fadl Allah, Shaikh Muhammad Husayn
Along with Shaikh Ibrahim al-Amin, Shaikh Fadlallah (Fadl Allah) leads the Hizbullah (Hizb Allah, Party of God), a shadowy umbrella organization in Lebanon of radical Shi'is with Iranian links. Hizbullah emerged after the 1985 TWA hijacking. Based in South Beirut, it aims to set up an Islamic state in Lebanon. From 14 to 19 January 1987 the British Archbishop of Canterbury's special envoy, Terry Waite, had talks with Fadlallah before his abduction on 20 January. In the following month, Fadlallah gave assurances that he was seeking Waite's release, and continued to repeat this assurance.

BIOGRAPHIES

Fahad: Sayyid Fahad ibn Mahmoud al-Said
Born 1944
Fahad is a member of the family of Oman's Sultan Qaboos. He studied in Cairo, Paris and The Netherlands and was appointed director of Oman's Foreign Ministry in 1971. In 1980 he was appointed deputy prime minister for legal affairs.

Fahd: King Fahd ibn Abd al-Aziz
Born 1923
Born in Riyadh, King Fahd of Saudi Arabia is the oldest son of the seven sons (the 'Sudairi Seven') of King Abd al-Aziz's favourite wife, Hasa bint Ahmad al-Sudairi. In 1953, aged 30, he joined Saudi Arabia's first Council of Ministers as education minister, becoming interior minister in 1963 and Second Deputy Premier in 1967. Effectively ruler since the assassination of his older half brother, King Faisal, in 1975, he became king on the death of his other half brother, King Khaled, on 13 June 1982. He also became prime minister and appointed his half brother, Abdullah, as crown prince and First Deputy Premier. Fahd's full brothers include the Second Deputy Premier and defence and aviation minister, Prince Sultan, Riyadh Governor Prince Salman, and deputy interior minister, Prince Ahmad.

Since 1975 he has played a key role in many aspects of the kingdom's modernization and industrialization programmes. He was a prime mover behind the creation of the Gulf Co-operation Council (GCC) in 1981. In February 1985 he visited Washington in an attempt to persuade the US to put pressure on Israel to make peace efforts acceptable to the Arabs. His disappointment over this meeting seems to have influenced secret talks held shortly afterwards with the Soviet Union in an attempt to diversify away from the kingdom's overwhelming dependence on the US.

Since the Islamic revolution in Iran in 1979 and the Mecca siege of Islamic fundamentalists later the same year, King Fahd has attempted to neutralize the Islamic militants who accuse the regime of decadence and financial corruption. Responsibility for various bomb attacks in the kingdom in 1985 was claimed by the Iran-based Islamic Jihad Organization. King Fahd's substitution of the title 'Custodian of the Two Holy Cities' for King in the following year was clearly aimed at innoculating the Saudi regime from further militant anger. However, the stationing of hundreds of thousands of mainly US troops in the kingdom after Iraq's invasion of Kuwait in August 1990 and Saudi Arabia's participation in the war with Iraq that started in January were to become the kingdom's severest tests.

Fahr: Sayyid Fahr ibn Teymour al-Said
Born 1928
Fahr is the brother of the late Sultan Said ibn Teymour of Oman. He studied at the Dehra Dun Military Academy in India in 1940, joining the Muscat Infantry eight years later. He then spent some years in Beirut before returning to join Muscat's Defence Department. In 1974 he was appointed deputy minister of the interior and then deputy prime minister for security and defence.

Faisal: King Faisal ibn Abd al-Aziz
Born 1904 – Died 25 March 1975
Born in the Saudi capital, Riyadh, King Faisal of Saudi Arabia was the fourth son of King Abd al-Aziz by his wife Bint al-Shaikh. At the age of 14, Faisal was sent by his father to Britain at the head of a mission to congratulate the Allies on their victory in the 1914–18 war. He enjoyed the absolute trust of his father and in 1925 commanded the siege of Jeddah. When the town surrendered later that year he became governor of Mecca and *wali* or viceroy of the Hejaz. In 1930 he became the kingdom's effective foreign minister

and in 1931 he became president of the Consultative Assembly and minister of the interior. In 1934 he led Saudi forces into Yemen and captured Hodeidah, compelling Imam Yahya to come to terms with King Abd al-Aziz.

In the London negotiations over Palestine in 1939, Faisal led the Saudi delegation. In 1943 he visited the US and represented his father when the conference of heads of Arab League states was held in Cairo in 1946. He became crown prince and prime minister when his father died and his half brother Saud became king in 1953. Because of Saud's failure to tackle Saudi Arabia's economic problems, Saud gave Faisal control of finance, internal and foreign affairs and defence in 1958. In December 1960 Faisal resigned as prime minister, only to be recalled in October 1962 at a time of emergency when the kingdom was embroiled on the side of the royalists in the Yemeni civil war. In March 1964 the Council of Ministers decreed that Faisal assume full powers and in November Saud was formally deposed and Faisal became king.

The 1960s saw conflict between the secular pan-Arabism of Nasser and the Islamic conservatism of Faisal. Faisal sought, through Islam, a middle way, maintaining: 'We have the Holy Qur'an and the Shari'a law. Why do we need socialism, capitalism, communism or any other ideology?' After the Arab disaster in the 1967 Arab-Israeli war, Faisal led the movement among Arab oil producers to offer subsidies to the principal losers in the war, Egypt and Jordan, and he refused to compromise over the status of Jerusalem, Islam's third holiest city, which the Israelis had taken in the war. He also agreed to cease supporting the royalists in North Yemen on condition that Nasser withdrew his Egyptian forces from the republican side. However, he was continually irked by left-wing movements, particularly in the form of the new hard-line regime in South Yemen. At the same time he encouraged progress, saying: 'Like it or not, we must join the modern world and find an honourable place in it.' On the break-out of the 1973 war, he led the oil producers in raising prices in order to put pressure on the Western oil companies, and he stopped all exports to the US for a period.

He was assassinated for no apparent political motive in the royal palace in Riyadh by his nephew, Faisal ibn Musaid, on 25 March 1975. He left many children, seven sons among them, by his three wives. He lived for many years with his third wife, Iffat, who was to influence the development of women's education in the kingdom. King Faisal was both a conservative and a realist and a man utterly committed to both Islam and his nation.

Faisal II: King Faisal ibn Ghazi ibn Faisal al-Hashim
Born 2 May 1935 – Died 13 July 1958

King Faisal, the last king of Iraq, was shot dead in the company of his uncle Abdulilah, and some of his womenfolk, in his palace at Baghdad in a coup led by Abd al-Karim Qasim. Faisal was born in Baghdad at Qasr al-Zuhur (the Palace of Roses), the only son of King Ghazi and Queen Aliyah. His grandfather, Faisal I, had led the Arab revolt against the Turks in 1916 and became, with British blessing, the first king of modern Iraq in August 1921.

When King Ghazi was killed in 1939, his three-year old son was proclaimed King Faisal II and Abdulilah, Ghazi's first cousin, was appointed regent. At the age of 12, Faisal went to Sandroyd 'Prep' school, then Harrow school, in England. On 2 May 1953 he formally acceded to the throne on the same day that his cousin Husayn became king of Jordan. In 1957 Faisal met King Saud of Saudi Arabia in Baghdad where they reaffirmed their commitment to independence and their hostility to Zionism and imperialism. In July of the same year it was announced that Faisal was to marry Princess Nabila Fazila, daughter of Prince Muhammad Ali Ibrahim.

In February 1958 he arrived in Amman where he, King Saud and King Husayn proclaimed the union of their three kingdoms as the 'Arab Federation' as a counter-weight to the recently created union of Egypt and Syria into the United Arab Republic (UAR). The federation was to be but a dream for on the night of 13 July the tanks of Qasim's deputy, Colonel Abd al-Salam Aref, surrounded the palace and massacred the royal family. On the following morning Qasim and Aref announced the creation of a republic.

Habibi, Hasan Ibrahim
Born 1937
Born in Iran, Habibi was a member of the Freedom Movement of Iran in the early 1960s and was active in the anti-shah movement abroad. He helped draft the Constitution of the Islamic Republic and became minister of culture and higher education in its provisional government. He was the Islamic Republican Party's candidate for the first presidential election in 1980 and became a member of the Republic's first parliament. He was appointed minister of justice in 1984 and first vice-president under Rafsanjani in September 1989.

Hamad: Shaikh Hamad ibn Khalifa al-Thani
Born 1950
Qatar's crown prince, Shaikh Hamad, was born in Doha, the Qatari capital. He is the first son of Shaikh Khalifa, the ruler. Educated in Qatar to secondary-school level, he graduated at Britain's Sandhurst Military Academy in 1971. In 1977 he became crown prince and defence minister. He has set up the Qatari air arm and sea arm as well as various specialist army units.

Hamed: Shaikh Hamed ibn Isa al-Khalifa
Born 1950
Shaikh Isa's son, Shaikh Hamed, is Bahrain's crown prince and defence minister. He was educated in Bahrain and later at Britain's Sandhurst Military Academy, the Mons Officer Cadet School and Fort Leavenworth, Kansas. He commanded the Bahrain National Guard from 1969 to 1971 and was a member of the State Administrative Council from 1970 to 1971.

Hammadi, Sa'doun
Born 1930
Born in Kerbala, Iraq, Hammadi studied in Lebanon and the US before returning to Baghdad to become a professor in economics at Baghdad University. He held various economic posts before becoming chairman of the Iraq National Oil Company in 1968, oil and minerals minister (1969–74) and foreign minister (1974–83). In mid-1986 Saddam Husayn strengthened his hand in a bloody purge in which Hammadi, now chairman of the National Assembly, was elected to the pivotal Revolutionary Command Council, replacing Na'im Haddad who was executed. Westerner observers then saw in Hammadi a possible successor to an increasingly ruthless but isolated Saddam Husayn.

In 1989 he replaced Adnan Khairallah (minister of defence and Saddam Husayn's brother-in-law) as deputy premier when Khairallah died in a mysterious helicopter crash in May 1989. Hammadi advocated compromise with Iran during the eight-year-long Gulf war.

Husayn, Saddam
Born 1937
Born in Al-Auja near Takrit on the Euphrates in northern Iraq, President Saddam Husayn of Iraq joined the Arab Ba'th Socialist Party in 1957 and was sentenced to death in 1959 for the attempted assassination of General Qasim, who founded the Iraqi republic in 1958. He played a prominent part in the revolution of 1968 and became vice-president of the

Revolutionary Command Council in 1969. The mid-1970s saw the Ba'th Party penetrating every sphere of Iraqi life from its smallest cell or *halqa* right up to the leadership in the form of Saddam Husayn whose cult of personality was by then at its height. On the retirement of his colleague and fellow Takriti, President Ahmad Hasan al-Bakr, he became sole president of Iraq in 1979.

His attack on Iran in the following year led to a bloody war which Husayn had hoped would end in a quick Iraqi victory but only ended, at a cost of 300,000 Iraqi lives, in 1988. In August 1990 he horrified the international community by invading Kuwait and apparently threatening to invade Saudi Arabia, bringing onto Iraq UN-sponsored sanctions and the deployment of US forces in Saudi Arabia. On 17 January 1991, with the approval of the UN Security Council, the multinational alliance launched a full-scale war on Iraq.

He has depended heavily on his Sunni followers from Takrit for his continued, ruthless hold on power within Iraq. Husayn brooks no opposition and has carried out systematic and bloody purges against his enemies, not least against the Kurds who have for long struggled for autonomy. In 1988 he used chemical weapons against the Kurds of Halabja, killing over 5,500. He is married to Sajida by whom he has two sons and two daughters.

Husayn: King Husayn ibn Talal
Born 14 November 1935
King Husayn of Jordan was educated at Amman, then the elite, British-style Victoria College in Alexandria, and Britain's Harrow school and the Sandhurst Military Academy. The son of King Talal and Queen Zein, Husayn succeeded his father on 11 August 1952 when the latter abdicated because of mental ill-health. Husayn took his formal oath as king on 2 May 1953 when he came of age at 18. He is today married to his third wife, the Syro-American Elizabeth Halaby, the present Queen Noor, by whom he has two sons, Princes Hamzeh and Hashem. Husayn's younger brother, Crown Prince Hasan, acts as regent when the king is absent.

King Husayn represents the Arab moderates although his army has taken much of the brunt of the wars fought with Israel. He greatly enhanced relations with his erstwhile foe, Iraq, by giving it support during its eight-year war with Iran. Despite periods of friction, he has been largely successful in absorbing the Palestinians who make up about 65 per cent of Jordan's population.

After the 1967 Arab-Israeli war (the 'June War'), the Palestinians became radicalized and militia groups belonging to the Palestine Liberation Organization (PLO) made increasing raids into Israel from Jordan. Eventually their power grew to such an extent in Jordan that the Jordanian army was ordered to move against them. In the wake of a short, bloody civil war which started in September 1970, the PLO's leadership fled abroad, mostly to Lebanon. Since then relations between the king and the Palestinians within Jordan have improved. Jordan's decison to cut links with the West Bank in 1988 prompted the PLO to establish a government in exile and later to recognize the State of Israel and renounce terrorism. After Iraq invaded Kuwait in August 1990 and the war that followed in January 1991, Husayn had to balance his good ties with the West with pragmatic ties with Saddam Husayn whom many Jordanians and Palestinians supported.

Iriani, Abd al-Karim al-
North Yemen's premier from 1980 to 1983, Iriani was also appointed chairman of the supreme council for reconstructing areas devastated by the 1982 earthquake. In late 1984 President Ali Abdullah Saleh appointed him prime minister, possibly feeling that he would suit Yemen's move towards a more democratic political system. He was later replaced by Abd al-Aziz Abd al-Ghani, himself becoming deputy premier and foreign minister, a portfolio he retained after the first general elections of July 1988.

BIOGRAPHIES

Isa: Shaikh Isa ibn Salman al-Khalifa
Born 1933

Bahrain's ruler (amir), Shaikh Isa was born in Bahrain. He has been the state's ruler since 1961 when he succeeded his father, Shaikh Salman. Educated in Manama, he became heir apparent in 1958, playing a key role in decision-making from 1959 onwards. Despite social tensions, particularly among Bahrain's majority Shi'i population after the Iranian revolution in 1979, Shaikh Isa has remained an essentially pro-Western moderate.

Jaber: Shaikh Jaber al-Ahmad al-Jaber al-Sabah
Born 1926

Born in Kuwait, Kuwait's ruler (in Arabic amir), Shaikh Jaber was educated at Kuwait's Al-Mubarakiya School and also with private tutors. In 1963 and 1965 he was minister of finance, industry and commerce and was prime minister from 1965 to 1967. He was crown prince in 1966/67, succeeding his uncle Shaikh Salem as amir in December 1977. Although he suspended Kuwait's National Assembly in 1986, he was considered to share the goals of Kuwait's progressive elements and allowed demonstrations in favour of the Assembly's restoration to take place in mid-1990. In August 1990 he escaped to Saudi Arabia as Iraq invaded Kuwait.

Kamil, Husayn

Brigadier-General Husayn Kamil was Iraq's acting minister of industry and minerals until July 1988 when his portfolio was changed to the key post of minister of industry and military industrialization to reflect Iraq's military might. As President Saddam Husayn's son-in-law, he enjoys considerable clout. His influence has increased since the death of Saddam Husayn's brother-in-law, Adnan Khairallah, in a mysterious helicopter crash in 1989. He advocated compromise with Iran during the eight-year-long Gulf war.

Karrubi, Hojatolislam Mehdi
Born 1937

Born in the Iranian town of Aligoodarz, Karrubi was incarcerated several times before the revolution in 1979 when he was imam in mass prayer meetings. He is member of parliament for Tehran and was deputy speaker of parliament before replacing Rafsanjani as speaker in August 1989. He is a hardliner who believes in exporting the Islamic revolution and has tended to act against Rafsanjani's pragmatism. He was reappointed speaker for a further year in May 1990 with an increased majority.

Kashani, Ayatollah Sayyid Abul-Qasim
Born c. 1881 – Died 14 March 1962

Kashani was born in Tehran. An ambitious patriarchal figure and a brilliant publicist with the common touch, Kashani was to play a key role in the oil crises of the early 1950s as well as in the return from brief exile of the shah. Kashani's father was a cleric. At the age of 15 the young Kashani went to the holy city of Najaf, in present-day Iraq, to continue his theological studies. He was in Iraq when a revolt among the tribes and towns of the Middle Euphrates River region against the British Mandate took place in 1920. His father was killed but the young Kashani escaped to Iran where he nursed a bitter loathing for the British. During the reign of Reza Shah, Kashani was muzzled but after the ruler's overthrow by the Allies in 1941 and the Anglo-Soviet occupation of Iran, Kashani intrigued with the Nazis. On one occasion he even escaped allied pursuit dressed as a woman. The British interned him during the war when they discovered that he was a top member of a pro-German organization in Iran. On his release he resumed his political activities.

After the war he helped to defeat proposals for a Soviet oil concession in the north and when the Anglo-Iranian Oil Company (AIOC) emerged, it became his natural enemy. In 1949 he was elected as a deputy to the Majlis (lower house). When the prime minister, General Razmara, was assassinated in March 1951 Kashani sided with the Fedayeen-e Islam who were responsible. Kashani had collaborated with the Fedayeen since the early 1940s. The Islamic fundamentalist organization had been founded by Sayyid Mujtaba Navvab-Safavi who had studied theology at Najaf in order to counter the influence of the late Ahmad Kasravi, an iconoclastic historian whom the Fedayeen had assassinated on 11 March 1946.

When Musaddiq nationalized the AIOC, Kashani became his natural ally and in August 1952 he became speaker of the Majlis. However, when Musaddiq demanded plenary powers in January 1953 he opposed him and in July, after the deputies had voted in the bill to give Musaddiq these powers, Kashani was ejected from the speakership. Indeed, Musaddiq regarded Kashani as responsible for the 1953 coup and according to one account the US Central Intelligence Agency passed $10,000 to Kashani to mobilize mob support against Musaddiq and for the shah (See Azimi's *Iran: The Crisis of Democracy 1941-53*). Kashani was, above all, an impassioned orator whose influence on the masses could challenge and even overthrow regimes.

Khalifa, al (Bahrain's ruling family). See under first names.

Khalifa: Shaikh Khalifa ibn Hamad al-Thani
Born 1932
Qatar's ruler (amir), Shaikh Khalifa, was born in the Qatari town of Rayyan. He deposed and succeeded his cousin Shaikh Ahmad ibn Ali al-Thani as amir in 1972, following the British withdrawal and the declaration of Qatari independence in September 1971.

Shaikh Khalifa was educated in Qatar before going to Britain's Sandhurst Military Academy. He became deputy ruler and minister of education in 1960 and became prime minister and minister of finance in 1970.

He takes a direct and firm hand in government affairs, with most matters decided by his own amiri decree after he has had discussions with members of the al-Thani ruling family. Although the Council of Ministers which he heads has the power to draw up legislation, it will usually leave him the initiative to do so. The advisory council which he appoints can comment on proposed legislation but has no power to make changes.

Khamenei, Ayatollah Sayyid Ali
Born 1940
Born in the Iranian town of Mashhad, Hojatolislam (later Ayatollah) Khamenei entered politics in the 1960s. He founded the Council of Militant Clergymen in Mashhad. After the revolution of 1979, he became a co-founder of the Islamic Republican Party and was appointed deputy minister of defence. He was appointed the Republic's third president in 1981 in the aftermath of the assassination of President Raja'i. On Khomeini's death, Khamenei inherited his spiritual position as Vali-e Faqih (Guardian and Jurisconsult) and in February and June 1990 reiterated Khomeini's *fatwa* (edict) against Salman Rushdie although he is more generally associated with Rafsanjani's pragmatism.

Khomeini, Ahmad
Born 1946
The younger son of Ayatollah Khomeini, Ahmad Khomeini was born in Qom. Over-shadowed in his father's affections by his elder brother, Mustafa, until the latter's death in 1977, Ahmad is married to the niece of Imam Musa Sadr, the late Lebanese Shi'i

leader. He backed President Bani Sadr during the 1981 crisis and supported Rafsanjani when he became president in 1989. He has also been close to the hardliners, however, and in May 1990 he asked both camps to forget their differences for the sake of national unity. In November 1989 he was appointed a member of the National Security Council dealing with security. His power lay in his control of access to Khomeini, during his father's lifetime. Ahmad's only legacy from him is a mandate to interpret his father's words.

Khomeini, Ayatollah Ruhullah Mousavi
Born 1902 – Died 3 June 1989

Some three million grief-stricken Iranians attended the funeral of the founder of the Islamic Republic of Iran, Ayatollah Khomeini. Since the Islamic revolution of February 1979 which saw the downfall of the Pahlavi monarchy, Khomeini was elevated by his followers to sainthood and near-prophethood, while his enemies saw him as a bloodthirsty tyrant. He displayed the contradictory characteristics of charisma, political expediency and mysticism. In adopting the title Vali-e Faqih (Trustee and Jurisconsult) he became God's spiritual representative on earth to Iranian Shi'is. He lacked eloquence, his 'peasant-like Persian accent' appealing to the masses but repelling the elite. Many early supporters became passionately disillusioned. Khomeini's hurried attempt to establish Islamic government quickly alienated his more secular followers.

Ironically, the brutality of the regime which acted in his name contrasted with the kindness of his private life. According to his son Ahmad, he would weep if you killed a fly but would not shed a tear if you killed 2,000 unbelievers.

Khomeini was born in the small town of Khomein in central Iran. His father was killed by bandits when he was a baby. He attended the local Qur'anic school, then several modern schools and his elder brother, Mustafa, introduced him to Arabic grammar and semantics. At the age of 20, he went to the holy city of Qom as a seminarian. During this period he was strongly influenced by Islamic mysticism. His most famous essays are *Kashf al-Asrar* (Key to Secrets) published in 1942 and *Hukumat-i-Islami* (Islamic Government) written in 1971. In 1927 he married Khadija by whom he had two sons and three daughters as well as three children who died.

Following the death in 1960 of the Grand Ayatollah Borujirdi whom his followers wanted him to succeed as religious leader, Khomeini entered the political arena. After serving a prison sentence for calling the shah an 'American stooge', he was sent into exile to Turkey in 1964. In the following year he was allowed to go to the holy Shi'i city of Najaf in Iraq where he remained until 1978.

In 1969 he developed his concept of Velayat-e Faqih (Trusteeship of the Jurisconsult, i.e. Islamic government). The basis of his teaching was that the clergy had the same authority as the Prophet Muhammad to administer the community, a philosophy which was a deviation from orthodox Shi'i thinking.

The shah's failure to establish a meaningful dialogue with his opponents, and the economic and political dissatisfaction which surfaced in 1977 both boosted the prestige of Khomeini whose sermons attacking the regime from his exile in Iraqi were being secretly distributed in Iran. The first anti-regime riots took place in Qom in January 1978 and by October the shah had persuaded the Iraqi regime to expel Khomeini who left Najaf for a village near Paris. From there he was to return in triumph to Tehran in February 1979.

The Islamic Republic of Iran and the Islamic Constitution were sanctioned in the following December and Khomeini's concept of Islamic leadership was incorporated into the Constitution. Khomeini's first prime minister was the veteran opposition leader, Mehdi Bazargan, but the new constitution soon alienated the secular forces and the take-over of the US embassy in November 1979 saw the beginning of the supremacy of the clergy over the secularists.

Khomeini's anti-US rhetoric, Iran's increasing world isolation and the emasculation of the army through purges, encouraged Iraq's President Saddam Husayn to launch an all-out war against Iran in September 1980. Within two years the Iranians were close to victory but Khomeini's refusal to discuss peace on terms remotely reasonable to the Iraqis allowed for a successful Iraqi counter-offensive backed up with Western help. It was the speaker of the Iranian Majlis (lower house), Hashemi Rafsanjani, who finally persuaded Khomeini to accept a humiliating cease-fire in July 1988 which Khomeini described as 'more bitter than drinking hemlock'.

Hopes of more moderate and pro-Western policies were soon dashed in early 1989 by Khomeini's *fatwa* (religious edict) condemning British author Salman Rushdie to death for apostasy in his book, *The Satanic Verses*. Clashes between the pragmatists and the hardliners ended in the dismissal of Khomeini's 'pragmatist' heir Ayatollah Hussein Ali Montazeri in March. Fears of a power struggle ended when Ayatollah Khamenei succeeded Khomeini as both political and spiritual leader although it was already clear that real power would lie with the powerful Majlis speaker, Hashemi Rafsanjani.

Maktoum: Shaikh Maktoum ibn Rashid ibn Said al-Maktoum
Shaikh Maktoum became ruler of Dubai on the death of his father, Shaikh Rashid, on 7 October 1990. He is the eldest of Shaikh Rashid's four sons.

Mohtashami, Hojatolislam Ali Akbar
Born 1946
Born in Tehran, Mohtashami worked in Khomeini's Paris office before the revolution in 1979, having studied theology under him during Khomeini's exile in Najaf. Ambassador to Syria from 1982, he forged strong links with Shi'i militants. He was interior minister from 1985 until dismissed by President Rafsanjani in August 1989. An extreme radical, he is a leader of Iran's Council of Militant Clergymen and inspires Lebanon's militant Shi'i Hizbullah (Party of God). He remains the focus of challenge to Rafsanjani's pragmatism. He writes for the radical *Kayhan* daily and has his own paper, *Bayan*. He was elected to the Majlis in late 1989 as member for Tehran.

Montazeri, Ayatollah Hussein Ali
Born 1922
Born in Najafabad, Iran, Montazeri demonstrated actively against the shah, and after 1966 was imprisoned and tortured. After spending a period in Najaf with Ayatollah Khomeini in exile, he returned to Iran and was again arrested and sentenced in 1975. On his release in 1978 by the shah's regime, Khomeini appointed him to the Council of the Islamic Revolution. After the revolution, he became speaker of the first Assembly of Experts. In 1981 he returned to Qom, but in 1985 the second Assembly of Experts chose him to succeed Khomeini as Rahbar (Supreme Leader). However, Khomeini dismissed him as his successor in March 1989 and he was confined to teaching in Qom. He is popular among modernist theologians but in 1990 came under fierce criticism for delivering a speech protesting against Rafsanjani's policy of borrowing money from abroad.

Musaddiq, Muhammad
Born 1876 – Died 5 March 1967
Muhammad Musaddiq was the son of a wealthy landowning commoner who had risen to become minister of court under the Qajars. His mother was a Qajar princess. After early schooling in Iran and France, Musaddiq held minor provincial appointments in Iran before returning to Europe in 1906 for higher studies in law in Liège and Neuchâtel, the latter awarding him a doctorate in law.

Returning to Iran in 1914 he held several senior appointments between 1917 and 1922 as under-secretary, governor of the Fars province, a deputy in the Majlis, governor of Azerbayjan province, minister of justice and, in 1922, minister of foreign affairs. He soon won a reputation for idealism and integrity, rejecting passionately any foreign interference in Iranian affairs. His criticism of Reza Khan (later Reza Shah) during the latter's rise to power led to the end of his mandate as a Majlis deputy (1923–28) and his banishment from the capital to his estates. From 1928 to 1939 he lived in the country in obscurity.

In 1939 he was imprisoned by Reza Shah and then condemned to house arrest at Ahmadabad. After the shah's forced abdication in 1941, he was elected to the Majlis in March 1943. As leader of the National Front Party, he collaborated with the Tudeh (Communist) Party. In October 1947 he took a prominent part in securing the rejection of the recently-initialled Soviet-Iranian oil agreement. The revised agreement with the Anglo-Iranian Oil Company, accepted by the Iranian cabinet in July 1949, was roundly attacked by Musaddiq. As chairman of the Majlis Oil Committee, Musaddiq had the agreement rejected.

After the murder of the prime minister, General Razmara, Musaddiq succeeded him. On 1 May 1951 he enacted the oil nationalization law which was to lead to the Iranian oil crisis, the brief exile of the shah (Reza Pahlavi) to Rome and, in late 1953, to Musaddiq's own downfall. Arraigned for treachery in December 1953, he was sentenced to death. But the sentence was promptly commuted to three years' imprisonment by the shah. He was freed at the end of his sentence in August 1956 and spent the rest of his life in virtual seclusion on his estates. He died in Tehran, leaving two sons and three daughters. Even in death Mussadiq continues to be a controversial figure.

Nahayan, al- (the ruling family of Abu Dhabi). See under first names.

Nayef: Prince Nayef ibn Abd al-Aziz
Born 1933
Born in the Saudi capital, Riyadh, Prince Nayef was its governor before various security posts led to the interior ministry portfolio. As son of King Abd al-Aziz by Hasa bint al-Sudairi, he is one of the elite 'Sudairi Seven'. After the incident in July 1987 when over 400 mainly Iranian *hajjis* (pilgrims) were killed by Saudi police in Mecca, Nayef responded to Iranian vitriole by openly called for the downfall of Iran's Islamic Republic.

Nazer, Shaikh Hisham
Born 1932
A sophisticated Saudi commoner, Hisham Nazer took two degrees at the University of California before becoming adviser to the director-general of the Ministry of Petroleum Mineral Resources in 1958. A director-general of the Central Planning Organization since 1968, Hisham Nazer launched the first five year plan in 1970, sensitive to the problem of Saudi Arabia's inadequate bureaucracy, primitive infrastructure and shortage of skilled manpower. Since late 1975 he has been minister of planning and vice-chairman of the Royal Commission for Jubail and Yanbu. Although Nazer voted for restraint after the 1973/74 oil boom, he was closely attached to the then Crown Prince Fahd, even earning himself the nickname 'Hisham abd al-Fahd' (Hisham, slave of Fahd).

Nidal, Abu
Abu Nidal, (formerly named Sabri Khalil al-Banna), founded an extremist terrorist group, 'Black June', which split from the mainstream Fatah in 1973. Its Baghdad headquarters was closed down by the Iraqis in 1983 and at the end of the year re-established in Damascus. In 1984, however, Abu Nidal was readmitted to Iraq, having fled Syria.

Since 1974 he has masterminded operations against the Fatah leadership, often in close co-operation with the Iraqi intelligence services. He has been allegedly behind the killings of Palestinian moderates, including the Palestine Liberation Organization's (PLO's) London representative, Said Hammami.

Nourbakhsh, Muhsen
Born in 1948

Born in Tehran, Nourbakhsh read economics at Tehran University followed by a Ph.D. at the University of California. A student activist in the US before the Iranian revolution, he returned to Iran in 1979 to work for the Ministry of Islamic Guidance and teach economics in the Computer College and National University of Iran. He was deputy minister of economy and finance and governor of the Central Bank for several years, resigning the latter post over differences with the then prime minister, Hussein Mousavi. Rafsanjani appointed him minister of economic affairs in 1989. He is in favour of controlling the money supply and enhancing economic production in line with Rafsanjani's economic policies.

Nouri, Abdullah Husseinabadi
Born 1949

Born in the Iranian town of Isfahan, Nouri taught theology before the revolution in 1979. Member of parliament for Isfahan, he replaced Ali Akbar Mohtashami in 1989 as minister of the interior. He is close to the radicals and to the late Ayatollah Khomeini's son, Ahmad Khomeini. Still young, his rapid rise to prominence came about through his work as Khomeini's representative to the Crusade for Construction.

Qaboos, Sultan ibn Said
Born 1940

Born in Muscat, Qaboos succeeded his father, Said ibn Teymour, in a palace coup in July 1970. Ibn Teymour had subjected Oman to a state of medieval darkness. Qaboos's first acts were to abolish restrictions on smoking in public as well as lifting bans on singing and the wearing of spectacles. The first five years of Qaboos's reign concentrated on defeating the Marxist-led rebellion in the southern province of Dhofar. Since then, with unstinted British support, he has raced his rugged nation into the twentieth century.

Qomi, Ayatollah Ahmad Azari
Born 1925

Qomi is member of parliament for the holy Iranian city in which he was born, Qom. He is also a member of the economy and finance parliamentary committee and the second Assembly of Experts. Arrested twice under the shah, he was a member of the Teachers' Association of the Qom Theological Seminaries. The proprietor of the conservative newspaper, *Resalat*, Qomi has challenged radicals within the establishment, openly exposing their financial misdeeds. He is the most articulate of the conservatives who kept their ties with Khomeini.

Rafsanjani, Hojatolislam Ali Akbar Hashemi
Born 25 August 1934

The most influential figure in Iran after Khomeini, Rafsanjani was born in the village of Bahraman, Rafsanjan, near Kerman. His parents made a fortune from pistachio-nut farming. He studied, and later taught, theology at Qom. Rafsanjani supported Khomeini after the latter's exile in 1963 and became a wealthy property speculator in the 1970s, operating through a company called Dezh-Saz (castle builders). He suffered imprisonments under the shah in the years 1963, 1967, 1970, 1972 and 1975.

After the Islamic revolution in 1979, he helped to found the ruling Islamic Republican Party. He also built the Pasdaran or Revolutionary Guards into a 250,000-strong force to neutralize any threat of a coup from the regular army. In 1980 he was chosen as speaker of the Majlis (lower house). Although of charming demeanour, he is capable of ruthlessness when necessary. In 1988, shortly after Khomeini had appointed him acting commander-in-chief of the army, he managed what many considered the impossible by persuading the inflexible Khomeini to 'drink poison' and agree to end the war with Iraq.

Although he represents the moderates who favour improved relations with the West, he has had to toe the line with the radicals and often dampen the Western media's enthusiasm for him. His wish to mollify the radicals may explain his support for Khomeini's *fatwa* (edict) condemning the British author, Salman Rushdie, to death for apostasy in 1989, and his suggestion later in the year that Palestinians would want to kill one Westerner for every Palestinian killed in the Intifada (literally 'tremor': the uprising in the Palestinian West Bank).

Ramadan, Taha Yasin
Born 1939
Born in the Iraqi city of Mosul, Yasin has been an RCC member since 1969. Today, as First Deputy Prime Minister and head of Iraq's Ba'th militia, a key post, he is widely considered to be President Saddam Husayn's number two. A hardliner who was totally dedicated to all-out conflict with Iran during the Gulf war, he is also deeply sceptical about attempts at political liberalization within Iraq. He led Saddam Husayn's publicity campaign after Iraq's invasion of Kuwait in August 1990.

Reyshahri, Hojatolislam Muhammad Muhammadi
Born 1946
Born in Rey, Reyshahri was imprisoned several times before the Iranian revolution in 1979. After the revolution he became president of the Islamic Revolution Courts and Military Tribunals in various Iranian towns – Dezful, Gachsaran, Behbahan, Khorramabad, Borujerd, Rasht and later Tehran. He is the son-in- law of Ayatollah Meshkini and was instrumental in the arrest, trial and execution of Mehdi Hashemi whose arrest led to the exposure of the 'Irangate' scandal in 1986. In 1989 Reyshahri refused to serve under Rafsanjani as minister of intelligence, a post he had held since 1984, but under pressure from Meshkini he accepted his present post of state prosecutor.

Sabah, al- (ruling family of Kuwait). See under first names.

Sabah: Shaikh Sabah al-Ahmad al-Jaber al-Sabah
Born 1929
Kuwait's foreign minister, Shaikh Sabah, was educated at the Al-Mubarakiya school in Kuwait. In 1962 he became minister of public information and guidance, and of social affairs, and in the following year foreign minister. In 1965–67 he was acting minister of finance and oil and in 1978 minister of the interior, and he has been deputy prime minister since February 1978. He escaped to Saudi Arabia as Iraq invaded Kuwait in August 1990.

Sa'd: Shaikh Sa'd al-Abdullah al-Salem al-Sabah
Born 1924
Kuwait's crown prince and prime minister, Shaikh Sa'd was born in Kuwait. He is the eldest son of a former amir, Abdullah al-Salem al-Sabah (1950–65) and is married to Shaikha Latifa al-Fahd al-Salem al-Sabah. Educated first in Kuwait, then at Britain's

Hendon Police College (1952–54), he returned to Kuwait to become assistant director of police. He was interior minister from 1962 and took on the additional role of defence minister in 1964. In 1978 he became crown prince and prime minister. Responding to calls for the re-establishment of Kuwait's National Assembly in early 1990, he reassured critics that the ruler was committed in principle to popular participation in public life. Shaikh Sa'd took the brunt of Iraqi diatribe before escaping to Saudi Arabia as Iraq invaded Kuwait in August 1990.

Said, ibn (ruling family of Oman). See under first names.

Saud: Prince Saud al-Faisal
Born 1943
Born in the Saudi capital, Riyadh, since 1975 Prince Saud has been Saudi Arabia's minister of foreign affairs. He is the eldest of the five sons of King Faisal by Iffat, Faisal's last and beloved wife. Like his four brothers, Saud is a progressive who believes, to a certain degree, in economic liberalization. Educated at the US Princeton University, he is both eloquent and glamorous and, therefore, highly effective with Western public opinion.

Sultan, Prince Sultan ibn Abd al-Aziz
Born 1924
Born in the Saudi capital, Riyadh, Sultan is the sixteenth son of King Abd al-Aziz of Saudi Arabia by Hasa bint Ahmad al-Sudairi, making him one of the elite 'Sudairi Seven'. On the day after the assassination of King Faisal in 1975 and the confirmation of Crown Prince Fahd as king, Sultan was appointed Second Deputy Premier, making him the kingdom's number three after his brother Abdullah. More importantly, perhaps, he has been defence and aviation minister since 1962. He had originally joined the cabinet in 1953 as agriculture minister, helping to settle Saudi Arabia's bedouin on modern farms. In 1955 he was appointed communications minister, a post he held until 1962.

Talabani, Jalal
In 1976 Talabani, arch rival to Mulla Mustafa Barzani, leader of the Iraqi Kurdish Democratic Party (KDP), formed the Patriotic Union of Kurdistan (PUK) which he announced would continue to kidnap Turkish workers in order to pressurize the Baghdad government to release Kurds from Turkish prisons. In November 1986 the PUK and the KDP agreed to unify their efforts, but the PUK's attempt to negotiate with the Iraqi Ba'th ended in failure. An amnesty offered by the Ba'th to all Kurds inside and outside Iraq in 1988 significantly excluded Talabani.

In November 1989 Talabani said that the PUK would take 'our urban guerrilla war to Arab cities' but added reassuringly that sensible Kurds would neither resort to terorrism, nor take the war outside Iraq's frontiers. Their fight would be restricted to military tagerts and economic installations.

Velayati, Ali Akbar
Born 1945
Born in Tehran, Velayati taught as an associate professor in Tehran's Hygiene Sciences College prior to the revolution in 1979. After holding various posts, he became foreign minister in December 1981. A moderate, he was retained when Rafsanjani became president in 1989 and shares the latter's wish for closer ties with the West.

Zawawi, Qais Abd al-Moneim
Born 1935

Born in Muscat, Zawawi belongs to one of Muscat's oldest merchant families. During the reign of Sultan Qaboos's father, Said ibn Teymour, he lived abroad, as did so many of Oman's intelligentsia, but returned to Muscat to manage the family business in 1966 on his father's death. In 1973 Sultan Qaboos made him minister of state for foreign affairs and in 1974 he became vice-chairman of the Development Council, a post which involved the co-ordination of Oman's five-year plans. Zawawi was also closely involved in setting up the Gulf Co-operation Council in 1981.

Zayed: Shaikh Zayed ibn Sultan al-Nayahan
Born c. 1915

Shaikh Zayed is Abu Dhabi's ruler and the president of the United Arab Emirates (UAE). He was born in Al-Ain's Jahili fortress. He was governor of Abu Dhabi's Eastern Province, based in Al-Ain, from 1946 to 1966 when he replaced his brother, Shaikh Shakbut (1928–66). On the formation of the UAE federation in December 1971 he was appointed head of state (president). He was re-elected president in 1976 and again in November 1981. His wife, Shaikha Fatima bint Mubarak, has played an important part in developing the status of UAE women and is president of the Abu Dhabi Women's Society founded in 1975. Shaikh Zayed's eldest son, Khalifa, has served as Abu Dhabi's prime minister, minister of defence and minister of finance. He is heir apparent and deputy supreme commander of the UAE armed forces. Shaikh Zayed's usual residence is the Bahar Palace in Abu Dhabi. His interests include falconry and hunting.

G L O S S A R Y

$A Australian dollars

abd (Arabic) slave or servant: (e.g. Abd Allah, Abdullah; the Servant of God and Abd al-Aziz, the Servant of The Most Powerful, i.e. God)

abu (Arabic) father: Commonly used in names (e.g. Abu Abbas)

ACC Arab Co-operation Council

ADMA Abu Dhabi Marine Areas

ADNOC Abu Dhabi National Oil Company

AIOC Anglo-Iranian Oil Company

Alawi SHI'I group founded in Syria where the Alawis form a minority elite today

Ali Son-in-law and cousin of the Prophet Muhammad (see also SHI'I)

Allah (Arabic) God

amir or emir (Arabic) ruler

ARAMCO Arabian American Oil Company

AWACS Airborne warning and control systems (aircraft)

ayatollah (Arabic) ayat Allah – sign of God: A SHI'I cleric who has reached the third level of SHI'I clerical education, is over 40 and is recognized as a MUJTAHID

basij (Arabic) mobilization: The auxiliary volunteer force of the Islamic Revolutionary Guards Corps (PASDARAN), the Basij-e Mustazafin (Mobilization of the Oppressed) was established in Iran in early 1980

ba'th (Arabic) rebirth or renaissance: The Ba'th is an Arab socialist political party founded by Michel Aflaq (see Biographies) in Syria. Also dominant in Iraq

bazaar (Persian) market

bedouin (Plural bedu) nomad

BP British Petroleum Corporation Limited

Caliph (Arabic Khalifa) successor: The Caliph inherited the Prophet Muhammad's leadership over the Islamic community but without direct, divine revelation

G L O S S A R Y

CFP   Compagnie Francaise des Petroles

CIA   Central Intelligence Agency

Council of Guardians   Iranian parliamentary upper house after the 1979 revolution (see MAJLIS and SENATE)

da'wa   (Arabic) call (missionary): Gave its name to the Islamic fundamentalist organisation Al-Da'wa al-Islamiyya

Dh   UAE dirham

£E   Egyptian pound

fajr   (Arabic) dawn: Iran named a series of offensives against Iraq Wa al-Fajr (By Dawn)

fatah   (Arabic) opening, conquest (i.e. opening by God): Fatah is the main Palestinian commando organization and an acronym of Haraka Tahrir Falastin

Fatima   Daughter of the Prophet Muhammad and wife of his cousin and son-in-law, ALI

fatwa   (Arabic) ISLAMIC edict, legal opinion

fedayeen   (Arabic, singular feda'i) Those who sacrifice their lives to achieve their goals. Fedayeen-e Islam, a militant Islamic organization

FLOSY   Front for the Liberation of Occupied South Yemen

GCC   Gulf Co-operation Council

hajj   (Arabic) Pilgrimage to Mecca incumbent on every MUSLIM once in his or her life who has the means and ability to perform it

hajji   (Arabic) Pilgrim who performs the HAJJ

Hasan   Elder son of Ali whose martyrdom is mourned by SHI'IS

Hizbullah   (Arabic Hizb Allah, Party of God) A radical SHI'I group in Lebanon.

hojatolislam   (Persian; Arabic hujjat al-Islam, meaning proof of ISLAM). Second rank in the SHI'I clerical hierarchy after AYATOLLAH

Husayn   (Arabic; Persian form Hussein) The younger son of ALI whose martyrdom is mourned by SHI'IS

ibn   (Arabic) son, son of: e.g. Ibn Saud, meaning the Son of Saud

imam   (Arabic) Literally a prayer leader. On another level (for Ismailis or Seveners, and for Twelver SHI'IS – those who await the return of the 'hidden', Twelth Imam) the Imam is a divinely guided infallible and sinless religious leader.

GLOSSARY

Intifada (Arabic) tremor: The term refers to the Palestinian uprising against the Israeli government in the Occupied Territories of the WEST BANK and Gaza

IPC Iraq Petroleum Company

IRNA Islamic Revolutionary News Agency (Iran)

Islam (Arabic) submission: Submission to the will of God and acceptance that MUHAMMAD is His prophet. Muslims believe that ISLAM was revealed by God in Mecca and Medina to the Prophet MUHAMMAD in the seventh century AD

IRP Islamic Republican Party (Iran's principal political party)

jihad (Arabic) struggle: Holy struggle for God enjoined on MUSLIMS to expand or defend ISLAM (sometimes translated as 'holy war')

Ka'ba Sacred, cube-shaped building in Mecca which is the qibla (direction of prayer) towards which MUSLIMS pray fives times a day

KD Kuwaiti dinar

KDP Kurdish Democratic Party

Knesset (Hebrew) Israeli parliament

Majlis (Arabic) assembly: Iran's parliamentary lower house

MI5/6 Military Intelligence 5/6

Muhammad Name of the Prophet Muhammad to whom the QU'RAN was revealed by God in the seventh century AD (see ISLAM and MUSLIM)

Mujahedeen-e khalq (Arabic/Persian) mujahedeen (those who conduct JIHAD); khalq (people). A leftist-ISLAMIC organization which helped overthrow the SHAH of Iran's regime in 1979.

mujtahid MUSLIM theologian who exercises his personal interpretation of the SHARI'A to form a legal opinion

mulla Member of the ULEMA, particularly among SHI'IS

Muslim (Arabic) one who submits to the will of God: Meaning one who accepts ISLAM

NIOC National Iranian Oil Company

NLF National Liberation Frout

OAPEC Organization of Arab Petroleum Exporting Countries

GLOSSARY

OPEC   Organization of Petroleum Exporting Countries

Pasdaran   (Persian) guards: Applies to the ISLAMIC Revolutionary Guards Corps founded in Iran after the 1979 revolution

PDRY   People's Democratic Republic of [South] Yemen

PFLOAG   Popular Front for the Liberation of Oman and the Arabian Gulf (later truncated to PFLO)

PLO   Palestine Liberation Organization

PUK   Patriotic Union of Kurdistan

Qur'an   The MUSLIM Holy Book, containing God's revelations in Arabic to the Prophet MUHAMMAD and considered by MUSLIMS to be the divine word of God

Ramadan   Ninth month of the MUSLIM year, when MUSLIMS must fast from dawn to dusk

RCC   Revolutionary Command Council

SAF   South Arabian Federation

SAS   Special Air Service

SAVAK   Sazman-e amniyat va ittilaat-e keshvar (Persian – Organization of National Security and Intelligence).

sayyid   (Arabic) master or lord: Also an honorific term for the descendants of the Prophet MUHAMMAD

Senate   Iran's parliamentary upper house until the 1979 revolution

Shafi'i   One of the four Islamic legal schools

shah   (Persian) king: Shahanshah means 'King of kings'

shaikh   (Arabic) old man: Also term of respect for head of a tribe. Today used for rulers (AMIRS) of the Arab Gulf states

Shari'a   ISLAMIC law

sharif   (Arabic) noble: came to refer to descendants of ALI's son, HASAN

shatt   (Arabic) bank or coast: e.g. Shatt al-Arab waterway, formed by the Tigris and Euphrates rivers and dividing Iran and Iraq

Shi'i   (Arabic adjective) partisan (of ALI): The SHI'A – sect (of ALI) – split from the rest of the ISLAMIC community in their belief that the CALIPHATE should have gone to ALI and his descendants (see also SUNNI)

sultan   (Arabic) ruler: Came to be associated with the Ottoman Sultan. Today used for the sultan of Oman

Sunni   (Arabic) One who follows the path or Sunna (of the Prophet Muhammad). The majority sect in ISLAM (see also SHI'I)

suq   (Arabic) market

tudeh   (Persian) masses: The Tudeh Party is Iran's Communist Party

UAE   United Arab Emirates

UAR   United Arab Republic (of Egypt and Syria); Egypt alone 1961–71

ulema   (Arabic) ISLAMIC clergy, religious-legal scholars (singular alim)

UN   United Nations

US   United States

vali   (Persian from Arabic wali) governor

Vali-e Faqih   (Persian) Governor or Trustee and Jurisconsult: In IRAN the term referred to Khomeini who believed that in the absence of the Twelth IMAM, it was the duty of the clergy, as trustees of the Prophet MUHAMMAD, to establish a social system to implement ISLAMIC laws. On Khomeini's death, this supreme religious leadership was transferred to AYATOLLAH Khamenei

Velayat-e Faqih   Guardianship or Trusteeship of the Jurisconsult

waqf   ISLAMIC religious endowment

West Bank   Palestinian West Bank region of the River Jordan occupied by Israel in the Arab-Israeli war of 1967

BIBLIOGRAPHY

General

Bacharach, J.L., *A Middle East Studies Handbook*, Cambridge University Press, Cambridge 1984.

Hourani, A., *Arabic Thought in the Liberal Age*, Oxford University Press, London 1962, 1967 (later edition Cambridge University Press 1983).

Keesings Archives, various years.

Mansfield, P., *The Arabs*, Penguin, Harmondsworth 1976, 1978.

The Middle East and North Africa, Europa Publications, London 1990.

The Middle East Review, The World of Information, Saffron Walden 1989.

Mostyn, T. and Hourani, A. (Eds.), *The Cambridge Encyclopedia of the Middle East and North Africa*, Cambridge University Press, Cambridge 1988.

Stephens, R. *Nasser*, Penguin, Harmondsworth 1973.

Journals

Arab Report and Record, London.

Middle East Economic Digest, London.

Middle East International, London.

Iraq

Committee Against Repression and for Democratic Rights in Iraq, Saddam's Iraq, Zed Books Limited, London 1989.

Farouk-Sluglett, M. and Sluglett, P., *Iraq since 1958, from Revolution to Dictatorship*, Kegan Paul International, London 1987. I.B. Taurus, London 1990 (extended edition).

Khadduri, M., *Republican Iraq*, Oxford University Press, London 1969.

al-Khalil, S., *Republic of Fear, The Politics of Modern Iraq*, Hutchinson Radius, London 1989.

Iran

Avery, P., *Modern Iran*, Ernest Benn, London 1967.

Azimi, F., *Iran: The crisis of democracy 1941–1953*, I.B. Taurus, London 1989.

Bakhash, S., *The Reign of the Ayatollahs*, Basic Books, New York 1979.

Chubin, S. and Tripp C., *Iran and Iraq at War*, I.B. Taurus, London 1988.

Hiro, D., *Iran under the Ayatollahs*, Routledge and Kegan Paul, London 1985.

Hiro, D., *The Longest War, The Iran–Iraq Military Conflict*, Paladin Books, London 1990.

Iran Yearbook, distributed by MENAS Associates, Cambridgeshire 1988.

Ramazani, R.K., *Iran's Foreign Policy 1941–1973*, University Press of Virginia, Charlottesville 1975.

Shawcross, W., *The Shah's Last Ride*, Chatto and Windus, London 1989.

Saudi Arabia

de Gaury, G., *Faisal: King of Saudi Arabia*, Barker, London 1966.

Holden, D. and Johns, R., *The House of Saud*, Sidgewick and Jackson, London 1981.

Lacey, R., *The Kingdom*, Hutchinson, London 1981.

Lackner, H., *A House built on sand: A political economy of Saudi Arabia*, Ithaca, London 1966.

BIBLIOGRAPHY

Mostyn, T. (Ed.), *Saudi Arabia – A MEED Practical Guide*, Middle East Economic Digest, London 1983.

United Arab Emirates
Abdullah, M., *The United Arab Emirates*: a modern history, Croom Helm, London 1978.
Fenelon, K.G., *The United Arab Emirates: an economic and social survey*, Longmans, London 1976 (second edition).
Hawley, D., *The Trucial States*, Allen and Unwin, London 1970.
Heard-Bey, F., *From Trucial States to United Arab Emirates*, Longman, London 1982.
Mostyn, T.(Ed.), *UAE – A MEED Practical Guide*, Middle East Economic Digest, London 1983, 1986.
Said Zahlan, R., *The Origins of the United Arab Emirates*, Macmillan Press, London 1978.
Sakr, N., *The United Arab Emirates to the 1990s*, London 1986.

Kuwait
Mansfield, P., *Kuwait*, Hutchinson, London 1990.
Rush, A., *Al-Sabah, The History and Genealogy of Kuwait's Ruling Family 1752–1987*, Ithaca, London 1987.
Whelan, J., *Kuwait – A MEED Practical Guide*, Middle East Economic Digest, London 1985.

Bahrain
Whelan, J., *Bahrain – A MEED Practical Guide*, Middle East Economic Digest, London 1984.

Qatar
Whelan, J., *Qatar – A MEED Practical Guide*, Middle East Economic Digest, London 1983.

The Yemens
Bidwell, R., *The Two Yemens*, Longman, Harlow 1983.
O'Ballance, E., *The War in the Yemen*, Faber and Faber, London 1971.

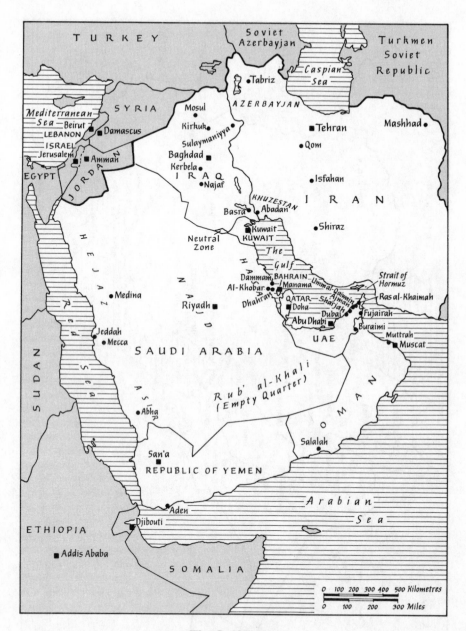

The Gulf Region

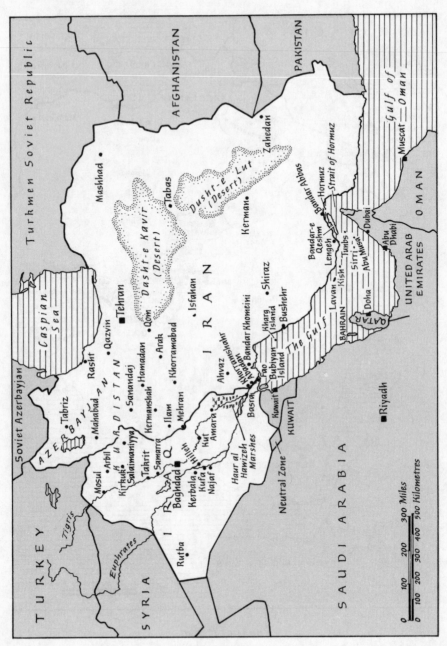

Iran and Iraq

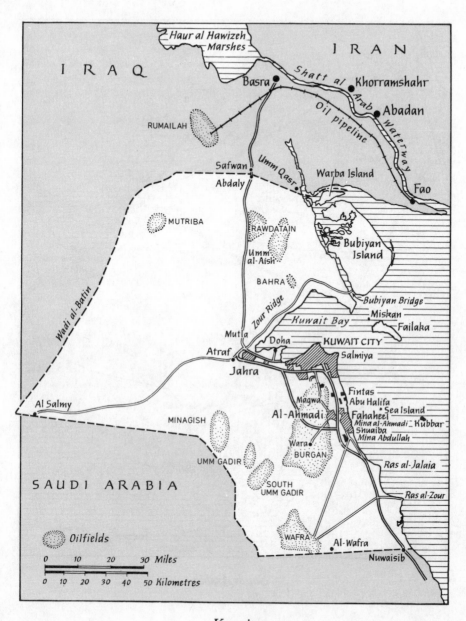

Kuwait

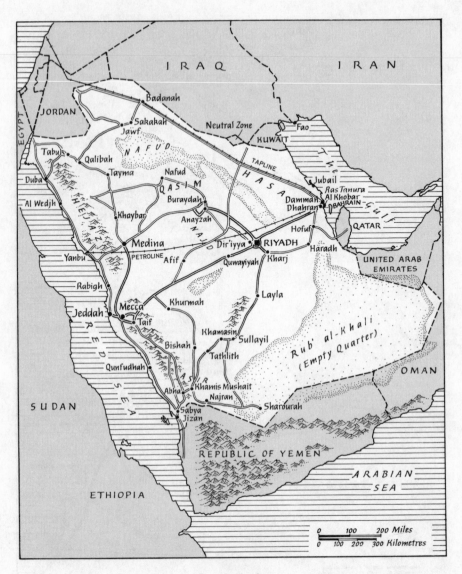

Saudi Arabia

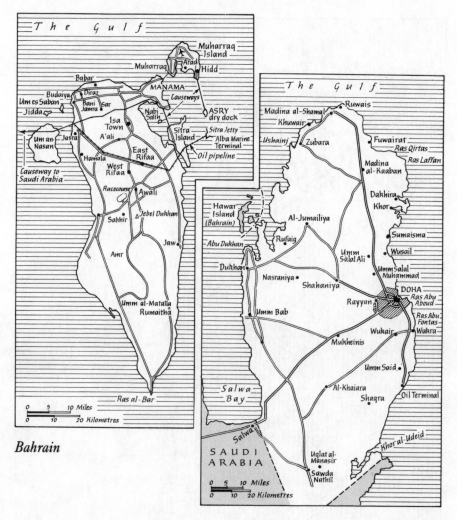

The Gulf

Muharraq Island
Muharraq
Hidd
Arad
MANAMA
Causeways
Babar
Budaiya
Diraz
Um es Saban
Bani Jamra
Jidda
Sar
Nabi Salih
ASRY dry dock
Isa Town
A'ali
Sitra Jetty
Alba Marine Terminal
Sitra Island
Oil pipeline
Um an-Nasan
Jasra
East Rifaa
Causeway to Saudi Arabia
Hamala
West Rifaa
Racecourse
Awali
Sakhir
△ Jebel Dukhan
Jaw
Amr
Umm al-Matalla Rumaitha
Ras al-Bar

0   5   10 Miles
0   10   20 Kilometres

Bahrain

The Gulf

Ruwais
Madina al-Shamal
Khuwair
Ushainj
Zubara
Fuwairat
Ras Qirtas
Madina al-Kaaban
Ras Laffan
Dahhira
Khor
Hawar Island (Bahrain)
Al-Jumailiya
Sumaisma
Abu Dukhan
Rufaig
Wusail
Umm Salal Ali
Dukhan
Umm Salal Muhammad
Nasraniya
Shahaniya
DOHA
Rayyan
Ras Abu Aboud
Umm Bab
Ras Abu Fontas
Wukair
Wahra
Mukheinis
Umm Said
Salwa Bay
Al-Khaiara
Shaqra
Oil Terminal
Salwa
Khor al-Udeid
SAUDI ARABIA
Uqlat al-Manasir
Sawda Nathil

0   5   10 Miles
0   10   20 Kilometres

Qatar

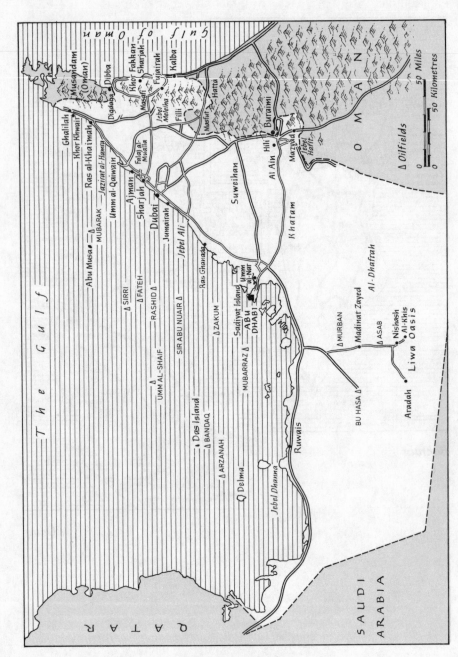

United Arab Emirates

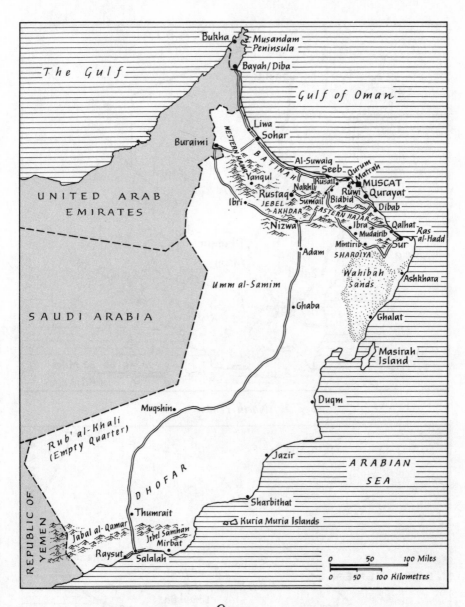

Oman

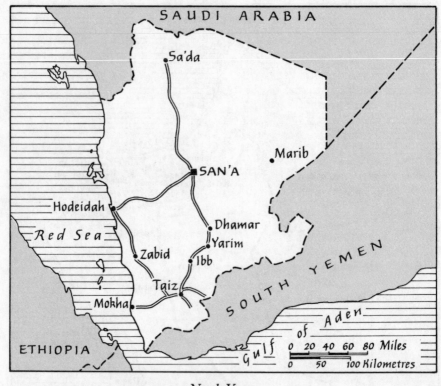

North Yemen

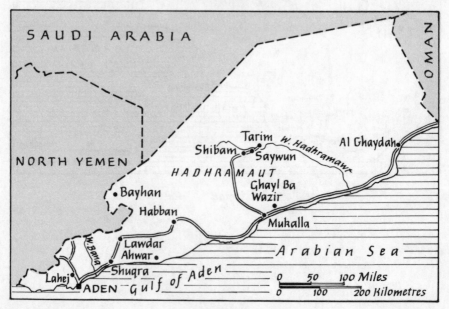

South Yemen

(On 22 May 1991 the two Yemens united as the Republic of Yemen)

INDEX

I N D E X